D1653905

SEMANTICS IN ACQUISITION

STUDIES IN THEORETICAL PSYCHOLINGUISTICS

VOLUME 35

Managing Editors

Lyn Frazier, *Dept. of Linguistics, University of Massachusetts at Amherst*
Thomas Roeper, *Dept. of Linguistics, University of Massachusetts at Amherst*
Kenneth Wexler, *Dept. of Brain and Cognitive Science, MIT, Cambridge, Mass.*

Editorial Board

Robert Berwick, *Artificial Intelligence Laboratory, MIT, Cambridge, Mass.*
Matthew Cocker, *Saarland University, Germany*
Janet Dean Fodor, *City University of New York, New York*
Angela Friederici, *Max Planck Institute of Human Cognitive and Brain Sciences, Germany*
Merrill Garrett, *University of Arizona, Tucson*
Lila Gleitman, *School of Education, University of Pennsylvania*
Chris Kennedy, *Northwestern University, Illinois*
Manfred Krifka, *Humboldt University, Berlin, Germany*
Howard Lasnik, *University of Connecticut at Storrs*
Yukio Otsu, *Keio University, Tokyo*
Andrew Radford, *University of Essex, U.K.*

The titles published in this series are listed at the end of this volume.

SEMANTICS IN ACQUISITION

Edited by

VEERLE VAN GEENHOVEN
*Radboud Universiteit, Nijmegen,
The Netherlands*

A C.I.P. Catalogue record for this book is available from the Library of Congress.

ISBN-10 1-4020-4484-4 (HB)
ISBN-13 978-1-4020-4484-7 (HB)
ISBN-10 1-4020-4485-2 (e-book)
ISBN-13 978-1-4020-4485-4 (e-book)

Published by Springer,
P.O. Box 17, 3300 AA Dordrecht, The Netherlands.

www.springer.com

Printed on acid-free paper

All Rights Reserved
© 2006 Springer
No part of this work may be reproduced, stored in a retrieval system, or transmitted in any form or by any means, electronic, mechanical, photocopying, microfilming, recording or otherwise, without written permission from the Publisher, with the exception of any material supplied specifically for the purpose of being entered and executed on a computer system, for exclusive use by the purchaser of the work.

Printed in the Netherlands.

to my late husband Bernd

CONTENTS

ACQUISITION AND INTERPRETATION: A BRIEF INTRODUCTION   1
   Veerle Van Geenhoven

PART I: THE DEVELOPMENT OF THE SYNTAX-SEMANTICS INTERFACE

'MISMATCHES' OF FORM AND INTERPRETATION   19
   Greg Carlson

WATCHING NOUN PHRASES EMERGE: SEEKING COMPOSITIONALITY   37
   Tom Roeper

CROSS-LINGUISTIC ACQUISITION OF COMPLEMENT TENSE   65
   Ayumi Matsuo

PART II: ACQUIRING UNIVERSAL QUANTIFICATION

EVERYBODY KNOWS   89
   Luisa Meroni, Andrea Gualmini, and Stephen Crain

THE EFFECT OF CONTEXT ON CHILDREN'S INTERPRETATIONS OF UNIVERSALLY QUANTIFIED SENTENCES   115
   Kenneth F. Drozd and Erik van Loosbroek

STRUCTURE AND MEANING IN THE ACQUISITION OF SCOPE   141
   Julien Musolino

PART III: TIME IN THE LANGUAGE OF A LEARNER

TIME FOR CHILDREN: AN INTEGRATED STAGE MODEL OF ASPECT AND TENSE   167
   Veerle Van Geenhoven

STATE CHANGE AND TEMPORAL REFERENCE IN INUKTITUT CHILD LANGUAGE Mary Swift	193
TEMPORAL ADVERBIALS AND EARLY TENSE AND ASPECT MARKERS IN THE ACQUISITION OF DUTCH Marianne Starren	219

PART IV: FINITENESS AND ITS DEVELOPMENT

ON FINITENESS Wolfgang Klein	245
FUNCTIONS OF FINITENESS IN CHILD LANGUAGE Petra Gretsch	273

PART V: FOCUS PARTICLES IN CHILD LANGUAGE

ADDITIVE PARTICLES AND SCOPE MARKING IN CHILD GERMAN Ulrike Nederstigt	303
(UN)STRESSED *OOK* IN CHILD DUTCH Wenda Bergsma	329
SUBJECT INDEX	349

VEERLE VAN GEENHOVEN

ACQUISITION AND INTERPRETATION

A Brief Introduction

Abstract. By raising a number of general questions as well as some of the specific questions addressed in the contributed papers, this introductory chapter shows the need for semantic thinking in language acquisition studies. I illustrate how insights in semantics can be related to findings and questions about language acquisition and how they can support particular solutions to puzzles in learners' data. I also illustrate the opposite case, namely, that semantic theories can broaden their empirical horizon by taking acquisition data into account.

1. SOME THEORETICAL AND METHODOLOGICAL ISSUES

By shifting the perspective in language acquisition research towards a semantic one, the present volume wants to show how acquisition research can gain from semantic research. The volume thus lays a basis for future investigations in the domain of the acquisition of semantic phenomena and interpretive skills, a field that so far has received little systematic attention within language acquisition research. This shift in perspective automatically leads to the additional insight that acquisition data can be a challenge for existing semantic theories. Investigating the semantics of acquisition data is an area that so far has been largely ignored by semanticists. Hence, by reconciling acquisition work with semantics work and by reconsidering 'old' findings about the language of a learner from a semantic perspective the book will be of interest to researchers studying language acquisition, to linguists interested in semantics and its interface with (morpho)syntax, and to cognitive psychologists who work on language interpretation.

In this introductory chapter, I first discuss some phenomena that trigger the general need for shifting the perspective on language data from a syntactic to a semantic one. Next, I point out how this shift is a prerequisite for our understanding of the development of the close interaction of structure and meaning that we find in natural language, an interaction which is known as the 'syntax-semantics interface'. A third issue I address is the issue of crosslinguistic variation, both in structure and meaning. Related to this, I discuss the crosslinguistic 'flavour' of learner data. The fourth question that I raise is what acquisitionists can learn from semanticists. For this purpose, I relate the semantic interpretation of adult focus to a number of questions about child focus. In the fifth subsection, I address the opposite question: Can, and if so, what do semanticists learn from acquisition theories and the data that support them? In the final subsection, I discuss some methodological aspects related to collecting and semantically interpreting child data in a reliable way.

1.1. From a Syntactic towards a Semantic Perspective

Due to the central role that the innateness hypothesis plays in Chomskyan approaches to syntax and, hence, in the syntactic theory of Universal Grammar, the formal study of language acquisition is characterized by a strong bias towards constituent structure and other aspects of language structure. As a consequence, formal acquisition studies have primarily contributed supporting evidence for or against particular answers to questions about natural language syntax. However, many phenomena and puzzles in natural language and hence also in the 'incomplete' language of a learner cannot be syntactically accounted for. Consider (1), a sentence that contains a universally quantified subject (*all candidates*) and a negation (*not*) in the VP:

(1)   All candidates did not pass the exam.

Ladd (1980) observed that a fall-rise intonation makes us understand this sentence that some but not all members of a contextually known set of candidates passed the exam. A simple falling contour gives rise to another reading, namely, one in which none of the candidates passed the exam. On the former interpretation, the negation has scope over the quantifier whereas on the latter the quantifier has scope over the negation. Interestingly, in German we find the same ambiguity corresponding to two intonational patterns (see Geurts, 1996):

(2)   Alle Kandidaten   haben   das Examen   nicht   bestanden.
      all candidates   *have*   *the exam*   *not*   *passed*

The normal declarative intonation pattern yields the reading in which none of the candidates was successful. With stress on *alle* ('all') and *nicht* ('not'), the sentence is understood in such a way that some but not all candidates out of a presupposed set of candidates passed the exam.

This observation about an interpretive similarity between the English example (1) and its German correspondent (2) gives rise to a number of questions. First, what is the nature of this similarity? Should it be attributed to similarities in these languages' syntactic components, or to similarities in how context and semantic principles are taken into account? And how do we account for the role of focus structure or of other prosodic devices that generate alternative interpretations? Independent of what is the exact division of labour between the various components of grammar, (1) and (2) show that the learner of English and the learner of German must establish and manipulate complex meaning representations of these sentences.

Further comparison of English and German scope patterns shows that these languages also demonstrate differences in semantic relations. This is illustrated in example (3):

(3)   A girl is holding every balloon.

This English sentence may either describe a picture in which a particular girl is holding all the balloons, or one in which every balloon is held by a girl. This ambiguity follows from whether the indefinite *a girl* takes scope over the universal quantifier *every balloon*, or not. Interestingly, this ambiguity is not available in German:

(4)   Ein Mädchen   hält   jeden Ballon   fest.
       a girl   *holds* *every balloon* *tight*

(4), which is the German equivalent of (3), can describe only a picture in which a particular girl is holding all the balloons. This shows that certain scope options may be available in one language but not in another and the question arises how language learners determine which options in the language they are acquiring are possible and which options are ruled out.

To the extent that we find crosslinguistic differences like the one between (3) and (4), we cannot explain the acquisition of scope options by referring to universal and innately known syntactic properties of languages. Even an innateness program that tries to explain the acquisition of different syntactic systems on the basis of innate knowledge (e.g., the syntactic parameter approach in Chomsky, 1986; Hyams, 1986) will not cover differences in scope assignment like the ones just discussed. This follows because the observed difference cannot be due only to a syntactic difference between English and German: If we replace the universal quantifier *every* in the English sentence (3) with a numeral determiner, such as *two*, the resulting sentence becomes as unambiguous as its German counterpart in (4).[1] This is shown in (5):

(5)   A girl is holding two balloons.

(5) describes only a situation in which a specific girl is holding two balloons.

The above observations may lead to (at least) two kinds of conclusions. Either one may conclude that whenever scope differences between languages cannot be attributed solely to differences in their syntax, researchers studying the acquisition of scope must take into account principles of learning that are not supported by innate knowledge of grammar. Or one may conclude that interpretive crosslinguistic differences indicate that innate knowledge of grammar is not restricted to syntax. It may very well be the case that in addition to syntactic variation semantic variation exists across languages. Hence, in addition to setting syntactic parameters languages may set semantic parameters in different ways and these semantic settings may capture exactly crosslinguistic variation in semantics.

1.2. The Development of the Syntax-Semantics Interface

Studying language acquisition from a semantic perspective does not only have an eye-opening effect with respect to the fact that syntactic theory may not have an answer to all the puzzles in natural language and its development. This shift of perspective is also a prerequisite if one wants to study the syntax-semantics interface in the grammar of a language learner. Understanding this interface and its mechanisms is a first step towards our understanding of whether and how the increase of syntactic complexity in the language of a learner goes hand in hand with an increase of semantic sophistication in this learner's grammar. To illustrate this, let us consider the semantic interpretation of nominal constituents.

It is a by now widespread belief in formal semantics that nominal constituents can be translated into expressions of different semantic types, namely, as individual-, quantifier-, and property-denoting expressions (Partee, 1987). A syntactic-semantic interface question that is directly related to this belief is how adult speakers manage to project phrases onto their interpretation. This is a complex cognitive capacity, one reason being that this kind of mapping from structure onto meaning is very often dependent on context-related factors. While at this point the syntax-semantics interface is still an issue of many debates, the question of how children manage to develop this mapping skill is less debated but of equal importance. In fact, the answer to this developmental question may bring us closer to answering the mapping question in general. Here is an example.

It is a well-known fact that children who acquire English first produce nominal phrases that lack a determiner (see Brown, 1973; Radford, 1990). That is, English learning children produce bare singulars and bare plurals, even though very often bare or determinerless nominal constituents are much less widespread or even ungrammatical in the corresponding adult language. This developmental fact gives rise to the question of whether the lack of determiners in child nominal expressions indicates their lack of semantic sophistication, namely, their inability to distinguish different semantic interpretations for nominal constituents. Widening our knowledge about a learner's command of the semantic sophistication of his or her target language requires that we model the learner's interface between the syntax of this learner's phrases and their semantic interpretation(s).

Clearly, the coverage of syntax and, hence, of the syntax-semantics interface is broader than the syntax of phrases. The structure of a language also consists of the word structure or the morphology of that language. Therefore, a full understanding of the development of a child's interpretive skills requires that we take into account the development of his or her morphological complexity and the potential impact of this morphological complexity on his or her command of semantic complexity. Again, let us consider an example.

It is a well-known fact about learners of English and some other languages that these learners first produce bare verbs, often called 'root infinitives'. This and the emergence of finite morphology are by themselves interesting morphosyntactic facts (see Hoekstra & Hyams, 1998; Radford, 1990; Wexler, 1998). However, these facts become even more interesting if we relate them to the question of what this lack and later the emergence of morphological complexity tell us about the semantic and pragmatic skills of a language learner. Looking at the primary lack of inflectional morphology in English we are once more confronted with the question of whether this lack of morphological complexity indicates a particular lack of semantic sophistication, or whether it does not. In particular, given that in English inflection often contributes aspect and tense information, we can ask whether English learning children lack the cognitive capacity to deal with time and to understand the ways in which time is integrated into language.

One way to reach a better understanding of the impact of morphology on the acquisition of various interpretive skills and on the development of the interface between structure and meaning is by looking into languages that are morphologically rich, that is, at agglutinating and polysynthetic languages. At a very young age learners of these languages are exposed to a highly complex morphological input and, interestingly, these young learners often turn out to be very sensitive to fine-grained semantic distinctions (for Turkish see Aksu-Koç, 1988; for Inuktitut see Allen, 1996; Swift, 2000). This then brings us to the topic of crosslinguistic variation across languages.

1.3. Crosslinguistic Variation and the Variety Status of Learner Data

The morphosyntactic visibility of particular semantic elements can bring about structural principles and interpretive mechanisms of natural language that are not visible in morphologically less complex languages. In section 1.1, I illustrated the notion of crosslinguistic semantic variation in light of interpretive differences between English and German. Another domain in semantics that illustrates many interesting cases of semantic variation is the domain of temporal aspect.

If we utter the Dutch sentence (6), its semantic paraphrases make clear that in Dutch the simple present form *rookt* ('smokes') can have an episodic and a habitual interpretation:

(6) Johan rookt.
    i.   'John is smoking.'
    ii.   'John smokes/is a smoker.'

In English, a simple present verb can receive only a habitual interpretation, as illustrated by *smokes* in (7); the episodic reading given in (6i) is expressed by means of a present progressive form, as shown by *is smoking* in (8):

(7) John smokes.
(8) John is smoking.

Moving from this observation about adult English to child English, it is commonly observed that children acquire the progressive form at a very young age and associate this form with atelic verbs (see Bloom et al., 1981). Relevant research questions here are: At which age does an English child start to use simple present tense forms; does he or she associate these forms with habitual aspect right away (like an English speaking adult does) or does this child go through a 'Dutch' present tense stage first by associating these forms with episodic interpretations? I raise these questions to show that child language can be seen as a variety of its adult target and that language learners may go through a number of stages before they reach their target. A child's so-called 'incorrect' or 'incomplete' use of a particular form may thus be an indication that from a crosslinguistic perspective — in this case a Dutch perspective — the child is correctly associating a particular form with a particular meaning. In fact, my idea that children may go through semantic stages representing particular semantic interpretations that are assigned to forms and constructions of non-target languages is a version of the idea that children go through syntactic stages representing syntactic configurations that we find in non-target languages (Hyams, 1994; Thornton & Crain, 1994). It would be interesting to check whether we can also regard the language developed by the learner of a second language as going through a number of stages which each correspond to an incomplete variety of the target language but perhaps to a complete variety of a non-target language. Note in this respect that in second language acquisition research we also find the opposite view, namely, the view that the first variety of all second language learners is a language-independent "Basic Variety" (Klein & Perdue, 1997). How basic and language-independent this variety really is can be determined only by investigating the second language of speakers of a large sample of fully unrelated source languages.

Finally, an interesting and novel research program within which the semantic variation that comes with the present tense form, as illustrated above for Dutch and English, could be investigated is the program that seeks evidence for semantic parameters (see Beck & Snyder, 2001).

1.4. Acquisition Questions Triggered by Semantic Theory

The degree of precision that has been achieved in formal semantic studies of various phenomena in natural language enables language acquisition researchers to develop and test complex hypotheses about the development of these phenomena. For example, ongoing acquisition studies of a particular peculiarity that has been observed in children's interpretation of universal quantifiers (see Philip, 1995; Crain *et al.*, 1996; Drozd, 2001) often relate their analyses of this peculiarity to existing semantic studies on the formal properties of universal quantification in natural language. Another domain in acquisition research that can gain from research in semantics is the acquisition of focus and focus particles. As an illustration, I will outline some notions of the large apparatus used in focus semantics and related phenomena. These notions are useful, if not indispensable, in formulating the relevant research questions in the study of the structure and the interpretation of child focus as well as in the investigation of focus particles in child language.

Theories of focus (Jackendoff, 1972; Jacobs, 1983; Rooth, 1985; Krifka, 1992) typically assume that focus marking partitions an utterance into at least two parts, namely, its focus and its background. The background is that part of an utterance that helps us to identify a set of alternatives to the focus, that is, the focus semantic value of the utterance. One way in which English marks focus overtly is by intonational prominence, which I have indicated by means of small caps in the examples below:

(9) a.   John introduced Bill to SUE.
    b.   John introduced BILL to Sue.

In (9a), SUE is the focus and the remaining part of the sentence is the background. Focus marking triggers a set of alternative introductions by John to Bill which each involve someone to whom John may have introduced Bill, for example, Sue, John, Fred, Mary, etc. Part of the meaning conveyed by focusing SUE in (9a) is that, in this particular context, it is important that it was Sue to whom John introduced Bill. In (9b), *BILL* is focused. In this case, the set of alternative introductions involves people who may have been introduced to Sue. Focus on *Bill* marks that he is the relevant person. Part of the meaning conveyed by (9b) is that it is relevant that it was Bill who was introduced to Sue. (9) thus illustrates that changes in a sentence's focus marking alter the meaning of this sentence by inducing different focus-background partitions of the sentence and by establishing different sets of alternatives. Turning to acquisition research, it has hardly been investigated how children learn that focus has the power to change the meaning of a particular sentence. Similarly, we do not know much about how children understand that different foci establish different sets of alternatives.

Within theories of focus, focus particles are regarded as elements that operate on a given sentence structure by modifying the semantic interpretation of the focus-background structure of the sentence they occur in (König, 1991). An 'exclusive' or 'restrictive' particle like *only* is used to assert that no member of the set of alternatives other than the focus satisfies the proposition expressed by the sentence. For example, what *only* contributes to the meaning of (10) is that it was Sue and no one other than Sue to whom John introduced Bill:

(10) John only introduced Bill to SUE.

In contrast, an 'inclusive' or 'additive' particle like *also* triggers the presupposition that the proposition to which it applies is true for at least one other member of the relevant set of alternatives which is not the focus. In (11), *also* contributes the presupposition that John introduced Bill to Sue and to someone other than Sue:

(11) John also introduced Bill to SUE.

Children must learn semantic contrasts like those between (10) and (11). A relevant question in this respect is whether the lexical meanings of some kinds of particles are acquired earlier than the meanings of other kinds.

In addition, children must learn that the meaning contribution of a focus particle to a sentence is determined not only by its lexical meaning and the focus-background structure of the sentence it occurs in, but also by the syntactic position of the focus particle in the sentence. The position of the focus particle determines which part of the sentence is in the scope of the focus particle, that is, which part is the particle's domain of application. In English, focus particles typically precede their scope and can adjoin to almost any major constituent. Consider therefore the examples in (12):

(12) a. Even John introduced Bill to Sue.
     b. John even introduced Bill to Sue.
     c. John introduced even Bill to Sue.
     d. John introduced Bill even to Sue.

In (12a), *even* takes scope over the subject *John*, yielding the meaning that it is amazing that John as well as other people introduced Bill to Sue. In (12b), *even* has scope over the VP. Here, the particle applies either to the complete VP, to individual constituents within the VP, or to combinations of individual constituents. In (12c) and (12d), the scope of *even* is reduced to the elements following it, thereby reducing the set of constituents that can be modified by the particle. Again, how do children learn that the syntactic position of a focus particle can determine its scope and, hence, its interpretation?

Another important issue one must raise with respect to the acquisition of focus and focus particles is the semantic contribution of stress. For instance, by putting stress on a particular particle its domain of application can be altered. This is illustrated in the following Dutch example:

(13) a. Het meisje   heeft   OOK   een koekje gegeten.
         The girl   has   also   a cookie eaten
         'The girl too ate a cookie.'

     b. Het meisje   heeft   ook   een koekje gegeten.
         The girl   has   also   a cookie eaten
         'In addition to eating something else, the girl ate a cookie.'

In (13a), the stressed particle OOK ('also, too') modifies the subject *het meisje* ('the girl') while the unstressed *ook* in (13b) modifies the object NP *een koekje* ('a cookie') or the VP *een koekje gegeten* ('a cookie eaten'). How and when do children command the fact that stress brings along this and other kinds of meaning contributions? Note that this brief discussion of stress and focus also illustrates the importance of the interface between sound structure and meaning and how this interface develops.

1.5. What Semantics can Learn from Acquisition Data

The above excursion into the domain of focus and focus particles shows that acquisitionists can take work that has been done in semantics as their guide. But semanticists too can learn a great deal from the study of acquisition data and the developmental hypotheses based on these data. Unlike many studies of the syntax of natural language, the field of natural language semantics has so far paid no attention to acquisition data. The empirical motivation for particular semantic theories has been largely drawn from English and languages related to English. In the past ten years, researchers in semantics have begun to consider also languages that are not related to English in order to create the basis for crosslinguistic semantic research. In this spirit, it seems to be a natural development to also let acquisition data provide empirical support for or against a particular semantic proposal.

In the ideal case, a semantic theory that presents an account of particular adult language data should be naturally extendable towards explaining semantic peculiarities in child varieties of that language. To illustrate this kind of extension, consider the following example of a semantic peculiarity that Krämer (2000) observed in Dutch child language. In (14), the reading paraphrases indicate that Dutch adults interpret the scrambled indefinite NP *een vis* ('a fish') as a wide scope expression, that is, as (14ii). The narrow interpretation given in (14i) is not available for (14):

(14) De jongen   heeft   een vis   niet   gevangen.
     the boy   has   a fish   not   caught
  i.   # 'It is not the case that the boy caught any fish.'   (# ¬ ∃)
  ii. 'There is a fish such that it is not the case that the boy caught it.'   (∃ ¬)

Krämer found out that more than 80% of the Dutch children (age 4;0–5;6) she investigated interpret scrambled indefinites in a nonadultlike way. The majority of children interpret *een vis* ('a fish') in (14) as if this indefinite, which is out of the scope of the negation particle *niet* ('not'), were in the scope of *niet*. In Dutch child language, singular indefinites thus seem to be interpreted as inherent narrow scope expressions. In a way, children interpret indefinites as if they were bare plurals, which are well-known for their inherent narrow scope behaviour (Carlson, 1977). For example, (15) can only mean that each boy caught some fish; it lacks the reading in which some fish were caught by every boy:

(15) Iedere jongen   heeft   vissen   gevangen.
     every boy   has   fish.PL   caught
  i.   'For every boy there were fish and he caught them.'   (∀ ∃)
  ii. #'There were some fish and every boy caught them.'   (# ∃ ∀)

The above peculiarity in child Dutch is a challenge for semantic theories of indefinites and bare plurals, and here is why.

In the semantic literature, we find two proposals for the interpretation of bare plurals. Building on Carlson's (1977) kind-based theory of the English bare plural, Chierchia (1998) proposes that all bare nominals across languages (i.e., bare singulars and bare plurals) are basically kind-denoting expressions — irrespective of whether they occur in a generic or in a nongeneric context. When used in a nongeneric context, a bare plural is re-interpreted as a predicate which receives its existential interpretation from the verb; this explains its narrow scope. In Chierchia's proposal, indefinites are never kind-denoting expressions but they introduce an existential quantifier or a choice function. Hence, adult indefinites and adult bare plurals have disjoint denotations and the source of a bare plural's narrow scope is different from the way in which an indefinite receives narrow scope. Alternatively, I argued in Van Geenhoven (1998, 2000) that in nongeneric contexts bare plurals denote a property; narrow scope indefinites denote properties as well. Property-denoting arguments receive their existential interpretation from the verb, which explains their inherent narrow scope (Carlson, 1977; McNally, 1992, 1998). I furthermore proposed that in addition to their property interpretation indefinites have a so-called free variable interpretation. The existential interpretation of these indefinites is the result of accommodation, a mechanism commonly used in presupposition projection theories (Heim, 1983; van der Sandt, 1992). A case in point is the wide scope interpretation of the indefinite in (14).

With these two approaches in mind, what happens if we now try to understand the Dutch child's inherent narrow scope interpretation of indefinite NPs. In a property-based approach the inherent narrow scope of a Dutch child's indefinites can be argued to have the same source as that of the inherent narrow scope of a Dutch adult's bare plurals. This is because a child's indefinites and an adult's bare plurals simply build a natural class: They denote properties. What Dutch children apparently do at some stage in their acquisition of the meanings of indefinites is that they ignore the structural scope position of indefinites while they overgeneralize the property interpretation. From a Chierchian perspective, in which indefinites and bare plurals are not a natural semantic class in adult grammar, one could explain the development from a child's indefinites as inherently narrow expressions to an adult's indefinites as expressions with narrow and wide scope as the result of type-shift. That is, while a child's indefinites may have at first the denotation of an adult's bare plural (i.e., a kind individual), later their semantic type is shifted to that of an adult's indefinite (i.e., an existential quantifier or a choice function).

Krämer (2000) has chosen the first approach. She argues that what Dutch children must learn is that in addition to their property interpretation indefinites receive a free variable interpretation and, moreover, that in Dutch these two interpretations correspond to two syntactic positions. If an indefinite NP is located to the left of a negation marker, as in (14), the indefinite receives a free variable interpretation. If it is located to the right of a negation marker, as shown in (16), the indefinite receives a property interpretation:

(16) De jongen   heeft   niet eens   een vis   gevangen.
     the boy   *has*   *not even*   *a fish* *caught*
   i.   'It is not even the case that the boy caught a fish.'   (¬ ∃)
   ii.   # 'There is a fish such that it is not even the case that the
            boy caught it.'   (# ∃ ¬)

Krämer relates the late emergence of interpreting indefinite NPs as free variable expressions to the late emergence of the ability to create discourse relations, that is, to the late command of variable binding mechanisms across sentences. Understanding discourse relations requires interpretive skills that go beyond the skills needed for the interpretation of a sentence. According to Krämer, the wide scope reading of *een vis* in (14) requires a command of these discourse skills and we seem to have an example in which growth of semantic sophistication is directly related to a growing awareness of syntactic complexity: Different structural positions map onto different semantic interpretations. We also seem to have an example of how child data can support a particular semantic theory of narrow scope nominals.

1.6. Methodology

Since semantic theories have begun to consider the data of unrelated an unfamiliar languages as a new way of gaining crosslinguistic empirical support of their hypotheses, there is a clear need for developing elicitation methods of semantic data and for setting up control mechanisms. These needs clearly also exist when we try to explain child data from a semantic perspective and when we want to use child data as supporting evidence for a particular semantic theory. In fact, we need more: For example, before we can study a child's understanding of the interaction between universal quantifiers and negation we must make sure that this child has some notion of universal quantification, on the one hand, and of negation, on the other.

A question that arises in this respect is whether we can adopt the methodology and experimental designs used in studies of the acquisition of syntactic phenomena. Interesting guides in this respect are McDaniel *et al.* (1996) and Crain & Thornton (1998). As we will see below, some of the contributions in this volume illustrate a variety of experimental designs and show how methods and experiments can lead to diverging conclusions of the same phenomena.

2. THE CONTRIBUTIONS

The volume is divided into five parts that correspond to the topics addressed in the previous section. In a first part, we find three papers (Carlson; Roeper; Matsuo) on topics related to the syntax-semantics interface. Part two contains three papers (Meroni, Gualmini & Crain; Drozd & van Loosbroek; Musolino) which focus on quantificational expressions in child language. A third set of papers (Van Geenhoven; Swift; Starren) takes a semantic perspective on temporal issues in first and second language acquisition. The fourth part consists of two papers (Klein; Gretsch) on the semantics and pragmatics of finiteness and its acquisition, a phenomenon that is closely related to temporality in language. The papers in the final part (Nederstigt; Bergsma) discuss the early presence and interpretation of focus particles and stress in German and Dutch child language.

Note that in many of the chapters in this volume the acquisition data are drawn from a variety of languages and their learner varieties, namely, Czech, Dutch, English, German, Inuktitut, Italian, Japanese, and Polish. Particular chapters make reference to a large number of languages. This shows that the volume aims at a crosslinguistic perspective on the phenomena under discussion.

2.1. Part I: The Development of the Syntax-Semantics Interface

As pointed out in the previous section, an important step for a child to master particular interpretations of natural language expressions, is that he or she learns to master the ways in which language structure is mapped onto language meaning. In the first chapter, Carlson outlines some of the challenges that the language learner encounters when he must figure out the way(s) in which a language form maps onto its meaning(s). Even though learners are confronted with many mismatches between structure and meaning, they seem to master these mismatches rather naturally in the end.

The acquisition of the syntax-semantics interface is also the topic of the chapter by Roeper, in particular, the interface between the syntax of nominal constituents and their meanings. Roeper hypothesizes that children first link nonspecific and kind meanings to nominals that have a NP structure and associate referential and specific meanings to nominal expressions which have a DP structure.

The paper by Matsuo addresses a well-known phenomenon in the interface between structure and meaning, namely, the sequence of tense

(SOT). In an SOT language, embedded past tense forms are ambiguous between a so-called overlapping reading and a real past reading. Matsuo investigates the question of whether an embedded past tense form is more difficult to interpret for children learning an SOT language (e.g., English, Dutch) than it is for children who are acquiring a non-SOT language (e.g., Japanese, Polish). Before interpreting an embedded tense correctly, children must, for example, command the distinction between a complement clause and an adjunct clause. One must try to closely pin down how the acquisition of an embedded tense proceeds and compare whether and where there is a difference in the acquisition of an embedded tense in SOT and non-SOT languages.

2.2. Part II: Acquiring Universal Quantification

Meroni, Gualmini & Crain examine a certain type of error children make in interpreting universally quantified sentences. When shown a picture with three boys riding a donkey and a donkey without a rider children often say 'no' when asked whether every boy is riding a donkey. They bring additional experimental support for Crain *et al.*'s (1996) view that this non-adult behaviour is an experimental artefact.

The chapter by Drozd & van Loosbroek argues for a different perspective on this error in the acquisition of universal quantification. In earlier work, they argued that the error reflects that children interpret universal quantifiers as weak quantifiers (see Milsark, 1974). In their chapter contributed to this volume, they argue that this non-adult behaviour follows from the fact that children do not manage to reorganize and update the context, skills that are required for the interpretation of universally quantified expressions.

In the chapter contributed by Musolino, the author discusses findings from an interconnected set of experiments designed to investigate children's (and adults') knowledge of scope phenomena involving the interaction of quantified NPs and negation. His main finding is that while adults can easily assign non-isomorphic interpretations to sentences containing a quantified NP and negation — that is, interpretations that cannot be directly read off the surface structure — children systematically interpret these sentences on the basis of the surface position of the quantificational elements.

2.3. Part III: Time in the Language of a Learner

The development of temporal expressions and their interpretation provides yet another interesting challenge both for acquisition and semantic theories of time in language. A first point of interest is the for acquisitionists well-known but by semanticists hardly known 'aspect before tense' hypothesis (Bloom *et al.*, 1980). This hypothesis captures the idea that children acquire lexical and grammatical aspectual distinctions before they command tense. All chapters contributed in this part examine this hypothesis.

Van Geenhoven's chapter examines the hypothesis from a theoretical semantic perspective. She presents a stage model that integrates the development of tense in that of aspect. In particular, she argues that an early lexical aspectual distinction 'telic versus atelic' stimulates the development of grammatical aspect (imperfective, perfective, perfect, and prospective). Furthermore, a child's command of the relational meanings of grammatical aspect (Klein, 1994) is said to be a necessary basis for his or her command of the relations expressed by present, past, and future tense.

Swift examines the hypothesis from a crosslinguistic perspective by addressing the development of temporality in the speech of children acquiring Inuktitut, a polysynthetic language spoken in East Canada. Looking into this language is interesting because aspect is expressed by means of explicit morphological markers. On the basis of a large set of Inuktitut data, Swift concludes that language structure can influence the developmental order of tense and aspect marking but that crosslinguistically the semantic processes in the development of tense and aspect are very similar.

Starren's chapter discusses the 'aspect before tense' hypothesis from the perspective of second languages learners, specifically, from the perspective of Moroccan and Turkish learners of Dutch. In this way, she shows that acquisition data of second language learners provide an interesting empirical basis for our understanding of the development of temporal expressions. A crucial difference between the acquisition of temporality by first as opposed to second language learners is that only the former already command a complete temporal system in their first language. Starren presents the structural embedding of early tense and aspect markers and of early temporal adverbials in varieties of Dutch acquired by untutored Turkish and Moroccan learners. She hypothesizes that the positioning of the temporal adverbials sets the skeleton for the acquisition of aspect and tense marking.

2.4. Part IV: Finiteness and its Development

As mentioned above, existing studies of the acquisition of finiteness typically focus on the emergence of finite morphology and narrow the role of finiteness to the issue of the much discussed 'root infinitives'. In his chapter, Klein points out that finiteness is not a mere fact of verb morphology but a grammatical category in its own right. He argues that it is the carrier of assertion — or, more generally speaking, of validity — in an utterance and that finiteness relates the descriptive content of a sentence to its topic time.

Klein then shows how most of the syntactic and semantic effects connected to finiteness naturally follow from this assumption.

Adopting Klein's view on finiteness, Gretsch compares the interpretation of finite child utterances with the interpretation of their infinitival utterances. Whereas the former are typically associated with conveying descriptions of the actual world, the latter are associated with commenting on ongoing events and with requests. Gretsch argues that this cannot be grasped in existing syntactic accounts of (non)finiteness in child language. She presents an alternative meaning-based functional account.

2.5. Part V: Focus Particles in Child Language

In section 1, I outlined how the study of the development of focus particles in the language of a learner can benefit from the findings and notions used in focus semantics. Many acquisition studies on focus particles examine restrictive particles like *only*. Both chapters in this part are innovative in that they investigate the acquisition of additive particles.

Nederstigt presents a study of the acquisition of the German additive particles *auch* ('also, too') and *noch* ('still, also') that is based on *auch*- and *noch*-utterances in the spontaneous production data of a German girl (age 1;10-3;06). She discusses a number of differences between the two particles. These differences concern the position of the particles and their scope, the notion of focus for their interpretation, and the influence of pitch accent on the particle.

The final chapter in this volume presents Bergsma's investigation of the acquisition of the Dutch additive particle *ook* ('also, too'). She presents the results of a comprehension experiment that was set up to examine the understanding of this particle by Dutch children (age 4;02-7;11).

Radboud Universiteit Nijmegen

3. ACKNOWLEDGEMENTS

The majority of papers that make up this volume have been presented at the workshop 'Semantics Meets Acquisition' that I organized at the Max Planck Institute for Psycholinguistics in Nijmegen in the Spring of 2000. Due to various circumstances it took me longer than expected to collect, comment, edit, and format the chapters and to turn them into this book. I thank the contributing authors for their patience during this process. I also wish to thank two anonymous reviewers whose critical comments improved the content of this introduction as well as the way in which I organized the volume. Finally, I owe thanks to Nigel Duffield and Hans Kamp for many helpful comments.

4. NOTES

[1] As a reviewer and N. Duffield both pointed out, one might argue that parametric difference in (covert) syntactic movement might solve the differences presented here for English and German. However, this would lead to a situation in which semantics rules syntactic movement, which in my view leads to a pseudo-syntactic explanation.

[2] Note that in (16) I am using *niet eens* ('not even') so that this example illustrates a case in which negation surfaces as the free morpheme *niet*. Without *eens*, negation is absorbed into the negative indefinite determiner *geen* ('no'), as shown in (i):

(i) De jongen heeft geen vis gevangen.
    The boy   has   no   fish caught
    'The boy didn't catch any fish.'

5. REFERENCES

Aksu-Koç, Ayhan. *The Acquisition of Aspect and Modality: The Case of Past Reference in Turkish*. Cambridge: Cambridge University Press, 1988.
Allen, Shanley. *Aspects of Argument Structure Acquisition in Inuktitut*. Amsterdam: Benjamins, 1996.
Beck, Sigrid, and William Snyder. "Complex Predicates and Goal PP's: Evidence for a Semantic Parameter." In Anna H.-J. Do, Laura Dominguez, and Aimee Johnson (eds.) *Proceedings of the 25th Annual Boston University Conference on Language Development*, 114–122, Sommerville: Cascadilla Press, 2001.
Bloom, Lois, Karin Lifter, and Jeremie Hafitz. "Semantics of Verbs and the Development of Verb Inflection in Child Language." *Language* 56 (1980): 386–412.
Brown, Roger. *A First Language: The Early Stages*. London: Allen and Unwin Ltd, 1973.
Carlson, Gregory N. *Reference to Kinds in English*. Ph.D. Diss., University of Massachusetss, Amherst, 1977.
Chierchia, Gennaro. "Reference to Kinds across Languages." *Natural Language Semantics* 6 (1998): 339–405.
Chierchia, Gennaro, Maria Teresa Guasti, and Andrea Gualmini, "Early Omission of Articles and the Syntax/Semantics Map." Paper presented at *Generative Approaches to Language Acquisition*. Potsdam, 1999.
Chomsky, Noam. *Knowledge of Language: Its Nature, Origin and Use*. New York: Praeger, 1986.
Comrie, Bernard. *Aspect*. Cambridge: Cambridge University Press, 1976.
Crain, Stephen, and Rosalind Thornton. *Investigations in Universal Grammar: A Guide to Experiments on the Acquisition of Syntax*. Cambridge: MIT Press, 1998.
Crain, Stephen, Rosalind Thornton, Carol Boster, Laura Conway, Diane Lillo-Martin, and Elaine Woodams. "Quantification without Qualification." *Language Acquisition* 5 (1996): 83–153.
Drozd, Kenneth F. "Children's Weak Interpretation of Universally Quantified Sentences." In Melissa Bowerman and Stephen Levinson (eds.) *Conceptual Development and Language Acquisition*, 340–376. Cambridge: Cambridge University Press, 2001.
Geurts, Bart. "On *No*." *Journal of Semantics* 13 (1996): 67–87.
Heim, Irene. "On the Projection Problem for Presuppositions." In Michael Barlow, Dan Flickinger, and Michael Wescoat (eds.) *Proceedings of WCCFL 2*, 114–126. Stanford: Stanford Linguistics Association, 1983.

Hoekstra, Teun, and Nina Hyams. "Aspects of Root Infinitives." *Lingua* 106 (1998): 81–112.
Hyams, Nina. *Language Acquisition and the Theory of Parameters.* Dordrecht: Kluwer, 1986.
Hyams, Nina. "V2, Null Arguments and C-Projections." In Teun Hoekstra and Bonnie Schwartz (eds.) *Language Acquisition Studies in Generative Grammar*, 21–56. Amsterdam: John Benjamins, 1994.
Jackendoff, Ray. *Semantic Interpretation in Generative Grammar.* Cambridge: MIT Press, 1972.
Jacobs, Joachim. *Fokus und Skalen: Zur Syntax und Semantik der Gradpartikeln im Deutschen.* Tübingen: Niemeyer, 1983.
Klein, Wolfgang. *Time in Language.* London: Routledge, 1994.
Klein, Wolfgang, and Clive Perdue. "The Basic Variety, or: Couldn't Natural Language be Much Simpler?" *Second Language Research* 13 (1997): 301–347.
König, Ekkehard. *The Meaning of Focus Particles: A Comparative Perspective.* London: Routledge, 1991.
Krämer, Irene. *Interpreting Indefinites: An Experimental Study of Children's Language Comprehension.* Ph.D. Diss., Universiteit Utrecht, 2000.
Krifka, Manfred. "A Compositional Semantics for Multiple Focus Constructions." In Joachim Jacobs (ed.) *Informationsstruktur und Grammatik, Sonderheft der Linguistischen Berichte* 4 (1992): 17–53.
Ladd, D. Robert. *The Structure of Intonational Meaning.* Bloomington: Indiana University Press, 1980.
McDaniel, Dana, Cecile McKee, and Helen S. Cairns. *Methods for Assessing Children's Syntax.* Cambridge, MA: MIT Press, 1996.
McNally, Louise. *An Interpretation for the English Existential Construction.* Ph.D. Diss., University of California, Santa Cruz, 1992.
McNally, Louise. "Existential Sentences without Existential Quantification." *Linguistics and Philosophy* 21 (1998): 353–392.
Milsark, Gary. *Existential Sentences in English.* Ph.D. Diss., MIT, 1974.
Partee, Barbara H. "Noun Phrase Interpretation and Type-Shifting Principles." In Jeroen Groenendijk, Dik de Jongh, and Martin Stokhof (eds.) *Studies in Discourse Representation Theory and the Theory of Generalized Quantifiers*, 115–143. Dordrecht: Foris, 1987.
Philip, William. *Event Quantification in the Acquisition of Universal Quantification.* Ph.D. Diss., University of Massachusetts, Amherst, 1995.
Radford, Andrew. *Syntactic Theory and the Acquisition of English Syntax.* Oxford: Blackwell, 1990.
Rooth, Mats. *Association with Focus.* Ph.D. Diss., University of Massachusetts, Amherst, 1985.
van der Sandt, Rob. "Presupposition Projection and Anaphora Resolution." *Journal of Semantics* 9 (1992): 333–377.
Swift, Mary. *The Development of Temporal Reference in Inuktitut Child Language.* Ph.D. Diss., University of Texas, Austin, 2000.
Thornton, Rosalind and Stephen Crain. "Successful Cyclic *Wh*-Movement." In Teun Hoekstra and Bonnie Schwartz (eds.) *Language Acquisition Studies in Generative Grammar*, 215–252. Amsterdam: John Benjamins, 1994.
Van Geenhoven, Veerle. *Semantic Incorporation and Indefinite Descriptions.* Stanford: CSLI Publications, 1998.
Van Geenhoven, Veerle. "Pro Properties, Contra Generalized Kinds." In Brendan Jackson and Tanya Matthews (eds.) *Proceedings of SALT 10*, 221–238. Ithaca: CLC Publications, 2000.
Wexler, Kenneth. "Very Early Parameter Setting and the Unique Checking Constraint: A New Explanation of the Optional Infinitive Stage." *Lingua* 106 (1998): 23–79.

GREG CARLSON

'MISMATCHES' OF FORM AND INTERPRETATION

Abstract. Much work in language acquisition has focused on the meanings of major lexical items (chiefly nouns, adjectives, and verbs). This chapter instead focuses on the types of issues and problems that arise when one focuses on the meanings of function words in a language (such as tense markers, conjunctions, articles, etc.). The issues that arise are very different from those surrounding the acquisition of major lexical items. It is pointed out that the function items interact with the syntax in complex ways that form a special challenge for any current view of language and meaning acquisition.

1. 'MEANING' AND SEMANTICS

The theme of the conference 'Semantics meets acquisition' that led to this volume has an amusing ring to it as it hearkens back to 'B' movie titles such as 'Wolfman meets Frankenstein'. This latent reference to movie monsters turns out to be apt, in a certain sense, as when I think about the twin issues of acquisition and semantics, and how to put them together, it does seem a frighteningly hard problem indeed. Were this presented to me as an abstract problem in a form that I didn't recognize as really about learning and meaning, I'm sure I would throw up my hands and soon declare the problem insoluble. But this of course would be a misjudgment, as it is contradicted daily by simple facts of the world.

In this chapter, I initially take a fairly superficial, perhaps even naive, perspective on matters of meaning and learning. I am going to assume that early language learners have, at best, access to knowledge of surfacy kinds of linguistic information (such as word boundaries), and some knowledge of context. I will present in overview style some of the challenges learners might face in trying to construct a consistent form-to-meaning mapping. (Throughout I take the point of view of someone trying to understand a language). One way to begin thinking about the issue is 'from the top', so to speak. The *experience* of extracting information from natural language utterances is a global one — the experience is that of understanding something you didn't before the utterance event occurred, and that's about it. This does not distinguish for instance among presuppositions, conveyed meanings, implicatures, literal, or metaphorical meanings, nor any other types of information derived from your encounter with the utterance, e.g. location, gender, emotional state of the speaker, etc. Some take this intuition about the unity of our experience at face value — this I take it is the underpinnings of "holism of meaning" (Chierchia & McConnell-Ginet, 2000) but I and many others believe that messages extracted from natural language are susceptible to analysis (the 'atomist' position) and it becomes clear that analysis leads to a view that meaning *in toto* is composed of a variety of distinguishable factors.

Let us draw a parallel. Upon hearing a single word, say, the English word *cats*, one has the experience of hearing a noise and pairing it with a certain type of animal, very roughly. There is nothing, I believe, in this experience that comes identified as also experiencing 'a word', 'two morphemes', 'a stem', 'the feature [-sonorant]', 'noun', and so on and so forth. Yet, upon analysis it becomes clear that this experience is somehow informed by a constellation of such factors, that all these factors or factors like them contribute their part to the whole. The experience of meaning is, I believe, likewise amenable to such analysis, and when one considers the factors it becomes clear that *meaning experienced* in its broadest sense results from a combination of similar factors, factors that do not wear their rank on their sleeves but which become apparent upon consideration through the lens of analysis. When we use the term 'semantics', we intend a certain *component* of meaning, that component which is in some sense referentially based and which is connected most intimately with the syntax of natural language: I'm going to refer to this as the truth-conditional aspect of meaning, a phrase I use here for convenience rather than in its fullest theoretical sense. This is the aspect of meaning which is absent from otherwise meaningful objects and events, such as the dark emotive colors in a painting, the rattling sound in my car, music, and, apparently (though I want to be a bit careful here), animal communication systems.

However, language clearly conveys meaning in ways in common with such other things, as well. Consider a point emphasized in Grice's work on conversational implicatures (Grice, 1975). He takes pains to point out that these implicatures apply to actions in general, not just the linguistic actions of executing utterances. For instance, one can congratulate someone by patting them on the back or shaking their hand, or one can do it linguistically by saying something like *Way to go there, Bob* or by using the stodgy performative utterance *I hereby congratulate you on your success*. Meanings of actions then, including linguistic actions, contribute one component to the meaning of the whole. Another type of meaning that is not commonly discussed in truth-conditional approaches is that of connotative or social/emotional meaning, associated primarily with words and set phrases. To learn a language is to learn, in part, facts like *rump* is a somewhat cruder way of making reference to a certain body part than *hind end*, and that *derrière* (in English) is almost affectedly silly, in most contexts, despite common reference. Such social/emotional meaning is omnipresent in language, is an essential part of its overall meaning, and seems most highlighted in poetry, song lyrics, and corporate presentations; but it is a type of meaning clearly present in nonlinguistic artistic objects and events as well. A further component of meaning arises from background cultural knowledge. For instance, the significance of the color red varies from culture to culture. And, in language, it is not a good idea (in English) to wish someone a refreshing night's sleep by saying *Rest in peace*, as this is a formulaic phrase that is associated with gravestones.

The purpose here is not to enumerate or catalogue the variety of meanings that the use of natural language gives rise to. Rather, it is to make the point that when we begin to talk about the semantics of a quantifier or the scope of tense marking, and how they might be acquired, we are already a long distance out of the starting gate in considering the general issue of meaning and language. Meaning comes at us — and people learning a language — from a variety of different directions, at a large numbers of levels, and only one among them is the subject of the kinds of semantic theories that are intimately connected with the syntax of language. Learners must somehow identify this level.

2. LEXICAL SEMANTICS

How this is accomplished remains something of a puzzle. But let us assume it gets done. Even then, when we restrict consideration to just this semantic, truth-conditional aspect of meaning, the difficulty of the problem of learning hardly abates. Obviously, perhaps most obviously, one must learn the meanings of the words of the language (or, a significant subset of them, at any rate), and there are many terrifically interesting learning issues that have been explored within this domain, at least in the area of learning meanings of the content words, nouns, verbs, adjectives, in the main (e.g., Gleitman, 1990; Bowerman, 1980; Clark, 1993; Bates, 1979). One absolutely immediate problem that comes up here is that of ambiguity. I would like to point out that the problem, even at the lexical level, is of mind-boggling proportions. In the early 1960's the linguist Charles Fries did a count of how many meanings were listed in the Oxford English Dictionary for the 500 most common words of English; there were in excess of 14,000, or about 28 different meanings per word, on average. Granted, many would be regarded as different 'senses' rather than different meanings proper, and a good many of them are low-frequency or even archaic usages that are learned later in life, if at all. Further, in context none are remotely as ambiguous as in citation form (though again, the question is how learners could marshal the context to narrow down the possibilities in the first place). On the other hand, many ambiguities are not included in this count. Type/token ambiguities are systematically associated with nouns (e.g., the ambiguity of *All the machines at the arcade are for sale*, whether it is those actual machines or other individual machines of the same design). Metonymic reference is not reflected there, as in the practice commonly cited of waitpersons referring to customers by their orders, resulting in ambiguities in sentences like *The ham sandwich is ready to eat*. Many ambiguities of thematic role assignment, which are extremely common, are missing. *John shoveled the cement* has the cement either as location cleared, or what was moved, *Sally packed the suitcases* can have the suitcases being put into things, or things being put into them, etc. Nor are many figurative meanings, on the whole, included in this count. It is hard to see offhand, or even on reflection, how any of this helps a language learner. To pair a new meaning with a word for which you already have a meaning, it appears one must notice there is an error, in the first place, which requires tremendous sensitivity to context *and* what is appropriate in a context. In the second place one must also localize the error: If one hears *That actor is a ham* and notes that the utterance is wrong in context for the 'smoked meat' sense of *ham*, why not conclude the error is due to *actor*, *that*, *is*, or *a*? Or perhaps it is a scope ambiguity, a topic/focus distinction?

The problem of learning words that are ambiguous has hardly gone unnoted, and in fact has received a huge amount of attention in the language learning literature (e.g., for a recent overview see Siskind, 2000). The chief focus, to this point, has been on the learning of ambiguous lexical items (nouns, verbs, adjectives, prepositions). But understanding an utterance of a sentence or discourse involves, of course, much more than just understanding the meanings of lexical items, and resolving their ambiguities in context. It involves consideration of the ways the lexical items are combined with one another, and here, as is well-known, the problem of ambiguity is likewise omnipresent — one could responsibly say that it has been a central problem in psycholinguistic and computational research in the past few decades. As we know the linear order of words can make an essential difference in meaning (*Dogs chase cats* vs. *Cats chase dogs*) but in many other instances there is no difference (*Mary put out the cat* vs. *Mary put the cat out*, Scrambling structures that appear in most languages, etc). But perhaps most interestingly, a vital part of learning this combinatory semantics is ferreting out the contributions of all those 'little' words to the meaning of the whole. Considering the contributions of these not so apparently referential things is a central focus of semanticists: What is the meaning of a past tense, a modal, an indefinite article, a reciprocal expression, *if*, *how*, *which*, what does an infinitival marker do, a plural ending, negation, interrogative pronouns?

3. NON-LEXICAL SEMANTICS

Consideration of these *functional* elements of meaning (Lebeaux, 1988; Carlson, 1983) introduces issues about the mapping between forms and meaning that are either absent or obscured when one concentrates primarily on the semantics of lexical items, or grosser aspects of sentence meaning such as argument structure. Consider the instance of the Classical Latin conjunctive particle *-que* (e.g., Hale & Buck, 1966). Latin had this alongside the conjunction *et,* but the syntax of the two was not the same. *Et* appeared, from a semantic point of view, 'right where it is supposed to', that is, between the elements conjoined, like most conjunctions we're used to seeing. The enclitic *-que*, on the other hand, appeared attached to the end of the first word of the phrase conjoined. Thus in (1) *-que* appears after the first word but signals that the whole phrase is a conjoined element, and not just the word *two*:

(1) *duasque ibi   legiones conscribit*
     two-and there   legions enrolled
     '... and there he enrolled two legions.'

In a slight wrinkle probably driven by prosodic considerations, it appeared attached to the second word if the first was a monosyllabic preposition:

(2) *ob   easque   res*
     because   these-and   things
     '... and because of these things'

If one treats *-que* as having the meaning of a conjunction, and compositionally combines it with whatever it is combining with on the surface syntax, one would not be able to get these meanings. Instead, one must in some sense 'raise' it up to a higher position in the tree structure, and put it in its rightful place. (This is a lot like Quantifier Raising, of course, with the notable difference that in the case of *-que* one does not wish to leave a variable in situ). Of course in such examples *-que* is not in any 'wrong' place — to put it elsewhere would be wrong — because the grammar says it is to be put where it is. But from a compositional semantic point of view, one needs to do some rearranging that one does not need to do with Latin *et*, English *and*, and German *und*.

This particular example is not simply an idle little curiosity to note and tuck away. The position of *-que* is of course a Wackernagel position phenomenon — a 'second position' phenomenon — a syntactic-morphological position so common it has a name (Anderson, 1993). But the phenomenon of having to 'rearrange' functional elements semantically extends well beyond Wackernagel position particles such as these. Consider how common it is to treat tense, for instance, both syntactically and semantically as a higher-level operator, and for good reason. A very common type of example from English Verb Phrase ellipsis will illustrate this point — the deleted VP in (3) does not carry the tense information of the (underlined) antecedent VP, even though tense is expressed as an inflection on the verb in that antecedent:

(3)   John *wrote a paper* because he had to (*wrote a paper).

Or, it appears plurality must be dissociated from the noun it appears attached to, by similar evidence:

(4)   John has two *dogs* and Fred has one (*dogs).

This listing of functional elements that appear 'out of place', from the point of view of where in the structure the meaning is contributed, is easily extendible to the point where one can easily conclude that it is a common and possibly essential feature of language that learners must somehow master. Is this something we are born knowing already? That would help, it seems, but how can one tell?

The appearance of items that do not seem to be 'in the right place' is but one of the issues learners must face in dealing with the meanings of functional items. Coalescence phenomena between adjacent functional elements are extraordinarily common — it is the classic definition of an inflectional language as opposed to an agglutinative one. Coalescence may also occur with otherwise free morphemes, as with the preposition/article coalescence found in Germanic and Romance; thus, French *du* is in some sense the equivalent of *de+le*. From the commonsense point of view taken here, a learner is required to assign a composite meaning to such elements as *du*, but not to other elements such as *le*, or any lexical items. A very similar process that well could cause increasing difficulties is when a sequence of two formally identical functional elements is reduced to one (a variant of haplology). This does not, to my knowledge, occur with lexical items (thus, *a bare bear* does not reduce to *a bear*, meaning 'a BARE bear'). Consider the case of Japanese -*no*, noted by Kuno (1973), Radford (1977), and others. It has two quite distinct functions, as a possessive postposition and as a pronoun (meaning some thing like 'one'). If these are juxtaposed, as in (5a), you get an ungrammatical sentence. But there is a nonperiphrastic way of expressing this, namely, (5b), with only one instance of -*no*. But both the possessive meaning and the pronominal meaning remain:

(5) a. *Kore wa anata no no desu ka.
This TOP you POSS one be Q
'Is this yours?' (lit. 'Your one')

b. Kore wa anata no desu ka.

Again, this is hardly a funny little isolated fact. One can multiply examples by the dozens in familiar and unfamiliar languages alike, and, as usual, when one looks for something like this, it seems to be everywhere. The Swahili negative past *ku* occurring right next to the infinitival marker *ku* reduces to a single *ku-* prefix, yet both meanings remain. In certain Turkish word forms (in the instance of NPs like *their books* where both the possessors and things possessed are plural) two plurals 'ought' to appear in a row, but only one appears; there are, however, two plurals, semantically. The special problem that examples like these raise is that, from a surfacy point of view, you have one element with two meanings, or the same meaning assigned two different scopes, as in the Turkish example. But I thought it was almost an axiomatic fact of perception that a single form could *not* be assigned two different meanings. Not only does this apply to lexical items. *He sat by the bank* cannot mean he sat by the river *and* a financial institution but this applies to perception more generally — this is Necker cube stuff. This would seem a prime case of putting the learner squarely behind the eight ball; yet, there it is.

We not only have the case of one form with two meanings to be concerned about, but also its converse. Two (or more) forms that add up to a single meaning. One reflection of this is discontinuous morphology. For instance, Nida (1978) cites the Kekchi examples in (6):

(6) a. *oçcoçc*
'house'

b. *roçcoçce'p*
'their house'

French *ne ... pas* would be a possible candidate for a more familiar example. But far more commonly this is found in agreement or concord forms: an agreeing plural article, two plural adjectives, and a plural noun add up to simply one plurality, not four. A definite article combined with the definite form of a noun still adds up to one definite. Multiple negations, as given in the Old English example in (7) add up to a one single negative:

(7)   Ac   he   ne   sealde nanum nytene ne
      and   he   NEG   gave   NEG   beasts NEG
      nanum fisce nane sawle.
      NEG   fish NEG   souls
      'And he did not give beasts or fish souls.'

Such examples are so familiar we might easily overlook the language learning problem: if we build a signal-detector that generates an associated meaning upon encounter with a certain form, we are going to get extra meanings generated which are not parts of the actual interpretation. Note that the strategy of treating certain forms as meaningless, and localizing the meaning to just one of the forms, may work in some instances but not generally. Let us take a really simple example, the English phrase *these houses*. Here we have two plural forms, so let us treat the one on the noun as 'real'. The problem is that *These have wooden doors* has a plural subject, semantically and in all other respects, and so does *Houses have wooden doors*.

It also appears on occasion that sounds are not paired with meanings. We are all used to work on expletives, so I will draw on examples from another domain, that of Classical Latin semi-deponent verbs. Latin had a productive inflectional passive marker that normally signalled passivization (i.e., the subject is semantically the direct object), but in many semi-deponents while the present tenses were formed from the usual active paradigms, the perfect forms required the passive morphology, but without a corresponding effect on passive meaning. Here is a textbook example:

(8)   a.   *audeo*   b.   *ausus sum*
           'I dare.'   'I dared.' (not, 'I was dared.')

Or, consider the habitual markers that appear in contrafactuals in some languages. In (9) is an example from Hindi cited in Iatridou (2000), due to R. Bhatt:

(9)   a.   ??Meera   do baje   bhaashaN   de
           Meeraa   2 o'clock   speech   give
           rahii   ho-tii (hai)
           PROG.F be-HAB.F (PRES)

      b.   agar   Meera   kal   do baje
           if   Meera   yesterday   2 o'clock
           bhaashaN   de   rahii ho-tii
           speech   give   PROG.F be-HAB.F

'... if Meera had been giving a speech yesterday at 2:00 ...'

Here, there is no discernible semantic contribution of the habituality marker HAB in (9b), while in (9a) its presence does make a semantic contribution, which makes the point-time adverbial sound strange (as generalizations are often odd if given point-time readings); but not so in (9b). English pluralia tanta (*scissors*, *pants*), or dependent plurals (as in *Unicycles have wheels*) would be possible examples of a plural making no semantic contribution. I will not go on, but language seems to have many instances of interpretable elements that, in given constructions, bear no such or seemingly any meaning.

Or, what they can do is bear *other* meanings instead. An illustrative case is the Spanish spurious *se*, first discussed to my knowledge in the generative literature by Perlmutter (1971). In sequences of Spanish clitics, if the third person indirect object clitic appears before a third person direct object clitic, it is realized as *se*, which is normally taken to be a reflexive form (though it has other functions as well). However, the meaning is not (necessarily) reflexive:

(10) Se   lo   mandas.
     REFL   3PERS.SG   SEND.2PERS
     'You send it to him/her/them.'

(11) * Le/*Les   lo   mandas.
     3PERS.SG/3PERS.PL   3PERS.SG   SEND.2PERS

Again, this might at first appear a funny little fact, but forms that are, from a transformational point of view, mapped to other forms in syntactic context are extraordinarily common. Consider sequence of tense phenomena, where a past tense appears in a subordinate clause, but it has a reading cotemporaneous with the interpretation of the higher tense as if, semantically, it were a present tense. In preposition/pronoun inversion in Germanic (now lost in English except in frozen forms like *thereupon* or *therefore*), a (neuter) personal pronoun seems expressed instead as a locative, as in German *damit, darauf*. In Modern Greek, we find in certain contexts imperfectives that appear to contribute perfective meaning, as in wishes and contrafactuals. Again, we are not looking at some spotty little curiosities, but rather some features which detailed analysis and study show recur time and again.

4. LEARNING

Even if one has a meaning, or a sets of meanings, paired with phonological forms, there remain serious issues about learning to put them together to form appropriate coherent meanings for the whole. The question I would like to pose is what minimal assumptions about the learning process can we make and account for the daily fact that language is, indeed, learned? Perhaps the most minimal assumption one could make is that this organization is also reflected in the learning of other domains (this is the 'there is nothing special about language' view). For example, perhaps there are organizational principles in learning to structure visual scenes, which encode this same arrangement of matters. My own impression of the state of such research, however, is that principles of learning based on work in other domains has proven of limited value to the learning of a full language. While there may be some spotty successes in, for instance, learning the location of word or morpheme boundaries, or learning certain word meanings demonstratively, it has yet to be shown that such mechanisms yield anything like a system capable of learning language, much less extracting appropriate full sentence meanings for anything beyond *Man bites dog* types of structures (and even those ignore the tense).

Lack of success is hardly an argument that something cannot be done eventually, and this must remain a possibility. As long as one views the learning task of language as a matter of learning the syntax of the language, that is, as an arrangement of forms, it is a seductively easy step to take to believe that learning language form arrangements is just like all the other form arrangements we learn as well that are not constituted of language. But when one focuses on meaning, particularly entire sentence meanings, the ground shifts, and I believe this step becomes much more difficult to take. This is because it is in a language, and only in a language, that one finds the essential ingredients of a semantics — truth, reference, and predication — and that these are inextricably bound up with the syntax of a sentence. No other naturally occurring object, including (in all likelihood) animal communication systems, has these properties and characteristics. It is in studying semantics, then, particularly non-lexical semantics, that the unique properties of language become most starkly evident, and thus it becomes increasingly reasonable to believe that special domain-specific language learning measures are called for.

Let us return then to the empirical issues raised above, and ask again what sorts of minimal assumptions might be necessary for the learning of a language. At this point I can at best speculate, but perhaps there is a general direction that may have some value. It has been long noted among grammarians that most (if not all) languages make a distinction between types of vocabulary items. This distinction has been characterized in various ways (e.g. 'full word' vs. 'particle', 'open class' vs. 'closed class'), but I will choose to use 'lexical item' vs. 'function item'. Lexical items consist most of prominently of nouns, verbs, and adjectives (with prepositions and adverbs sometimes included), and function items are all those little words that accompany them, such as articles, conjunctions, infinitive markers, the copula, auxiliary verbs, pronouns, and so forth. As suggested by the terms 'open class' and 'closed class', the lexical items tend to allow the relatively easy addition of new members of the category, via productive processes of the language or borrowing, Function items, on the other hand, lack the internal productivity of the language to add new items, and are generally much more resistant to borrowing (for example, current English lexical vocabulary is about 60% of non-native origin, but among the function items nearly 100% is of native Germanic origin). Whether a simple two-way distinction is an appropriate characterization remains unclear (e.g., prepositions, a closed class, nevertheless appear to have some lexical characteristics as well). This said, I am going to outline things in these binary terms.

Among the closed-class items are not only words, or free forms, but also inflectional morphology and clitics. As the discussion in the previous section indicates, these function items have syntactic/semantic properties not shared by open-class lexical items. Chief among these is that their interpretation may take place at a 'higher' level of syntax than the interpretation of their host word (in the case of inflectional morphology and clitics). It is not fully certain, but appears a fact that their interpretation may not appear 'lower' in the syntax than surface constituency would indicate. In Carlson (1983), a point of view is developed which is designed to express this distinction between lexical items and function items in which the function items form a part of the *structure* in which the lexical items appear. One formalization of this idea is to treat the function items as expressions of features that appear on the syntactic categories. A rough representation of what a plural definite NP might look like is not the usual, as in (12) but rather as in (13):

(12)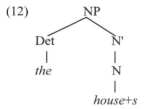

(13)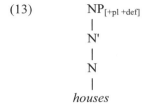

It is the features that are then interpreted by the semantics, and not the phonological forms of the expressions of those features. Thus, *the* and *-s* as phonological forms do not have meanings assigned to them (unlike the phonological form *house*, which does), but the features themselves do have meanings associated with them. One reflection of this is that many function items might have (and commonly do have) a nonanaphoric null expression, which provides no phonological form for interpretation but nevertheless provides a feature as surely as when there is phonological expression.

In order for these features to receive expression, they may be 'passed down' to nodes or heads of phrases (this is simply the reverse of 'feature percolation') to determine the forms. Thus, in the rough example, the representation might look as follows:

(14)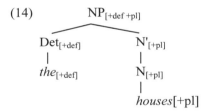

The features then are phonologically interpreted 'at the bottom', and semantically interpreted 'at the top'. In Carlson (1983), the use of features was inspired by work in GPSG but the basic idea can easily be translated into other frameworks, some of which may not make use of discrete features such as those exemplified.

What, then, would be possible assumptions that language learners might bring to the task of learning how to interpret language? One thought is that language learners have some type of foreknowledge of this basic architecture of a language (however represented, it need not be a Cartesian idea, but could be more indirectly expressed in the architecture of the learning mechanism itself), combined with some understanding of the types of meanings that can be expressed by features versus those that may be expressed by lexical items. For instance, feature meanings tend to be context-sensitive in a way that distinguishes them from meanings of lexical items. Once this is understood, one of the first tasks is to identify those elements in the speech stream which express lexical items versus those that serve as expressions of features, and it is at this task level that a relatively weak and non-domain-specific learning strategy could well turn out to be of considerable value, making use of such notions as intonation, stress and tone assignment, opportunities for phonological assimilation, statistical patterning, etc. However, on this view, the more general mechanisms themselves do not provide an account of the *significance* of what is found, that is provided by the larger and domain-specific prior understanding of the nature of the object being learned.

These comments are of course highly speculative, and their value is found only in the extent to which they might provide a productive means of accounting for how a person might end up learning the semantics of a language, despite its challenging, even daunting, complexity.

5. AN EXERCISE IN DEFINITE ARTICLES

The point of this final section is to illustrate, using a certain domain of data, the types of problems of matching forms and interpretations that learners might encounter. The data we are going to examine first has to do with nouns that appear without any articles before them. As there is a vast literature in semantics on the topics of mass terms and bare plurals, I am going to focus on a somewhat lesser-studied topic: singular count noun forms without articles. While these are the norm in many languages that lack plural marking and articles, such as Chinese and Japanese, in Indo-European languages, for instance, they appear less often and in fewer contexts (see Kallulli, 1999; Borthen, 1998; Schmidt & Munn, 1999; Dayal, 1999). English presents in own special issues with the bare singular construction. An excellent overview of the English data and many theoretical matters is found in Stvan (1998).

The basic facts seem to be these. Bare singulars are both lexically and positionally restricted. Hence, we have contrasts such as those in (15):

(15) a. They put him in *jail/prison/*penitentiary*.
     b. I took my son to *school/college/*university* (Am. English)
     c. The men were found on *shore/*beach*.

These lexical restrictions are subject to considerable dialect (such as American vs. British English) and social variation (e.g., if one is a member of the art world, one is more likely to say or hear *She is in studio*, which to my inartistic ears sounds strange).

Syntactically, they often follow certain verbs and prepositions (as in (15) above), but may appear occasionally as subjects of certain verbs:

(16) a. *Prison* has little to offer in the way of recreation.
   b. *College* is a good place to learn.
   c. *School* makes Jimmy very happy.

They may not be modified (unlike bare plurals); this follows from Stvan's arguments that these are, in fact, full one-word phrases and not simply nouns:

(17) a. They sent him to *(big) jail.
   b. I watched it on television *(that had a 31" screen)

Bare singulars can also appear, to a certain stylistic effect, in conjunction constructions and a couple others. In these particular instances the lexical restrictions are eliminated or reduced:

(18) a. University and high school alike require much study.
   b. Neither television nor radio has become serious educational tools.

Impressionistically, these structures appear to share many of the positional constraints of bare plurals in Spanish and Italian that have been analyzed as properly governing and empty D position (Contreras, 1986), and they seem to share the lexical constraints of incorporated and incorporation-like structures found in other languages.

The main semantic observation is that bare singulars appear to be non-referential, in the following way. Consider a situation in which Bob is watching television. There is a definite TV he is then watching, and one can refer back to that TV, e.g., by continuing *and then he turned it off and went to bed*. However, if we use this sentence as the antecedent of VP ellipsis, consider the result:

(19) Bob was watching television, and Fred was, too.

There is no reading of this where both had to have been watching exactly the same television set. This is exactly what you would expect if *television* were treated as a narrow-scope, nonspecific indefinite.

The meanings are actually more subtly articulated than just this. Stvan (1998) lists three main meanings. One is an 'activity' meaning. If someone is *in bed*, for example, it does not mean just a person is located in a certain place, but is also partaking of a certain activity or relationship that is canonically associated with that location — in this instance, sleeping or at least trying to. If one is *in prison*, then one is incarcerated, not simply in that location. This 'activity' meaning is not always present, and a 'familiarity' meaning may appear instead. If John is *at home*, or *in town*, or *out of state*, there is no special activity or relationship implied. However, a seemingly deictic meaning is intended, i.e., he is at *his* home, he is in *our* town, or out of *this* state. It is not just any home, any town, or any state. In these instances, the meaning of the bare singular, a maximally unmarked construction, is actually *more* complex than similar constructions with determiners (such as being in *a* prison, or in *a* bed), not less. Finally, there is the generic reading that lacks both of these dimensions. If tape recordings are not admissible *in court*, or if religious teaching is questionable *in prison*, all prisons or courts (of law) are under discussion.

Now let us move to the title of this section, cases involving overtly definite noun phrases. If we use VP ellipsis in such cases, identity of reference is preserved. This is intuitively obvious because definite articles are used to pick out something salient or familiar or unique in the context; the English word *the* signals this:

(20) a. Bob attended the old brown school, and Sam did, too.
     b. Max liked the Brecht play a lot, and Susan did, too.

Naturally, they went to the same school, liked the same play, because of the definiteness. Or so the usual story goes.

However, certain unmodified, lexically selected nouns seem to work differently (the basic intuitive observations can be found in Birner & Ward, 1994):

(21) a. Sam is in the hospital again, and so is Mary.
     b. I heard about the riot on the radio, and Sharon did, too.

Sam and Mary need *not* be in the same hospital, and while Sharon and I did hear about the same riot, our radios may well have been different, as if that phrase is an indefinite. But we have this definite article, what are we to make of that?

Note that in the presence of restrictive modification, this indefinite reading disappears, and the truly definite reading emerges as the only option:

(22) a. Sam is in the Red Cross hospital again, and so is Mary.
     b. I heard about the riot on the radio sitting on my desk, and Sharon did, too.

Suddenly, for American English speakers, Sam and Mary must be in the same hospital, and have heard the very same radio. These examples illustrate two hallmarks of the bare singular construction: lack of modification and lexical restriction (e.g. *riot* vs. *radio*). The other hallmark, syntactically restricted distribution, may likewise be established. Thus, we have some instances of definite articles which lack their usual semantic effect.

It seems many noun phrases with definite articles work this way in English, but others (such as *the riot*) do not. There is a certain amount of work, e.g., by Longobardi (1994) and Vergnaud & Zubizarreta (1992), that introduces the notion of 'expletive article', one put in to produce a noise in an otherwise empty D position. What I am suggesting here is that in instances such as (17), there is a reading (the most natural one) where the definite article is expletive, that is, we *really* have an instance of a bare singular in each case, the semantics of which is similar to that of bare plurals.

It is misleading to think of such constructions as 'idioms', being surprisingly highly productive and lacking the figurative or clearly non-compositional meanings often associated with clear instances of idioms. One way of thinking about what is going on here is to think of the construction as a complex predicate of the type examined in Snyder (2001) regarding first language acquisition. (Snyder also includes a cross-linguistic comparison of a variety of languages). Snyder considers the acquisition of a series of English constructions that have been suggested by syntacticians to be complex predicates, that is, single predicates made up of two or more syntactic parts. For instance, one among them is the resultative construction, as in *He hammered the metal flat*, where *hammer flat* appears to function as a single predicate. Verb-particle constructions are another example. Based on theoretical concerns as well results of the cross-linguistic study, Snyder notes that there is a close connection between the availability of productive root compounding in nominals, and the appearance of what are analyzed as complex predicates in a language. Snyder's study with children indicates that there is a highly positive correlation in children learning English between the time of appearance of both productive root compounding, and of the verb-particle construction (as a representative of complex predicates). If the non-referential definites discussed above form a complex predicate with the verb, then there should also be a positive correlation between acquisition of compounds, complex predicates, and this particular reading of definites. Whether this (speculative) prediction is correct is presently unknown, but it would provide one starting place for further investigation.

To return to the overall point, how could one see through the complexity of language to learn such facts, though? There would appear to be considerable usefulness in such notions as meaningful things that occasionally mean nothing, and things like null determiners, as such seem a persistent part of the design of language. But how could this ever actually help a learner acquire an appropriate syntax and interpretations? From a surfacy point of view, things like this appear to be roadblocks to learning, as if messages which easily could have been encoded in a straightforward signal-to-meaning relationship have been cleverly garbled and disguised. But I am suggesting a perspective that is perhaps the opposite of this — that such 'mismatches' in fact contain cues and clues to meaning that enable learning the whole system, particularly the non-lexical semantics, and are not there to hinder it, as a surface signal-to-meaning notion would suggest.

6. CONCLUSION

Natural languages, from a commonsensical point of view, seem treacherously designed. We have some things that mean nothing, and nothings that mean something. We have two things meaning one thing, and one thing meaning two things. We have things in disguise, meaning in highly constrained contexts what something else means that it normally contrasts with. We have things, even if the meaning is a single, normal seeming meaning, that are put in the 'wrong' place and have to be figured instead for another.

Things like this are learned by scores of millions annually, and one task of language learning research is to produce sensible and effective ideas about how this could be. It would appear that such work would be most effective if embedded within a larger and comprehensive framework articulating the form-to-meaning mapping of the general sort worked on by semanticists and syntacticians, if only to provide some appreciation of the sheer difficulty of the task ahead.

University of Rochester

7. ACKNOWLEDGEMENTS

I wish to thank the many workshop participants who commented on the presentation. Special thanks go to Veerle Van Geenhoven and Tom Roeper. This material is based upon work supported by the National Science Foundation under Grant No. 0082928.

8. REFERENCES

Anderson, Stephen. "Wackernagel's Revenge: Clitics, Morphology, and the Syntax of Second Position." *Language* 96 (1993): 68–98.
Bates, Elizabeth. *The Emergence of Symbols: Cognition and Communication in Infancy.* New York: Academic Press, 1979.
Birner, Betty, and Gregory Ward. "Uniqueness, Familiarity, and the Definite Article in English." In *Proceedings of the 20th Annual Meeting of the Berkeley Linguistic Society*, 93–102. Berkeley: BLS, 1994.
Bloom, Lois. *One Word at a Time.* The Hague: Mouton, 1973.

Borthen, Katja. *Bare Singulars in Norwegian*. Cand. Phil. Thesis, Norwegian University of Science and Technology, Trondheim, 1998.
Bowerman, Melissa. "The Structure and Origin of Semantic Categories in the Language-Learning Child." In Mary L. Foster and Stanley Brandes (eds.) *Symbol as Sense*, 277–300. New York: Academic Press, 1980.
Carlson, Gregory. "Marking Constituents." In Frank Heny and Barry Richards (eds.) *Linguistic Categories: Auxiliaries and Related Puzzles, Volume 1: Categories*, 69–98. Dordrecht: Reidel, 1983.
Chierchia, Gennaro, and Sally McConnell-Ginet. *Meaning and Grammar (2nd Edition)*. Cambridge, MA: MIT Press, 2000.
Clark, Eve. *The Lexicon in Acquisition*. Cambridge: Cambridge University Press, 1993.
Contreras, Heles. "Spanish Bare NP's and the ECP." In Ivonne Bordelois, Heles Contreras, and Karen Zagona (eds.) *Generative Studies in Spanish Syntax*, 25–49. Dordrecht: Foris, 1986.
Dayal, Veneeta. "Bare NP's, Reference to Kinds, and Incorporation." In Tanya Matthews and Devon Strolovitch (eds.) *Proceedings of SALT 9*, 35–52. Ithaca: CLC Publications, 1999.
Gleitman, Lila. "The Structural Sources of Verb Meanings." *Language Acquisition* 1 (1990): 3–55.
Grice, Paul. "Meaning and Conversation." In Peter Cole and Jerrold Sadock (eds.) *Syntax and Semantics 3: Speech Acts*, 41–58. New York: Academic Press, 1975.
Hale, William G., and Carl D. Buck. *A Latin Grammar*. Alabama: University of Alabama Press, 1966.
Iatridou, Sabine. "The Grammatical Ingredients of Counterfactuality." *Linguistic Inquiry* 31 (2000): 231–270.
Kallulli, Dalina. *The Comparative Syntax of Albanian: On the Contribution of Syntactic Types to Propositional Interpretation*. Ph.D. Diss., University of Durham, 1999.
Kuno, Susumo. *The Structure of the Japanese Language*. Cambridge, MA: MIT Press, 1973.
Lebeaux, David. *Language Acquisition and the Form of Grammar*. Ph.D. Diss., University of Massachusetts, Amherst, 1988.
Longobardi, Giuseppe. "Reference and Proper Names: A Theory of N-Movement in Syntax and Logical Form." *Linguistic Inquiry* 25 (1994): 609–669.
Nida, Eugene. *Morphology: The Descriptive Analysis of Words*. Ann Arbor: University of Michigan Press, 1978.
Perlmutter, David. *Deep and Surface Structure Constraints in Syntax*. New York: Holt, Rinehart, Winston, 1971.
Radford, Andrew. "Counter-Filtering Rules." In John Green and Stephen Harlow (eds.) *York Papers in Linguistics* (7), 7–45. York: Department of Linguistics, University of York, 1977.
Schmitt, Cristina, and Alan Munn. "Against the Nominal Mapping Parameter: Bare Nouns in Brazilian Portuguese." In Pius Tamanji, Masako Hirotani, and Nancy Hall (eds.) *Proceedings of NELS 29*, 339–353. Amherst: GLSA, 1999.
Siskind, Jeffrey Mark. "Learning Word-to-Meaning Mappings." In Peter Broeder and Jaap Murre (eds.) *Models of Language Acquisition: Inductive and Deductive Approaches*, 121–153. Oxford: Oxford University Press, 2000.
Snyder, William. "On the Nature of Syntactic Variation: Evidence from Complex Predicates and Complex Word Formation." *Language* 77 (2001): 324–342.
Stvan, Laurel. *The Semantics and Pragmatics of Bare Singular Noun Phrases*. Ph.D. Diss., Northwestern University, Evanston, 1998.
Vergnaud, Jean-Roget, and Maria Luisa Zubizarreta. "The Definite Determiner and the Inalienable Constructions in French and English." *Linguistic Inquiry* 23 (1992): 595–652.

TOM ROEPER

WATCHING NOUN PHRASES EMERGE

Seeking Compositionality

Abstract. An argument is presented that the child moves from nonspecific to specific in a series of compositional steps that builds a language-specific Determiner Phrase. The child must select a subset of language-specific nodes from a larger set provided by UG. Every node, it is argued, requires semantic information to justify a language particular projection. In the process the child reverts to Defaults, maintains Multiple Grammars, and uses pragmatic information to confirm hypotheses about structure. Acquisition evidence for many decisions about DP nodes is reviewed, with a special emphasis upon how the child learns that definite articles allow temporal displacement. The larger argument provides a step toward building a model that reflects both semantic generalizations and acquisition evidence.

1. QUESTIONS

How does a child project the myriad semantic and syntactic properties of Noun Phrases? We will argue that there is a tremendously intricate process required to capture the varieties of possible 'reference' that confront the child. At various points non-target options are taken from Universal Grammar (UG) that are consistent with syntactic/semantic defaults. Here are a few questions linked to what children say:

(1) a. Why do children say *I want cookie* instead of *a cookie*? Or, why does a child answer *towel* instead of *a towel* when asked *What do you need to wash?*?
 b. Why do children say *yes* to the question *Does a dog have tails?*? Or, why does a child refer to his parents as *husbands and wives*?
 c. Why do children say *yes* to the question *Mary's bike is broken. Is John riding the bike?* (a different bike)? Why does a child say *the dog* in this situation? [3 dogs, 2 cats on a fence, one dog falls off] *What fell off the fence?*

These examples are at the level of subtlety that motivates many modern theories, particularly in semantics. It is one thesis of this essay that children, at every moment, make subtle distinctions of interpretation like these examples imply and seek to map them onto grammar. Most syntactic acquisition theories vastly understate the semantic distinctions for which children seek a grammatical representation.

1.1. Overview

Our theory develops a theory of Minimal Default Grammar (MDG), where MDG is the Initial State projected from UG. MDG contains nodes that are universal (basic form of CP, IP, VP, NP) in a hierarchical relation. A classic example of a Default projection is a phrase like *Me want* which often occurs in children's grammars, but which adults never use.

We will propose Defaults at three levels of nominal projection:

N = Kind (*want cookie*)
NP = Predicate (*Joshua home*)
DP = Proper Name/deixis (*Johnny, that*)

These claims reflect the fact that children begin with particular DPs, namely, names (e.g., *Johnny*), pronouns (e.g., *that*), and nonspecific bare nouns (e.g., *cookie*), all of which do not have an article. Then children pursue a series of hypotheses about possible forms of specificity that are linked (in part) to a fixation of the article system in a syntactic tree. Above N lies NP. NP has a Spec, which we argue has an anaphoric link that allows what is called a predicate reading for words like *home*. As we show below, anaphoric *home* appears very early and therefore we suggest that it represents a Default projection.

Between NP and DP come a variety of nodes (see below) that, for instance, permit Degree phrases and guarantee Agreement and are notably absent in early phases of grammar. Their hierarchical order is (by hypothesis) fixed in UG but not every one is present in every grammar, and so the child needs evidence to determine which ones are present in his grammar.

The MDG theory leads naturally to a theory of Multiple Grammars (Roeper, 1999; Yang, 2003; Chomsky, 2001). The theory assumes that grammars are not completely resolved, but allow lexically limited domains where other grammars exist (for instance, English has Latin, Greek, and Anglo-Saxon morphology). One of the grammars that remains, is the MDG itself. The existence of Headline Grammar is a common example of where adult language uses Default structures and resembles children's language.

1.2. Compositionality

How does a child compose syntactic structures into semantic ones? Our goal will be to maintain an allegiance to the data from children and begin with a less formal notion of Child Compositionality which we expect will eventually meet semantic theories.[1] We assume the following broad principle:

(2) Nodes in a tree are linked to semantic distinctions.

2. SYNTACTIC AND SEMANTIC PERSPECTIVES

To orient our approach with respect to syntax, consider at one extreme the concept of 'autonomy of syntax', which was part of the original model of generative grammar (Chomsky, 1955). Under this conception a child might learn the entire syntax of a grammar from the radio without ever assigning meaning to a structure. No stepwise compositionality is required for adult or child. To orient our approach with respect to semantics, a Fregean approach to compositionality is adopted as explicated in Heim & Kratzer (1998), where higher nodes are strictly composed of the contents of lower ones.

(3) Locality
Semantic interpretation rules are local; the denotation of any non-terminal node is computed from the denotation of its daughter nodes.

And they add Frege's conjecture as well:

(4) Semantic composition is Function Application

This approach will naturally capture phrases where each element has an independent denotation:

(5) eat raisin

But more complex forms of composition are needed to capture phrases where a functional element, without an independent denotation, occur:

(6) the hat

Heim & Kratzer argue that if one denotation has no value, then a false presupposition is present, which then requires the inclusion of a contextual variable. Thus the interpretation is more complex.

Modern syntactic structures have become increasingly sensitive to semantic distinctions. Cinque (1999) advocates 62 different Adverb positions, each capturing refined semantics.[2] The range of possibilities is highly constrained because the Functional Categories in effect subcategorize each other: a verb carries the potential for certain kinds of adverbs.

A recent semantic account can be found in the work of Morzyki (2003) who argues that the syntactic nodes are part of what undergoes semantic composition. For instance, an adverb such as *remarkably* combines with a Degree node to produce a reading of intensification in an AP, as in (7):

(7)   DP [Deg [AP [NP]]]
      a.   this is a remarkably big tree
      b.   ≠ *Remarkably this is a big tree

The reading in (7a) is not possible for the adverb in any other position (7b). Therefore, he argues that the adverb combines with a Feature in the Degree Phrase to produce the degree interpretation of the adverb. Only just before the adjective is the intensification of Degree a possible reading. A Degree Phrase is an example of the distinctions that the child must seek between a DP and a NP node.

Our view is that UG does provide a fixed hierarchy of Functional Categories, but that not all grammars instantiate every node in this hierarchy. Not all the possible adverb categories are independently represented, nor is there an Agreement node for adjectives if they do not agree (as in English). Therefore the acquisition challenge is for the child to determine both the content of elements to be combined *and* exactly what node dominates them. The errors children make in word-order never involve an error in the hierarchy of FCs. We never see children misplace articles, as in *apple the*.

2.1. Child Evidence

In fact, children do exhibit expressions like *eat raisin* before *the hat* and therefore the compositional rules that combine words with separate denotations does seem to precede those where a contextual variable must be included. Therefore, prima facie, the semantic theory mirrors an important part of the acquisition process. Moreover, young children show knowledge of just the kind of adverb composition that Morzyki (2003) discusses with the adverb *really*:

(8)   *Adjectival degree intensifier*:
      It's really heavy.   (Shem, 2;8,3)
      That was really funny.   (Nina, 2;9,13)

Cause you're really tired.   (Nina, 2;9, 26)

Verbal modifier:
Yeah, really she didn't.   (Nina, 3;2,12)
Is Paul really just a baby?   (Adam, 3;4,18)

These facts and arguments point toward the idea, not far from common sense, that we need a real conception of how semantic composition figures into the acquisition process.

Now, keeping a steady eye on what the data tells us, we can ask the question of how much of the path of composition can we see? A great deal more careful experimentation will be needed before it is completely clear, but first let us try intuitively to grasp what the act of composition might look like.

2.2. Compositional Implications of Merge

What happens when a child hears two nouns, like *doll* and *house*? We assume the following:

(9)   known word + known word => composed compound
      doll + house => dollhouse

This seems like common sense, but a close look shows that a number of other steps are possible. A child could make three different steps. In a first step, he might erroneously see phrases as single words; in a second step, as conjunctions; in a third step, function composition.

(10) idiom: no analysis
      conjunction: *doll* and *house*
      composition: Modifier and Head

If the child recognized the two parts, *doll* and *house* morphologically, then the idiomatic analysis would itself call for dropping a compositional analysis, and treating it as a single word. Were this the child's first assumption — make any sequence into a single word if possible — many erroneous compounds should arise. Imagine a parent who hands a child a spoon and says *Eat rice* and the child understands *eatrice* as 'spoon' and says *Where my eatrice?* We find amazingly few such errors.

Were the child to assume that a sequence of words were linked as conjunctions, then we predict the false conclusion that two objects are implied:

(11) *dollhouse* = *doll* and *house*

Conjunctions are notoriously rare in children's utterances. We do not have:

(12) Mommydaddy
spoonfork
hatcoat

The examples in (12) would be the utterances we would expect if the child were pursuing simple conjunction as a basis for initial word combinations. Therefore we conclude that the child must first seek to identify a Head and then add something to it:

(13) Merge to Head: X + Head

This analysis entails the semantic differentiation of a Head. Is the Merged X, added by a rule of semantic composition or just syntactic analysis? A look at the grammar of compounds provides a clue from the adult grammar. In a series of papers originating in Snyder (1995) on how English children acquire productive compounds and how French children never project productive compounds (see Roeper, Snyder, & Hiramatsu (2000); Roeper & Snyder, 2003), we realized the importance of Namiki's (1994) observation:

(14) There are no three-term idioms.

That is, we may have many two-term idioms, as shown in (15), but a three-term compound has some compositional analysis, as shown in (16):

(15) turncoat, fatcat, footloose, slapdash
(16) turncoat brigade [brigade + turncoat]

Based on this claim, Snyder examined the input to children and found that children who produce novel, compositional two-term compounds (e.g., *animal cup*, *ribbon hat*, *BigBird book*) are exposed to three-term compounds from adults (e.g., *Christmas tree cookie*, *peanut butter sandwich*, *baby doll napkin*, *nursery school book*). In other words, it appears that compositionality *must* apply when Merge of a Noun applies twice (a suggestion of Barbara Partee, p.c., circa 1976):

(17) Recursion (e.g. repeated Merge) entails compositionality

We argue that children know this principle and seek recursive structures to differentiate lexical idioms from productive rules by requiring that recursive structures submit to compositional analysis. An important corollary for acquisition is a point of non-compositionality:

(18) Merge: No composition is required for the first Merge.

Where more hierarchy is present, recursive Merge must have applied, therefore a compositional decision is entailed (see Roeper & Snyder, 2003):

(19) Claim: Hierarchical structure requires a compositional decision.

Therefore we argue that children first carry out a morphological analysis:

(20) word + X

In essence, children carry forth the operation of Merge, or decompose it without a necessary compositional output. So far, we have an autonomous syntax.

(21) a.
```
        word
        /  \
     word   affix
```

b.
```
        *word
        /  \
       X    word
            /  \
         word   Y
```

However, once again, we cannot have a *mystery x* and *mystery y* at the same time because recursion requires compositionality. This is a strong claim, and it is possible that there are exceptions. This argument arrives at what is seen as almost 'common sense' for the acquisition of morphology. It is an old observation that children misidentify morphemes when they initially recognize them. Slobin (1973) claims:

(22) New morphemes first take *old* functions.

Slobin observes that morphemes are added without meaning change for gender in Russian:

(23) noun+feminine

The affix is treated as either masculine or feminine. In English, the *-ed* is added to verbs without a clear intension of past reference, but rather continuing the present. The most straightforward suggestion is that in all languages (24) holds:

(24) New morphemes at first take *no* function.

In other words, this evidence points toward our claim that the Primary Linguistic Data problem forces an initial moment of non-compositional analysis. We can assign a minimal structure to two elements without (a) knowing what one of them means, and (b) consequently not knowing what the combination means.³

2.3. Compositionality Predictions

The recursive compositionality requirement has an immediate implication for acquisition theory, a Compositionality Filter:

(25) Compositionality eliminates all non-compositional material.

This forces the child to eliminate most of what he first hears because he cannot make sense of it. Note, paradoxically, that the child might in fact 'understand' the sentence but still not enter it into his grammar revision machine. A child that looks at a bottle of milk and hears a parent say (26), may be pragmatically able to see exactly what is meant.

(26) Will you please finish your milk?

Nevertheless, the sentence contains all sorts of things beyond his grammar, and therefore is rejected as an input to grammar change. A series of first order predictions are available from this analysis. First, we predict (27):

(27) No second morpheme should be added without the first Merge being assigned a meaning.

For instance, German involves both Tense and Agreement morphemes. It has been argued that each may appear without a clear meaning (which, of course, does not guarantee that it has no meaning):

(28) sag + te + st
V + Tense + AGR

However it has never been claimed to my knowledge that the AGR is added before the Tense receives a meaning.

Second, we predict that articles may appear without meaning. Matthewson & Schaeffer (2000) report that 20% of the child Adam's first definite articles do not have a clear antecedent. This evidence is compatible with the idea that the expletive *the* initially has no meaning.

2.4. Acquisition Model for DP

We will now project the model of NP/DP acquisition that we regard as an idealization of the real process, which we expect to be far more refined. One of our goals is to avoid understating the true intricacy of the grammar to be acquired. Therefore we cast our net wide at first and imagine the largest range of distinct possibilities that a child may confront (still surely too small). Consider this array of discernibly different meanings that NPs can have (we shall discuss them in greater detail below).

(29) a. Bare Noun, kind (*want cookie*)
 b. NP, predicate with anaphoric control (*go home*)
 c. NP, generic (*I like cats*)
 d. NP, existential (*cats are in the yard*)
 e. NP, member of a set (*see a dog*)
 f. NP member of an introduced set (not English)
  (*There are three dogs. The dog is big*)
 g. NP, expletive definite (*I have the ability to do this*)
 h. DP, part-whole Reference
 i. DP, Point of View Link
  (*John has four dogs. He thinks the best is the worst.*)
 j. DP, Discourse familiar object (*I have a hat. The hat green*)
 k. DP, Unique object focal stress: (*did he get THE bike*)
 l. DP, Culturally familiar object (*where is the sun*)

A full exploration of these distinctions and how their acquisition reflects upon semantic theories will require many years of work. In principle each of these forms could be marked with special morphology (and may be in other languages). If we conceive of syntactic projections as a bundle of Features that in turn may represent a distinct semantic formula, then we might expect that each one would project a distinct syntactic node. We imagine a range of NP nonspecific projections and DP specific projections. The projection system might look like this, reflecting our hypothesis that there is a progression between Nonspecific and Specific:

(30) DP
       \
        D => Proper Name
         \
          D => Demonstrative deictic
         / \
     Spec   D => Definite unique
             \
              D => Part-whole
               \
                D => Definite member of a set
                 \
                  D => Definite expletive
                   \
                    NP
                   / \
               Spec   NP => Indefinite specific
                       \
                        NP => Indefinite member of a set
                         \
                          NP => Default, Nonspecific, or Predicate
                           \
                            N => Default Kind

The tree in (30) resembles more articulated trees suggested in several theories, i.e., in Categorial Grammar (Drozd, 1993), in Minimalist Grammars without Node labels (Collins, 1997; 2001), in Cinque's proposals for 62 semantically distinguishable Adverb nodes (Cinque, 1999), and in articulated trees in which DP contains Number, Agreement, Adjective, Gender, Case, and Degree nodes (Moore, in prep.). If we add these to the one proposed above, the child would need to locate and instantiate at least 16 different nodes within the DP.

This rough sketch of a tree would be motivated by the notion that increasing specificity adds information and the idea that the child moves roughly from lower to higher nodes. What is missing is exactly what semantic properties would motivate each node. We take the acquisition sequence itself as a first suggestion about what increasing complexity should capture.

3. BARE NOUNS ARE KINDS

A child's first utterances are the most linguistically opaque. It is extremely difficult to know just what information the words carry and how much is supplied by inference. If a parent walks into a teenage party and says *Beer!* an entire mindset may be implied, but it is not actually mapped onto that word, rather the word is interpreted according to the situation. The same is true when a small child says *Milk*. Similarly, older disordered children persist with bare nouns (Schaeffer, 2001; Leonard *et al.*, 2001). We argue that the first stage reflects the notion of kind, primarily to differentiate the bare noun from the meaning of definite reference.

The notion of kind is a traditional one and it reflects the idea that one should not attribute definite reference if it is not present — though people commonly do say the child deleted *the* in the expression *Want cookie*, although the intentional verb (*want*) itself suggests the notion of kind.

There are modern theories that reduce or replace the notion of kind (Carlson, 1977; Dayal, 1999) with the notion of property, for instance, Van Geenhoven (1998).[4] This discussion reaches beyond what the acquisition data reveals. One can simply impose one theory or another upon the data whose origins are outside of acquisition, but that provides no insight unless some clear prediction is made to distinguish our concept (we can call it Child-Kind (Ch-Kind)) to indicate that the acquisition evidence may be compatible with more than one perspective. Nevertheless, two factors incline us to favor the traditional notion of kind:

(i) The notion of property is broader and includes many other constructions. (It applies to the *predicate* constructions and pertains to our discussion of NPs and words like *home* below.).

(ii) The notion of kind reflects the task of partitioning the world into sets from different perspectives. If one asks about the kind of a car, one might ask if it is a sedan, SUV, station wagon, convertible, or one might ask if it is a Ford, Buick, or Pontiac. The notion of kind aims at something different from property (G. Carlson, p.c.).

It is certainly true that some finer information involving properties separates one kind from another (e.g., tigers from lions). Such information must be used by the child to differentiate classes, which may at first fail when a child calls cows *dogs*. It is possible that the notion of a property functions as a trigger to a larger concept of kind. It could thus have a special role to a play in a Language Acquisition Device that is unlike its role in grammar.

3.1. Expletive Articles

What information does a child's first use of articles carry? There are several possibilities. Matthewson & Schaeffer (2000) have pointed out that children seem to use articles incorrectly without a prior reference. Marinis (2000) points out that determiners undergo 'spreading' in early Greek (e.g., *the big the yellow the house*) where the determiner does not have a compositional reading for each adjective (see also Eisenbeiss, 2000). Carlson (this volume) makes the interesting suggestion that form/meaning mismatches are helpful to the child in acquisition, which in general seems very likely. For instance, articles appear to function as empty expletives in constructions:

(31) All the victims went to the hospital.

They could in fact go to different hospitals. Such a form/meaning mismatch could be seen to trigger a syntactic node that would then be home to a number of semantic constructs. We are not sure exactly what expletives entail, but our approach would suggest that they do have meaning, albeit a less specific one. The language has hundreds of examples like: *John showed the ability, the audacity, the acumen, the capacity*, where no prior referent is entailed. Moreover, children show no difficulty in using sentences with expletive NP's like *I'll show you the way, I have the idea, Here's the plan, What's the difference*. A brief search for *the way* revealed these cases:

Sarah:	is that the right way?	(4yrs old)
	here's the way you play the game	
	that the way that people go	
Adam:	does it go just like the other way	(4yrs old)
	that's the wrong way (note: *wrong ways* are infinite)	

In many instances, children seem to be using a generic concept (e.g., *the hospital*). Evidently, just as we predict, children do not seem to stumble in the slightest over this kind of expletive definite article.

In experimental work, de Villiers & Roeper (1995) and Baauw (2000) showed that these expletives were not barriers to extraction in cases like:

(32) How did John make the decision to wash himself => how-wash

They showed an interaction with binding theory as well. De Villiers & Roeper argue that extraction is consistent with an analysis of expletive Determiner as an NP and not a DP (see *home* evidence below). Understanding expletive articles follows our prediction: Less specific interpretations emerge very early.

3.2. Reference and Sets

Our broad proposal is that the child moves from Ch-Kind to indefinites and gradually to unique discourse referents. The next stage involves selecting a member of a set. We are able to discern the relevance of sets in three different situations:

(33) a.   indefinite (*I want a dog*)
      b.   specific indefinite (*I want a specific dog*)
      c.   member of a mentioned set (*John has 3 hats. He is wearing the biggest hat.*)

A great deal of research has addressed how children comprehend indefinites and definites (Maratsos, 1971; Krämer, 2000; Matthewson, Bryant & Roeper (2001) and references therein). Matthewson & Schaeffer (2000) provided evidence that Adam used definites for non-introduced nouns, and that children were able to use the definite article when it was a member of a set, but not as a unique item. In Salish the discourse *John took a book from the shelf, and then Bill took the book* allows Bill to take a *different* book, as long as some book has been mentioned. Precisely this meaning is possible in Salish (Matthewson, 1998). They showed that 4-5 year old children would allow this reading for (35a) but not (35b):

(34)   Mary has a broken bike.

(35) a.   Did Billy ride the bike (he is on a different bike.) => yes
      b.   Did Billy ride it => no

The Salish definite is less specific and therefore on the path from the most general reference, Ch-Kind, to the most specific, Unique Referent DP (*the*).[5]

Finally, Schafer & de Villiers (2000) found a similar response with Smith College students. When contrastive sets were present, a definite was chosen for a member of a set:

(36)   Three ducks and two dogs were walking across a bridge. One of the animals fell off the bridge and said *Quack*. Guess which or what was it?

While 70% gave *a duck* as an answer 30% said *the duck*. This suggests that this may remain as a residual grammatical option in adult English as well.

By contrast, we do not believe that the Unique Referent option would constitute a stage of acquisition in an Asian language without articles. It is not impossible without a DP because, as Brun & Avrutin (2001) show, it is possible to define specificity by movement rather than by morphology. It is simply not a natural stage in the way that nonspecificity is a natural stage because of Default Economy representations.

In sum, children do not randomly explore other grammars: There is a fundamental asymmetry in the acquisition of grammars that reflects a UG division:

(A) Some grammars have rich Determiner Systems (overt DP)
(B) Some grammars have no Determiners (NP only)

The DP itself, we argue, is projected by Specificity and therefore does not require an article and can house Proper Names. Because the child prefers minimal structure, it will seek to connect overt determiners with nonspecific NPs if possible. Therefore the acquisition of determiner rich DP grammars will pass through an NP-only phase, but no NP-only grammars will pass through a phase of projecting DPs.[6] We predict that children will fail to recognize markers of specificity and treat them as nonspecific.[7]

3.3. NP Defaults

Although Longobardi (1994) and others (e.g., Baauw, 2000) argue for a universal DP, de Hoop (1992) has argued for a distinction between Strong and Weak NP's, and Chomsky (1998) has explicitly connected the specific/nonspecific distinction to NP/DP.[8] Our concept of NP reflects discussions in which it is claimed that an NP is a predicate that carries a property. In Romance, it is common to find bare nouns predicated of a subject:

(37) John is a fool = John is fool

English has many instances of bare nouns, though often in larger phrases:

(38) a. I pronounce you man and wife
 b. He came, gun in hand
 c. Make war against king and country
 d. The president stayed on message, off television, on radio...

These constitute a neglected, but very real, corner of English in which we find a Romance grammar. The construction either states an equivalence between subject and predicate or there is implicit control: *gun in hand* means 'his gun in his hand', or *at home* means 'at his home'.[9] We argue that this kind of control requires an NP that is available as a Default to the child, for which we now provide an overview of theoretical evidence.[10] First, the crucial distinction between N and NP can be seen in these two sentences:

(39) a.   John likes singing at home
     b.   John likes home-singing

In (39a), John sings at his own home, but in (39b) it can be anyone's home. Thus the N is incorporated but not the NP, which retains a 'controlled' reading:

(40) a.

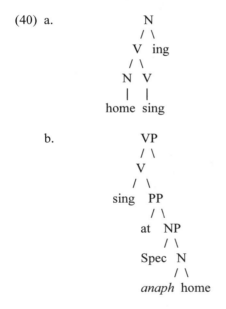

b.

In general, the word *home* is an NP like many others which is 'controlled' in the sense that it is linked to the subject and distributes (*Everyone went home* means 'to different homes'). We capture the control property of a NP, but not a N, by arguing that the NP has a Spec position containing a hidden Anaphor that is co-indexed with the subject. If it is an anaphor, then it immediately predicts obedience to Principle A of the binding theory (clause-boundedness). This prediction is the subject of the experiment from Perez & Roeper (1999).

Our earliest evidence in the two-word stage, in fact, suggests that children are able to grasp the anaphoric control reading which we associate with NP and not N (see below). In each instance, the child has either subject or speaker control, but not an undifferentiated kind interpretation.

Table 1. Two-word interpretation

Speaker oriented (Adam's home)	*ADA: Cromer home. *MOT: Cromer's at your [!!] home.
Speaker oriented (Adam's home)	*ADA: bike home. *MOT: bike is home. *MOT: yes.
Subject oriented (Man's home)	*ADA: Man tractor drive tractor over dere home. *MOT: Yes # man driving tractor over ther.
Subject oriented (Joshua's home)	*ADA: Jowha home. *MOT: Joshua's at his [!!] home.

Although two-word utterances are hard to interpret, the following experiment shows that children understand the difference between the controlled NP form (*home*) and uncontrolled DP form (*his home*).

In a pilot experiment by Blumenfeld (1999), there is evidence that children will make this distinction in the 6-8-year range where the context allows both:

(41) a.   He gave her cookies made at home.
     b.   He gave her home-made cookies.

(42) Prompt: *Where were the cookies made?*
     Bare nouns: 100% of responses 'at his house.'
     Compounds: 12% responded 'at his house.'
     Majority of responses: 60% 'at the bakery' (or similar)

This evidence contributes to the claim that children are sensitive to the N/NP distinction, although it needs to be replicated with younger children (see also Burns & Soja, 1997, who show sensitivity to the NP/DP distinction). At the syntactic level, we have argued that there is an Anaphoric element in the Spec position linked to the Subject (or possibly to the Speaker), because *home* obeys Principle A like other anaphors (see experiment below). Obligatory control is blocked with an indefinite in the Spec or if a DP is present:

(43) John went to a home / John went to the home. (may not be John's)

The anaphoric properties that we link to Spec-NP (blocked by compound incorporation) can best be seen with quantifiers:

(44) Everybody went home.
for every x, x a person, x goes to [x home].
interpretation is more strict than narrow scope

(45) Everybody walks to a home.
every x, x a person, There is a y, y a home [x walks to y]
narrow scope (no restrictions on selection of y)

46) Everybody walks to a different home.
(y is different for each x)

There are a variety of diagnostic contexts that support this NP analysis pragmatically and syntactically.

(47) Diagnostics (see Perez & Roeper, 1999):

1. A bound interpretation is stable and not sensitive to context:

    a. John lost the audience's interest. (disjoint interests)
    b. John lost interest. (John's interest)
    c. The audience was enthralled, but as John's voice turned to a monotone, John lost interest. (anti-pragmatic, still John's interest)

2. NP is incompatible with restrictive relatives & restrictive adjectives:

    a. Ellen visits a beautiful home.
    b. *Ellen visits beautiful home.
    c. *Ellen visits home that sits near the lake.

3. NP exhibits local binding: *Home* is subject to principle B (Jackendoff *et al.*, 1993).

    a. John told Bill to work on vacation. (on Bill's vacation)
    b. John told Bill to work on his vacation. (John's, Bill's, etc.)

4. It obeys C-command.

    Peter's fiancee went home. (the fiancee's home, not Peter's)

5. NP allows extraction where it is blocked by DP (the+NP).

    a. How does John like t [$_{DP}$ the advice *t from his mother]?
    => 'very much', i.e., 'how does he like it?'
    Cannot be interpreted as 'how is the advice?'
    b. How does John like [$_{NP}$ advice t from his mother]?
    => 'very much', i.e., 'how does he like it?'
    => 'with no ulterior motives', i.e., 'how is advice?'

A wide variety of evidence supports this distinction between NP and DP.

3.4. The Home Experiment (Perez & Roeper, 1999)

Stories were constructed to test distributed interpretation and local binding. They are anti-pragmatic in one condition in terms of the question in which children reject an invitation to go to one person's home and go to their own instead:

(48) One-Clause Story

> The sheep lives in the barn, the dog lives in the doghouse and the chickens live in the chicken coup. Grover lives in the house, and he loves to play with his animal friends. Some days they play outside, other days they play at Grover's house. Today they played outside until it started to rain. Grover said: 'Lets play at my house for a little longer.'

(49) Target sentence:
    a. Everybody went home.
    b. Everybody went to his home.
Prompt: Can you show me?

Table 2. Possible responses to One-Clause stories

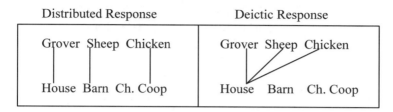

With two-clauses, we are examining whether children obey the Principle A restriction for anaphors, effectively not allowing *home* to link to *everybody*, which is outside the clause:

(50) Two-Clause Story

The Next day, each animal invited the Lion King to come play at his village. It is getting late, so he does not know if he can.

(51) Target sentence:
 a. Everybody hoped the Lion King would go home, and he did.
 b. Everybody hoped the Lion King would go to his home, and he did.
Prompt: Can you show me what the Lion King did?

Table 3. Possible responses to Two-Clause stories

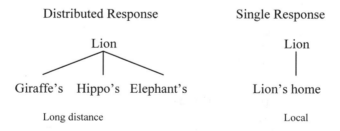

The results comparing the two experiments show strongly that the children take distributed responses and obey binding conditions. This is shown in Table 4:

Table 4. Distributed responses in%

Age	Experiment 1 (One-Clause) bare N	Experiment 2 (Two-Clause) bare N
3-4	72.2	–
4-5	63.2	17.6
5-6	88.9	11.1
adult	94.0	8.16

These results are compatible with the view that the anaphorically bound NP is available as a Default, and it is consistent with the naturalistic data (*Joshua home*) cited above for even younger children.

4. DP PROPERTIES

We can put our theory to a fairly extreme test. We proposed two fundamental Default projections and a semantic interpretation for each:

Default DP => Proper Name with Unique Antecedent
Default NP => Member of a set or a Kind

A subtle experiment by Romero & Bock (2001) puts these two possibilities in competition to see whether either, or both, will be selected by children. The concept of a Default means that the options remain available to older children. The experiment is built around the use of a Definite Determiner to allow a temporal displacement.

4.1. Temporal Nouns

Musan (1995) showed that nouns can be time-independent, if they are not in an expletive environment:

(52) a. DP: Time-Independent:
Some professors were radical in the sixties.
(those who are professors *now*)
b. Bare Noun: Time-Dependent
There were radical professors in the sixties.
(those who were radical professors *then*)

These examples show that articles can enable a referential displacement that is contradicted by the current context. For a child to master them, they must not only understand that definiteness creates a link to an entity introduced in the discourse, but that the truth of the phrase may be defined exclusively in the earlier context.[11]

While such sentences may seem unusual, they are certainly a part of the daily life of the child. They will hear from teachers utterances like (53):

(53) Good morning. Isn't it nice that all the sick children are well again?

Or they might hear on a playing field about children who were injured the previous week, but are now recovered:

(54) It is good that all the injured children are playing again.

4.2. The Temporal Noun Experiment

12 stories with pictures were created with 121 questions, counter-balanced, of the following kind and given to 29 children (age 3;2-5;6):

> It's warm and these mice are playing in their favorite swimming hole. See this mouse? He's playing on a swing. And this one is hopping from stone to stone. This mouse is splashing in the water. This one is playing in the waterfall. And see this one? Look! He's eating a piece of cheese. They are all enjoying the cool spray of the waterfall. Later in the afternoon, the mice go to a field. The sun is shining. See how bright the sun is? After a while, the mice in the field get very hot. See this mouse. He's sweating. This one is giggling; he always giggles when he is hot. And this one is so hot he can't move.

The same mice are cool when they are swimming, but become hot by hiking. The bare noun *hot mice* should allow no time shift, while *the hot mice* allows for reference to the later hiking state. These are the adult responses, assuming specificity in the DP, and nonspecificity for the Adjective+Noun:

(55) a.   Were *the* hot mice in the swimming hole? YES
    b.   Were *there* hot mice in the swimming hole? NO
    c.   Are *the* hot mice in the swimming hole? YES
    d.   Are *there* hot mice in the swimming hole? NO

Single time pattern (= default NP, no Specificity):

(56) a.   Were *the* hot mice in the swimming hole? NO
    b.   Were *there* hot mice in the swimming hole? NO
    c.   Are *the* hot mice in the swimming hole? NO
    d.   Are *there* hot mice in the swimming hole? NO

Name pattern (= default DP = all are Proper Names):

(57) a.   Were *the* hot mice in the swimming hole? YES
b.   Were *there* hot mice in the swimming hole? YES
c.   Are *the* hot mice in the swimming hole? YES
d.   Are *there* hot mice in the swimming hole? YES

In Romero & Bock (2001), results are linked to a preponderant *yes* or *no*. They found three patterns without strong age variation, but with trends. They found 12 children who gave us the adult yes/no variation (Bare Noun = nonspecific / Determiner = specific), who on the whole were older. Two children who gave the opposite interpretations (Bare Noun = specific, Determiner = nonspecific), and they were very young. Their answers could be close to guessing.

The other two major groups were those who consistently took a 'name' interpretation for both cases, and those who took a nonspecific 'single time' interpretation. They would answer (58) with *No because they were cool*:

(58) Were the hot mice in the swimming hole?

These results are more impressive because we regard the stories as (unavoidably) pragmatically imperfect. For instance, one could still be hot for awhile in the cool pool before cooling took effect. We take this to explain some of the variation that was found. Nonetheless there are very clear groups that fit into the Name = DP, and the Nonspecific = NP which we take to be the semantic Default, and therefore is construed as referring to the single, present time of the question, ignoring the article:

(59) No = NAME (8 children) = Chinese Pattern of Name
Ages: 3;4, 3;4, 3;6, 4;0, 6;0, 4;1, 4;6, 5;5

Yes = SINGLE TIME (7 children) = Bare Noun, Nonspecific
Ages: 3;5, 3;9, 3;9, 3;9, 4;7, 4;7, 4;7

Yes/no adult (12 children) subjects = *the* = specific,
there = nonspecific
Ages: 3;3, 3;6, 3;9, 3;11, 3;11, 3;11, 4;1, 4;3, 4;6, 4;7, 5;2, 5;6

No/yes Opposite to adult (2 children)
Ages: 3;2, 3;8

Let us address these results with a series of questions. First, why would the child not associate Specificity immediately with DP *the*?[12] We argue precisely that NP without a definite article is the preference for economic representations: It involves less structure and constitutes both a syntactic and semantic Default.[13] Second, why would some of the children do the opposite and take every reference to be a Name? Our results suggest the DP (Proper Name) is also a Default that is available to them. Third, why does the child not get definite and indefinite articles right immediately? There is an intricate variety of possible sets and it is not immediately clear what sort each grammar has.[14] Preference is for the NP nonspecific because of less structure.

In conclusion, we have seen the appearance of Default syntactic/semantic representations in very subtle environments.

5. PARTIAL CONCLUSIONS

Our theoretical model and acquisition data are far from painting a complete picture. We remain uncertain about what steps are taken by children and we expect the ultimate DP map to be heavily influenced by their decisions. Moreover, we cannot be completely sure that children all follow the same path, nor do we see clearly how Defaults reappear and how Multiple Grammars connect. Nevertheless we have shown that children's grammar operates with great semantic subtlety at all times. We have argued that there is clear and strong evidence for the following, namely:

(60) a. that children move from less specific to more specific,
 b. that this path mirrors the tree from N to NP to DP,
 c. that defaults play a prominent role in grammar, and
 d. that the concept of compositionality is natural and should play a central role.

We have also sought to articulate what it means for semantics to meet acquisition. In part, one accepts UG as a statement of defaults and innate structure. However beyond that the best method is to seek definitions of core concepts that reflect acquisition data and theory rather than to impose existing semantic theories. In this way, semantic theory can benefit from the insights that subtle steps in development reveal about semantic formulations.

If, however, both the child and adult really tolerate a mixture of grammars for their language, then the child is really considering several grammars at once. Acquisition analysis often abstracts away from age differences because they are difficult to explain, and it abstracts away from percentage responses for the same reason. A natural explanation for percentage responses is that children revert to the default some of the time, but at other times they exhibit a more adult grammar. At some point one grammar is defined more broadly and one grammar is linked to specific lexical items. We think, as we said, that recursion plays a crucial role here.

In sum, we have argued that the child is overtly maintaining a series of grammar types and must decide which part of his language goes with which grammar type. The term *grammar*, in this context, seems to say too much, since we are usually referring to a very limited option. As with most scientific enterprises, the vocabulary begins to miss the target as the analysis becomes more refined. We need to abandon the notion of grammar in favor of more refined descriptions of variation within modules.

University of Massachusetts at Amherst

6. ACKNOWLEDGEMENTS

Thanks to Emmon Bach, Manfred Bierwisch, Greg Carlson, Bart Hollebrandse, Hans Kamp, Wolfgang Klein, Angelika Kratzer, Irene Krämer, and to the audience of the Semantics Meets Acquisition Conference, for comments, to Veerle Van Geenhoven and anonymous reviewers, and for editorial assistance to Casey Hill and Vanessa Cargill. Also my thanks to Jill de Villiers and to the UMass Acquisition Lab members for comments. The perspectives here evolved out of joint work with Jill de Villiers, Ana Perez, Maribel Romero, Jeanine Bock, Lisa Matthewson, Tim Bryant, and Robin Schafer. Mistakes and errors, particularly in my non-technical exposition of semantic ideas are, obviously, my responsibility.

7. NOTES

[1] This approach reflects in part the fact that I write primarily from the perspective of acquisition and syntax and therefore the use of the notion of compositionality is rudimentary.
[2] Categorial Grammars (Drozd, 1993), Minimalist approaches (Chomsky, 1995, 2001; Roeper, 1996).
[3] Technically this initial stage in acquisition fails to *converge* in minimalist terms. It is therefore a part of grammar acquisition that deviates slightly from UG, and therefore would be a part of a separate component of LAD.
[4] My own work on incorporation has assumed that incorporated nouns are bare heads (Roeper & Siegel, 1978; Roeper, 1988; Keyser & Roeper, 1992; van Hout & Roeper, 1999). The concept of the First Sister evolved into the Abstract Clitic hypothesis which argued that in order to capture the fact that we generate: *homerebuilding* and not *rehomebuilding or *homeuplifting* but *uphomelifting, an argument must be moved into a Clitic position that allows only Heads, after a particle has been fronted from that position. The semantic consequences of this could be that there is type-shifting or theme-suppression as Dayal (1999) suggests. Empirically the contrast between sentences like *John enjoyed singing at home* and *John enjoyed home-singing* is that in the latter sentence *home* is interpreted generically, while in the former it is controlled by *John* which we attribute to the distinction between incorporated N and non-incorporated NP (with an

anaphor in the Spec position). Arguments from Van Geenhoven (1998) about existential properties of incorporated nouns reflect one kind of incorporation, namely phrasal incorporation, which can be seen in English in the following contrast:
    a. John saw a quickly-flowing river   b. John saw a quick-flowing river
In (a) an event is implied, but not in (b). The same contrast is found in the difference between nominalizations and compounds:
    c. a saver of lives   d. a life-saver
In (c) the event must have transpired, but not in (d). The arguments in favor of treating incorporated nouns as referential often refer to definite articles in discourse:
    e. John enjoyed apple-picking. The apples were beautiful.
Here, however, there is a part-whole relation between the event and the definite article. Consequently *the apples* can refer to those still on trees, as well as those actually picked, which means that the incorporated *apple* could still be a Kind. In sum, these arguments suggest that the Kind interpretation remains viable. It is clear that Kinds must involve properties in order to be fully specified, but it is less clear that the notion of properties is sufficiently refined to capture the nature of partitioning. (Thanks to Emmon Bach, Greg Carlson for discussion.)

[5] Their responses to presupposition-violation sentences like *Do you want more soup?* when they had none was often *What soup?* and therefore their acceptance of definites does not reflect a failure to recognize presupposition violation.

[6] In general, a variety of further NP nodes could be warranted under the strict view that these semantic differences lead to differences in how these elements are labeled. Schmitt & Munn (2000) argue in depth for language particular variation pivoting around the interaction of AgrP and NumP, showing that variation within Romance responds to these nodes. Hoekstra & Hyams (1999) and Schafer & de Villiers (2000) argue for a NumP node in acquisition as an explanation for both early phases of root infinitives and DP's. — Our analysis tends in the direction of Chomsky (1998), Collins (2001), Cinque (1999) and the Categorial Grammar tradition where the labels are much more refined (see Drozd, 1993). The ultimate claim is that we have Bare Phrase structure with no labels but rather a bundle of properties. The crucial issue in that case is whether the label itself functions in a further rule, such as a barrier to extraction.

[7] Schaeffer (2001) argues that SLI children who use the bare Noun have the cognitive requirements for definite articles but do not use them. We would argue that in both the normal and SLI cases, children prefer a more economical structure without a DP node that is accomplished by using just the bare noun. A more interesting question is whether it is just a NP or an N.

[8] "[...] categories lacking interpretable features should be disallowed. [...] The argument carries over to other cases, among them semantically null determiners D_{null}. If true D relates to referentiality/specificity in some sense, then an indefinite nonspecific nominal phrase (*a lot of people, someone*) that enters into scopal interactions must be a pure NP, not DP with null D." (Chomsky, November 1998, 55).

[9] See Roeper (2000) for numerous further examples.

[10] See Roeper (2000), de Villiers & Roeper (1995), Perez & Roeper (1999).

[11] See Romero and Bock (2001) for a formulation of truth conditions for temporal nouns in terms of a tripartite structure.

[12] Not only are there expletive determiners, possible forms of Agreement, but as mentioned above complex aspects of Point of View can be linked to the DP (Hollebrandse, 2000; de Villiers, 1999; Speas, 2000; Tenny, 1997). For instance, a Speaker POV is involved in a sentence like *John thought the new hat was old*. It is the Speaker who knows that the hat is new. Therefore it is sensible that the child, unsure of what the Determiner *the* carries, would wait until a narrow, particular-language appropriate form appears.

[13] An interesting hypothesis by Chierchia (1998a,b) has been advanced. He claims that there is a parameter such that a Definiteness feature is attached to Bare Nouns in Asian languages where

there are no articles. If one combined that view with a notion of economy of structure, then his view would also predict that English children might pass through a Chinese phase. Crucially, we predict that Chinese children will not project an invented piece of morphology to represent a Determiner, thereby passing through an English phase. Bottari *et al.* (1993) have in fact provided evidence that Italian children spontaneously project a schwa in the position of a Determiner. We suspect this would not be a direct projection of UG, but a version of a Determiner that they have heard and begun to project.

[14] It is possible, as Brun & Avrutin (2001) argue, that movement can impose specificity, which makes the child's task even more complex.

8. REFERENCES

Baauw, Sergio. *Grammatical Features and the Acquisition of Reference.* Ph.D. Diss., Universiteit Utrecht, 2000.

Blumenfeld, Ann. *Acquisition of Compounds and Home.* Ms., Haverford, 1999.

Bottari, Pierro, Paolo Cipriani, and Anna M. Chilosi. "Protosyntactic Devices in the Acquisition of Italian Morphology." *Language Acquisition* 3 (1993): 285–315.

Burns, Tracy, and Nancy Soja. "The Role of Determiner in the Interpretation of NP-type Nouns." In Elizabeth Hughes, Mary Hughes, and Annabell Greenhill (eds.) *BUCDL 21 Proceedings*, 35–55. Somerville, MA: Cascadilla Press, 1997.

Brun, Dina, and Sergey Avrutin. "The Expression of Specificity in a Language without Determiners." In Anna H.-J. Do, Laura Dominguez, and Aimee Johansen (eds.) *BUCLD 25 Proceedings*, 70-81. Somerville, MA: Cascadilla Press, 2001.

Chierchia, Gennaro. "Plurality of Mass Nouns and the Notion of Semantic Parameter." In Susan Rothstein (ed.) *Events in Grammar*, 53–103. Dordrecht: Kluwer, 1998.

Chierchia, Gennaro. "Reference to Kinds across Natural Languages." *Natural Language Semantics* 6 (1998): 339–405.

Chomsky, Noam. *The Logical Structure of Linguistic Theory.* New York: Plenum Press, 1955/1978.

Chomsky, Noam. *Reflections on Language.* New York: Pantheon Books, 1976.

Chomsky, Noam. *The Minimalist Program.* Cambridge, MA: MIT Press, 1995.

Chomsky, Noam. *Minimalist Inquiries.* Cambridge, MA: MIT Press, 1998.

Chomsky, Noam. "Beyond Explanatory Adequacy." Ms., MIT, Cambridge, MA, 2001.

Cinque, Guglielmo. *Adverbs and Functional Heads: A Crosslinguistic Perspective.* Oxford: Oxford University Press, 1999.

Collins, Chris. *Local Economy.* Cambridge, MA: MIT Press, 1997.

Collins, Chris. "Eliminating Labels." *MIT WPL 20*, 1–25. Cambridge, MA: MIT, 2001.

Crain, Stephen, and Rosalind Thornton. *Investigations in Universal Grammar.* Cambridge, MA: MIT Press, 1998.

Dayal, Veneeta. "Bare NP's, Reference to Kinds, and Incorporation." In Tanya Matthews and Devon Strolovitch (eds.) *Proceedings of SALT 9*, 35–52. Ithaca: CLC Publications, 1999.

Drozd, Kenneth. *A Unification Categorial Grammar of Child English Negation.* Ph.D. Diss., University of Arizona, Tucson, 1993.

Eisenbeiss, Sonja. "The Acquisition of the Determiner Phrase in German Child Language." In Marc-Ariel Friedemann and Luigi Rizzi (eds.) *The Acquisition of Syntax*, 26–63. London: Longman, 2000.

Heim, Irene. *The Semantics of Definite and Indefinite Noun Phrases.* Ph.D. Diss., UMass, Amherst, 1982.

Heim, Irene, and Angelika Kratzer. *Semantics and Generative Grammar.* Oxford: Blackwell, 1998.

Hoekstra, Teun, and Nina Hyams. "The Eventivity Constraint and Modal Reference Effects in Root Infinitives." In Annabell Greenhill, Heather Littlefield, and Cheryl Tano (eds.) *BUCLD 23 Proceedings*, 240–252. Somerville, MA: Cascadilla Press, 1999.

Hollebrandse, Bart. *The Acquisition of Sequence of Tense*. Ph.D. Diss., UMass, Amherst, 2000.

de Hoop, Helen. *Case Configuration and Noun Phrase Interpretation*. Ph.D. Diss., RijksUniversiteit Groningen, 1992.

Hyams, Nina. "The Underspecification of Functional Categories in Early Grammar." In Harald Clahsen (ed.) *Generative Perspectives on Language Acquisition*, 91–129. Oxford: John Benjamins Publishing, 1996.

Jackendoff, Ray, Joan Maling, and Annie Zaenen. "Home is Subject to Principle A." *Linguistic Inquiry* 24 (1993): 173–177.

Keyser, Samuel J., and Tom Roeper. "Re: The Abstract Clitic Hypothesis." *Linguistic Inquiry* 23 (1992): 89–125.

Krämer, Irene. *Interpreting Indefinites: An Experimental Study of Children's Language Comprehension*. Ph.D. Diss., Universiteit Utrecht, 2000.

Leonard, Lawrence, Eva-Kristina Salameh, and Kristina Hansson. "Noun Phrase Morphology in Swedish-Speaking Children with Specific Language Impairment." Ms., Purdue, 2001.

Longobardi, Giuseppe. "Reference and Proper Names." *Linguistic Inquiry* 25 (1994): 609–665.

Maratsos, Michael. *The Use of Definite and Indefinite Reference in Young Children*. Cambridge: Cambridge University Press, 1974.

Marinis, Theo. *The Acquisition of the DP in Modern Greek*. Ph.D. Diss., Universität Potsdam, 2000.

Matsuo, Ayumi, and Nigel Duffield. "VP-Ellipsis and Anaphora in First and Second Language Acquisition." *Language Acquisition* (to appear).

Matthewson, Lisa. *Determiner Systems and Quantificational Strategies: Evidence from Salish*. The Hague: Holland Academic Graphics, 1998.

Matthewson, Lisa, Tim Bryant, and Tom Roeper. "A Salish Stage in the Acquisition of the English Determiner: Unfamiliar 'Definites'." In Ji-Yung Kim and Adam Werle (eds.) *Proceedings of the first SULA Conference*, 63–72. Amherst: GLSA, 2001.

Matthewson, Lisa, and Jeannette Schaeffer. "Grammar and Pragmatics in the Acquisition of Article Systems." In Jeanette Gilkerson, Misha Becker, and Nina Hyams (eds.) *Language Development and Breakdown 1, UCLA Working Papers in Linguistics No. 5*, 1–39. Los Angeles: Linguistics Department, 2000.

Montague, Richard. *Formal Philosophy: Selected Papers of Richard Montague*. New Haven: Yale University Press, 1974.

Moore, Deanna. *The Acquisition of Comparatives*. Ph.D. Diss., UMass, Amherst, in prep.

Morzyki, Marcin. *Mediated Modification: Functional Structure and the Interpretation of Modifier Position*. Ph.D. Diss., UMass, Amherst, 2003.

Musan, Renate. *On the Temporal Interpretation of Noun Phrases*. Ph.D. Diss., MIT, 1995.

Namiki, Taka. "Heads and Subheads of Compounds." In Shuji Chiba (ed.) *Synchronic and Diachronic Approaches to Language: A Festschrift for Toshio Nakao on the Occasion of his Sixtieth Birthday*, 239–265. Tokyo: Liber Press, 1994.

Penner, Zvi. "The Ban on Parameter-Resetting, Default Mechanisms, and the Acquisition of V2 in Bernese Swiss German." In Jürgen Meisel (ed.) *The Acquisition of Verb Placement*, 245–283. Dordrecht: Kluwer, 1992.

Pérez-Leroux, Ana, and Tom Roeper. "Scope and the Structure of Bare Nominals: Evidence from Child Language." *Linguistics* 37 (1999): 927–960.

Roeper, Tom. "The Role of Universals in the Acquisition of Gerunds." In Eric Wanner and Lila Gleitman (eds.) *Language Acquisition: The State of the Art*, 267–287. Cambridge: Cambridge University Press, 1982.

Roeper, Tom. "Compound Syntax and Head Movement." In *Yearbook of Morphology*, 120–128. Dordrecht: Foris, 1987.

Roeper, Tom. "Universal Bilingualism." *Bilingualism: Language and Cognition* 2 (1999): 169–186.
Roeper, Tom. "Leftward Movement in Morphology." In Vivienne Lin, Charles Krause, Benjamin Bruening, and Klaus Arregi (eds.) *Papers on Morphology and Syntax*, 35–66. Cambridge, MA: MITWPL, 2000.
Roeper, Tom. "Multiple Grammars, Feature-Attraction, Pied-Piping and the Question: Is AGR inside TP?" In Natascha Müller (ed.) *(In)Vulnerable Grammars in Multilingualism*, 355–361. Oxford: John Benjamins Publishing, 2003.
Roeper, Tom, and Muffy E.A. Siegel. "A Lexical Transformation for Verbal Compounds." *Linguistic Inquiry* 9 (1978): 199–260.
Roeper, Tom, and William Snyder. "Recursion as an Analytic Device in Acquisition." In Janine van Kampen and Peter Coopmans (eds.) *Proceedings of GALA 2003*. 158–168. Utrecht: LOT, 2003.
Roeper, Tom, William Snyder, and Kazuko Hiamatsu. "Learnability in a Minimalist Framework: Root Compounds, Merger, and the Syntax-Morphology Interface." In Inge Lasser (ed.) *Proceedings of Gala*, 25–37. Berlin: Peter Lang, 2001.
Romero, Maribel, and Jeannine Bock. "Temporal Noun Phrase Interpretation and Theory of Mind." In Margareta Almgren, Andoni Barreña, María-José Ezeizabarrena, Itziar Idiazabal, and Brian MacWhinney (eds.) *Proceedings of the VIIIth Conference for the Study of Child Language*, 1026–1037. Somerville, MA: Cascadilla Press, 2001.
Schaeffer, Jeanette. "Articles in English Child Language." LSA, Los Angeles, 1999.
Schaeffer, Jeanette. "Pragmatics and SLI." In Yonata Levy and Jeanette Schaeffer (eds.) *Towards a Definition of SLI*, 135–151. Hillsdale, NJ: Lawrence Erlbaum, 2001.
Schafer, Robin, and Jill de Villiers. "Imagining Articles: What *a* and *the* can Tell us about the Emergence of DP." In Catherine Howell, Sarah A. Fish, and Thea Keith-Lucas (eds.) *Proceedings of the 24th BUCLD*, 609–620. Somerville, MA: Cascadilla Press, 2000.
Schmitt, Cristina, and Alan Munn. "Against the Nominal Mapping Parameter." In Pius Tamanji, Masako Hirotani, and Nancy Hall (eds.) *Proceedings of NELS* 29, 339–355. Amherst: GSLA, 1999.
Schmitt, Cristina, and Alan Munn. "Bare Nominals and the Morpho-Syntax of Number." In Diana Cresti, Teresa Sattersfield, and Christina Tortora (eds.) *Current Issues in Romance Linguistics*, 1–15. Oxford: John Benjamins, 2000.
Slobin, Dan. "Cognitive Prerequisites for the Development of Grammar." In Dan Slobin and Charles Ferguson (eds.) *Studies of Child Language Development*, 175–277. New York: Holt, Rinehart, and Winston, 1973.
Snyder, William. *Language Acquisition and Language Variation: The Role of Morphology*. Ph.D. Diss., MIT, 1995.
Speas, Margaret. "Person and Point of View in Navajo Direct Discourse Complements." Ms., UMass, Amherst, 2000.
Tenny, Carol. "Short Distance Pronouns, Point of View, and the Nature of Pronominal Reference." Ms., UMass, Amherst, 1997.
Thrainnson, Höskuldur. "On the Nonuniversality of Functional Categories." In Werner Abraham, Samual Epstein, Hoskur Thrainsson, and Jan-Wouter Zwart (eds.) *Minimal Ideas*, 253–281. Oxford: Benjamins Publishing, 1996.
Van Geenhoven, Veerle. *Semantic Incorporation and Indefinite Descriptions*. Stanford: CSLI Publications, 1998.
de Villiers, Jill. "On Acquiring the Structural Representations for False Complements." In Bart Hollebrandse (ed.) *New Perspectives in Language Acquisition*, 125–136. Amherst: GSLA, 1997.
de Villiers, Jill, and Tom Roeper. "Barriers, Binding and Acquisition of the NP/DP Distinction." *Language Acquisition* 4 (1995): 73–104.
Yang, Charles. *Knowledge and Learning in Natural Language*. Oxford: Oxford University Press, 2003.

AYUMI MATSUO

CROSS-LINGUISTIC ACQUISITION OF COMPLEMENT TENSE

Abstract. This chapter discusses how young Polish children (age 3;3-6;11) interpret a past tense when embedded in the complement clause of an intensional attitude verb. Past research by Hollebrandse (1988) on English and Dutch has found a strong relationship between having an adult-like understanding of the past tense in a complement clause and having an adult-like Theory of Mind. By contrast, Matsuo & Hollebrandse (1999) did not find the same correlation in Japanese. The aim of this chapter is to gain a better understanding of the relationship between having an adult-like understanding of the past tense and having an adult Theory of Mind, by looking at another language, namely, Polish.

1. INTRODUCTION

This chapter concerns the acquisition of a complex tense system by young children learning Polish as their first language; the results are compared to the results of previous experiments on Dutch, English and Japanese. The complex tense construction under investigation is illustrated by the examples in (1): intensional attitude verbs taking a complement clause. In these examples past tense subordinate clauses are embedded under past tense matrix clauses (we call these 'past under past sentences' following Abusch, 1988):[1]

(1) a. John said that Bill was happy.   (English)

 b. Jan   zei dat Bill gelukkig   was.   (Dutch)
    John   said that Bill happy   be-PST
    'John said that Bill was happy.'

 c. John-wa   Bill-ga   siawase
    John-TOP   Bill-NOM   happy
    datta   to   itta.
    be-PST   that say-PST   (Japanese)
    'John said that Bill was happy.'

d. Jan   powiedział   że Bill   był
    John   say-PST-PERF   that Bill   be-PST-IMP
    szcześliwy.   (Polish)
    happy
    'John said that Bill was happy.'

The construction introduced in (1) is quite complex. First, these sentences involve sentential complementation, which many researchers argue does not appear until Stage IV (MLU 3-3.5) of the grammatical development proposed by Brown (1973). Second, they also involve a sophisticated temporal relationship between two tensed predicates. Furthermore, there is a language variation as to whether the language displays the Sequence of Tense (SOT) phenomenon or not.

The SOT phenomenon is observed only in certain languages, which include English and Dutch. In these languages, the same (past) tense in the matrix and embedded clause can indicate that the two events overlap in time. One of the interpretations of examples (1a) and (1b) is that where the time of John's saying and of Bill's being happy overlap with each other: although the embedded clause verb is marked with past tense morphology — due to the application of the SOT rule (Abusch, 1988; Ogihara, 1996) — at an interpretive level, the complement may be interpreted as present tense.[2] The SOT rule makes English and Dutch examples (1a) and (1b) ambiguous. The most prominent reading is the one where a matrix event time overlaps with the embedded event time (see (3a) below). This is called the 'overlapping' reading. The second reading is the one where Bill's being happy precedes John's saying so. Ogihara (1996) argues that this type of interpretation is especially obvious when an adverbial such as *last week* is added, as in (2):

(2)   John said [that Bill was happy last week]

This is called a 'real past' reading (see also (3b) below).

The SOT phenomenon is not observed in most other languages, including Polish and Japanese, and examples (1c) and (1d) are unambiguous. They only permit the real past reading (see (3b)):

(3) a.   there is a time t_1 such that $t_1 <$ Utterance Time (UT) and John said at t_1 that [there is a time t_2 such that Bill was happy at t_2 and $t_2 = t_1$]. (overlapping)

     b.   there is a time t_1 such that $t_1 <$ UT and John said at t_1 that [there is a time t_2 such that Bill was happy at t_2 and $t_2 < t_1$]. (real past)

As briefly mentioned right after example (1), acquiring the correct inter-interpretation of complex tense constructions should be especially difficult for children. There are several reasons for believing this. First, (1) involves a form-meaning mismatch in the temporal domain (see Carlson, this volume, concerning such mismatches). The examples in (1) are either ambiguous or unambiguous depending on whether or not the language displays the SOT phenomenon. For example, English and Dutch children must learn that a past tense can show an overlapping interpretation only when it appears in the position where another past tense has scope over. Japanese and Polish children, on the other hand, must find out that a present tense shows an overlapping reading under the same circumstances. This involves a successful lexical learning of present and past tense as well as a sophisticated syntactic analysis, including the notion of c-command. Second, in all languages, a past tense meaning changes or becomes more restricted when it is embedded under another past tense; a complement clause in isolation in (1c) shown in (4a) has the interpretation in (4b):

(4) a. Bill-wa siawase datta.
Bill-TOP happy be-PST
'Bill was happy.'

b. there is a time t_1 such that $t_1 <$ UT and Bill was happy at t_1.

Simple sentences involving one situation time are rather easy because all that needs to be done is to relate one time point (t_1) to the time of utterance (UT). By contrast, when two situation time points (t and$_2$ t) are involved in a complex sentence, it is necessary for children to relate the two points appropriately for each language ($t_1 < t_2$ in Japanese and Polish; $t_1 \leq t_2$ in English and Dutch). Moreover, children will have to distinguish complex constructions involving a complement clause from those involving a relative clause, as in (5a). The sentence in (5a) permits a wider set of interpretations than in (1); namely, it allows the interpretation where embedded event takes place in the past without any temporal dependency on a matrix event time as observed in (5b). We call this an 'independent' interpretation:

(5) a. John fed the animal that was in the garden.

b. there is a time t_1 such that $t_1 <$ UT and John fed the animal at t_1. There is also a time t_2 such that $t_2 <$ UT and the animal was in the garden at t_2.   (independent)

Since both t_1 and t_2 can be past with respect to the utterance time in (5b), one can have sentences such as (6a), where there is no relative ordering between two events. Compare (6a) with (6b), where there is a strict temporal ordering between t_1 and t_2:

(6) a. Yesterday, John already fed the animal that was in the garden just now.
b. *Yesterday, John said that Bill was happy just now.

Children acquiring a complex temporal system must discover that the complex sentences in (6a) and (6b) display different temporal interpretations, even though they are superficially similar.[3]

Table 1 summarizes the temporal interpretations past-under-past-sentences can have:

Table 1. Different temporal interpretations

		interpretation(s) of past-under-past-sentences	interpretation of the sentences with relative clauses
SOT languages	Dutch, English	overlapping reading (3a) real-past reading (3b)	independent reading (5b)
Non SOT languages	Japanese, Polish	only real-past reading (3b)	independent reading (5b)

The aim of this chapter is to examine more closely the problems that young children face in interpreting past-under-past-sentences. Previous research in Hollebrandse (1998) relates the difficulty that the Dutch and English children had to their non-adultlike Theory of Mind. Matsuo & Hollebrandse (1999), after conducting the same experiment in Japanese, found that adult-like Theory of Mind is not the only prerequisite for correctly interpreting past-under-past-sentences. They proposed that Japanese past-under-past-sentences are more difficult for the children to interpret than those of Dutch and English due to the syntactic characteristics of CPs (they call this "a syntactic account"). The aim of this chapter is to investigate the validity of the syntactic account by looking at Polish past-under-past-sentences and to compare a syntactic account with a processing account. The processing account proposes that it is the word order of the language that causes the

CROSS-LINGUISTIC ACQUISITION OF COMPLEMENT TENSE 69

difficulty for the children in interpreting past-under-past-sentences. Polish is an ideal language for distinguishing the two accounts since it should behave like Japanese under the syntactic account, but should pattern with English or Dutch under the processing account, given its word order characteristics. If Polish children face the same level of difficulty as the Japanese children in interpreting the sentences, we can confirm the validity of the syntactic account. By contrast, if Polish children face less difficulty than the Japanese children, then we may conclude that Japanese is exceptional in this comparison due to its word order.

The chapter is organized as follows. Section 2 includes a brief outline of the four different readings manipulated in our experiment, following Hollebrandse (1998). Section 3 discusses previous experiments on Dutch, English and Japanese by Hollebrandse (1998) and Matsuo & Hollebrandse (1999). Section 4 introduces the results of a new Polish experiment and compares them with the previous results. Section 5 concludes the paper.

2. TEMPORAL INTERPRETATIONS

As discussed in section 1, past-under-past-sentences have different readings depending on whether or not it is an SOT language. This section sets out these different interpretations, as used in Hollebrandse (1998).

2.1. Past-under-Past in SOT Languages

The complex sentences in (1a) and (1b) allow both real past and overlapping readings as shown in diagrams (8b) and (9b). The diagram in (8) schematizes the reading where the embedded event takes place before the matrix event and it should represent a situation equivalent to the interpretation of the direct quotation in (8a). Following Hollebrandse (1998), we call (8) an E1 reading.

(8) a.   John said "Bill was happy."
    b.   E1 (real past reading)

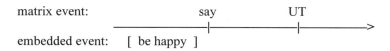

The next reading, the overlapping reading, is equivalent to the interpretation of the direct quotation in (9a) and is schematized in the diagram in (9b). We call this an E2 reading:

(9) a. John said "Bill is happy."
  b. E2 (overlapping reading)

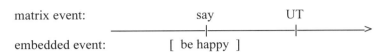

Unlike (6a), (1a) and (1b) cannot have a forward shifted reading (also called an E3 reading). A forward shifted reading is a subset of an independent interpretation. It allows the embedded event time to follow the matrix event time. Such a reading is represented in (10). This interpretation is only possible when the two past tenses do not need to interact with each other or when the embedded clause has a modal *would* as in (10a).

(10) a. John said that Bill would be happy.
  b. E3 (forward shifted reading)

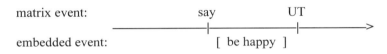

It is also clear that the E4 reading — where the embedded predicate involves a future situation time — is not a possible interpretation for (1a) and (1b). As a matter of fact, even (6a) does not allow the E4 interpretation. To have an E4 reading, the embedded clause must include a future tense as in (11a).

(11) a. John said that Bill will be happy.
  b. E4 (future reading)

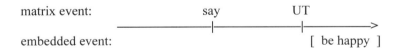

Two impossible readings of (1a) and (1b) are in (10), where the embedded event takes place between the matrix situation time and the utterance time, and (11), where the embedded event takes place after the utterance time.

2.2. Past-under-Past in non-SOT Languages

The Japanese and Polish examples in (1c) and (1d), respectively, allow more restricted interpretations due to the absence of the SOT phenomenon in these languages. In other words, sentences (1c) and (1d) only have the real past reading (E1). In order to express the overlapping reading (E2), we need to use a present tense in a complement clause, as in (12):

(12) Taroo-wa   Hanako-ga   byooki-da-   to   it-ta.
     Taroo-TOP   Hanako-NOM   be-sick-PRS   that   say-PST
     'Taroo said that Hanako was sick (at that time).'
     only overlapping reading (Ogihara, 1996, 69)

Interestingly, though, Japanese complex sentences containing *relative clauses* behave in the same way as in Dutch or English. The Japanese equivalent of (6a), given in (13), permits three readings: real past, overlapping and forward shifted (E1, E2 and E3):

(13) Taroo-wa   niwa-ni   i-ta   doobutu-ni   esa-o
     Taro-TOP   garden-LOC   be-PST   animal-DAT   food-ACC
     yat-ta.
     give-PST
     'Taro fed the animal that was in the garden.'

In (13), the time when the animal was in the garden may precede, overlap or follow the time of Taro's feeding that animal.

The different readings in these languages discussed so far are summarized in Table 2, which is slightly modified from Hollebrandse (1998):

Table 2. Interpretations of complex sentences (past-under-past)

	E1	E2	E3	E4
English/Dutch complement clauses	√	√	*	*
Japanese/Polish complement clauses	√	*	*	*
English/Dutch/Japanese/Polish relative clauses	√	√	*	*

In the following section, we will discuss how young children perform in assigning correct interpretations to past-under-past-sentences. I will briefly summarize the findings in Hollebrandse (1998) and Matsuo & Hollebrandse (1999). Section 3.2 discusses how the experiments in Hollebrandse (1998) were carried out. Section 3.3 includes a syntactic account and a processing account in a discussion on cross-linguistic variety on the results of the experiment.

3. PAST EXPERIMENTS

This section summarizes two previous experiments conducted on the acquisition of complex temporal structure by Hollebrandse (1998) and Matsuo & Hollebrandse (1999). These studies employed the Theory of Mind (ToM) task and the Sequence of Tense (SOT) task in experiments with Dutch, English and Japanese children.

3.1. Dutch and English Experiments: Hollebrandse (1998)

Following work by de Villiers (1995) and Gale, de Villiers, de Villiers & Pyers (1996), Hollebrandse (1998) claims that having an adult-like ToM is strongly related to the syntactic development of a clause structure. A cognitive notion, ToM is something that children have to develop in order to represent somebody else's belief that they know to be false. Hollebrandse (1998) goes further to claim that an adult-like ToM is necessary to link two past events in a sentence with a complement clause. The ToM test Hollebrandse (1998) employed was the 'unexpected-content-in-a-familiar-box-task', developed in Wimmer & Perner (1983). In this task, a child is shown a bandage box that contains a fish. Then she is asked what her best friend (who has not seen the box) will say is in the box. The successful children should answer *bandages*. The children without a developed ToM should answer *a fish* to the question because it should be difficult for them to relate a false belief, namely, the bandages are in the box, to others.

For the SOT test, Hollebrandse (1998) used a 'yes/no' judgement task. The different event sequences E1 through E4 that have been outlined in section 1 were acted out to the participants with hand-puppets and toys and the participants were asked to answer *yes* or *no* to the question such as *Did Bill say that John was happy?* The questions always involved two past tenses in matrix and complement clauses.

Hollebrandse (1998) predicts a strong relationship between having an adult like ToM and succeeding in the SOT experiment. By hypothesis, both ToM and SOT require embedding under an intensional attitude verb. If the child lacks adult ToM, she should interpret complex sentences as mono-clausal. He predicts that ToM failers should interpret (1a), repeated here in (14a), as if it is (14b):

(14) a. John said that Bill was happy. (English)
     b. Bill was happy.

The prediction is that although adults and ToM passers should accept only E1 and E2 readings for (14a), ToM failers should accept E1, E2 and E3 readings. These are the readings that (14b) has. In other words, ToM failers should treat relative Past as an absolute Past.

Hollebrandse (1998) reports results from 62 Dutch subjects ranging in age from 2;7 to 7;2 and 62 English subjects ranging in age from 2;10 to 7;8. He found a significant effect of ToM on the future shifted reading before UT (E3) ($F = 11.79$, $p < .001$), as predicted. He also found a small effect on E4 reading after UT ($F = 4.95$, $p < .05$). In a multiple regression he found that ToM had an almost-significant effect ($p = .060$) only on the dependent variable E3. For the dependent variable E4, he found no effect of ToM, but a significant effect of age ($p < .005$).

Hollebrandse concludes that passing or failing a ToM test is a reliable predictor for allowing a forward shifted reading before UT (E3) in past-under-past-sentences. His results support the prediction that when the child fails in ToM, she does not have an adult-like CP system and in consequence is not able to interpret embedded tense as a relative tense. The child treats the embedded past in an SOT construction as absolute and thus allows a wider range of possible readings for past-under-past-sentences than an adult does.

3.2. Japanese Experiment: Matsuo & Hollebrandse (1999)

Using the same experimental method and stimuli as in Hollebrandse (1998), Matsuo & Hollebrandse (1999) investigate how Japanese children interpret past-under-past-sentences. 32 Japanese children (3;4-6;2) were tested, together with 7 adult controls. Matsuo & Hollebrandse (1999) predict that when Japanese ToM failers hear a sentence in (1c) repeated here in (15), they should accept E1, E2 and E3 readings; however, passers should accept only E1 reading:

(15) John-wa   Bill-ga   siawase-datta   to   itta. (Japanese)
     John-TOP   Bill-NOM   happy-be-PST   that say-PST
     'John said that Bill was happy.'

A regression analysis showed that ToM is not a variable that can account for responses given by Japanese children for E1-3 readings. For E4 readings, ToM had only a marginal effect on correct performance ($p = .061$). In other words, there was no relationship between ToM and SOT in Japanese. Matsuo & Hollebrandse conclude that ToM is not the only prerequisite for Japanese children to interpret an embedded past tense correctly. The only similarity between Japanese and Dutch/English was that, in acquiring past-under-past-sentences, the participants all followed the same pattern, excluding the future reading (E4) first.

3.3. Why are Japanese Children Different from Dutch/English Children?

The results of the two experiments above lead us to question why there was no correlation in the results of ToM and SOT in Japanese, as was found in Dutch/English. Matsuo & Hollebrandse (1999) argue that the contrast was due to the fact that Japanese complement clauses are syntactically different from those of Dutch/English (this is called "a syntactic account"). Matsuo & Hollebrandse trace this difference to the fact that Japanese complement clauses are opaque/strong islands. They use two pieces of evidence to support their claim, namely, constraints on *wh*-movement and on negative polarity item (NPI) licensing. First, Japanese, being a *wh*-in-situ language, allows *dare* 'who' to stay in the complement clause as shown in (16a). The English equivalent of (16a), (16b), is not allowed except as an echo question:

(16) a. John-wa   Mary-ga   dare-ni   atta   to
         John-TOP   Mary-NOM   who-DAT   meet-PST   that
         omotta   no.
         think-PST Q
         'Who did John think that Mary met?'

   b.   *John thought that Mary met who? (as a *wh*-question)

Second, Japanese does not allow an NPI item to be separated from its licensor across a CP boundary. Sentence (17a) is possible because an NPI item: *nani-mo* 'any' is in the same clause as its licensor, i.e., negation. The same is true in the English example (17b):

(17) a. John-wa   Mary-ga   *nani-mo*   kawa*n*akatta
         John-TOP   Mary-NOM   *anything-NPI*   buy-*NEG*-PST
         to   iwanakatta.
         that say-NEG-PST
         'John didn't say that Mary didn't buy anything.'

   b.   John didn't say that Mary did*n't* buy *anything*.

However, (18a) shows that *nani-mo* must not be on the other side of a CP boundary from its licensing negation. The equivalent of (18a) in English, that is (18b), is grammatical:

(18) a. *John-wa [_CP_ Mary-ga   nani-mo   katta to]
         John-TOP   Mary-NOM   anything-NPI   buy-PST that
         iwanakatta.
         say-NEG-PST
         'John didn't say that Mary bought anything.'

   b.   John didn't say that Mary bought anything.

Based on these different constraints concerning Japanese CPs, Matsuo & Hollebrandse (1999) claim that the opaque nature of Japanese CPs makes it harder for Japanese children to acquire the correct CP structure.

There are certain problems with this account. First, this account predicts that Japanese children should acquire all types of embedded sentences later than English children. However, this prediction is disconfirmed by a brief search in the CHILDES corpus (MacWhinney & Snow, 1990; Ishii, 1999). Bowerman (1979) points out that most studies indicate that the ability to produce complex sentences in English emerges between the ages of about 2 and 4 (stage IV-MLU from 3-3,5 in Brown, 1973). Jun, a Japanese boy in the CHILDES database (MacWhinney & Snow, 1990; Ishii, 1999), produces his first embedded clause with *if* at age 2;2, when his MLU is 1.58. This suggests that Japanese children do not seem to face any problems in acquiring a CP structure.

The second problem with the syntactic account is more theory internal. Since Huang (1981), it is widely believed that *wh*-in-situ languages such as Chinese and Japanese have *wh*-movement at the level of Logical Form (LF). In (16a), the *wh*-element *dare* 'who' moves to the matrix CP Specifier position to get its *wh*-feature checked. This means that a CP boundary in Japanese does not block LF *wh*-movement. Hornstein (1995) argues that NPIs also undergo an LF movement to the specifier position of negation. The reason that (18a) is ungrammatical is that an NPI cannot cross a CP boundary in Japanese. This means that for NPI licensing, Japanese CPs are islands but for *wh*-movement, they are not. So, considering CPs to be simply opaque islands is inconsistent with more sophisticated recent analyses.

In this chapter, I argue that the reason that Japanese children perform differently from Dutch/English children is related to linear order rather than hierarchical structure. I call this 'a processing account'. Under the processing account, Japanese speakers are disadvantaged compared to Dutch/English speakers in two respects. First, Japanese sentences remain ambiguous until most of the structure is revealed. When we process the Dutch/English sentences in (1a) and (1b) repeated here in (19a) and (19b), we notice quickly that this is not a simple sentence but a complex sentence. The processor encounters with a complementizer *that/dat* much earlier in Dutch/English than in Japanese. Notice that in a head-final language such as Japanese, the complementizer *to* 'that' comes close to the end of a sentence:

(19) a. John said that Bill was happy.   (English)

   b. Jan   zei   dat Bill gelukkig   was. (Dutch)
       John   said   that Bill happy   was
       'John said that Bill was happy.'

   c. John-wa   Bill-ga   siawase-datta   to itta.   (Jap.)
       John-TOP   Bill-NOM   happy-be-PST   that say-PST
       'John said that Bill was happy.'

The example in (20) supports the same point. Notice that (20) looks exactly the same as (19c) up to *siawase* 'happy'. However, (20) does not involve an embedded CP (see Nakayama, 1999): [4]

(20) John-wa   Bill-ga   siawase-ni   natte   hosii.
     John-TOP   Bill-NOM   happy-to   become   want
     'John wants Bill to be happy.'

Second, Japanese has a disadvantage compared to English/Dutch in terms of processing because the temporal ordering of a matrix and an embedded predicate is much more straightforward in English/Dutch. In (19a) or (19b), when we hear a matrix verb, namely, *said/zei*, we position the matrix event time (the time of saying) on the time line as in (21):

(21) matrix event: say   UT

What we hear next is the embedded predicate, namely, *was happy/gelukkig was*, and it is comparatively easy for us to position the embedded event time on the time line on (22), relating the matrix and the embedded event times:

(22) E1 (real past reading)

   matrix event: say   UT
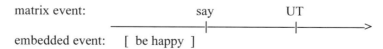
   embedded event: [be happy]

However, the same ordering procedure is not possible with the Japanese example in (19c). In processing (19c), we hear an embedded predicate first and we position an embedded predicate with a past marking on the time line as in (23):

(23)
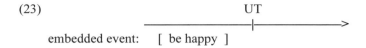
embedded event: [be happy]

When we finally hear the matrix predicate, i.e., *itta* 'said', it is very difficult to position the matrix event time on the time line. What we need to do is to position the embedded event time with respect to the matrix event time, which is straightforward if we are processing Dutch/English sentences; however, this is a very complicated task for Japanese speakers (especially for children). In a way, we need to position the matrix event time as in (24) and readjust the embedded event time in (23) with respect to the matrix event time in (24). I suggest that this readjustment process places higher demands on the processor:

(24) matrix event:

If we position the embedded event time as in (23) and position the matrix event time independently (past with respect to the UT) without a readjustment, we should rule in impossible interpretations such (25a) and (25b), which are E3 and E2 readings, respectively:

(25) a.
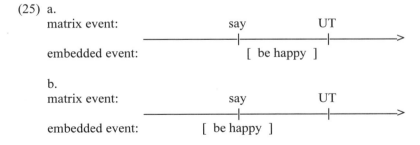

I propose that this extra processing difficulty involved in readjusting the two event times accounts for the developmental delay in assigning correct temporal interpretations to past-under-past-sentences in Japanese.

The next section looks at Polish, which is similar to Dutch and English in terms of word order but is similar to Japanese in terms of the opacity of CPs.

4. POLISH EXPERIMENTS

In order to tease apart the language characteristics that support the syntactic account from those that support the processing account, the same experiment was carried out in Polish, which is a non-SOT, head-initial language.

4.1. Experiment Details

The Polish experiment was run from November to December 1999.[5]

4.1.1. Subjects

32 Polish children (ages ranging from 3;3 to 6;11) participated in this experiment.[6] Instead of adult controls, 12 older children (ages ranging from 9;3 to10;1) took part in the experiment as control subjects.

4.1.2. Procedure

The same methodology as in Hollebrandse (1998) was used. For the ToM task, the 'unexpected-content-in-a-familiar-box' task was used and for the SOT task, the yes-no judgement task was used. The stories included the same four situations (E1-E4) and after each story, the children were asked to say *yes* or *no* to the comments made by a puppet. The puppet's comments always had the same form, namely, there was a past tense in a complement clause of the verb: said. The English stimuli used by Hollebrandse (1998) were translated as closely as possible into Polish by two native speakers.

According to Weist (1986), Polish involves a complicated tense system and there are five possible combinations of tenses (past, present and future) and aspects (perfective and imperfective). There is no combination of present tense and perfective aspect. Temporal and aspectual markings are realized by prefixation, suffixation, full or partial suppletion, vowel alternation and/or a combination of these devices. Our test sentences shown in (26) involve a past perfective matrix verb, i.e., *powiedzia* 'said', and a past imperfective embedded verb such as *by* 'was/were'. The sample stories for E1-E4 are listed in (26):

(26) Piotrusiu: Wiecie co,
Know-2-PRES what,
mam nowy garaż
have-1SG-PRES new garage.
A to są moje samochody.
Andthese be-PRES my cars.

CROSS-LINGUISTIC ACQUISITION OF COMPLEMENT TENSE

	Wprowadzę	je	do garażu.
	put-1SG-PRES-PERF	them	in the garage.

'You know what? I have a new garage. And these are my cars. I will put them in my garage.'

Karolcia: Cześć, Piotrusiu! Co słychać?
hi Peter! how listen-PRES-IMP

'Hi Peter, what is going on?'

Piotrusiu: W porządku. Właśnie wprowadziłem
all right. Just put-1SG-PST-PERF
swoje auta; teraz wszystkie są w
my cars; now be-PRES all in
garażu.
the-garage.

'Well, I just put away my cars. Now they are all in the garage.'

Experimenter: Czy Piotruś powiedział, że jego auta
whether Peter say-PST-PERF that his cars
były w garażu?
be-PST in the-garage

'Did Peter say that his cars were in the garage?'

Target answer: No

Piotrusiu: A teraz wyprowadzam auta.
and now put-out-1SG-PRES-IMP cars.
moje auta były przed chwilą w
my cars be-PST ago a-while in
garażu.
the-garage

'And now I am taking out my cars. They used to be in the garage a while ago.'

Experimenter:	Czekaj, czy Piotruś powiedział, że wait, whether Peter say-PST-PERF that jego auta były w garażu? his cars be-PST in the-garage?	

'Did Peter say that his cars were in the garage?'

Target answer:	Yes.
Karolcia:	Piotrusiu, już późno, chodź Peter already late come-PRES-IMP na podwieczorek. to breakfast

'Peter, it is already late. Come to have breakfast.'

Piotrusiu:	Ale ja jeszcze chcę schować but I still wish-PRES hide-INF moje koniki przed podwieczorkiem. Wtedy my horses before tea-time then koniki będą w garażu. the-horses be-PRES-PERF in the-garage.

'But I want to put my horses away before lunch. Then the horses will be in the garage.'

Karolcia:	Nie, teraz nie ma czasu. no now no have-PRES time

'No, there is no time.'

Experimenter:	Czy Piotruś powiedział że jego whether Peter say-PST-PERF that his koniki były w garażu? (E4) horses be-PST in the-garage?

'Did Peter say that his horses were in the garage?'

Target answer:	No.

Karolcia:	Poczęstuję	cię	bananem,
	offer-1SG-PRES-PERF	you	a-banana,
	Piotrusiu.		
	Peter		

'I will offer you a banana, Peter.'

Karolcia kładzie banana nazielonymtalerzu.
'Caroline is putting a banana on a green plate.'

Experimenter:	Czy	Karolcia	powiedziała	że
	whether	Caroline	say-PST-PERF	that
	poczęstowała		Piotrusia	bananem?(E3)
	offer-3SG-PST-PERF		Peter	a-banana?

'Did Caroline say that she gave Peter a banana?'

Target answer: No.

4.1.3. Predictions

The syntactic and the processing accounts above lead us to two different predictions. The Polish data below show that Polish involves opaque CPs like Japanese. First, a *wh*-question in (27a) shows that *wh*-movement is not allowed in Polish when there is a complementizer: [7]

(27) a. *Z kimś Marek powiedział że ona
with whom Mark say-PST-PERF that she
rozmawiała?
talk-3SG-PST-IMP
'With whom did Mark say that she talked?'

b. Marek powiedział że ona z kimś rozmawiała?
Mark say-PST-PERF that she with whom talk-3SG-PST-IMP
'Mark said that she talked to whom?'

(28) a. Z kimś Marek powiedział ona rozmawiała?
with whom Mark say-PST-PERF she talk-3SG-PST-IMP
'With whom did Mark say she talked?'

b.   Marek powiedział ona z kimś rozmawiała?
Mark say-PST-PERF she with whom talk-3SG-PST-IMP
'Mark said she talked with whom?'

In both (27a) and (28a), *z kimś* 'with whom' has undergone *wh*-movement. (28a) shows that Polish allows *wh*-movement only when a head position of CP is empty and not filled with *że* 'that' (see (27a)). (27b) and (28b) are instances of *wh*-in-situ sentences (with and without complementizers). Based on this data, I conclude that Polish CPs are opaque islands when their head positions are filled with lexical items.

Second, the data below involving NPI licensing also favour the claim that Polish CPs are opaque islands:

(29) a.   Marek nie powiedział że ona *nic* *nie*
Mark not say-PST-PERF that she *anything* *not*
kupiła.
buy-3SG- PST-IMP
'Mark didn't say that she didn't buy anything.'

    b.   Marek *nie* powiedział że ona *coś*
Mark *not* say-PST-PERF that she *something*
kupiła.
buy-3SG- PST-IMP
'Mark didn't say that she bought something.'

    c.   *Marek *nie* powiedział że ona *nic*
Mark *not* say-PST-PERF that she *anything*
kupiła.
buy-3SG-PST-IMP
'Mark didn't say that she bought anything.'

(29a) shows that an NPI item *nic* is licensed clause-internally by its licensor, namely, *nie*. (29c) shows that it cannot be licensed across a clause boundary, similar to the Japanese example in (18a). Finally, (29b), in which a non-NPI *coś* 'something' is used instead of *nic*, is perfectly grammatical. Summing up, the data concerning *wh*-movement and NPI-licensing show that Polish CPs are opaque islands.[8] The syntactic account predicts that Japanese and Polish children should perform in the same way in the experiments.

Let us next move to the prediction of the processing account. As the Polish example (1d) shows (repeated here as (30)), Polish word order resembles that of English, with a tensed matrix verbs appearing before the embedded tensed verb:

(30) Jan   powiedział   że Bill był   szczęśliwy.
     John   say-PST-PERF that Bill be-3SG-PST happy
     'John said that Bill was happy.'

The processing account predicts that Dutch/English and Polish should pattern together. In other words, we should see a correlation between ToM and SOT in Polish. Polish children should perform better in assigning correct temporal interpretations to complex sentences than Japanese children.

Table 3 sums up the predictions discussed so far:

Table 3. Predictions

	Dutch/English	Japanese	Polish
syntactic account	no delay	delay	delay
processing account	no delay	delay	no delay

Briefly summarizing, the syntactic account in Matsuo & Hollebrandse (1999) predicts that Polish and Japanese children should exhibit some delay in performing well in the SOT task compared to Dutch/English children because in both Polish and Japanese, CPs are opaque islands. On the other hand, the processing account predicts that Polish children should show no delay in performing well in the SOT task; in other words, this account predicts that Dutch, English and Polish should fall on one side and Japanese on the other. The word order of the former three is head initial whereas the latter is head final. The head-final order must call for an extra processing ability in ordering two temporal predicates.

4.2. Results

Among the 44 participants, there were 31 ToM passers and 13 failers. The 12 control subjects all passed the test. Table 4 shows the results (percentage correct) of the SOT experiment by ToM passers, failers and control subjects:

Table 4. Percentage correct for E1-E4 trials (ToM passers vs. failers)

	passer (n=19)	failer (n=13)	control (n=12)
E1	80.7	79.4	91.6
E2	26.3	20.5	97.2
E3	28.0	5.1	100
E4	60.5	50.0	100
average	49	39	97

A control group (12 children age ranging from 9;3 to10;1) performed almost perfectly on E1-E4 conditions with a 97% average of correct responses; however, the 32 test subjects did not perform as well. Especially, the results diverged dramatically between ToM passers and failers on E3 trials (28% correct for passers; 5.1% correct for failers).

Table 5 shows the performance of the children from four age groups:

Table 5. Percentage correct for E1-E4 trials (different age groups)

age group	Group 1 (3;3-3;8)	Group 2 (4;0-4;9)	Group 3 (5;0-6;11)	Control (9;3-10;1)
E1	87.5	78	83	91.7
E2	12	21.4	40	97.2
E3	4	19	30	100
E4	16	45	90	100
average	29.8	40.8	60.7	97.2

Table 5 makes clear that there is a gradual development across age groups on E2-E4 trials. As seen in Dutch, English and Japanese, Polish children performed best on E1 trials and then next best on E4 trials. Statistical analyses investigated whether or not there is any correlation between ToM and SOT in Polish. A 2-way ANOVA showed that a significant interaction between ToM and SOT on both E2 and E3 readings exists: E2: ($F(1, 126) = 7.576$, $p < .01$; E3: ($F(1, 126) = 22.86$, $p < .0001$). This means that having an adult-like ToM is a good indicator in succeeding in E2 and E3 trials of the SOT experiment. Also, a regression analysis revealed that ToM is a significant factor on performing well on E2 and E3 readings but not on E1 and E4 readings. This kind of contingency between ToM and SOT was not found in Japanese.

4.3. Discussion

After the Polish experiment, further statistical analysis was carried out to see whether or not language difference could account for the results obtained in Polish and Japanese experiments. We found that a highly significant effect of language on correct response: $F (1, 1028) = 12.57$, $p < .0001$. This again supports the finding that having an adult ToM is a significant factor for Polish children to give correct answers to E2 and E3. For Japanese children, ToM was not a reliable predictor for their successful performance on the SOT task.

I argue that the results we obtained are more consistent with the processing account. The syntactic account cannot account for why Polish children did not perform as Japanese children given CPs are opaque islands in both languages. Children in general have very more limited processing capacities; it seems that positioning the two events relative to one another in a head final language is a hard task.

Although this chapter was not concerned with an independent experiment to measure the processing abilities of the young children, the processing account has following testable consequences. I list two experiments that could be carried out to support the claim.[9] First, it is a well-known fact that Japanese displays a relatively free word order. For example, (31), the test sentence used in Matsuo & Hollebrandse (1999) can be re-ordered as (32):

(31) Kuma-wa   kuruma-wa   ouchi-no   naka-ni   at-ta
     bear-TOP   car-TOP   house-GEN   inside-LOC be-PST
     to   iimasita ka.
     that say-PST Q
     'Did Mr. Bear say that the cars are in the house?'

(32) Kuma-wa   iimasita ka/ kuruma-wa   ouchi-no   naka-ni
     bear-TOP   say-PST Q/   car-TOP   house-GEN   inside-LOC
     at-ta   to.
     be-PST   that
     'Did Mr. Bear say that the cars are in the house?'

In (32), the embedded CP is extraposed to the sentence final position and it resembles a word order of a head initial language (Dutch, English, Polish). If the processing account is correct, then young Japanese children should show less difficulty in processing (32) because they do not need to readjust a matrix and an embedded event times as discussed in (23) and (24). If the syntactic account is correct, then the Japanese children should not perform differently between (31) and (32). The processing account predicts that even adults should be influenced slightly. I propose that (32) should be easier to process than (31) for both adults and children, although the influence on adults might be observed only within sophisticated experimental methods.

The second testable implication of the processing account concerns the following contrast in English:

(33) The child who stole the cat two weeks before saw the man a month ago.

(34) A month ago, the child who stole the cat two weeks before saw the man.

(33) includes a positional temporal adverb, namely, *before*, that calls for an event to be positioned in relation to other time spans. In other words, the time of the child stealing the cat must be positioned two weeks prior to the time of the child seeing a man: a month ago. In processing (33), we need to wait to position the event time of the child stealing a cat on the time line until we hear *a month ago*, which does not appear until the end of the sentence. Conversely, the processing account predicts that (34) should be much easier to process because we do not need to put a hold on positioning any event time on the time line since the adverbial: *a month ago* appears in the beginning of the sentence. For both adults and children, example (34) should call for lesser burden on the processor.

5. CONCLUSION

In this chapter, I reviewed previous experiments on ToM and SOT reported in Hollebrandse (1998) (for Dutch and English) and Matsuo & Hollebrandse (1999) (for Japanese). In Section 4, new results from Polish children were introduced. The main results were that there was a correlation between having an adult ToM and succeeding in the SOT task in three languages: Dutch, English and Polish; however, the same correlation was not found in Japanese. Matsuo & Hollebrandse (1999) claim that Japanese children showed a delay because Japanese CPs show island effects. It takes longer for Japanese children to acquire a CP because of this additional trait. I challenged this idea by showing that the syntactic account leads to two additional problems: one within language acquisition and the other within a syntactic theory. I proposed an alternative account in terms of processing. The results of the Polish experiment were shown to be more compatible with the processing account than with the syntactic account. Finally, I introduced some possible experiments that will confirm the processing account.

University of Sheffield

6. ACKNOWLEDGEMENTS

I would like to express my gratitude to Wolfgang Klein who made it possible to run the Polish experiments. Many discussions with various people helped to develop this paper. My thanks go to Maria Bittner, Nigel Duffield, Bart Hollebrandse, Romuald Skiba, Veerle Van Geenhoven, Jill de Villiers, and Sandro Zucchi. Christopher Miller and Nigel Duffield kindly helped me with statistical analyses. Finally, I would like to thank Veerle Van Geenhoven, who did an amazing job in editing the volume, and two anonymous reviewers for valuable comments. Needless to say, all errors and shortcomings are my own.

7. NOTES

[1] Abreviations used are DAT (Dative); ACC (Accusative); GEN (Genitive); NOM (Nominative); TOP (Topic); LOC (Locative); PRS (Present); PST (Past); IMP (Imperfect); PERF (Perfect); UT (Utterance Time); INF (Infinitive); 1SG (1st person singular); 3SG (3rd person singular); NEG (Negation); NPI (Negative Polarity Item); Q (Question).

[2] An SOT rule is "responsible for the shift of present tense morphology into past tense in complements of matrix clauses which have past tense morphology (Abusch, 1988, 4)."

[3] One of the reviewers asked what complex sentences with relative clauses and complement clauses have in common. Not only they both involve two finite predicates, the world languages tend to use the same lexical item (such as *that* in English, *dat* in Dutch, *qu'* in French among others) to introduce both relative and complement clauses.

[4] (19) involves an embedded IP.

[5] My appreciation goes to Dr. Dorota Kiebzak-Mandera, Mgr. Greta Lemanaite-Deprati, and especially to Dr. Magdalena Smoczynska for running the actual experiments.

[6] These subjects include eight subjects between 3;3 and 3;8, 14 subjects between 4;0 and 4;9 and 10 subjects between 5;0 and 6;11.

[7] I thank Romuald Skiba and Maria Bittner for their help with the Polish examples.

[8] *Wh*-movement is allowed when the head of CP is not filled as in (26a); however, we treat this as an exception. This exception concerning headless CPs will not be considered further in this chapter because all the test items used in the experiment contain a lexical complementizer: *że* 'that' as shown in (25).

[9] I appreciate the comments by two reviewers for giving me a chance to think more about this issue.

8. REFERENCES

Abusch, Dorit. "Sequence of Tense, Intensionality and Scope." In Hagit Borer (ed.) *Proceedings of the 7th West Coast Conference on Formal Linguistics*, 1–14. Stanford: The Stanford Linguistics Association, 1988.

Bowerman, Melissa. "The Acquisition of Complex Sentences." In Paul Fletcher and Michael Garman (eds.) *Language Acquisition Studies in First Language Development*, 285–306. Cambridge: Cambridge University Press, 1979.

Brown, Roger. *A First Language: The Early Stages.* Cambridge, MA: Harvard University Press, 1973.

Gale, Elaine, Peter de Villiers, Jill de Villiers, and Jenny Pyers. "Language and the Theory of Mind in Oral Deaf Children." In Elizabeth Hughes, Mary Hughes, and Annabel Greenhill (eds.) *Proceedings of the 21st Boston University Conference on Language Development*, 213–224. Somerville, MA: Cascadilla Press, 1996.

Hollebrandse, Bart. "On the Relation between the Acquisition of Theory of Mind and Sequence of Tense." In Annabel Greenhill, Mary Hughes, Heather Littlefield, and Hugh Walsh (eds.) *Proceedings of the 22nd Boston University Conference on Language Development*, 374–384. Somerville, MA: Cascadilla Press, 1997.

Hornstein Norbert. *Logical Form*. Oxford: Blackwell Publishers, 1995.

Huang, James. "Move *Wh* in a Language without *Wh* Movement." *The Linguistic Review* 1 (1981): 369–416.

Ishii, Takeo. *Jun Corpus*. www.kyoto-su.ac.jp/ishii/index.html, 1999.

MacWhinney, Brian, and Catherine Snow. "The Child Language Data Exchange System: An Update." *Journal of Child Language* 17 (1990): 457–472.

Matsuo, Ayumi, and Bart Hollebrandse. "Children's Acquisition of SOT in Japanese." In Annabel Greenhill, Heather Littlefield, and Cheryl Tano (eds.) *Proceedings of 23rd Boston University Conference on Language Development*, 431–442. Somerville, MA: Cascadilla Press, 1999.

Nakayama, Mineharu. "Sentence Processing." In Naoko Tsujimura (ed.) *The Handbook of Japanese Linguistics,* 398–424. Oxford: Blackwell Publishers, 1999.

Ogihara, Toshiyuki. *Tense, Attitudes and Scope*. Dordrecht: Kluwer Academic Publishers, 1996.

de Villiers, Jill. "Questioning Minds and Answering Machines." In Dawn MacLaughlin and Susan McEwen (eds.) *Proceedings of the 19th Boston University Conference on Language Development*, 20–36. Somerville, MA: Cascadilla Press, 1995.

Weist, Richard. "Tense and Aspect: Temporal Systems in Child Language." In Paul Fletcher and Michael Garman (eds.) *Language Acquisition, 2nd Edition*, 356–174. Cambridge: Cambridge University Press, 1986.

Wimmer, Heinz, and Josef Perner. "Beliefs about Beliefs: Representation and Constraining Function of Wrong Beliefs in Young Children's Understanding of Deception." *Cognition* 13 (1983): 103–128.

LUISA MERONI, ANDREA GUALMINI AND STEPHEN CRAIN

EVERYBODY KNOWS

Abstract. Much current research is devoted to children's non-adult responses to sentences containing the universal quantifier *every*. In this chapter we review two alternative views: one that attributes children's responses to non-adult grammars and one that focuses on extra-linguistic factors to explain children's non-adult responses. We argue that the grammatical view faces several theoretical difficulties and, in light of new experimental findings, we demonstrate that it also suffers from limited explanatory power.

1. INTRODUCTION

Children's interpretation of the universal quantifier *every* has been the subject of abundant investigations of child language. These investigations start from the observation, due to Inhelder & Piaget (1964), that some children show a systematic non-adult interpretation of sentences containing the universal quantifier *every*. In particular, Inhelder & Piaget discovered that pre-school and even school-age children sometimes respond *No* to the question *Is every boy riding an elephant?* in a context where three boys are each riding an elephant and a fourth elephant (referred to as the 'extra-object') is not being ridden.

This chapter scrutinizes two alternative accounts of this phenomenon. First, we introduce the original findings and the alternative views that have been proposed to explain the findings. Then we turn to the current debate. In particular, we raise several theoretical concerns about the recent accounts of children's 'errors' that attribute them to non-adult linguistic principles. Another view, which we endorse, emphasizes non-linguistic factors that have been found to affect children's performance in certain experimental contexts, but not in others. Finally, we turn to the laboratory to follow up some predictions of the current linguistic accounts of children's behavior. The findings of the present experiments resist explanation on the linguistic accounts of children's non-adult responses. Therefore, they provide further support for a non-linguistic account of children's non-adult responses.

2. BACKGROUND

A good deal of work in language acquisition has been devoted to children's interpretation of sentences that contain the universal quantifier, e.g., *every* in English. It has been observed in several experimental studies and across several languages that some school-age children experience difficulty in interpreting such sentences (e.g., Inhelder & Piaget, 1964; Roeper & de Villiers, 1991; Philip, 1995). Non-adult responses from children have been found in various conditions, including the circumstance exemplified in the picture in Figure 1, where three boys are each riding an elephant and a fourth elephant (referred to as the 'extra-object') is not being ridden. Some children who are shown such a picture sometimes respond *No* to the question in (1) relative to this picture:

(1) Is every boy riding an elephant?

Figure 1. The Extra-Object Condition

To justify their negative answer to the question in (1), children often point to the extra object, i.e., the elephant that is not being ridden. This reply has been called the s*ymmetrical response* or the *exhaustive pairing response* since children who give this kind of response seem to interpret the question to be about the symmetry (i.e., one-to-one relation) between the set of entities denoted by the subject noun (the boys) and the set denoted by the object noun (the elephants). It should be noted, however, that children who produce the symmetrical response to questions like (1) often produce adult-like *Yes* responses in the same circumstances. It is also noteworthy that these same children sometimes produce a symmetrical-type response even when they are asked a question that mentions just one set of entities, as in *Is every boy riding?*[1]

Several accounts of children's non-adult responses have been offered. Broadly speaking, these accounts can be divided into ones that attribute children's responses to deviant linguistic analyses of quantified expressions, and ones that attribute them to non-linguistic factors. A noteworthy example of the non-linguistic kind of account is offered by Freeman, Sinha & Stedmon (1982), who propose that the experiments that evoke errors violate conventional rules of discourse. Crediting John Locke (1690) and William James (1892) with relevant observations about principles of discourse, these authors suggest that children's non-adult responses arise because children adhere to discourse principles that are not met in the experimental context; on this view, children's 'errors' reflect their rational attempt to understand "the speaker's purpose and intended frame of reference" (Freeman *et al.*, 1982, 54) in contexts that flout the usual discourse practices of natural language.

On the account advanced by Freeman *et al.* (1982), children are credited with adult-like knowledge of linguistic principles of syntax and semantics, as well as adult-like knowledge of the pragmatic principles that govern language use in ordinary conversational contexts. When children produce non-adult responses, on this account, it is because they are confronted with circumstances in which grammatical principles are at odds with principles of discourse. In such circumstances, children are left to infer the discourse topic that the speaker intends, because it appears to the child that the discourse topic that is ordinarily associated with the sentences in question cannot be the one that is actually intended by the speaker. Children are therefore forced to either violate principles of grammar (i.e., syntax and semantics) or principles of discourse. When confronted with dilemmas of this kind, Freeman *et al.*, argue that children frequently ignore the discourse topic that is usually assigned to such sentences and respond, instead, to an inferred discourse topic. In short, based on their knowledge of "conventional rules of use which encompass the perceived purposes and intentions of the speaker ... children try to understand what people mean, not only what words mean" (Freeman *et al.*, 1982, 69). Children's non-adult behavior, however, should not be interpreted as evidence that they lack linguistic knowledge, according to Freeman *et al.* (1982, 70-71):

> Whenever children give strange answers in such studies, it is up to the psychologist to *prove* that he or she has really established joint reference with the child in the way that was intended, if faulty semantic/syntactic comprehension is to be invoked as an explanation. It is essential to work towards independent evidence of this, and it is not sufficient to say that children must have miscomprehended the semantics solely on the grounds of a context-free truth-value violation somewhere. ... Only if there is independent evidence that the relevant frame of reference has been set up, and the relevant

distinctions have been drawn, and that still the answer is wrong, are we on safe grounds in producing a purely linguistic analysis.

To adjudicate between linguistic and non-linguistic accounts of children's non-adult responses to linguistic expressions, Freeman *et al.*, adopt a dual-route approach. If a non-linguistic account of children's non-adult behavior is correct, then it should be possible "to get adults to give child-like answers, and children to reverse their strategies." (1982, 66). We postpone discussion of ways to induce children to reverse their performance strategies. Suffice it to say that most researchers agree that this can indeed be done, though there is considerable disagreement on the method and on the interpretation of children's adult-like behavior. As for eliciting child-like behavior from adults, this too has proven to be straightforward. For example, Freeman *et al.*, interviewed twenty adults, showing them a picture of four saucers, three with one cup on them. In responding to the question *Are all the cups on the saucers*? 17 of the 20 adults replied *No*. That is, adults were duped into giving a symmetrical response, when real-world knowledge was sufficiently biased towards this response.[2] In view of the circumstantial evidence favoring a non-linguistic account of children's 'errors' in the previous literature, and in the absence of compelling evidence that children continue to make such 'errors' when the rules of discourse are followed, Freeman *et al.*, conclude that a linguistic account of children's non-adult behavior cannot be sustained.

Nevertheless, several researchers have defended linguistic accounts of children's non-adult responses to sentences with the universal quantifier. One proposal is the Event Quantification account advanced by Philip (1995). This account explains symmetrical responses by children to sentences with transitive verb phrases, such as the question in (1), as the product of a non-adult linguistic analysis. On the Event Quantification account, sentences with the universal quantifier *every* are ambiguous for children. One interpretation of such sentences is similar to that of adults. However, the Event Quantification account maintains that children can also assign an interpretation that is exclusive to child grammar, and this interpretation accounts for the symmetrical response. Roughly, the proposal is that children can analyze the universal quantifier *every* as an unselective binder, on analogy with temporal adverbs like *always* and *usually* in the adult grammar. In extending the analysis of quantificational adverbs to the universal quantifier, Philip (1995) contends that the determiner *every* quantifies over events (as well as individuals) in child grammar, whereas it only quantifies over individuals in the adult grammar. On the Event Quantification account, the sentence *Every boy is riding an elephant* can be assigned the truth conditions represented in (2):

(2) For every event *e* in which either an elephant or a boy participates, or which is a possible sub-event of a boy-riding-an-elephant, a boy is riding an elephant in *e*.

As (2) indicates, *Every boy is riding an elephant* is false whenever an event involving a boy or an elephant is not an event in which a boy is riding an elephant. Since Figure 1 involves an event in which an elephant (the 'extra' elephant) participates but which is not an event in which a boy is riding an elephant, children give a negative answer to the question in (1) (see Philip, 1995; 1996, for a more complete explanation).

The Event Quantification account is criticized by Crain *et al.* (1996) on both empirical and theoretical grounds. They point out that only 87 of the 276 (37%) child subjects that were tested in the Philip (1995) study were 'pure' cases of 'Symmetry Children,' i.e., children whose predominant type of response was the symmetrical response. These Symmetry Children produced such responses only 57% of the time, however. These children produced adult-like responses on the remaining trials. In addition, roughly half of the Symmetry Children's non-adult responses should be chalked up to noise, since these children continued to produce 'symmetrical' responses almost half the time when they were responding to questions with *intransitive* verb phrases, like *Is every boy riding*? The Event Quantification account does not extend to such sentences, so children's non-adult responses to them are attributed by Philip (1995) to "carry over effects" or "response strategies". Once we factor out children's adult-like responses and responses due to noise, it turns out that only about one-fifth of the responses of the Symmetry Children are governed by the Event Quantification analysis.

Besides the limited quantity of children's non-adult responses that are explained by the Event Quantification account, Crain *et al.*, raise several theoretical shortcomings with the account. First, it is difficult to see how the linguistic analysis attributed to children could be purged from children's grammars. The problem of learnability arises because, as we noted, Symmetry Children produce adult-like *Yes* answers much of the time. According to the Event Quantification account, both adult and non-adult analyses are accessed by these children in response to sentences with the universal quantifier. In other words, such sentences are ambiguous for them, whereas the same sentences are unambiguous for adults. To converge on the target grammar, therefore, children have to 'unlearn' the non-adult interpretation. This is problematic, however, since all of the parental input is consistent with one of the interpretations generated by the grammars of these children, namely the adult interpretation. To purge their grammars of the non-adult interpretation, then, children would seem to need some form of negative evidence, informing them that adults do not access the non-adult interpretation under any circumstance. Even if negative evidence proved to be robustly available to children, however, it would miss the mark, because the non-adult interpretation makes sentences true in a subset of the circumstances that verify these sentences for adults. So, for example, if children produced a sentence with the universal quantifier in a circumstance that corresponds to the symmetrical interpretation, the sentence would be acceptable for adults. It is difficult to see, therefore, how children could expunge from their grammars the non-adult interpretation proposed by the Event Quantification account.

A second problem with the Event Quantification account is that the linguistic analysis attributed to children violates a principle of Universal Grammar. Crosslinguistic research on formal semantics has concluded that the meanings of all natural language determiners, including the universal quantifier *every*, adhere to the property of conservativity (see e.g., Barwise & Cooper, 1981; Keenan & Stavi, 1986). We will discuss conservativity in section 2.4. For the present purposes it is worth observing that of all the logically possible relations that could constitute determiner meanings, the language faculty has apparently evolved such that all determiners in natural language are conservative. In particular, the principle of conservativity eliminates the meaning *equinumerous* as a possible meaning of a natural language determiner, but it is precisely this meaning that is assigned to the universal quantifier on the Event Quantification account. Accounts of differences in the behavior of children and adults should not compromise putative linguistic universals, such as the conservativity of determiner meanings, in the absence of compelling evidence. Similar remarks pertain to the principle of compositionality.[3]

In view of the empirical limitations and theoretical concerns with linguistic accounts of children's non-adult responses to sentences with the universal quantifier, such as the Event Quantification account, some researchers have conjectured that non-linguistic factors are the source of children's symmetrical responses, on those occasions when such responses occur. One conjecture, by Freeman *et al.*, focuses on the inappropriateness of the discourse contexts used in previous research. Crain *et al.*, make a similar proposal. Both call attention to a *felicity condition*. The particular felicity condition that inspired these researchers has a long and venerable history, dating back to Russell (1948). It was called "plausible denial" by Wason (1965). This felicity condition was extended by Freeman *et al.*, and by Crain *et al.*, to explain children's non-adult behavior in studies that evoked symmetrical responses by children. Let us stick with the Freeman *et al.*, (1982, 64) proposal for the moment. They contend that symmetrical responses are produced because children attempt to follow a "conventional rule for interpreting quantified expressions," which is flouted in the experiments that evoke non-adult responses from children:

> When a speaker asks a question about the presence of 'all the Xs', he is implicitly requesting the hearer to carry out an exhaustive search to check that no X is missing. Asking someone such a question is only legitimate 'socio-dialogically' if there is at least the possibility that some X is (or some Xs are) in actuality missing.

According to Freeman *et al.*, earlier studies that evoked symmetrical responses from children (and adults, in some cases) failed to satisfy the felicity conditions associated with questions with the universal quantifier, because the context did not include *the possibility* that some element in the relevant set was "in actuality missing." As a consequence of this infelicity, children were led to override the meaning provided by their grammars in order to provide a plausible interpretation of the questions. To derive a plausible interpretation of sentences with the construction 'all the Xs,' children were compelled to modify their mental model of the discourse context, by mentally conjuring up additional entities, beyond those that are depicted in Figure 1, for example. As Freeman *et al.* (1982, 64) put it:

> If the hearer's task is to check the context for cues which might indicate the absence of one of the items, then there is a conventional discourse bias towards giving a negative reply. Effectively the situation provides a context for plausible denial (Wason 1965) in view of the speaker's apparent concern that nothing is missing. ... 'all the Xs' is taken to mean 'all the Xs which ought to be present' or 'all the Xs which the speaker intends to be present.' ... Hence answering a question about 'all the Xs' is likely to entail ignoring irrelevant Xs and searching for cues which indicate a missing X.

On this account, children's non-adult behavior is simply due to the difficulty they experience in responding to sentences in infelicitous contexts. This means that there is just one difference in the linguistic skills of children and those of adults — adults are apparently better able to ignore infelicities than children are. By minimizing the differences in the language apparatus of children and adults, Freeman *et al.*, and Crain *et al.*, try to avoid the potential pitfalls of a linguistic analysis of children's non-adult behavior, such as the Event Quantificational account: Children's grammars would not need to change over time; they would obey compositionality (where adult grammars do), and they would adhere to putative universal properties of determiner meanings (including conservativity). In short, children and adults would access the same UG-based linguistic analysis of sentences with the universal quantifier.

The proposal by Crain *et al.*, is similar in spirit to Freeman *et al.*, The two accounts differ, however, in that Crain *et al.*, contend that the infelicity of a question like *Is every boy riding an elephant?* does not follow from the use of the universal quantifier. Rather, the infelicity derives from posing the question in a context that does not include any alternative outcome. This is called the condition of Plausible Dissent, a pragmatic prerequisite to posing *yes-no* questions. In absence of an alternative outcome, children might try to satisfy the condition of Plausible Dissent by positing the existence of a fourth boy. This boy would make the sentence false because he is not riding an elephant, but the boy would also make the sentence felicitous, in that the 'revised' context would suggest how the sentence might have been true. The 'extra' elephant in Figure 1 provides further encouragement to children to infer the existence of a boy who is not present in the picture. Children who go to the trouble to make this inference will produce negative replies to the question. Such responses will be inhibited if there is no 'extra' elephant or if there are too many 'extra' elephants (because, in that case, children are less likely to infer that the speaker thinks that there is a large number of boys missing).[4] Nevertheless, the question remains odd in both such circumstances.

To assess the role of the felicity condition under discussion, Crain *et al.*, introduced a new feature of experimental design. As we noted, for example, the question *Is every boy riding an elephant?* would be felicitous if some boy(s) considered riding a donkey even if, in the end, every boy rode an elephant. In such a circumstance, children would be expected to produce appropriate "Yes" answers as often as adults do. This way of satisfying the condition of Plausible Dissent is easily implemented in one experimental technique, the Truth Value Judgment task (see Crain & McKee, 1985; Crain & Thornton, 1998). Using the Truth Value Judgment task, Crain *et al.*, conducted a series of experiments to assess children's comprehension of the universal quantifier *every*. Several of the experiments satisfied the felicity condition associated with the test sentences. The finding was that children performed as well as adults in interpreting sentences containing the universal quantifier in these experiments. Crain *et al.*, concluded that the improvement in children's performance resulted from the satisfaction of the felicity conditions associated with judgments of truth or falsity and that children's non-adult behavior in previous research was due to the failure to satisfy those felicity conditions, rather than to any difference between child and adult grammar.

3. THE CURRENT DEBATE

The condition of Plausible Dissent, and the general notion of felicity, has been widely criticized in the literature on child language. Researchers have argued that it is vague, unfalsifiable, and lacks independent empirical support. Here are two representative statements:

> It attempts to explain the conditioning of a strange phenomenon by means of an equally strange hypothesis. They do not define what they mean by 'felicity'. ... Moreover utterances are never felicitous or infelicitous per se. This is not altogether surprising since there are no in principle falsifiable theories by means of which one can measure the 'felicity value' of an utterance. There are only intuitions about felicity ... (Philip, 1996, 572)

> Contrary to what Crain *et al*., contend, it is doubtful that a *yes-no* question is pragmatically infelicitous unless both the affirmative and the negative answer are 'under consideration' in any substantial sense. In my own experience, children are rather good at answering all manner of questions that would be infelicitous according to Crain *et al*., (Geurts, 2001, 5)

These quotes question the account of children's non-adult responses proposed by Crain *et al*., and by Freeman *et al*., We will therefore take this opportunity to clarify the account, though it should be understood that the main thrust of this line of research has been to question the need for a *linguistic* analysis of children's behavior, rather than to provide a *non-linguistic* analysis of children's behavior. That said, it will be useful to place the condition of Plausible Dissent in a broader perspective. In addition, we will illustrate alternative accounts of children's non-adult responses, highlightening theoretical problems and empirical inadequacies.

3.1. The Plausibility of Plausible Dissent

As indicated earlier, the condition of Plausible Dissent is an extension of the observation by Bertrand Russell (1948) that a negative judgment is felicitous only if the alternative positive judgment has been made or is under consideration. One kind of linguistic expression that requires a potentially negative judgment is a *yes-no* question. If the answer (either *yes* or *no*) is already known, the hearer is likely to infer that what the speaker intends is not conveyed by the literal meaning of the question. As an example, consider the following question, which is a familiar joke in Italian:

(3) What color was Napoleon's white horse?

Italians who are asked this question often take a long time to respond, trying to recall relevant facts from their high school classes in French history. This delay reveals that people do not expect questions to contain their own answers.

The point can be put more formally, drawing upon work by Robert Stalnaker (1999). In a discussion of the role of assertions in conversational exchanges, Stalnaker (1999, 78) states that "assertions affect, and are intended to affect the context." The 'context' at issue is the conversational or discourse context. The participants who are engaged in a conversation bring with them a shared set of beliefs or assumptions, which Stalnaker calls the *common ground* (also see Heim, 1982). The common ground includes propositions that have not been challenged or withdrawn by any of the participants in the conversation. As the conversation progresses, new propositions are added to the common ground. If a proposition is inconsistent with what is already included in the common ground, either that proposition is rejected or some proposition contained in the common ground is abandoned. So at each stage during a conversation, the common ground contains a set of coherent and connected propositions. Adopting a different terminology, the common ground is a set of possible worlds, possible situations, or *live possibilities*:

> A *live possibility* at a given discourse stage is any circumstances v such that all the propositions in the common ground at that point of the discourse are true in v. (Chierchia & McConnell-Ginet, 2000, 216)

The role of an assertion in discourse is to reduce the set of *live possibilities*: an assertion eliminates all propositions that are incompatible with it. Among the principles that regulate the interaction of assertions and the common ground, Stalnaker (1999, 88) introduces the principle in (4):

(4) "A proposition asserted is always true in some but not all of the possible worlds in the context set." [5]

As (4) makes clear, a speaker is not expected to assert a proposition that is already part of the common ground. If a speaker violates this rule, he has done "something that, from the point of view of the conversation, was unreasonable, inefficient, disorderly, or uncooperative" (ibid 89).

The role of a *yes-no* question in a conversation is similar. It is an attempt by the speaker to reduce, by half, the set of live possibilities. Roughly, a *yes-no* question and its corresponding answer, taken together, can be viewed as an assertion that such-and-such is, or is not, the case. Therefore, question/answer pairs should be governed by the principle in (4): a *yes-no* question is "unreasonable, inefficient, disorderly, uncooperative," if its answers are already contained in the common ground. The condition of Plausible Dissent is designed to introduce a possible outcome in the stories presented to children, in addition to the actual outcome. On this view, when a child participates in a Truth Value Judgment task, his job is to evaluate whether the puppet's statement reflects the particular way in which the common ground has been affected by the events described in the story. By satisfying the condition of Plausible Dissent, the experimenter ensures that the principle in (4) is met for the propositions that children are asked to judge.

3.2. Empirical Support for the Felicity Account

Another objection to the account advocated by Freeman *et al.*, and Crain *et al.*, is that the failure to satisfy felicity conditions is not troublesome for older children and adults. This creates a learnability problem, it is claimed:

> ...their diagnosis still leaves open some of the most intriguing issues raised by the empirical facts. Why is it, for example, that older children and adults aren't bothered by an experimental set-up that, by Crain et al.'s lights, is hopelessly flawed? (Geurts, 2001, 5)

> On their account, a child has extremely nonadult-like notions of 'felicity'. How does the child acquire adult-like notions of 'felicity' then? (Philip, 1996, 572)

In our view, the main point of the accounts by Freeman *et al.*, and by Crain *et al.*, is to minimize the differences in the language apparatus of children and adults, including discourse principles. We have already seen that adults can be induced to commit errors like the ones children make. The difference is a matter of degree. To underscore this point, we review two recent experimental investigations of how adults are influenced by changes in the conversational context.

The first study was by Guasti & Chierchia (2000), who studied the interpretation assigned by children and adults to sentences governed by Principle C of the binding theory. One finding of the Guasti & Chierchia study was that adults accepted violations of Principle C in sentences like (5) significantly more often when the condition of Plausible Dissent was not satisfied than when it was satisfied:

(5) Andava   sul cavallo   a dondolo   mentre un
    went-3SG on-the horse   rocking   while   a
    musicista suonava.
    musician played-3SG
    'He was riding a rocking horse while a musician was playing.'

For example, adults failed to reject referential dependence between *un musicista* and the implicit subject, as dictated by Principle C, if the story did not provide a possible outcome in which a salient character considered riding a rocking horse while the musician was playing; there was only a 41% rate of rejection. In stories that provided this possible outcome, adults rejected the test sentences 94% of the time, revealing knowledge of Principle C.

Another study was conducted in our own laboratory, where we examined the influence of the condition of Plausible Dissent on adults' interpretation of sentences with the universal quantifier, using a free head eye-tracking system (Meroni, Crain & Gualmini, 2001; Meroni, 2002). Eye-movements were monitored on-line, as subjects verified sentences that were paired with visually presented scenes. We analyzed the pattern of eye-movements and the fixation durations that were associated with various objects depicted in the scenes. With a scene in front of them, subjects were asked to judge whether the test sentence was an accurate description of the scene. In evaluating a sentence like *Every boy is riding an elephant* we anticipated that subjects would fixate longer on the 'extra' elephant in a picture like Figure 1, than they would in an alternative scene that depicted another object, e.g., a horse, in addition to the 'extra' elephant as in Figure 2. This is precisely what happened. Fixation durations on the 'extra' objects were significantly longer in response to pictures like Figure 1 than in the alternative condition. We interpret these results as evidence that subjects were mentally attempting to satisfy the condition of Plausible Dissent, but were unable to in response to scenes like Figure 1:

Figure 2. The Plausible Dissent Condition

These findings are consistent with the proposal that children and adults have equivalent cognitive mechanisms. The fact that adults are sensitive to the same felicity conditions as children casts doubts on the claim that children have a "nonadult-like notion of felicity" (Philip, 1996, 572). Therefore, we continue to embrace the non-linguistic account of children's nonadult responses in earlier studies. By minimizing differences in the cognitive mechanisms of children and adults, it is possible to avoid the kinds of learnability problems that confront linguistic accounts of children's non-adult responses, such as the Event Quantification account. We continue to stick to our original claim, therefore, that young children are subject to the same discourse constraints as adults and older children; younger children are just less successful in making the necessary accommodations when discourse principles are flouted.

3.3. The Salience Account

An alternative explanation of the improvement in children's performance in the Crain *et al.*, study has emerged in recent work (e.g., Gordon, 1996; Drozd & van Loosbroek, 1999; Krämer, 2000; Philip & Lynch, 2000; Geurts, 2001). The alternative accounts of children's increased success attribute the improvements in performance to the salience of the objects that figure into children's interpretation of sentences like *Every boy is riding an elephant*. When children's attention is drawn to the set denoted by the object noun (e.g., the elephants), children assign one interpretation, yielding non-adult responses. When children focus on the set denoted by the subject noun (e.g., the boys), however, children assign another interpretation, yielding adult-like responses. Despite some minor differences in detail, we will lump these various accounts together, calling them the Salience account. Here are a few excerpts from studies that advocate the Salience account:

> ... it could be hypothesized that the reason that children ignored the extra [objects - MGC] in the latter study [Crain *et al.*, 1996 - MGC] is simply that the [extra objects - MGC] were backgrounded and did not figure significantly in the story. On the other hand, when the extra [objects - MGC] are presented statically..., they are foregrounded and likely to distract the child into thinking they are relevant. (Gordon, 1996, 217)

> But the contexts in [Figure 1 - MGC] fail to invite children to represent the set of boys in visual context as discourse-active. In addition, the visual context in [Figure 1 - MGC] makes it easy for children (and adults) to represent the set of elephants or elephant-riders as discourse-active. (Drozd & van Loosbroek, 1999, 189)

> Crain *et al.*'s (1996) experimental findings may have been an artifact of subtle manipulations of relevance. Their subjects may have shown highly adult-grammatical performance in their second experiment session simply because the extra object-which the child must notice if she is to give a nonadult response-was inadvertently made highly irrelevant. (Philip & Lynch, 2000, 589)

> children do better on Crain *et al.*'s stories simply because they provide clear contextual support for the presuppositional interpretation [the adult

interpretation – MGC] of a universal quantifier ... Children largely abandon exhaustive pairing [symmetrical response - MGC] on this condition because the intended restriction for the universal quantifier ... was presented to them before the universally quantified proposition. (Drozd & van Loosbroek, 1998, 15)

The Salience account carries with it much of the theoretical baggage that weighed down the Event Quantification account. First, children's grammars assign more than one analysis to such sentences, so one analysis must be 'unlearned.' Second, depending on which particular analysis is attributed to children, children's grammars might violate compositionality on the non-adult interpretation, and they violate conservativity on that interpretation — a putatively universal linguistic constraint on determiner meanings.[6]

We would not deny that salience plays an important role in language understanding. For example, quantificational adverbs have the flexibility to target different indefinite NPs, depending on the theme-rheme structure of the discourse. Salience is not a relevant factor for unambiguous sentences, however. As in the adult grammar, if children's grammars assign a single interpretation to a sentence like *Every boy is riding an elephant*, then that is what the sentence means, regardless of the discourse topic. Like adults, children may be compelled in certain circumstances to abandon the literal meaning of a sentence, if the assignment of that meaning makes the sentence pragmatically odd, but such problems should arise only in circumstances that do not adhere to principles of discourse; these problems should not arise in run-of-the-mill discourse contexts.

Based on these observations we expect children to access the correct interpretation of sentences like *Every boy is riding an elephant* whenever discourse principles are satisfied, regardless of the salience of the objects denoted by the different NPs in the sentence. In fact, studies reported in Crain *et al.*, did attempt to control for salience, in two ways: (a) by 'highlighting' the set of objects during the story and (b) by mentioning them at the end of each trial, thereby directing children's attention to the 'extra' object (see Crain *et al.*, 125). Nevertheless, the issue of felicity versus salience is worth pursuing, because the Salience account has been invoked by several researchers to motivate linguistic accounts of children's non-adult performance.

To pit the Felicity account against the Salience account, we conducted an experiment using the Truth Value Judgment task (see Meroni, Gualmini & Crain, 2000). In the experiment, the objects in the denotation of the object noun phrase were made highly salient and, at the same time, the condition of Plausible Dissent was satisfied. If salience is the critical factor, then a non-adult interpretation of the quantifier *every* is expected to emerge in the study, as in previous research. If children's non-adult responses surface only in infelicitous tasks, however, then children are expected to respond correctly to the test sentences, regardless of the heightened salience of the denotation of the object noun phrase. In a typical trial, children were told a story about a rodeo competition. The story involved three farmers, four horses and two dinosaurs. When the set of characters is introduced to the child subject, it is pointed out that one of the four horses has no saddle and is probably a wild horse. Each farmer has to choose an animal to ride in the rodeo. Here is how the storyline unfolds in real time. One farmer considers riding a dinosaur, because he knows he will win the competition if he can ride a dinosaur. But the dinosaur is quite angry, so the farmer decides to ride one of the horses (the condition of Plausible Dissent is satisfied when the farmer considers riding a dinosaur). First, he considers riding the wild horse, but the horse proves to be unfriendly, so the farmer decides to ride one of the other horses. In the remainder of the story, the two remaining farmers also consider riding a dinosaur and the wild horse, but they too realize the risks involved in riding these animals. In the end every farmer rides a 'regular' horse.

When the story is completed, the child can see in the experimental workspace that every farmer is riding a horse and also that no farmer chose to ride the wild horse (keeping the wild horse salient in the experimental workspace). At the conclusion of the story, the puppet, Kermit the Frog, produced the target sentence, preceded by a linguistic antecedent, as illustrated in (6):

(6) This was a story about three farmers, two dinosaurs and four horses and one of them was a wild horse! I know what happened. Every farmer rode a horse.

Sixteen children ranging in age between 3;10 and 6;3 (mean age: 5;1) participated in the experiment. Each child was presented with one warm-up, two fillers and three target sentences. The results are unexpected under the hypothesis that the salience of the denotation of the object noun is the critical factor in children's judgments. Children rarely produced non-adult responses, regardless of the salience of the denotation of the object noun. The child subjects correctly accepted sentences like *Every farmer rode a horse* on 43 out of 48 trials (90%). These results show that the satisfaction of felicity conditions, rather than salience, determines children's (adult-like) responses, when each factor meets the other head on.

3.4. The Weak Quantification Account

So far, we have introduced three accounts of children's failures in understanding of the universal quantifier *every*. We will review one more linguistic account, called the Weak Quantification account (WQA, henceforth). The WQA was advanced by Drozd & van Loosbroek (1999). The account incorporates the Salience account, but it makes a number of further theoretical assumptions that are worth closer examination, to illustrate the value of linguistic principles in constraining children's grammatical hypotheses. One relevant linguistic principle is conservativity, or the 'lives on' relation (Barwise & Cooper, 1981; Keenan & Stavi, 1986). Determiner meanings are conservative functions, according to the following definition:

(7) A determiner meaning is *conservative* iff:
Y ∈ DET(X) iff Y ∩ X ∈ DET(X)
(where X, Y are sets, DET is a function from sets into sets of sets and ∩ is set intersection)

According to the definition in (7), determiners verify inferences of the following kind: D(A)(B) ⇔ D(A)(A ∩ B). Thus determiners validate the following inferences:

(8) Few/every/no Americans smoke ⇔ Few/every/no Americans are Americans who smoke.

The meaning of the quantifier *many*, has resisted being labeled as conservative, however. The troublesome phenomenon can be illustrated with the following example, due to Westerståhl (1984):

(9) Many Scandinavians have won the Nobel Prize in literature.

It is sometimes assumed that (9) allows the three readings reported below:

(10) a. |Scandinavians ∩ Nobel- Prize winners in literature| > n
 b. (|Scandinavians ∩ Nobel-Prize winners in literature|) > p
    |Scandinavians|
 c. (|Scandinavians∩Nobel-Prize winners in literature|) > q
    |Nobel-Prize winners in literature|

The interpretation in (10a) requires the number of Scandinavians who won the Nobel Prize to be higher than a value n, where n is a context-dependent variable. Under this reading, *many* is used as a vague numerical quantifier. This can be called this the *intersective* interpretation of the quantifier *many*. By contrast, the interpretation in (10b) requires the ratio of the number of Scandinavians who won the Nobel Prize to the number of Scandinavians available in the context to be higher than p, where p is a context-dependent variable. This is called the *proportional* reading. The two readings differ in the number of sets that needs to be considered in order to evaluate sentences containing the quantifier *many*. Despite this difference, both the intersective and the proportional readings express conservative functions.

In addition to the two readings described above, some linguists have assumed that sentences containing the quantifier *many* can have an additional reading, which is not conservative (see Partee, 1988). This is the reading in (10c), which requires the ratio between the number of Scandinavians who won the Noble Prize and the number of Noble Prize winners to be higher than q. The interpretation in (10c) violates conservativity[7] because in order to determine the truth value of (10c) on this reading, one must take into consideration entities that potentially lie outside the set denoted by the restrictor, namely the entire set denoted by the nuclear scope.[8]

This flexibility of interpretation allowed by the quantifier *many* plays a crucial role in the account advanced by Drozd & van Loosbroek. The non-conservative reading of *many* illustrated in (10c) results when speakers rely on real-world knowledge or on the notion of normal expectations to evaluate sentences containing the weak quantifier *many*. For example, the sentence *Many students passed the exam* is ordinarily false relative to a situation in which only four students succeeded on the exam. However, the same sentence might be true in the same situation if it is known that the exam was very difficult.

Taking stock, we have discussed the properties of the quantifier *many* and we have illustrated the interpretations that this quantifier has in the adult language. Let us now turn to child language. As we anticipated, Drozd & van Loosbroek (1998) claim that the quantifiers *every* and *many* behave in a similar way for 4- and 5-year-old children. They propose that children find the universal quantifier *every* as at least two ways ambiguous. The two readings licensed by children's grammar are the adult reading and a non-conservative reading which is similar in spirit to the non-conservative reading of the weak quantifier *many*. The non-conservative reading is claimed to explain children's symmetrical response to universally quantified sentences.[9] Consider the sentence in (11):

(11) Every boy is riding an elephant.

When adults are presented with (11), they consider the set of boys available in the context (denoted by the restrictor) and the set of boys who are riding an elephant (intersective set). This is the conservative interpretation. On this interpretation the sentence is true in the context in Figure 1. According to Drozd & van Loosbroek (1999) and Drozd (2000) children can resort to an additional interpretation, which involves the comparison of the set of boys who are riding an elephant against the set of expected elephant-riders or elephant-riding-boys. Since the domain of discourse contains an 'extra' elephant, children infer that an additional elephant-rider (or elephant-riding-boy), albeit one who is not present in the picture, must exist. As a consequence, children evaluate the target sentence against an expected set of elephant-riders. Therefore children judge the sentence in (11) to be 'false,' thus providing the basis for the symmetrical response, because "the number of elephant-riding boys does not match their expectations" (Drozd, 2000, 359).

Notice that on the adult interpretation, the proposal is that two sets need to be considered: the intersective set (elephant-riding-boys) and the set denoted by the restrictor (boys). Here is where the context comes into play, according to the WQA. In a typical Truth Value Judgment task, the set denoted by the restrictor (boys) is presented to children separately from the set of elephant-riding-boys. This feature of the experimental design draws children's attention to this set (boys), making it discourse-active. This prompts children to adopt the adult interpretation of the universal quantifier. In the original experiments (e.g., Philip, 1995), children were presented with a picture in which the boys were already riding elephants. The set denoted by the restrictor (boys) and the intersective set (elephant-riding-boys) were presented as the same set. Under these circumstances, children seem to be unable to distinguish the set of the boys from the set of elephant-riding boys and, as a consequence, they consider the former to be the restrictor of the quantifier. The next step in the WQA is to apply the non-conservative reading of *every* which involves the comparison between the set of elephant-riding boys with the set of expected of elephant-riding boys. Importantly, the presence of the 'extra' elephant strongly invites children to assume that the set of boys who ought to be riding an elephant should be constructed from the number of elephants in the picture. Put slightly differently, according to Drozd & van Loosbroek when the set denoted by the restrictor (boys) is made salient or discourse-active, as in the Crain *et al.*, study, children apply the adult conservative reading; but when the set of boys is not salient enough, children resort to the non-conservative reading that is provided by their grammar.

The WQA raises by now familiar theoretical and methodological concerns. One problem is learnability, which arises anytime children are hypothesized to have grammars which differ from those of adults. A second concern is given by the differences between *every* and *many*. As we suggested above, the flexibility allowed by the quantifier *many* is mainly due to the fact that *many* is a vague quantifier. However, it is hard to see how the same could hold for the universal quantifier *every*.[10] A further concern stems from the fact that, according to Drozd & van Loosbroek, children's misinterpretation of the universal quantifier in the Extra Object Condition is due to the fact that the set denoted by the restrictor of *every* (e.g., the boys) is not perceived by children as discourse-active, so children interpret the set of elephant-riding-boys to be the restrictor. It is not clear why this should be so. If children do not perceive the set of boys as discourse-active, because the context fails to establish the salience of this set, this reduces to a variant of the Salience Hypothesis. If so, there is no need to assume that children have a non-adult grammar in order to justify their peculiar interpretation of the universal quantifier *every*. In fact, many experimental studies have shown that in infelicitous or ambiguous contexts, *salience* can affect the language understanding of both children and adult.

Let us sidestep these observations for now and consider a different possibility. It could also be the case that children do not find the set of boys to be discourse-active because they are unable to distinguish this set from the set of elephant-riding-boys.[11] In other words, children find it difficult to identify the boys as entities simply because they are presented as elephant-riding-boys. We find this suggestion problematic.[12] In fact, this hypothesis assumes that children perceive entities in different ways when they are engaged in different actions, i.e., elephant-riding boys are not 'boys' anymore. This possibility also arises if one assumes that

> explicitly mentioning a perceptually available set, or specifying the cardinality of that set when the members are portrayed as already engaged in the action described in the test question. (Drozd, 2000, 349)

We wish to raise one further empirical concern. If children estimate the number of boys who should be riding an elephant on the basis of the number of elephants in the context, the presence of 'extra-agents', i.e., boys who are not riding an elephant, should not matter in verifying the sentence.[13] As a consequence, the WQA predicts that children will accept a sentence like *Every boy is riding an elephant* even in a situation in which some boy is not riding any elephant, as long as the number of elephant-riding-boys is the same as the number of elephants (henceforth *the extra-agent condition*). On this account, then,

> knowing a property of every elephant-riding-boys does not provide enough information to allow us to make a valid inference about every boy. This is because the set of elephant-riding-boys may be only a subset of the set of boys. (Drozd, 2000, 360)

Children's mistakes in the extra-agent condition are, however, rarely attested in previous research (see also Philip, 1995).[14]

An experiment explicitly designed to examine this prediction of the WQA was conducted by Meroni, Gualmini & Crain (2000). The extra-agent condition was constructed using pictures to evaluate the proposal by Drozd & van Loosbroek using their own methodology. Two experimenters participated in the study. One presented pictures to the child and to Kermit the Frog, the puppet who was manipulated by the second experimenter. Then, Kermit described the picture. The child's task was to judge whether or not Kermit's description was correct. To illustrate, on one trial children were presented with the picture of four tigers and three balloons. Only three of the four tigers were holding a balloon, so there was an 'extra' tiger in the picture. Children were then asked to evaluate the sentence in (12), produced by Kermit the Frog:

Figure 3. The Extra-Agent Condition

(12)   Every tiger is holding a balloon.

Nineteen children, ranging in age between 3;08 and 5;10 (mean age: 4;11), participated in the experiment. Each child was presented with three target sentences and two fillers. The children correctly rejected the target sentences 46 times out of 51 trials (90%). In short, children did not behave as predicted by the Weak Quantification account.

4. CONCLUSION

A central question in child language is whether possible mismatches between children and adults are due to non-adult linguistic analyses, or to non-linguistic factors to which adults are also sensitive. We have argued in favor of a non-linguistic account of children's behavior that invokes discourse principles that govern both child and adult performance. We would challenge, on grounds of parsimony, any account of children's behavior that does not comport with principles that are also known to influence adults. We have presented the findings of two new experiments that are consistent with the view that the source of children's 'errors' lies outside the language faculty.

In recent work we have been exploring, from a different angle, the empirical predictions of the competing accounts of children's interpretation of sentences with the universal quantifier. One prediction that is common to the Event Quantification account and the Weak Quantification account is that the restrictor of the universal quantifier extends beyond its internal argument, to include its external argument as well. The upshot is that asymmetries between the internal and external arguments of the universal quantifier should be blurred in child grammars, if either of these accounts is correct. However, if children's errors are the artifacts of experimental infelicities, as we maintain, then children are expected to observe the same differences in interpretation that arise in the two arguments of the universal quantifier in adult languages.

One relevant semantic property is downward entailment, because the universal quantifier is downward entailing on its internal argument, but not on its external argument. To see this one can observe that the internal argument of *every* licenses inferences from a set to its subsets (as long as the relevant presupposition of existence is satisfied); the external argument does not:

(13) Every boy who ate pizza got sick.
    $\Rightarrow$ Every boy who ate pepperoni pizza got sick.

(14) Every boy ate pizza. * $\Rightarrow$ Every boy ate pepperoni pizza.

As a consequence the internal argument of the universal quantifier *every* alllows the conjunctive interpretation of the disjunction operator *or* as in (15), but the external argument does not require this interpretation; the external argument ordinarily licenses the exclusive-*or* interpretation of disjunction, as illustrated in (16):

(15) Every boy who ate cheese pizza or pepperoni pizza got sick.
⇔ Every boy who ate cheese pizza got sick and every boy who ate pepperoni pizza got sick.

(16) Every ghostbuster will choose a cat or a pig.
*⇔ Every ghostbuster will choose a cat and every ghostbuster will choose a pig.

The contrast in (15)-(16) is the subject of two recent investigations of child language. Boster & Crain (1993) designed a Truth Value Judgment task to investigate children's interpretation of (16). The results obtained by Boster & Crain provide evidence that children assign the exclusive interpretation to the disjunction operator *or*, when it appears in the external argument of *every*. That is, children do not treat the nuclear scope of the universal quantifier *every* as downward entailing. In a second study, Gualmini, Meroni & Crain (2003) focused on (15). The findings of a truth Value Judgment task show that children assign an inclusive interpretation of the disjunction operator, when it occurs in the internal argument of the universal quantifier. Based on these findings, we conclude that children younger than four assign the conjunctive interpretation to the disjunction operator only when *or* occurs in the internal argument of the universal quantifier *every*. Taken together, the findings by Boster & Crain (1993) and Gualmini *et al.* (2003) show that children know that the two arguments of the universal quantifier *every* differ with respect to downward entailingness. This research finding adds to the empirical weakness of linguistic accounts of children's non-adults responses to sentences with the universal quantifier.

5. ACKNOWLEDGEMENTS

We wish to thank the children, staff and teachers at the Center for Young Children at the University of Maryland at College Park and Lia Gravelle for her assistance as puppeteer. We also thank Nadia Shihab for reading the manuscript, and we are indebted to Paul Pietroski for extensive discussion of the issues raised in this chapter.

University of Maryland at College Park

6. NOTES

[1] We follow the literature in calling 'symmetrical' children's rejections of sentences containing an intransitive verb, as in *Every boy is riding* in the same context. In this case one can

describe children behavior by saying that they demand a symmetry between the set of boys and the set of entities that could be ridden.

[2] One reviewer pointed out that the example under consideration may be analysed as an instance of a relational plural, as discussed by Scha (1984). Consider (i):
(i) The squares contain the circles.
Scha (1984) proposes that (i) is true just so long as each circle is contained in some square. In other words, whereas (i) is true if there is an extra square which contains no circle, it becomes false if there is a circle that is not contained in any square. By analogy, the sentence *All the cups are on the saucers* is false since there is a saucer with no cup on it. However, as Scha & Stallard (1988, 17) observes, sentences containing plurals "often require entirely different semantic treatments depending upon the particular verbs (or adjectives or prepositions) that these plurals are combined with." In particular, sentences containing the preposition "on" differ from the one exemplified in (i) in that the roles of the first and the second plural nouns are reversed. Under this analysis, the sentence *All the cups are on the saucers* means that every cup is on some saucer and does not require that every saucer has some cup on it. As a consequence, the sentence is true in the situation used by Freeman *et al.*, in which each cup is on the saucer but there is an extra saucer with no cup on it (see Beck, 2000, for a different approach).

[3] In set theoretic terms, the function expressed by the universal quantifier makes the sentence true if the set of boys (first argument) is a subset of the set of entities that are riding an elephant (second argument). On this view, the syntactic structure of the sentence contributes to the logical form, and hence the semantic interpretation, in a transparent fashion. By contrast, the Event Quantification account assumes that children can access an interpretation in which the two arguments of the universal quantifier *every* do not reflect the syntax in a transparent way. The semantic representation in (2) does not restrict the application of the universal quantifier *every* to the events in which a boy participates; rather, it extends the application of the universal quantifier *every* to include events in which an elephant participates. In other words, the first argument of the universal quantifier not only contains the semantic value of the noun that combines with the universal quantifier *every* in the overt syntax (i.e., *boy*), but it also contains the semantic value of the noun phrase that resides in the direct object position in the overt syntax (i.e., *elephant*), i.e., in the second argument.

[4] See Sugisaki & Isobe (2000); Gouro, Norita, Nakajima & Ariji (2001) for experimental evidence that confirms this prediction.

[5] The context set is the set of propositions which constitute the live options relevant to the conversation.

[6] We would not hold all advocates of the Salience account to each of these claims; however, this is our reading of the work by Philip & Lynch (2000), Drozd & van Loosbroek (1998), and Geurts (2000). We are less certain of the claims made by Gordon (1996).

[7] One reviewer points out that, according to the definition in (7), conservativity is a property of lexical items. On this view, (10c) would not violate the semantic property of conservativity, but it would represent a different case of violation of Principle of Universal Grammar that govern the mapping between syntax and semantics. For ease of exposition, we continue to describe the issue as involving conservativity.

[8] The acceptability of (9) in a context in which many of the Nobel Prize winners are Scandinavians is taken by Drozd & van Loosbroek as evidence that this sentence allows the non-conservative interpretation in (10c). The availability of the reading in (10c) is not a necessary condition for the acceptability of (9) in the context under consideration, however. In particular, given a value q that makes (10c) true, it is always possible to obtain a value n which will make (10a) true, or a value p that makes (10b) true in the same context (see Löbner, 1987; Partee, 1988). Importantly, both interpretations of *many* illustrated in (10a) and (10b) do not violate conservativity. Current semantic research has not reached conclusive evidence on whether it is necessary to assume (10c), or if the relevant truth conditions can be obtained via (10a) or (10b).

[9] See Crain (2000) and Meroni, Gualmini & Crain (2000) for further empirical discussion.

[10] This concern is relevant in light of the following quote from Drozd & van Loosbroek (1998, 10): "In other words, they attempt to verify the universally-quantified proposition ... by checking if the cardinality of the set of elephant-riding boys constitutes what the interlocutors would consider to be 'every', i.e., EVERY AB iff| A∩B | = 'every'".

[11] Most children's mistakes are produced when they are presented with pictures in which boys are already riding elephants.

[12] See also Brooks & Braine (1996) who show that children are perfectly able to distinguish the two sets even when these sets are represented as the same set.

[13] Along the same lines, the presence of numerous elephants (extra-objects) should not change children's response. Children should in fact infer from the presence of 'many' extra elephants the existence of 'many' boys. However, as we have seen, this prediction goes unfulfilled. As Gouro *et al.*, and Sugisaki *et al.*, show (and the condition of Plausible Dissent predicts), children's performance dramatically improves in such circumstances.

[14] Freeman *et al.*, report some cases of children's mistakes in the extra-agent condition, although a low percentage (10%). It is attested that, in infelicitous situations, different strategies may be used by children to make sense of the linguistic input. In particular, these strategies rely on pragmatic cues, such as salience, which are inferred from the visual scene (see Donaldson & Lloyd, 1974; Freeman *et al.*). However, on the account proposed by Drozd (2000), children's mistakes in the extra-agent condition should emerge consistently and regardless of salience.

7. REFERENCES

Barwise, John, and Robin Cooper. "Generalized Quantifiers and Natural Language." *Linguistics and Philosophy* 4 (1981): 159–219.

Beck, Sigrid. "Exceptions in Relational Plurals." In Brendan Jackson and Tanya Matthews (eds.) *Proceedings of SALT X*, 1–20. Ithaca: CLC Publications, 2000.

Boster, Carole, and Stephen Crain. "On Children's Understanding of *Every* and *Or*." In *Proceedings of Early Cognition and Transition to Language*. Austin: University of Texas, 1993.

Brooks, Patricia J., and Martin D.S. Braine. "What do Children Know about the Universal Quantifiers *All* and *Each*?" *Cognition* 60 (1996): 235–268.

Chierchia, Gennaro, and Sally McConnell-Ginet. *Meaning and Grammar, 2nd Edition*. Cambridge, MA: MIT Press, 2000.

Crain, Stephen. "Sense and Sense Ability in Child Language." In S. Catherine Howell, Sarah A. Fish, and Thea Keith-Lucas (eds.) *Proceedings of the 24th Boston University Conference on Language Development*, 22–44. Somerville: Cascadilla Press, 2000.

Crain, Stephen, and Cecile McKee. "The Acquisition of Structural Restrictions on Anaphora." In Steve Berman, Jae Woong Choe, and Joyce McDonough (eds.) *Proceedings of NELS 15*, 94–110. Amherst: GLSA, 1985.

Crain, Stephen, and Paul Pietroski. "Nature, Nurture and Universal Grammar." *Linguistics and Philosophy* 24 (2001): 139–186.

Crain, Stephen, and Rosalind Thornton. *Investigations in Universal Grammar*. Cambridge, MA: MIT Press, 1998.

Crain, Stephen, Rosalind Thornton, Carol Boster, Laura Conway, Diane Lillo-Martin, and Elaine Woodams. "Quantification without Qualification." *Language Acquisition* 5 (1996): 83–153.

Donaldson, Margaret, and Peter Lloyd. "Children's Judgments of Match and Mismatch." In F. Bresson (ed.) *Problèmes Actuels en Psycholinguistique*. Paris: Presses Universitaires de France, 1974.

Drozd, Kenneth. "Children's Weak Interpretation of Universally Quantified Sentences." In Melissa Bowerman and Stephen Levinson (eds.) *Conceptual Development and Language Acquisition*, 340–376. Cambridge: Cambridge University Press, 2000.

Drozd, Kenneth, and Erik van Loosbroek. "The Effect of Context on Children's Interpretation of Universally Quantified Sentences." Ms., Max Planck Institute for Psycholinguistics and Nijmegen University, Nijmegen, 1998.

Drozd, Kenneth, and Erik van Loosbroek. "Weak Quantification, Plausible Dissent, and the Development of Children's Pragmatic Competence." In Annabel Greenhill, Heather Littlefield, and Cheryl Tano (eds.) *Proceedings of the 23rd Boston University Conference on Language Development*, 184–195. Somerville: Cascadilla Press, 1999.

Freeman, Norman H., Sinha, C.G. and Jacqueline A. Stedmon. "All the Cars – Which Cars? From Word to Meaning to Discourse Analysis." In Michael Beveridge (ed.) *Children Thinking hrough Language*, 52–74. London: Edward Arnold Publisher, 1982.

Freeman, Norman H., and Jacqueline A. Stedmon. "How Children Deal with Natural Language Quantification." In Ida Kurcz, Grace Wales Shugar, and Joseph H. Danks (eds.) *Knowledge and Language*, 21–48. Amsterdam: Elsevier Science Publishers, 1986.

Geurts, Bart. "Quantifying Kids." Ms., Humboldt University, Berlin and Nijmegen University, Nijmegen, 2001.

Gordon, Peter. "The Truth Value Judgment Task." In Dana McDaniel, Cecile McKee and Helen Smith Cairns (eds.) *Methods for Assessing Children's Syntax*, 211–231. Cambridge, MA: MIT Press, 1996.

Gouro, Takuya, Hanae Norita, Motoki Nakajima, and Ken-ichi Ariji. "Children's Interpretation of Universal Quantifier and Pragmatic Interference." In Youkio Otsu (ed.) *Proceedings of the Second Tokyo Conference on Psycholinguistics*, 61–78. Tokyo: Hituzi Syobo Publishing Company, 2001.

Gualmini, Andrea, Luisa Meroni, and Stephen Crain. "An Asymmetric Universal in Child Language" To appear in *Proceedings of Sinn und Bedeutung VI.* Konstanz: Arbeitspapiere des Fachbereichs Sprachwissenschaft, 2003.

Guasti, Maria Teresa, and Gennaro Chierchia. "Backward Versus Forward Anaphora: Reconstruction in Child Grammar." *Language Acquisition* 8 (2000): 129–170.

Heim, Irene. *The Semantics of Definite and Indefinite Noun Phrases*. Ph.D. Diss., University of Massachusetts, Amherst, 1982.

Inhelder, Bärbel, and Jean Piaget. *The Early Growth of Logic in the Child*. London: Routledge, Kegan and Paul, 1964.

James, William. *Psychology*. New York: Harper and Brothers, 1892.

Keenan, Edward L., and Jonathan Stavi. "A Semantic Characterization of Natural Language Determiners." *Linguistics and Philosophy* 9 (1986): 253–326.

Krämer, Irene. *Interpreting Indefinites. An Experimental Study of Children's Language Comprehension*. Ph.D. Diss., Universiteit Utrecht.

Löbner, Sebastian. "Quantification as a Major Module of Natural Language Semantics." In Jeroen Groenendijk, Dick de Jongh, and Martin Stokhof (eds.) *Studies in Discourse Representation Theory and the Theory of Generalized Quantifiers*, 53–85. Dordrecht: Foris, 1987.

Locke, John. *An Essay Concerning Human Understanding*. London, 1690.

Meroni, Luisa. "Children's and Adults' Interpretation of the Universal Quantifier: Grammatical Non-adult Principles vs. Non-grammatical Adult Principles." Doctoral Research Paper, University of Maryland at College Park, 2002.

Meroni, Luisa, Andrea Gualmini, and Stephen Crain. "A Conservative Approach to Quantification in Child Language." In Michelle Minnick Fox, Alexander Williams, and Elsi Kaiser (eds.) *Proceedings of the 24th Annual Penn Linguistics Colloquium*, 171–182. Philadelphia, University of Pennsylvania, 2000.

Meroni, Luisa, Stephen Crain, and Andrea Gualmini. "Felicity Conditions and On-line Interpretation of Sentence with Quantified NPs." Paper presented at the *14th Annual CUNY Conference on Human Sentence Processing*, Philadelphia: University of Pennsylvania, 2001.

Partee, Barbara. "Many Quantifiers." In Joyce Powers and Kenneth de Jong (eds.) *Proceedings of ESCOL* 5, 383–402. Columbus: Ohio State University, 1988.
Philip, William. *Event Quantification in the Acquisition of Universal Quantification*. Ph.D. Diss., University of Massachusetts, Amherst, 1995.
Philip, William. "The Event Quantificational Account of Symmetrical Interpretation and a Denial of Implausible Infelicity." In Andy Stringfellow, Dalia Cahana-Amitay, Elizabeth Hughes, and Andrea Zukowski (eds.) *Proceedings of the 20th Boston University Conference on Language Development,* 564–575. Somerville: Cascadilla Press, 1996.
Philip, William, and Emily Lynch. "Felicity, Relevance, and Acquisition of the Grammar of *Every* and *Only*." In S. Catherine Howell, Sarah A. Fish, and Thea Keith-Lucas (eds.) *Proceedings of the 24th Boston University Conference on Language Development*, 583–596. Somerville: Cascadilla Press, 2000.
Roeper, Tom, and Jill de Villiers. "The Emergence of Bound Variable Structures." In Thomas Maxfield and Bernadette Plunket (eds.) *University of Massachusetts Occasional Papers: Papers in the Acquisition of WH*, 267–282. Amherst, MA: GLSA, 1991.
Russell, Bertrand. *Human Knowledge: Its Scope and Limits*. London: Allen and Unwin, 1948.
Scha, Remko. "Distributive, Collective and Cumulative Quantification." In Jeroen Groenendijk, Theo Janssen, and Martin Stokhof (eds.) *Truth, Interpretation and Information*, 483–512. Dordrecht, Netherlands: Foris, 1984.
Scha, Remko, and David Stallard. "Multi-level Plurals and Distributivity." In *Proceedings of the 26th Annual Meeting of the Association for Computational Linguistics*, 17–24. Buffalo: Association for Computational Linguistics Publisher, 1988.
Stalnaker, Robert C. *Context and Content*. Oxford: Oxford University Press, 1999.
Sugisaki, Koji, and Miwa Isobe. "Quantification without Qualification without Plausible Dissent." In Ji-Yung Kim and Adam Werle (eds.) *Proceedings of SULA 1: The Semantics of Under-represented Languages of the Americas*. University of Massachusetts Occasional Papers in Linguistics 25. Amherst: GLSA, 2001.
Wason, Peter C. "The Context of Plausible Denial." *Journal of Verbal Learning and Verbal Behaviour* 4 (1965): 7–11.
Westerståhl, Dag. "Logical Constants in Quantifier Languages." *Linguistics and Philosophy* 8 (1985): 387–413.

KENNETH F. DROZD AND ERIK VAN LOOSBROEK

THE EFFECT OF CONTEXT ON CHILDREN'S INTERPRETATIONS OF UNIVERSALLY QUANTIFIED SENTENCES

Abstract. This chapter investigates the effects of perceptual and discourse context on children's Exhaustive Pairing interpretation of universally quantified sentences. Two experiments compared the predictions of two recent accounts of Exhaustive Pairing. In one account, Crain *et al.* (1996) argue that children make the Exhaustive Pairing error because the experiments used to elicit the error do not satisfy a felicity condition called the Condition of Plausible Dissent. In another account, Drozd (2001) argued that children adopt Exhaustive Pairing when they fail to evaluate the presuppositions adults normally use to constrain the interpretation of a universal quantifier. We argue that the results support Drozd's account.

1. INTRODUCTION

Children's comprehension of universally quantified expressions like *All the circles are blue* and *All the cars are in the garages* has long been a research topic in developmental psychology (Inhelder & Piaget, 1964; Donaldson, 1978; Freeman, Sinha & Stedmon 1982; Brooks & Braine, 1996) and has recently drawn the attention of developmental psycholinguists (e.g., Philip, 1995; Crain, Thornton, Boster, Conway, Lillo-Martin, and Woodams, 1996; Drozd & van Loosbroek, 1999; Drozd, 2001; Kang, 2001). Much of the research in this area has focused on one interesting puzzle, recently named the Symmetrical Interpretation (Philip, 1995), or Exhaustive Pairing (Drozd, 2001).

Exhaustive Pairing is commonly elicited anywhere from 39% to 80% of the time in experimental trials like (1) (see Drozd, 2001, for a review). While adults respond *Yes* to *Is every boy riding an elephant*? or judge statements like *Every boy is riding an elephant* as true on such trials, many children incorrectly say *No* and justify their response by pointing out either that the unridden elephant is left over or that there is no boy matched with the unridden elephant. Henceforth, we refer to the actors in the scene as 'actors', the objects acted upon as 'objects', and the actors and objects as 'participants'.[1]

(1) Extra Object Trial

Figure 1. Extra Object Context.

Experimenter:	Here's some boys and some elephants. Is every boy riding an elephant?
Adult:	Yes.
Exhaustive Pairing:	No. Not this one.

One question raised by Exhaustive Pairing is what kind of grammatical analysis children assign to universally quantified sentences when they make the error. Some researchers have proposed that children misanalyze the determiner quantifier *every* syntactically as an adverb (Roeper & de Villiers, 1991) or as a modifier in a Noun Phrase (NP) rather than a functional head in a Determiner Phrase (DP) (Kang, 2001). Other researchers have argued that children misanalyze *every* and *all* semantically as quantifiers over events rather than individuals (Philip, 1995) or interpret these quantifiers as weak rather than strong quantifiers (Drozd, 2001). Still others have proposed that children who make the error modify the choice functions adults normally assign to direct objects like *an elephant* in sentences like *Every boy is riding an elephant* (Crain et al., 1996, 107).

A second question is how children's analysis of perceptual and discourse context influences their judgments of universally quantified sentences. Researchers generally agree that the presence of the extra object draws children's attention to the disparity in the actual and expected number of participating actors in context. When asked to explain Exhaustive Pairing responses, children typically either point out that there is an extra object or that an actor is not associated with the extra object (Philip, 1995; Drozd, 2001). Moreover, children perform no differently than adults on similar trials where no extra object appears in context, or when the actors outnumber the objects (Philip, 1995). What researchers presently disagree about is how contextual information influences children's semantic interpretations and why children's performance improves on some experimental trials but not others.

In this chapter, we report the results of two experiments designed to explore this second question. The experiments test the predictions of two different accounts of Exhaustive Pairing. One account offered by Crain *et al.* (1996) claims that children make the Exhaustive Pairing error because Extra Object trials do not satisfy a felicity condition called the Condition of Plausible Dissent. This account predicts that children's performance should improve if the Condition of Plausible Dissent is satisfied. A second account offered by Drozd (2001) claims that children make the error because they do not always analyze the domain presuppositions conveyed by universal quantifiers when presented with Extra Object trials, and, as a result, do not constrain their interpretation of the quantifier in the expected way. This account predicts that children's performance should improve in contexts that make it easy for them to resolve the domain presuppositions conveyed by the quantifier. The results suggest that children's performance improves in contexts in which the presuppositions conveyed by the quantifier are easily resolved, supporting Drozd's account. The results also suggest that satisfying Plausible Dissent is neither a necessary nor a sufficient condition for reducing the rate of Exhaustive Pairing.

2. TWO ACCOUNTS OF EXHAUSTIVE PAIRING

Crain *et al.* (1996) proposed that children have full competence with universal quantification, but make the Exhaustive Pairing error because the design of the Extra Object trial violates the 'Condition of Plausible Dissent' (henceforth, Plausible Dissent), a general felicity condition on the presentation of sentences for truth-value judgements. Plausible Dissent states that the presentation of a sentence which is true is felicitous for an addressee only if she can conceive of a possible outcome or situation other than the actual outcome described in the proposition (Crain *et al.*, 1996, 116).[2]

According to Crain *et al.*, the problem with Extra Object trials like (1) is that no possible outcome other than the actual outcome is brought to the child's attention during the task. Whereas adults and older children can recover from the infelicity created in such situations, younger, less experienced children are sometimes unable to "perform the necessary accommodations as successfully or rapidly" (Crain *et al.*, 1996, 117). Instead, children find it felicitous to construe questions like *Is every boy riding an elephant?* as a request to check if there is a one-to-one correspondence between actors and objects and incorrectly reject the proposition as a description of the Extra Object context on this basis.

To back up their claim, Crain et al., presented experimental evidence which showed that Exhaustive Pairing is drastically reduced when a story which satisfied Plausible Dissent was acted out in front of a child before she was asked to judge a universally quantified sentence about that story. In one such story, three skiers, a mother and her two daughters, each ski down a mountain and under an arch before heading to the ski lodge for a drink. Each of the two girls chooses a bottle of soda before their mother convinces them to choose a cup of hot apple cider instead. At the end of the story, each skier is drinking a cup of hot apple cider in the presence of additional cups of cider, a situation type similar to that portrayed in Figure 1. When the story is finished, children are asked to judge whether Kermit's statement *Every skier drank a cup of hot apple cider* is correct given the story. Crain et al., reported that children correctly accepted Kermit's descriptions on conditions like the Skiers Condition 88% of the time. Children's performance generally improves on such conditions, they argued, because the story satisfies Plausible Dissent. In the story, two of the three skiers initially expressed a preference for soda before all three ended up drinking hot apple cider. According to Crain et al., this turn of events introduced the children to the possibility that some of the skiers may have ended up drinking sodas rather than apple cider, a possible outcome other than the actual outcome described in the test sentence.

An alternative view favored by many researchers is that Exhaustive Pairing reflects children's analysis of universal quantification on trials like (1). In one recent account, Drozd (2001) proposed that children make the Exhaustive Pairing error because they do not always analyze the domain presuppositions which speakers normally use to constrain their interpretations of universal quantifiers. Universal quantifiers like *every*, *all*, and *each* are typically viewed as 'strong' or 'essentially relational' quantifiers (e.g., Barwise & Cooper, 1981; Partee, 1995), which are analyzed semantically as operators which denote binary relations between subsets of the universe of discourse (Zwarts, 1983). Under this view, the truth conditions for the sentence *Every boy is riding an elephant* specify that each individual in the quantifier's 'restriction' or domain of quantification, in this case the set extension of the N *boy*, is also an individual in the quantifier's 'nuclear scope', the set extension of the VP predicate *is riding an elephant*. When used in nongeneric contexts, strong quantifiers introduce the presupposition that the quantifier's domain of quantification is nonempty (Strawson, 1952) or that there exists some set of entities in discourse context, commonly called a 'witness set', which can serve as the domain for the quantifier (Szabolcsi, 1997). Henceforth, we refer to such presuppositions as 'domain' presuppositions. For example, the use of the quantifier *every* in the sentence *every boy is riding an elephant* introduces the domain presupposition that there exists some witness set of boys in discourse context which can serve as the domain for *every*. To verify the sentence in context, it is assumed that speakers must represent two distinct sets, a presupposed set of boys (corresponding to the quantifier's restriction) and a set of elephant-riding boys (corresponding to the quantifier's nuclear scope) and check if they are identical. If they are, the sentence is true.

Drozd observed that children who make the Exhaustive Pairing error, unlike adults, seem to arrive at a response to questions like *Is every boy riding an elephant?* in (1) by comparing the set of elephant-riding boys they see not with a presupposed set of boys but with what they consider to be the normal or expected frequency of elephant-riders given that context. Drozd proposed that children may, in fact, forego a presuppositional interpretation of the quantifier in *Is every boy riding an elephant?* because verifying that interpretation in (1) requires representing the set of boys they see in Figure 1 in two different guises, as a set of elephant-riding boys (nuclear scope) and as a presupposed set of boys (restriction). According to Drozd, children correctly represent the set of boys they see as the nuclear scope for the quantifier, but they do not always have this set in mind as a presupposed set of boys when they come to the task of analyzing the quantified question. Moreover, children do not always update their discourse model to resolve the relevant domain presupposition under these conditions. As a result they have no presupposed set in mind to compare to the nuclear scope (see Freeman *et al.*, 1982, for a similar account).

According to Drozd, children's performance improves on conditions like Crain *et al.*'s Skiers Condition because the set the children need to represent as the domain of quantification for the quantifier *every* is presented as presupposed before Kermit presents the test sentence for judgment. This makes it possible for children to establish the restriction and nuclear scope arguments for the quantifier as independent sets and to proceed with the presuppositional interpretation of the quantifier. In Extra Object trials like (1), Drozd proposed that children end up assigning an interpretation to universally quantified questions similar to those proposed for sentences with weak quantifiers, which do not convey domain presuppositions. For example, Westerståhl (1985a; 1989, 45) proposed that sentences like *Many Scandinavians have won the Nobel Prize in literature* can be assigned a context-dependent 'frequency' interpretation which compares the set of Nobel prize-winning Scandinavians (the nuclear scope), not with a presupposed set of Scandinavians (restriction), but with some normal or expected frequency of Nobel prize winners. Drozd suggested that children assign a similar interpretation to questions like *Is every boy riding an elephant?* on Extra Object trials.

3. PREDICTIONS OF THE ACCOUNTS

The Plausible Dissent account (Crain *et al.*) and the Presuppositionality account (Drozd) make different predictions about what kind of contextual manipulations will improve children's performance on Extra Object trials like (1). If the Plausible Dissent account is correct, then satisfying Plausible Dissent should be a sufficient and, perhaps, a necessary condition for improving children's performance on such trials. If the Presuppositionality account is correct, children's performance on Extra Object trials should significantly improve if the intended domain of quantification is clearly established in context as presupposed before the quantified question is presented.

The two accounts also lead to different predictions regarding how children evaluate distributive quantification in different contexts. We assume that *every* is an obligatorily distributive quantifier (e.g., Vendler, 1967; Gil, 1992; Partee, 1995) and that distributivity is built into the lexical meaning of *every* as a scopal function involving two syntactic constituents, the 'distributive-key' and the 'distributive share' (Choe, 1987; Gil, 1992; Beghelli & Stowell, 1997). Under this view, the scopal function conveyed by *Every boy is riding an elephant* assigns at least one case of elephant-riding in the extension of the distributive share VP *is riding an elephant* (or alternatively, one elephant in the extension of the distributive share *an elephant*) to each individual boy in the extension of the distributive key *Every boy*. If no such function can be established, the sentence is false. The scopal function distinguishes distributive universal quantifiers from the 'collective' universal quantifier *all* (Vendler, 1967).

The Plausible Dissent account claims that children have full competence with distributive universal quantification. This predicts that children presented with an *every*-sentence will always represent the scopal function conveyed by *every* and distinguish the appropriate distributive key and distributive share arguments of the function. The Presuppositionality account, in contrast, raises the possibility that children may not always follow through with a distributive interpretation of *every* across discourse contexts. Drozd was specifically concerned with connecting Exhaustive Pairing with how and when children analyze universal quantifiers as presuppositional quantifiers. A key point in Drozd's account is that a child may not always analyze universal quantifiers as presuppositional in contexts in which the presuppositional interpretation is not unambiguously supported and may require updating the discourse model. In our view, this proposal may apply more generally. We hypothesize that children may also not always recover the distributive interpretation of *every* in similar contexts. Let us call this the 'Distributivity Hypothesis.' Notably, Crain *et al.*'s Skiers Condition does not test children's knowledge of distributive meaning. In the Skiers Condition, each skier is introduced independently on at least two different occasions, when they ski under the arch and when they choose to drink apple cider. This makes it impossible to tell whether Crain *et al.*'s children identified the individual skiers because they controlled the scopal function expressed by the universal quantifier or because they simply preferred to match *Every skier drank a cup of hot apple cider* with contexts in which each skier is matched with her own cup. The Distributivity Hypothesis predicts that children may perform less well when they have to rely on the scopal function of the universal quantifier alone to build a distributive interpretation. For example, children may make considerably more errors when asked to judge a question like *Is every boy riding an elephant?* with respect to the 'collective' context in Figure 3 below, where the actors are not matched independently with different situations, than with respect to Figure 1, where the actors are matched in this way.

To test these predictions, we conducted two experiments which investigate Dutch children's understanding of sentences with universal quantification in distributive and collective contexts. In Experiment 1, we investigated the Distributivity Hypothesis by comparing children's interpretations of questions with distributive and collective universal quantifiers in distributive and collective contexts. This experiment is presented first so that the results can be statistically compared with the results of Experiment 2. In Experiment 2, we investigated the Plausible Dissent and Presuppositionality accounts by comparing children's interpretations of statements with distributive universal quantifiers across contexts which made the presuppositional interpretation felicitous but varied in whether Plausible Dissent was satisfied or not.

4. EXPERIMENT 1

In this experiment, we compared Dutch children's judgments of *yes-no* questions quantified with either the distributive universal quantifier *iedere* 'every' or the collective universal quantifier *alle* 'all' in distributive and collective contexts which neither satisfied Plausible Dissent nor made a presuppositional quantifier interpretation felicitous.[3] Comparing children's responses to *iedere* and *alle* questions allowed us to determine if children were sensitive to the distinction between obligatorily distributive and collective universal quantification. Asking children questions in both distributive and collective contexts allowed us to examine whether children responded differently to questions with distributive universal quantifiers in different contexts.

4.1. Subjects

Fifty-two Dutch children, consisting of twenty-six 4-year-olds (Group 1, mean age: 4;4) and twenty-six 5-year-olds (Group 2, mean age: 5;6) and twenty-six adult controls participated in this experiment. All of the children were drawn from a school in Nijmegen. The adults were also living in Nijmegen.

4.2. Method

The children were tested individually in an isolated room in their school for approximately twenty minutes. Each child first received four warm-up trials designed to determine whether the children had a basic understanding of *iedere* 'every' and *alle* 'all' and to get the children used to the task. On each warm-up, the experimenter presented a child with a pictured context like Figure 1 and introduced the participants in context to the child by pointing them out and naming them or by asking the child who the actors were or what they were doing. Then, the experimenter used Cookie Monster to ask the child to judge whether an intransitive question like *Slapen alle meisjes?* 'Are all the girls sleeping?' correctly described the context (correct answer was *nee* 'no'). Two of the warm-up questions included the quantifier *iedere* 'every' and two questions included *alle* 'all' in subject determiner position. Each of twelve different warm-up orders were given to roughly the same number of subjects.

Each child then received eight experimental trials. On each trial, the child was asked to answer a *yes-no* question with respect to a pictured context. The eight trials represented the combinations of two factors. The first was whether the question was quantified with *iedere* 'every' or *alle* 'alle' (as in (2) or (3), respectively). The second was whether the actors were depicted in one-to-one correspondence with individual objects (as in Figure 2) or as a collection associated with a single object (as in Figure 3). Henceforth, we refer to these conditions as the *iedere*-distributive, *iedere*-collective, *alle*-distributive, and *alle*-collective conditions. Each child received two trials of each condition:

(2) Question Type 1: Rijdt iedere jongen op een olifant?
('Is every boy riding (on) an elephant?')

(3) Question Type 2: Rijden alle jongens op een olifant?
('Are all the boys riding (on) an elephant?')

Figure 2. A distributive context   *Figure 3. A collective context*

Collective and distributive contexts were used to determine if children found it easy to adopt a distributive interpretation for *every* simply because each individual in the domain of quantification was already mapped in one-to-one correspondence with a different object. In contexts like Figure 3, there is no unambiguous visual support for conceptualizing any boy as riding an elephant independently of the others and, hence, no ambiguous visual support for a one-to-one distributive interpretation of *every*. However, if a child knows that *every* is obligatorily distributive, she should be able to correctly respond *Yes* on *iedere*-collective trials, even if she initially did not perceive each boy as an independent elephant rider.

On each trial, the experimenter first introduced the participants as on the warm-up trials. These introductions neither brought alternative possible outcomes to a child's attention nor presented the intended domain of quantification to a child independently of the set they needed to establish the nuclear scope for the quantifier. Thus, the contexts neither satisfied Plausible Dissent nor pragmatically supported the presuppositional interpretation of the quantifier. The experimenter then used Cookie Monster to pose an *iedere* or *alle* question to the child. *Ja* 'yes' was the expected response on all eight trials. Two versions of the trials were prepared to control for the combined effect of using a particular question with a particular context. Contexts paired with *iedere* questions in Version One were paired with the *alle* questions in Version Two. Half of the subjects in each group received Version One and half received Version Two. Roughly every three subjects received a different order of experimental trials.

4.3. Scoring

Children who incorrectly responded *Nee* 'no' to a test question were always asked why they did so. A negative response was scored as an Exhaustive Pairing response if the child referred to the disparity in the number of actors and objects in context in explaining her response, e.g., *Nee, één olifant is alleen* 'No, one elephant is alone', *Nee, één jongen moet nog bij deze olifant* 'No, one boy has to be with this elephant', *Nee, alleen deze olifant heeft een jongen* 'No, only this elephant has a boy', *Nee, deze, deze en deze* 'No, this one, this one, and this one (boys)'. Explanations including no reference to the disparity were coded as 'other'. Negative responses followed by either no explanation or unclear explanations were marked 'unclear'.

4.4. Results

Table 1 presents a summary of how often the children gave correct *yes* responses to the test questions across conditions:

Table 1. Proportions of correct responses to test questions

	Iedere		Alle	
Age	Collective	Distributive	Collective	Distributive
4-year-olds	.35	.56	.52	.63
5-year-olds	.48	.65	.42	.62

Using the scoring procedures, 85% of the children's *no* responses were coded as Exhaustive Pairing responses and 15% as unclear. Since none of the children gave explanations, which were inconsistent with Exhaustive Pairing, we regarded all of the children's negative responses as Exhaustive Pairing responses in the analyses.

A mixed-design factorial analysis (ANOVA) with question type (*iedere* question/*alle* question) and context (distributive, collective) as within-subjects factors and age (Group 1, Group 2) between subjects was performed to determine if the children responded differently to *alle* and *iedere* questions and if the children responded correctly more often on the *iedere*-distributive condition than the *alle*-distributive condition, as we predicted. The dependent measure was the proportion of correct responses. The results revealed a main effect of context, $F(1,50) = 15.01$, $p < .001$. The children responded correctly significantly more often in distributive contexts than in collective contexts. There was also a significant interaction of age and question type, $F(1,50) = 4.83$, $p < .04$. Although the 5-year-olds' responses did not differ across question type, the 4-year-olds answered *alle* questions correctly more often than *iedere* questions, $t(25) = 2.05$, $p < .05$. The 4-year-olds also answered correctly significantly less often on the *iedere*-collective condition than on the *iedere*-distributive condition, $t(25) = 2.39$, $p < .03$. Thus, of the two age groups only the results for the 4-year-olds support the Distributivity Hypothesis.

One question is why the 4-year-olds may have adopted Exhaustive Pairing more often on the *iedere*-collective condition than on the *iedere*-distributive condition. One possibility consistent with the Distributivity Hypothesis is that the children found the *iedere*-collective condition infelicitous because the actors were not matched independently with different actions. To investigate, we calculated how often the children explained their Exhaustive Pairing responses by referring to the way the participating actors were depicted in context. If children found the *iedere*-collective trials infelicitous because the actors were not depicted unambiguously as independently performing an action, we would expect them to mention this fact more often on *iedere*-collective trials than on *iedere*-distributive trials. Next, we calculated how often children replaced *iedere* with collective terms like *alle* and *samen* ('together') in *iedere*-distributive and *iedere*-collective trials. If the children had a dispreference for *iedere* on the *iedere*-collective trials, we would expect them to have used collective terms in their explanations more often on *iedere*-collective than on *iedere*-distributive trials.

The proportion of children's explanations including references to participating actors is given in Table 2:

Table 2. Number and proportion of explanations including reference to participating actors on 'iedere' conditions

	Context	
Age	Collective	Distributive
4-year-olds	12 (.36)	2 (.08)
5-year-olds	17 (.63)	4 (.22)

The data suggest that the 4-year-olds referred significantly more often to the participating actors on the *iedere*-collective condition than on the *iedere*-distributive condition, $z = 2.43$, $p < .05$. A similar result was found for the 5-year-olds, $z = 2.99$, $p < .05$. Typically, the children explained that the participating actors were involved with a single object, *Nee, (alle) drie (de jongens) op één (olifant)* 'No, (all) three (boys) on one (elephant)'. This is expected if children initially construed the actors on the *iedere*-collective condition as performing the action as a group and found *iedere* infelicitous.

The proportion of explanations in which the children used collective terms in their explanations is given in Table 3:

Table 3. Number and proportion of explanations including collective terms

	Condition			
	Collective		Distributive	
Age	Alle	Iedere	Alle	Iedere
4-year-olds	4 (.16)	6 (.18)	0 (.00)	0 (.00)
5-year-olds	13 (.43)	13 (.48)	0 (.00)	0 (.00)

These results show that the children used collective terms in their explanations only in collective contexts. This result is consistent with the view that at least some of the children may have preferred to use collective terms rather than distributive quantifiers to describe the collective context.

4.5. Summary

We conducted this experiment to determine if children interpret *iedere* and *alle* questions differently across contexts and if children adopt Exhaustive Pairing more often when asked *iedere* questions in collective than in distributive contexts, as predicted by the Distributivity Hypothesis. The results partially support the hypothesis. Of the two age groups tested, only the 4-year-olds showed a sensitivity to question type and adopted Exhaustive Pairing more often when asked *iedere* questions in collective rather than in distributive contexts. Children's explanations for their Exhaustive Pairing responses suggest that although all of the children may have initially conceptualized the action portrayed in the collective contexts as a group action on some occasions, the 4-year-olds were more likely to incorrectly respond *nee* to an *iedere* question in this context than the 5-year-olds. This suggests that the 4-year-olds, in particular, were sensitive to the meaning difference between *iedere* and *alle* (see also Brooks & Braine, 1996), but did not always analyze *iedere* as obligatorily distributive.

5. EXPERIMENT 2

Experiment 2 was designed to investigate whether satisfying Plausible Dissent or making it clear to children that the intended domain of quantification for a quantifier is presupposed is responsible for improving children's performance on Extra Object trials. We compared children's responses to *iedere* questions in distributive and collective contexts using a modified version of the Extra Object conditions. Before giving a child an Extra Object trial like in Figure 1 and (1), the experimenter drew the child's attention to the set of actors they would need to recall on that trial to resolve the domain presupposition for *iedere*. However, only some of the children were given trials that also satisfied Plausible Dissent. Comparing children's responses to *iedere* questions in distributive and collective contexts allowed us to further examine how variation in perceptual and discourse context affects children's interpretation of distributive universal quantification.

5.1. Subjects

The participants were seventy-eight Dutch children consisting of thirty-nine 4-year-olds (mean 4;6, range 4;0-4;11) and thirty-nine 5-year-olds (mean 5;7, range 5;0-5;11) from various preschools in the Nijmegen area. The children in each age group were divided into three subsets of thirteen. Each subset was randomly assigned to one of the three conditions described below.

5.2. Method

Each child was given nineteen sentence judgment trials, consisting of three warm up trials, eight experimental trials and eight filler trials. The warm-ups were identical to the *iedere* warm-up trials of Experiment 1 and were presented first. All children received the same warm-ups. Each experimental trial consisted of a modified Extra Object trial consisting of two parts. The second part consisted of an Extra Object trial in which the child is first presented with a pictured context like those in Figures 2 and 3 and asked what the actors are doing. Then the experimenter asks Cookie Monster, who has been listening in, if he sees what's happening in the picture. Cookie Monster then presents the test sentence to the child. In the first part of each trial, a child was either directed to identify or asked an *iedere* question about a set of actors which the child would need to recall as the intended domain of quantification for *iedere* on the second part. The second part immediately followed the first part.

Three different sets of eight experimental trials were prepared: the 'Show Me Condition', the 'Irrelevant Property Condition', and the 'Relevant Property Condition'. On the first part of each condition, the child's attention is drawn to the intended domain of quantification in some manner. The second part of each condition consisted of an Extra Object trial like (1). Thus, each condition provided contextual support for the presuppositional interpretation of the universal quantifier presented in the second part. Only on the Relevant Property Condition was Plausible Dissent satisfied.

In the first part of the Show Me Condition (see (4)), the experimenter presented a child with a pictured context including the intended domain of quantification, e.g., a group of boys. The experimenter first identified the nature of the context for the child and asked questions about the identity of the individuals in context. After the child successfully answered these questions, she is asked by Cookie Monster to identify the intended domain of quantification, e.g., *Point to the boys*. After the child successfully identified the intended domain of quantification, she is immediately presented with the second part. The problem for the child was to recall the set she just pointed out as the intended domain of quantification and proceed with a presuppositional interpretation of the universally quantified statement:

(4) The Show Me Condition

Figure 4. Context for the Show me Condition (First Part)

Experimenter: Dit lijkt wel een woestijn.('This looks like a desert.')
          Allemaal zand en bergen. ('All sand and mountains')
          En dit zijn jongens? ('And these are boys?')
          Hier zie je ...? (olifanten) ('Here you see...? (elephants)')
Cookie Monster: Wijs de jongens eens aan. ('Point to the boys.')

The Irrelevant Property Condition (see (5)) is identical to the Show Me Condition except that, on the first part, the experimenter introduces the child to the intended domain of quantification by asking her an *iedere* question about that set, e.g., *Heeft iedere jongen schoenen?* 'Does every boy have shoes?'. The property introduced by this question is 'irrelevant' in the sense that it does not introduce a possible outcome to the child. Therefore, this condition, like the Show Me Condition, does not satisfy Plausible Dissent:

(5) The Irrelevant Property Condition

Figure 5. Context for the Irrelevant Property Condition (First Part)

Experimenter: Dit lijkt wel een woestijn.('This looks like a desert.')
Allemaal zand en bergen. ('All sand and mountains')
En dit zijn jongens? ('And these are boys?')
Hier zie je...? (olifanten) ('Here you see ...? (elephants)')
Cookie Monster: Heeft iedere jongen schoenen? ('Does every boy have shoes?')

The Relevant Property Condition in (6) differs from the first two in that the question presented in the first part and second parts of the condition is the same. The first part of this condition explicitly introduces the child both to the intended domain of quantification and to a possible outcome other than the actual outcome described in the *iedere* question presented in the second part. Thus, the Relevant Property Condition satisfies Plausible Dissent and provides contextual support for the presuppositional interpretation of the universal quantifier:

(6) The Relevant Property Condition

Figure 6. Context for the Relevant Property Condition (First Part)

Experimenter: Dit lijkt wel een woestijn. ('This looks like a desert.')
Allemaal zand en bergen. ('All sand and mountains')
En dit zijn jongens? ('And these are boys?')
Hier zie je ...? (olifanten) ('Here you see...? (elephants)')
Cookie Monster: Zit iedere jongen op een olifant? ('Is every boy sitting on an elephant?')

Subjects from each age group were randomly assigned to the three experimental conditions. Each child received four trials with a distributive context and four trials with a collective context.

The pictures in the eight filler trials were identical in design to the Show Me Condition. However, the *iedere* statements were replaced by those with plural definite subjects, e.g., *De jongens rijden op een olifant* 'The boys are riding an elephant'. Filler trials were mixed in with the experimental trials. Fifteen different orders of filler and experimental trials were created and distributed across the seventy-eight subjects.

5.3. Scoring

The children's responses were scored in the same way as in Experiment 1.

5.4. Results

The Plausible Dissent account predicts that children given the Relevant Property Condition (distributive or collective) should respond correctly significantly more often than the children given either the Show Me or Irrelevant Property Conditions, since only the Relevant Property condition satisfies Plausible Dissent. Let us call this Prediction 1. The Presuppositionality account predicts that the children in Experiment 2 should give more correct responses on the distributive trials than the children in Experiment 1 did on the *iedere*-distributive trials, since only the trials of Experiment 2 unambiguously support the presuppositional interpretation of the quantifier. Let us call this Prediction 2. The Distributivity Hypothesis predicts that children should make fewer correct judgments on the collective trials than on the distributive trials, since the collective trials provide no unambiguous contextual support for the distributive interpretation of *iedere*. Let us call this Prediction 3. This hypothesis also predicts that there should be no difference in responses on the *iedere*-collective trials across the two experiments. Let us call this Prediction 4.

How often the children correctly responded to the questions across conditions is given in Table 4. As in Experiment 1, all of the children's denials were analyzed as Exhaustive Pairing responses:

Table 4. Proportion correct responses (standard deviations in parentheses)

Condition		Context	
	Age	Collective	Distributive
Show me	4-year-olds	.29 (.37)	.75 (.31)
	5-year-olds	.37 (.42)	.65 (.47)
Irrelevant property	4-year-olds	.44 (.40)	.65 (.47)
	5-year-olds	.48 (.44)	.77 (.53)
Relevant property	4-year-olds	.63 (.40)	.87 (.19)
	5-year-olds	.56 (.47)	.81 (.33)

Three separate ANOVAs were performed to test the predictions. First, a 3 x 2 x 2 ANOVA using context (distributive, collective) as a within-subjects factor and age (4 years, 5 years) and condition (Show me, Irrelevant Property, Relevant Property) between subjects was performed to test Predictions 1 and 3. A main effect of context was found, $F(2, 76) = 34.66$, $p < .001$. The children responded correctly in distributive contexts significantly more often than in collective contexts, in support of Prediction 3. There was no statistically significant difference in scores across conditions, contra Prediction 1. No other significant main effects or interactions were found.

A 2 x 2 ANOVA using age (4 years, 5 years) and experiment (No contextual support (Experiment 1), contextual support (Experiment 2)) between subjects was performed to test Prediction 2. Because no main effect of condition was revealed by the first ANOVA, and no main effect of version was found in Experiment 1, we compared the responses of all 52 subjects of Experiment 1 with those of all 78 subjects of Experiment 2 in this analysis. Age was included as a factor to determine whether the responses of the 4- and 5-year-olds differed across contexts, as found in Experiment 1. The results revealed a main effect of condition, $F(1,126) = 3.98$, $p < .05$. The children from Experiment 2 responded correctly significantly more often on the *iedere* distributive trials than the children in Experiment 1. This supports Prediction 2.

A second 2 x 2 ANOVA using age (4 years, 5 years) and experiment (No contextual support (Experiment 1), contextual support (Experiment 2)) between subjects was performed to test Prediction 4. This time, the proportion correct response on collective contexts was the dependent variable. No main effect of experiment was found, supporting Prediction 4. No other main effects or interactions were found.

As in Experiment 1, the children's uses of collective terms in their explanations were tabulated to determine if children's relatively lower scores on *iedere*-collective trials when compared to *iedere*-distributive trials could be traced to a dispreference for *iedere* on *iedere*-collective trials across conditions. As we found in Experiment 1, the children in Experiment 2 produced collective terms only in their explanations on *iedere*-collective trials, suggesting that the children may have preferred to use collective terms rather than distributive quantifiers to describe the context on these trials. Table 5 shows the proportional use of collective terms in explanations across collective conditions:

Table 5. Number and proportion of all explanations including collective terms on 'iedere' collective trials

	Condition		
Age	Show Me	Irrelevant Property	Relevant Property
4-year-olds	11 (.30)	6 (.32)	3 (.16)
5-year-olds	16 (.48)	6 (.22)	3 (.13)

The table shows that the children overall used collective terms in their explanations least often on the Relevant Property condition and less often on the Irrelevant Property condition than on the Show Me condition. Moreover, there is a negative correlation between the relative improvement in children's scores (Table 4) and the relative proportion of collective terms in children's explanations across *iedere*-collective conditions. This suggests that the children were less likely to have conceptualized the actors as performing an action as a group on the Irrelevant Property and Relevant Property collective conditions and more likely to have done so on the Show Me collective condition.

One explanation for these observations consistent with the Distributivity Hypothesis is that the Irrelevant and Relevant Property conditions required children to analyze *iedere* questions on both parts of the conditions. Analyzing *iedere* on the first part is likely to have prepared children to analyze the actors as the intended domain of quantification and as a set of independent individuals on the second part, thereby improving their performance and reducing any tendency to analyze the actors as a group. An alternative hypothesis consistent with the Plausible Dissent account is that the children were least likely to construe the actors as a group and more likely to respond correctly on the Relevant Property *iedere*-collective trials because the trials satisfied Plausible Dissent.

A statistical comparison revealed that the children used collective terms significantly more often in their explanations on the Show Me condition than on the Relevant Property Condition, $z = 2.00$, $p < .05$, supporting Plausible Dissent. However, no significant difference was found between the proportional use of collective terms on the Relevant and Irrelevant Property conditions, $z = 1.09$, $p > .05$. This suggests that the presentation of *iedere* on both parts of the Irrelevant Property and Relevant Property Conditions rather than satisfaction of Plausible Dissent was responsible for both the reduced number of collective terms appearing in the children's explanations on these conditions and the observed negative correlation between the proportion of collective terms used and the children's relative performance across conditions.

5.5. Summary

The results from Experiment 2 show that satisfying Plausible Dissent is neither a necessary nor sufficient condition for improving children's performance on Extra Object trials, contra the Plausible Dissent account. However, the results do support the Presuppositionality account. The results show that children's performance significantly improves on Extra Object trials like (1) if the intended domain of quantification for the quantifier is presented as presupposed before the child encounters a universally quantified question, as the account predicts. The results also support the Distributivity Hypothesis. The children's performance did not significantly improve when children are asked to evaluate *iedere* with respect to collective contexts, as the hypothesis predicts.

6. GENERAL DISCUSSION

We would like to discuss two questions in this section. The first question is whether our results actually provide strong evidence against the Plausible Dissent account, as we have claimed. In a recent response to an earlier presentation of our Experiment 2 results, Crain (2000) has argued that our findings support the Plausible Dissent account. We would like to briefly address some of these arguments here. The second question has to do with children's analysis of universal quantification. Our results suggest that a central factor in Exhaustive Pairing is children's evaluation of a universal quantifier in context. But why should children's evaluation of universal quantifiers be subject to contextual manipulations like the ones we have performed in our experiments?

Crain's comments concern our conclusion that satisfying Plausible Dissent is neither a necessary nor a sufficient condition for improving children's performance with Exhaust Pairing. We have argued that satisfying Plausible Dissent cannot be a sufficient condition for improving children's performance on the grounds that children's performance remains poor when Plausible Dissent is satisfied, such as the Relevant Property collective condition. However, Crain argued that the children's performance failed to improve on this condition because it did not satisfy Plausible Dissent. According to Crain, the first part of the condition required children to build a universal wide-scope interpretation for a question like *Is every boy sitting on an elephant?* To satisfy Plausible Dissent, the children mentally constructed a possible outcome that was consistent with the universal wide-scope interpretation. The second part of the condition required children to build an existential wide-scope (collective) interpretation for the same question. For this interpretation to be felicitous, a child must conceive of a possible outcome consistent with the existential wide-scope interpretation. But the possible outcome they mentally constructed on the first part was appropriate only for the universal wide-scope interpretation, not for the existential wide-scope interpretation. This rendered the Relevant Property collective condition infelicitous.

We find this explanation unlikely. We see no reason why a child would necessarily represent a possible outcome constructed on the basis of one presentation of a question as a possible outcome for another. Second, if, as Crain contends, a child is able to mentally construct a possible outcome on the first part of the condition without contextual support — the first part of the *iedere*-collective conditions doesn't satisfy Plausible Dissent — she is also able to mentally construct a possible outcome on the second part without such support, and need not rely on previously constructed possible outcomes to render test questions felicitous.

Crain also argued against our conclusion that satisfying Plausible Dissent was not a necessary condition for improving children's performance. We reported that children's performance did not significantly differ across our distributive context conditions, whether Plausible Dissent was satisfied or not. Crain observed that the Relevant Property distributive condition seemed to do a better job of reducing Exhaustive Pairing than the Show Me- and Irrelevant Property distributive conditions (see Table 4), suggesting that satisfying Plausible Dissent was indeed a factor in the improvement in children's performance on this condition.

We agree with Crain that children's improvement on the Relevant Property distributive condition deserves an explanation. But we also think our conclusions regarding Plausible Dissent remain the appropriate ones. Table 4 also shows that the Relevant Property Collective condition seemed to do a better job of reducing Exhaustive Pairing than the other two collective conditions. Yet, the children's performance on the collective condition remained far poorer than expected given the Plausible Dissent account. If we assume, as Crain does, that the Relevant Property collective condition did not satisfy Plausible Dissent, then satisfying Plausible Dissent could not have been responsible for children's improved performance on the Relevant Property collective condition. But then there is no reason for thinking that it is responsible for the similar improvement in performance on the distributive condition. We maintain that Plausible Dissent was satisfied on all Relevant Property trials, and that satisfying Plausible Dissent has no influence on the frequency of Exhaustive Pairing.

Our results don't permit us to make anything more than an educated guess at why children's performance improved on the Relevant Property conditions. We find it likely that the improvement was due at least in part to the fact that the same question was presented on the first and second parts of the condition. Having just analyzed the question, the children presented with the second part were already familiarized not only with the intended domain of quantification, but also the objects they would need to fix as the extensions of the DPs in the question on the second part. We leave this matter for further research.[4]

The second question we want to address is why children's analysis of universal quantifiers should be influenced by the kinds of contextual manipulations we performed in our experiments. We consider it unlikely that children simply lack the grammatical knowledge necessary for building the appropriate grammatical representations for universal quantification. Children judge universally quantified sentences no differently than adults on numerous experimental conditions other than Extra Object conditions. This suggests that children do, in fact, have the grammatical knowledge necessary for constraining the interpretation of universally quantified sentences. Another problem is that children at least as old as six continue to make the Exhaustive Pairing error at considerable rates (e.g., Freeman & Schreiner, 1988). Children at this age have sophisticated linguistic competence and are unlikely to lack knowledge of quantificational syntax and semantics.

We would like to suggest a second possibility, which is that children have the requisite grammatical knowledge but lack or do not invoke the pragmatic principles adults use to constrain the interpretation of universal quantifiers at the discourse level. A common view is that the interpretation of a quantified sentence like *Every boy is riding an elephant* invokes two kinds of restrictive devices, the standard restriction contributed by the denotation of the common noun *boy*, and a context set or resource domain variable, whose value further restricts the domain of quantification to a set of entities within the NP denotation (Westerståhl, 1985b; von Fintel, 1994). In von Fintel's formulation, each quantificational determiner is indexed in the lexicon with a hidden resource domain variable C whose set value is supplied by context. The resource domain set intersects with the denotation of the quantifier's NP argument to further constrain the interpretation of the quantifier. Applying this view to the standard truth conditions for *Every A is B* gives us (7):

(7) $\text{EVERY}_C (A)(B) \Leftrightarrow (A \cap C) \, B$

Resource domain variables, like free variables more generally, are construed as gaps in semantic representation which are filled at the discourse-pragmatic level to complete the semantic interpretation (establish a proposition) of a sentence. As von Fintel notes, the resource domain variable introduced by *everyone* in the sentence *Everyone is so quiet* is likely to be resolved deictically if the sentence is uttered upon entering a room. But it is likely to be resolved anaphorically if it is introduced by *everyone* in the sentence *When I walked into my class today, everyone was really quiet.* In this case, *everyone* is anaphorically restricted to people in my class.

We assume that resource domain variables associated with distributive universal quantifiers like *every* and *each* are subject to two presuppositions. The first is the familiar domain presupposition. The second is the presupposition that the resource domain for the quantifier is represented as a set of individuated entities. Such a presupposition is also responsible, we assume, for the infelicity created by the use of distributive quantification to talk about collective actions, such as the use of *Every mover is lifting a piano* in a context where the movers are all lifting a single piano.

This view of universal quantifier interpretation makes it possible to explain Exhaustive Pairing without assuming that children lack grammatical knowledge. When children make the Exhaustive Pairing error on the Extra Object trial, they attempt to semantically evaluate universal quantification as presuppositional and distributive without having first represented the intended domain of quantification in their mental discourse model in a way which satisfies the presuppositions conveyed by the quantifier. Whereas speakers normally make the effort to resolve the resource domain variable (e.g., deictically) via presupposition accommodation, the computational cost of performing accommodation is prohibitive for children (Hamburger & Crain, 1982). In some cases, children infer the intended resource domain on the basis of other salient information in context, such as a disparity between agents and objects, as in Figure 1. When this strategy is used, children make the Exhaustive Pairing error. When the intended resource domain is explicitly presented to a child as individuated before the child is asked to judge a universally quantified sentence, the child can easily resolve the presuppositions associated with the resource domain variable and proceed with a presuppositional interpretation of the quantifier. This explains children's improved performance on Crain *et al.*'s Skiers Condition and our finding that children's scores significantly improved on the Distributive Conditions from Experiment 2. Children continue to make the Exhaustive Pairing error on the Collective Conditions from Experiment 2 at relatively high rates because they tend to represent the intended domain of quantification initially as a collection and do not attempt to represent the set again as independent individuals. Instead, they construe the presence of nonparticipating objects in context as a salient clue for how to distribute the actors in the domain of quantification.

Further research is needed to determine the viability of this explanation. However, recent studies of children's sentence comprehension suggest that it may be on the right track. Their findings imply that children have a limited ability or reluctance to revise initial syntactic or referential commitments during on-line sentence comprehension due to limited processing capacity (e.g., Trueswell, Sekerina, Hill & Logrip, 1999; Hurewitz, Brown-Schmidt, Thorpe, Gleitman & Trueswell, 2000; Lidz & Musolino, 2002). For example, Trueswell *et al.*, discovered that 5-year-old children do not make use of the Referential Principle (Crain & Steedman, 1985), a pragmatic principle that guides speakers to choose that interpretation of an ambiguous sentence which violates the fewest presuppositions. Trueswell *et al.*, presented children wearing eye-tracking equipment with a visual array of objects including two frogs, one of which was sitting on a napkin, and instructed the children to *put the frog on the napkin in the box*. They reported that children rarely utilized the modifying phrase *on the napkin* to select the appropriate frog, but instead tended to select the frog they happened to notice first. Furthermore, these children never recovered from their initial misanalysis (see Hurewitz *et al.*, 2000, for similar findings). In a different set of studies, Lidz & Musolino (2002, 143) found that children asked to evaluate scopally ambiguous sentences like *Donald didn't find two guys* often fail to access the inverted scope or non-isomorphic readings, e.g., there are two guys that Donald didn't find, because they "initially access the isomorphic reading and end up being stuck with it for lack of the ability to revise that initial interpretation." We tentatively suggest that children's inability or reluctance to revise initial commitments also applies at the discourse level when they encounter the task of resolving presuppositions. Under this view, children presented with an Extra Object trial like (1) initially construe the actors in context as satisfying the quantifier's nuclear scope. However, they do not always revise this initial commitment and represent the actors again as the intended domain of quantification. The disparity between actors and objects in context becomes relevant information to children because it is presupposed information which can be accessed at little processing cost. Similarly, children presented with our *iedere*-collective condition may have initially construed the actors as a collection and failed to revise this interpretation during the processing of the quantified test question.

7. CONCLUSION

Our goal in conducting the experiments we reported on in this chapter was to come to a better understanding of how differences in perceptual and discourse context affect children's comprehension of universally quantified sentences. The results of our experiments support the view that the primary factor in children's Exhaustive Pairing error is their analysis of universal quantification. We suggest that children turn to Exhaustive Pairing because they do not update or revise their discourse models in contexts which may initially be construed as incompatible with either the presuppositional requirements or distributive meaning conveyed by universal quantifiers like *every*. Many questions still need to be answered before we have a complete picture of why children adopt Exhaustive Pairing. We hope to find answers to these questions in further research.

Århus University
Maastricht University

8. ACKNOWLEDGEMENTS

We would like to thank the teachers and parents at the Sterrendans School in Nijmegen, the Adelbert School in Mook, and the De Raamdonk School in Grave, for their help and permission to conduct experiments. We would especially like to thank the children at these schools for participating in our experiments. Finally, we thank Cornelia Hamann and Irene Krämer for helpful comments and discussion regarding previous drafts of this paper.

9. NOTES

[1] Exhaustive Pairing is one of three similar errors reported in the literature. The 'Underexhaustive Pairing' error (Freeman *et al.*, 1982, Drozd, 2001) occurs when children incorrectly agree that every boy is riding an elephant when one boy is not riding an elephant. The 'Perfectionist' error (Philip,1995) occurs when children deny that every boy is riding an elephant if every boy and a girl are each riding an elephant. We do not discuss these errors in this chapter.
[2] Importantly, Plausible Dissent is fundamentally different from the more well-known notion 'context of plausible denial' (Wason, 1965) and from Freeman *et al.*'s (1982) less well-known 'context of plausible denial effect' (but see Meroni *et al.*, this volume, for an alternative view). Plausible denial specifically concerns the appropriateness of negative utterances and the plausibility or accessibility of their positive counterparts (Horn, 1989, 172). In contrast, Plausible Dissent is a general felicity condition on the presentation of either affirmative or negative sentences. Freeman *et al.*, were specifically concerned with the conventional rules for interpreting universally quantified expressions, not general felicity conditions on the presentation of statements and questions. Freeman *et al.*'s own experiments don't satisfy Plausible Dissent and were never intended to (see Drozd, 2001).
[3] Dutch has three universal quantifiers, *iedere*, *alle*, and *elke*, which are commonly translated by English *every*, *all*, and *each*. Dutch *alle* is typically used where English speakers use either (generic) *all* or *all the*, and the uninflected *al* is used more typically to express the partitive meaning, e.g, *al de meisjes* 'all the girls'. Contrary to English *every*, *iedere* occurs in positions normally reserved for *each* in English, such as floated quantifier position, e.g., *De jongens rijden ieder een olifant* 'The boys are each riding an elephant'. However, *iedere*, like *every*, can occur

in generic constructions, e.g., *Iedere man is sterfelijk* 'Every man is mortal'. It is unknown at present if these differences between *iedere* and *every* play any role in their acquisition. Unfortunately, a more detailed discussion of this interesting issue is beyond the scope of this paper.

4   We would like to take this opportunity to correct a misunderstanding. Crain (2000) and Meroni *et al.* (this volume) claim that we advocate the view that the Exhaustive Pairing response to *Every boy is riding an elephant* is associated with the truth conditions [BOY ∩ IS-RIDING-AN-ELEPHANT] = EVERY (Discourse Topic: [ELEPHANT]). We have never proposed such truth conditions. Furthermore, we find that they are incoherent and certainly do not capture Exhaustive Pairing.

10. REFERENCES

Barwise, John, and Robin Cooper. "Generalized Quantifiers and Natural Language." *Linguistics and Philosophy* 4 (1981): 159–219.
Beghelli, Filippo, and Tim Stowell. "Distributivity and Negation: The Syntax of *Every* and *Each*." In Anna Szabolcsi (ed.) *Ways of Scope Taking*, 71–98. Dordrecht: Kluwer, 1997.
Brooks, Patricia J., and Martin D.S. Braine. "What Do Children Know about the Universal Quantifiers *All* and *Each*?" *Cognition* 60 (1996): 235–268.
Choe, Jae-Woong. *Anti-Quantifiers and a Theory of Distributivity*. Ph.D. Diss., University of Massachusetts, Amherst, 1987.
Crain, Stephen. "Sense and Sense Ability in Child Language." In S. Catherine Howell, Sarah A. Fish, and Thea Keith-Lucas (eds.) *Proceedings of the 24th Conference on Language Development*, 22–44. Somerville, MA: Cascadilla Press, 2000.
Crain, Stephen, and Mark J. Steedman. "On Not Being Led up the Garden Path." In David Dowty, Lauri Karttunen, and Arnold Zwicky (eds.) *Natural Language Parsing: psychological, Computational, and Theoretical Perspectives*, 320–385. Cambridge: Cambridge University Press, 1985.
Crain, Stephen, Rosalind Thornton, Carol Boster, Laura Conway, Diane Lillo-Martin, and Elaine Woodams. "Quantification without Qualification." *Language Acquisition* 5 (1996): 83–153.
Donaldson, Margaret. *Children's Minds*. London: Fontana, 1978.
Drozd, Kenneth F. "Children's Weak Interpretation of Universally Quantified Sentences." In Melissa Bowerman and Stephen Levinson (eds.) *Conceptual Development and Language Acquisition*, 340–376. Cambridge: Cambridge University Press, 2001.
Drozd, Kenneth F., and Erik van Loosbroek. "Weak Quantification, Plausible Dissent, and the Development of Children's Pragmatic Competence." In Annabel Greenhill, Heather Littlefield, and Cheryl Tano (eds.) *Proceedings of the 23rd Annual Boston University Conference on Language Development*, 184–195. Somerville, MA: Cascadilla Press, 1999.
von Fintel, Kai. "Restrictions on Quantifier Domains." Ph.D. Diss., University of Massachusetts, Amherst, 1994.
Freeman, Norbert H., and Schreiner K. "Complementary Error Patterns in Collective and Individuating Judgements: Their Semantic Basis in 6-year-olds." *British Journal of Developmental Psychology* 6 (1988): 341–350.
Freeman, Norman H., Chris G. Sinha, and Jackie A. Stedmon. "All the Cars - which Cars? From Word Meaning to Discourse Analysis." In Michael Beveridge (ed.) *Children Thinking Through Language*, 52–74. London: Edward Arnold, 1982.
Gil, David. "Scopal Quantifiers: Some Universals of Lexical Effability." In Michel Kefer and Johan van der Auwera (eds.) *Meaning and Grammar: Crosslinguistic Perspectives*, 303–346. Mouton: Berlin, 1992.
Hamburger, Henry, and Stephen Crain. "Relative Acquisition." In Stan Kuczaj (ed.) *Language Development: Syntax and Semantics*, 245–274. Hillsdale, NJ: Lawrence Erlbaum, 1982.
Horn, Lawrence. *A Natural History of Negation*. Chicago: Chicago University Press, 1989.

Hurewitz, Felicia, Sarah Brown-Schmidt, Kirsten Thorpe, Lila R. Gleitman, and John C. Trueswell. "One Frog, Two Frog, Red Frog, Blue Frog: Factors Affecting Children's Syntactic Choices in Production and Comprehension." *Journal of Psycholinguistic Research* 29 (2000): 597–626.

Inhelder, Bärbel, and Jean Piaget. *The Early Growth of Logic in the Child*. London: Routledge, Kegan and Paul, 1964.

Kang, Hye-Kyung. "Quantifier Spreading: Linguistic and Pragmatic Considerations." *Lingua* 111 (2001): 591–627.

Lidz, Jeffrey, and Julien Musolino. "Children's Command of Quantification." *Cognition* 84 (2002): 113–154.

Partee, Barbara H. "Quantificational Structures and Compositionality." In Emmon Bach, Eloise Jelinek, Angelika Kratzer, and Barbara H. Partee (eds.) *Quantification in Natural Languages: Volume II*, 541–601. Dordrecht: Kluwer, 1995.

Philip, William. *Event Quantification in the Acquisition of Universal Quantification*. Amherst, MA: GLSA Publications, 1995.

Roeper, Thomas, and Jill de Villiers. "The Emergence of Bound Variable Structures." In Thomas Maxfield and Bernadette Plunkett (eds.) *UMOP Special Edition: Papers in the Acquisition of WH*, 225–265. Amherst, MA: GLSA Publications, 1991.

Strawson, Peter F. *Introduction to Logical Theory*. London: Methuen, 1952.

Szabolcsi, Anna. *Ways of Scope Taking*. Dordrecht: Kluwer, 1997.

Trueswell, John C, Irina Sekerina, Nicole M. Hill, and Marian L. Logrip. "The Kindergarten-Path Effect: Studying On-line Sentence Processing in Young Children." *Cognition* 73 (1999): 89–134.

Vendler, Zeno. *Linguistics in Philosophy*. Ithaca: Cornell University Press, 1967.

Wason, Paul C. "The Contexts of Plausible Denial." *Journal of Verbal Learning and Verbal Behavior* 4 (1965): 7–11.

Westerståhl, Dag. "Logical Constants in Quantifier Languages." *Linguistics and Philosophy* 8 (1985a): 387–413.

Westerståhl, Dag. "Determiners and Context Sets." In Johan van Benthem and Alice ter Meulen (eds.) *Generalized Quantifiers in Natural Language*, 45–72. Dordrecht: Foris, 1985b.

Westerståhl, Dag. "Quantifiers in Formal and Natural Languages." In Dov M. Gabbay and Franz Guenthner (eds.) *Handbook of Philosophic Logic, Volume IV*, 1–131. Dordrecht: Reidel, 1989.

Zwarts, Frans. "Determiners: A Relational Perspective." In Alice ter Meulen (ed.) *Studies in Model-Theoretic Semantics*, 63–84. Dordrecht: Foris, 1983.

JULIEN MUSOLINO

STRUCTURE AND MEANING IN THE ACQUISITION OF SCOPE

Abstract. This chapter presents results from a series of interconnected experiments designed to investigate the development of quantificational competence. Focusing on the case of scope relations between multiple quantificational elements, I present a new account of a systematic and pervasive non-adult pattern previously believed to reflect a grammatical difference between preschoolers and adults (e.g., Musolino, 1998; Musolino, Crain & Thornton, 2000).

1. INTRODUCTION

In this chapter, I examine the development of a fundamental aspect of our linguistic capacity — our ability to use the words of our language, not simply to refer to the individuals and objects that surround us, but, more interestingly, to express abstract generalizations about *quantities* of individuals or objects. In English, for example, I can say of a particular dog, Fido, that it has four legs, that it is black and that it does not meow. I can also say, without referring to any particular dog, that every dog has four legs, that some dogs are black or that no dog meows. Linguistic expressions such as *every dog*, *some dogs* or *no dog* belong to the class of *quantified* expressions or *quantifiers*. An important property of quantificational determiners such as *every*, *some* and *none*, for example, is that they express abstract relations among *sets* of individuals. Accordingly, *Every dog has four legs* expresses the idea that the set of dogs is properly contained within the set of four-legged individuals. *Some dogs are black* states that there is only partial overlap between the set of dogs and the set of black things and, finally, *No dog meows* indicates that there is no overlap between the set of dogs and the set of meowers. Because of the abstract nature of their meaning and the rich set of inferences to which they give rise, natural language quantifiers have been of central concern to logicians, philosophers and linguists, and their analysis has played an important role in the investigation of the principles underlying natural language semantics (Barwise & Cooper, 1981; Keenan & Stavi, 1986; van Benthem, 1986).

In addition to puzzling logicians and students of language, quantified expressions also raise serious psychological issues, in particular in the domain of conceptual development and language acquisition. Consider for example the problem of a child trying to determine the meanings of words. First, children must realize that quantificational determiners, unlike most of the other words of their language, do not refer to individuals or objects, such as cats and chairs for example, or even to properties of individuals like fluffy or tall. Rather, they express abstract relations among *sets* of individuals. This, in turn, creates an interesting problem since, as Bloom (2000, 213) remarks:

> Sets are notoriously abstract entities. One can see and hear cats, but nobody has ever been wakened in the middle of the night by the yowling of a set. The apprehension of sets might therefore require some cognitive capacity above and beyond the normal apprehension of entities in the world ...

To complicate matters further, since the conceptual generalizations underlying the meaning of quantified expressions are abstract, the learner's ability to map these concepts onto phonological form depends on cognitive development having reached the point at which such concepts can be mastered and put to use (Carey, 2001).

What is particularly interesting about the development of quantificational competence is that children's adult-like comprehension of quantified expressions lags far behind their early spontaneous use of such expressions. As the examples below illustrate, the use of quantified expressions occurs early in the speech of children:

(1)　*Two knife* out the box　　　　　　　　　　(Eve, 1;11)
(2)　Because there *no pictures*　　　　　　　　(Eve, 2;01)
(3)　Then Eve have *some milk*　　　　　　　　(Eve, 1;11)
(4)　I drink *all grape juice*　　　　　　　　　　(Eve, 1;10)
　　　　　　(Eve, Brown Corpus, CHILDES database)

In spite of these precocious first steps however, children's comprehension of quantified expressions does not reach a fully mature level until a much later point in development. Consider for example the case of universally quantified expressions (i.e., *every boy, all the girls*). It is a well-known fact in the developmental literature that children often give strikingly non-adult responses to statements or questions containing such expressions (see Drozd & van Loosbroek, this volume; Meroni *et al.*, this volume). A classic illustration of this phenomenon comes from children's behavior on a typical class-inclusion task (Inhelder & Piaget, 1958, 1964). In this task, subjects are asked of an array composed of blue squares and blue circles whether all the circles are blue. While adults answer affirmatively (all the circles are indeed blue!), children as old as 7 or 8 often answer negatively and, when asked to justify their answers, they point to the fact that there are also blue squares in the array. This kind of observation, initially due to Piaget, has since been reported, under various labels, by a large number of investigators and has been attested in a variety of languages (see Philip, 1995; Drozd & van Loosbroek, this volume, for reviews).

Why then do quantified expressions take children so long to master, in spite of the fact that they appear so early in their production? Answers to this question depend on whether children's difficulty with quantified expressions is viewed as reflecting a problem at the *conceptual* or the *linguistic* level. Proponents of the conceptual view include Piaget and his collaborators for whom children's difficulty with the universal quantifier stems from a lack of ability to distinguish part-whole relationships. More recently, a number of investigators have proposed that children's difficulties with quantifiers stem from their immature linguistic representations. For example, Bucci (1978) proposes that children and adults often parse statements such as *All the circles are blue* as simple strings of words lacking any syntactic structure, i.e., *all, circles, blue* and that the universal quantifier, *all*, is free to apply to either or both of the remaining terms in the array. According to Roeper & de Villiers (1993) children fail to represent the syntactic connection between the quantificational determiner and the noun with which it combines. On this account, children treat the universal quantifier as an adverb of quantification like *always*, which allows them to quantify either the subject or the object NP. Philip (1995) offers a semantic explanation, arguing that children's non-adult interpretation of sentences containing the universal quantifier corresponds to a linguistic representation in which the child overgeneralizes a tendency to quantify over individual events rather than individual objects. Drozd & van Loosbroek (this volume) propose that children initially analyze the universal quantifier as a weak quantifier like *some* or *many*, and that this misanalysis gives rise to children's non-adult interpretations of sentences containing *all* or *every*. Finally, the positions described above have been challenged by Crain *et al.* (1996), Crain (2000) and Meroni *et al.* (this volume) who argue that children have full adult linguistic competence in the domain of universal quantification. According to Crain *et al.*, earlier observations of children's non-adult behavior in tasks involving the comprehension of universally quantified propositions are pragmatic in nature; they are due to violations of the felicity conditions associated with the use of such expressions (for a similar view, see Freeman *et al.*, 1982).

One of the hallmarks of the literature on the development of quantificational competence, reflected in the positions described above, is the remarkable lack of consensus regarding the exact nature of children's difficulty with quantified expressions. Another concern regarding previous developmental work is that, as noted by Brooks & Braine (1996), the vast majority of studies on children's comprehension of quantified expressions have focused almost exclusively on children's comprehension of the universal quantifier. However, the set of natural language quantifiers is not limited to elements such as *all* and *every*. In order to gain a broader understanding of the development of children's quantificational competence, it is therefore necessary to look beyond children's comprehension of the universal quantifier.

This is what I propose to do in this chapter. First, in response to the selective focus of previous studies, I present here a systematic investigation of a set of phenomena involving the interaction of multiple quantificational elements. In addition to producing a broader picture of development, this study also aims at addressing the more challenging issue of trying to tease apart the contribution of the various factors that have been claimed to affect children's performance on tasks involving the comprehension of quantified expressions. On a more general level, and in keeping with the theme of the present volume, my goal in this chapter is to show how insights from linguistic theory — in particular from syntactic and semantic theory — can lead to the formulation of precise and interesting developmental questions and how such questions can be addressed empirically using the tools of experimental psychology. By doing so, my hope is to show how acquisition and semantics can be brought together in a fruitful interdisciplinary marriage.

The discussion is organized as follows. Section 2 lays out the theoretical and methodological foundations of this study. Section 3 presents the core developmental phenomenon discussed throughout the study, namely the fact that preschoolers, unlike adults, systematically interpret sentences containing negation and quantified NPs on the basis of the position that these elements occupy in surface syntax. I call this phenomenon 'isomorphism'. The remaining four sections are devoted to an account of the phenomenon. Section 4 presents evidence that isomorphism reflects a problem at the linguistic rather than at the conceptual level. In section 5, I show that isomorphism is a pervasive phenomenon in the sense that it manifests itself across a range of quantificational expressions and that it can also be observed in the acquisition of languages other than English. Drawing on evidence from Kannada (Dravidian), section 5 also demonstrates that isomorphism stems from an over-reliance on the surface c-command relations between quantified NPs and negation. In section 6, I present the grammatical account of isomorphism originally proposed by Musolino (1998). I then show, on the basis of new evidence, that this earlier account must be abandoned and that isomorphism does not reflect a grammatical difference between children and adults. In section 7, I sketch an account of the developmental transition leading the isomorphic child to the adult system and I show that an important ingredient of this account lies in the realization that in spite of its apparent descriptive uniformity, isomorphism may be not a homogenous phenomenon after all.

2. THEORETICAL AND METHODOLOGICAL BACKGROUND

To preface the set of experiments presented here, I begin by introducing the phenomenon whose study constitutes the backbone of this chapter. To further set the stage for our discussion, this section also provides a description of the essential aspects of the experimental methodology used throughout this study.

A well-known and important property of quantificational expressions is their ability to interact with one another to create scope ambiguity (Horn, 1989; Jackendoff, 1972; Lasnik, 1972; May, 1977). Consider for example the sentence in (5):

(5) Every student can't afford a new car.
    a. $\forall x$ [student (x) → ¬ can afford a new car (x)]
    b. $\neg\forall x$ [student (x) → can afford a new car (x)]

On one reading, (5) can be paraphrased as *Every student is such that s/he cannot afford a new car*. In this case, the universally quantified subject is interpreted outside the scope of negation (abbreviated *every > not*), as indicated by the logical representation in (5a). I call this an *isomorphic* interpretation since in this case, the scope relation between *every student* and negation can be directly read off their surface position. On another reading, (5) can be paraphrased as *Not every student can afford a new car*. Here, *every student* is interpreted within the scope of negation (abbreviated *not > every*), as shown in (5b). I call this a *non-isomorphic* interpretation since in this case, the surface position of *every student* and negation does not coincide with their semantic interpretation.

The example in (6) illustrates the fact that the availability of non-isomorphic interpretations depends in part on the lexical nature of the quantificational element involved. That is, replace *every student* in (5) by *some students*, as in (6), and the sentence is no longer perceived to be ambiguous. The most natural interpretation of (6) is an isomorphic one on which the sentence can be paraphrased as *There are some students who cannot afford a new car*:

(6) Some students can't afford a new car.
    $\exists x$ [students(x) ∧ ¬ can afford a new car (x)]

Another factor determining the availability of non-isomorphic interpretations is the syntactic position of the quantified expression. This can be seen by comparing (5), which finds the universally quantified NP in subject position and is perceived to be ambiguous, and (7), which finds the universally quantified NP in object position and is not perceived to be ambiguous. Indeed, the most natural interpretation of (7) is one on which the professor talked to some of the students but not to others. In other words, *every student* is interpreted within the scope of negation, an isomorphic interpretation:

(7) The professor didn't talk to every student.
$\neg \forall x$ [student (x) $\rightarrow$ talked to (professor, x)]

As in the case of quantified subjects, the lexical nature of a quantified object also affects its scopal properties with respect to negation. If *every student* in (7) is replaced by *some students*, as in (8), the most natural interpretation becomes a non-isomorphic one on which (8) can be paraphrased as *There are some students to whom the professor didn't talk* (abbreviated *some > not*). Replacing *some students* by *any students*, as in (9), now forces an isomorphic interpretation. In this case, *any students* must be interpreted in the scope of negation:

(8) The professor didn't talk to some students.
$\exists x$ [students (x) $\wedge \neg$ talked to (professor, x)]

(9) The professor didn't talk to any students.
$\neg \exists x$ [students (x) $\wedge$ talked to (professor, x)]

Finally, a numerally quantified object, like *two students*, gives rise to scopal ambiguity and hence to both an isomorphic and a non-isomorphic interpretation, as shown in the example below. The example in (10) can be paraphrased as meaning that it is not the case that the professor talked to two students. In this case, *two students* receives a narrow scope interpretation with respect to negation (abbreviated *not > two*) which corresponds to an isomorphic interpretation. Alternatively, (10) can be paraphrased as meaning that there are two particular students to whom the professor didn't talk. Here, *two students* receives a wide scope interpretation with respect to negation (abbreviated *two > not*), which corresponds to a non-isomorphic interpretation:

(10) The professor didn't talk to two students.
    a. $\neg \exists_2 x$ [students (x) $\wedge$ talked to (professor, x)]
    b. $\exists_2 x$ [students (x) $\wedge \neg$ talked to (professor, x)]

In sum, quantified expressions interact with other logical operators such as negation. These interactions result in complex interpretive patterns determined in part by the nature of the quantificational expressions involved and their syntactic position.

In order to investigate children's (and adults') interpretation of sentences containing negation and quantified NPs, the studies presented in this chapter are based an experimental technique known as the Truth Value Judgment task (TVJT), (Crain & Thornton, 1998). The TVJT is a technique that was specifically developed to investigate the meaning that children assign to the sentences of their language. The TVJT typically involves two experimenters. The first experimenter acts out short stories in front of the subjects using small toys and props. The second experimenter plays the role of a puppet who watches the stories alongside the subjects. At the end of the story, the puppet makes a statement about what he thinks happened in the story. The subjects' role is to determine whether the puppet's statement is *right*, or whether the puppet was *wrong*. Finally, the subjects are asked to justify their answers by explaining why they think that the puppet was right or wrong.[1]

3. CHILDREN'S ISOMORPHIC INTERPRETATIONS OF SCOPE RELATIONS

In order to determine whether preschoolers are aware of the complex mappings between form and meaning involved in sentences containing quantified expressions and negation, Musolino *et al.* (2000) (based on Musolino, 1998) tested children's comprehension of sentences like (11) and (12) using the TVJT methodology:

(11) Every horse didn't jump over the fence.
    a. $\forall x \, [\text{horse}(x) \rightarrow \neg \text{jump over the fence}(x)]$
    b. $\neg \forall x \, [\text{horse}(x) \rightarrow \text{jump over the fence}(x)]$

(12) The detective didn't find someone.
    $\exists x \, [\text{person}(x) \land \neg \text{find}(\text{detective}, x)]$

One of the stories used to test subjects' comprehension of sentences like (11) involved three horses trying to jump over a fence. Two of the horses jumped over the fence but the third one didn't. At the end of the story, a puppet described the situation as follows: *Every horse didn't jump over the fence.* Notice that this statement is true on the non-isomorphic (i.e., *not all*) interpretation since it is true that not all of the horses jumped over the fence. However, the puppet's statement is false on the 'none', isomorphic, interpretation since two horses did jump over the fence. A *yes* response to the puppet's statement that every horse didn't jump over the fence (along with appropriate justification) would therefore indicate that subjects are accessing the *not all*, non-isomorphic interpretation while a *no* response (along with appropriate justification) would indicate that they are accessing the 'none', isomorphic interpretation.

Musolino *et al.*, tested a group of 20 English-speaking children between the ages of 4;0 and 7;3 (mean 5;11) and a control group of adults on their interpretation of sentences like (7). What they found is that while adults always accepted the puppet's statement (i.e., 100% of the time), showing that they could easily assign these sentences a non-isomorphic interpretation, children almost never accepted the puppet's statements (i.e., 7.5 % of the time). On average then, children rejected the puppet's statements 92.5% of the time. When asked to justify their answers, children typically said that the puppet was wrong because two of the horses did jump over the fence. Children, therefore, unlike adults, systematically accessed the isomorphic interpretation of sentences like (7).

Turning to sentences like (8), one of the stories involved a detective playing hide-and-seek with two of his friends. As the story unfolds, the detective finds one of his friends but fails to find the other. At the end of the story, the puppet described the situation as follows: *The detective didn't find someone*. Notice that this statement is true on a non-isomorphic interpretation since there is indeed someone that the detective didn't find. However, the puppet's statement is false on an isomorphic interpretation since it is not the case that the detective didn't find anyone. Therefore, a *yes* response to the puppet statement that the detective didn't find someone (along with appropriate justification) would indicate that subjects access a non-isomorphic interpretation while a *no* response (along with appropriate justification) is indicative of an isomorphic interpretation.

The subjects were 30 English-speaking children divided into two groups: Children in group 1 (n = 15) ranged in age between 3;10 and 5;2 (mean 4;7) and children in group 2 (n = 15) were between the ages of 5;2 to 6;6 (mean 5;7). The experiment also involved a control group of adults. What was found is that while adult subjects always accepted statements like (8) (i.e., 100% of the time), showing that they were systematically assigning such sentences a non-isomorphic interpretation, children accepted the puppet's statements significantly less often (i.e., 65% of the time for children in group 2 and 35% of the time for children in group 1). Children, therefore, often rejected the puppet's statements. When asked to justify their negative answers, children typically explained that the puppet was wrong because the detective had indeed found someone. Thus, children, unlike adults, often assigned statements like (12) an isomorphic interpretation.

Children's interpretations of sentences like (11) and (12) led Musolino *et al.*, to propose "The Observation of Isomorphism" as a descriptive generalization. This observation states that children, unlike adults, have a tendency to interpret negation and quantified NPs on the basis of their surface syntactic position (see Table 1):

Table 1. The observation of isomorphism

SENTENCE TYPE	CHILDREN	ADULTS
Every horse did<u>n't</u> jump over the fence.	$\forall \neg$	$\neg \forall$
The detective did<u>n't</u> find <u>someone</u>.	$\neg \exists$	$\exists \neg$

The Observation of Isomorphism and, more generally, the existence of any systematic difference in the linguistic behavior of children and adults raises two important questions. First, one needs to determine what causes children to differ from adults. This is what I call the *causal* question. The second question is to explain how children eventually manage to converge on the adult system in the course of language development. I call this question the *developmental* question. As mentioned earlier, the origin of children's difficulty with quantified expressions has traditionally been viewed as falling on either side of the divide between linguistic and conceptual knowledge. Consequently, our first task in addressing the causal question is to determine whether the Observation of Isomorphism reflects a problem at the conceptual or at the linguistic level.

To the extent that the Observation of Isomorphism reflects a linguistic problem, rather than a conceptual one, a number of additional, more specific questions need to be considered. The first one involves the traditional Chomskyan distinction between linguistic competence and linguistic performance (Chomsky, 1965). In the case at hand, this question asks whether children's isomorphic interpretations reflect a stage in linguistic development during which children do not have implicit knowledge of non-isomorphic interpretations (a competence account). Alternatively, the Observation of Isomorphism may be due to limitations in the computational resources that children deploy during language comprehension (a performance account). This is what I call the *competence* question.

A second, important question concerns the scope of the phenomenon observed by Musolino *et al.*, and, in particular, the extent to which the 'isomorphism' effect is bound to the lexical properties of the quantified NPs investigated by these authors, i.e., *some N* and *every N*. Following Lidz & Musolino (2002), I call this the *lexical* question.

Another question raised by Musolino *et al.*'s findings is whether Isomorphism obtains as a consequence of the linear arrangement of the quantificational elements involved or whether children's interpretations are constrained by the surface c-command relations holding between these elements. This is what Lidz & Musolino (2002) call the *structural* question. This question arises because linear and hierarchical (i.e. c-command) relations are systematically confounded in the examples used by Musolino *et al.*

A fourth question, also related to the scope of the phenomenon observed by Musolino *et al.*, is whether the isomorphism effect can be observed in the acquisition of languages other than English, provided of course that such languages manifest the same kind of scope phenomena as English does with respect to negation and quantified NPs. Following Lidz & Musolino (2002), I call this the *cross-linguistic* question. In the discussion that follows, I present a series of experiments designed to refine our understanding of children's developing quantificational competence by addressing the questions raised above.

4. ISOMORPHISM AND THE DISTINCTION BETWEEN CONCEPTUAL AND LINGUISTIC KNOWLEDGE

I begin here by addressing a crucial aspect of what I called the causal question, namely the issue of whether the Observation of Isomorphism reflects a problem at the conceptual or at the linguistic level. Recall that children typically assigned sentences like *Every horse didn't jump over the fence* and *The detective didn't find someone*, a *none* interpretation, i.e., none of the horses jumped over the fence and the detective found no-one, instead of a 'not all' and a 'some not' interpretation, i.e., *not all the horses jumped over the fence* and *there is someone who was not found by the detective*. This finding raises the possibility that children experience difficulty with the abstract conceptual relations underlying the 'not all' and the 'some not' interpretations. Alternatively, children may possess the conceptual wherewithal to apprehend such relations, but they may not yet know that sentences like *Every horse didn't jump over the fence* and *The detective didn't find someone* can be assigned a 'not all' and a 'some not' interpretation because such (non-isomorphic) interpretations involve a mismatch between surface form and semantic interpretation.

In order to tease these two possibilities apart, Musolino (1998) conducted two experiments designed to test children's interpretations of sentences like (13) and (14) below:

(13) The Smurf didn't buy every orange.
 $\neg \forall x \, [\text{orange}(x) \rightarrow \text{buy}(\text{Smurf}, x)]$

(14) Some girls didn't ride on the merry-go-round.
 $\exists x \, [\text{girls}(x) \wedge \neg \, \text{ride}(x, \text{the merry-go-round})]$

Notice that in both cases, the *not all* and the *some not* interpretations correspond to isomorphic interpretations. If children's difficulty with sentences like (11) and (12) is conceptual in nature, then changing the position of the quantified expressions, as in (13) and (14), should have no effect. That is, children should interpret these sentences to mean that the Smurf bought none of the oranges and that none of the girls rode on the merry-go-round. On the other hand, if children's difficulty has to do with the fact that the *not all* and the *some not* interpretations of (11) and (12) correspond to non-isomorphic interpretations, they may find it easier to assign such interpretations to (13) and (14) because in this case, these interpretations correspond to isomorphic ones.

One of the stories used to test subjects' interpretation of sentences like (13) involved a Smurf who went to the grocery store to buy some fruit. The Smurf considered buying apples and oranges and ended up buying one of three oranges. At the end of the story, the puppet described the situation as follows: *The Smurf didn't buy every orange*. Notice that this statement is true on an isomorphic (i.e., *not all*) interpretation, since the Smurf didn't buy all the oranges. However, the statement is false on a non-isomorphic (i.e., *none*) interpretation since it is not true that the Smurf bought none of the oranges. Therefore, a *yes* response to the puppet's statement that the Smurf didn't buy every orange would indicate that subjects interpret *every orange* in the scope of negation and therefore assign the sentence a *not all*, isomorphic interpretation. A *no* answer, on the other hand, (along with appropriate justification) would indicate that subjects assign the sentence a *none* interpretation.

What Musolino (1998) found in the case of sentences like (13) is that a group of 20 English-speaking children ranging in age between 3;11 and 6;0 (mean 4;10) overwhelmingly accepted the puppet's statements, i.e., 85% of the time, and therefore systematically assigned sentences like *The Smurf didn't buy every orange* a 'not all' interpretation. Moreover, when asked to justify their answers, children pointed to the fact that the Smurf had only bought one of the three oranges. Recall that when the universally quantified NP occurs in subject position, as in sentences like *Every horse didn't jump over the fence,* children almost never assigned a 'not all' interpretation, i.e. only 7.5% of the time.

Turning to sentences like (14), one of the stories involved three girls and a merry-go-round. As the story unfolds, each of the girls considers riding on the merry-go-round but only one of them ends up doing so. At the end of the story, the puppet describes the situation as follows: 'Some girls didn't ride on the merry-go-round'.[2] In this case, the puppet's statement is true on an isomorphic interpretation (i.e., *some* > *not*) since there are indeed some girls who didn't ride on the merry-go-round. On the other hand, a 'none', non-isomorphic interpretation falsifies the puppet's statement, since one of the girls did ride on the merry-go-round. While 4 and 5-year-old children only accessed the *some* > *not* interpretation of sentences like *The detective didn't find someone* 35% and 65% of the time respectively, a group of 20 English speaking children ranging between the ages of 4;0 and 6;2 (mean 4;10) assigned sentences like *Some girls didn't ride on the merry-go-round* a *some* > *not* interpretation 100% of the time. Children's interpretation of sentences like (13) and (14), compared to their interpretation of (11) and (12), clearly demonstrates that they can entertain the conceptual relations underlying interpretations like 'not all' and *some not*. These results therefore provide solid evidence that isomorphism reflects a linguistic rather than a conceptual problem.

5. THE SCOPE OF ISOMORPHISM AND ITS STRUCTUAL UNDERPINNING

Having determined that isomorphism reflects a linguistic problem, I now ask whether the phenomenon is bound to the lexical properties of the quantified NPs examined by Musolino *et al.* (the lexical question); whether children's overly isomorphic interpretations reflect the linear arrangement between the different quantificational elements or the c-command relations between them (the structural question) and, finally, whether isomorphism is a phenomenon restricted to the acquisition of English (the cross-linguistic question). I now turn to a study by Lidz & Musolino (2002) designed to address these questions.

5.1. The Lexical Question

In order to address the lexical question, Lidz & Musolino (2002), following Musolino (1998), tested children's (and adults') interpretation of sentences like (15). As discussed earlier, examples like (15) are ambiguous between an isomorphic interpretation, as shown in (15a), and a non-isomorphic interpretation, as shown in (15b). The question of interest here is whether the Observation of Isomorphism extends to children's interpretation of sentences like (15):

(15) Cookie Monster didn't eat two slices of pizza.
    a. $\neg \exists_2 x$ [slices of pizza (x) $\wedge$ eat (Cookie Monster, x)]
    b. $\exists_2 x$ [slices of pizza (x) $\wedge \neg$ eat (Cookie Monster, x)]

The experiment conducted by Lidz & Musolino had two conditions. In the first condition, called the isomorphic condition, sentences like (15) were true on the isomorphic interpretation but they were false on the non-isomorphic interpretation. One of the stories used in this condition involved Cookie Monster and two slices of pizza. As the story unfolds, Cookie Monster eats one of the slices but not the other. At the end of the story, the puppet describes the situation by stating that Cookie Monster didn't eat two slices of pizza. In this case, the puppet's statement is true on the isomorphic interpretation since Cookie Monster ate only one slice of pizza (and not two) and it is false on the non-isomorphic interpretation since it not the case that there are two slices of pizza that Cookie Monster didn't eat (there is in fact only one such slice).

In the second condition, called the non-isomorphic condition, sentences like (15) were true on the non-isomorphic interpretation but they were false on the isomorphic interpretation. One of the stories used in this condition involves a situation in which Cookie Monster tries to eat four slices of pizza but only manages to eat two. As before, the puppet described the situation by stating that Cookie Monster didn't eat two slices of pizza. In this case, the non-isomorphic interpretation is true since there are indeed two slices of pizza that Cookie Monster didn't eat; but the isomorphic interpretation, which states that it is not the case that Cookie Monster ate two slices of pizza, is false since he ate exactly two slices.

The situation described above gave rise to a 2 by 2 design in which the factors were age (4-year-olds vs. adults) and scope condition (isomorphic vs. non-isomorphic). The subjects were 24 English-speaking children between the ages of 3;11 and 4;11 (mean 4;4) and 24 adult native speakers of English. Scope condition was treated as a between-subject factor. In other words, the children and the adults were divided into two groups and randomly assigned to each scope condition.

Turning to the results, Lidz & Musolino found that adult subjects overwhelmingly accepted the puppet statements, i.e., sentences like (15) in both the isomorphic and the non-isomorphic condition, and displayed no significant preference for one scope interpretation over the other (i.e., 97% acceptance rate in the isomorphic condition and 93% acceptance rate in the non-isomorphic condition). 4-year-olds, on the other hand, displayed a significant preference for the isomorphic interpretation of sentences like (15) (i.e., 81% acceptance rate in the isomorphic condition vs. 33% acceptance rate in the non-isomorphic condition). When asked to justify their answers, children who rejected the puppet's statements in the non-isomorphic condition typically explained that the puppet was wrong because Cookie Monster had indeed eaten two slices of pizza. By contrast, in the isomorphic condition, children almost always said that the puppet was right and they justified their answers by explaining that Cookie Monster had eaten only one slice of pizza.

These results extend Musolino *et al.*'s Observation of Isomorphism to the case of numerally quantified objects, thereby addressing the lexical question (for a more detailed discussion and further implications, see Lidz & Musolino, 2002).

5.2. The Structural and the Cross-Linguistic Question

In order to address the structural and the cross-linguistic question, Lidz & Musolino went to India to test child and adult native speakers of Kannada.[3] Kannada is a Dravidian language spoken by approximately 40 million people in the state of Karnataka in south-western India. The canonical word order in Kannada is Subject-Object-Verb (SOV) and Kannada displays the same kind of scope ambiguities as English with respect to negation and quantified NPs (Lidz, 1999).

The crucial difference between Kannada and English for our purposes is that in Kannada, linear order and c-command relations are not confounded. Consider the tree diagrams given in (16). In English, negation both precedes and c-commands the object position, as discussed earlier. In Kannada, however, negation c-commands the object but does not precede it. This means that in Kannada, a c-command account of isomorphism would predict a preference for the narrow scope reading of the object with respect to negation whereas a linear (i.e., precedence) account of isomorphism would predict a preference for the wide scope reading of the object:

(16)

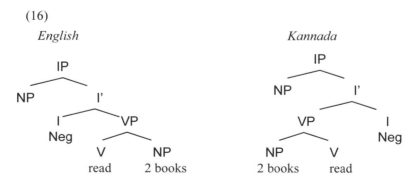

24 Kannada-speaking 4-year-olds between the ages of 4;0 and 4;11 (mean 4;5) along with 24 adult native speakers of Kannada were tested using the paradigm described above for English. Apart from the fact that the language used was now Kannada, the design of the two experiments was identical.

What Lidz & Musolino found is that Kannada speaking adults, like their English-speaking counterparts, displayed no significant preference for either scope interpretation (i.e., 87.5% acceptance rate for the wide scope reading of the object vs. 85.4% for the narrow scope reading). By contrast, Kannada-speaking 4-year-olds, like their English-speaking counterparts, displayed a significant preference for one of the two interpretations. Crucially, this preference was for the narrow scope reading of the object with respect to negation (i.e., 75% acceptance rate for the narrow scope reading of the object vs. 22.9% for the wide scope reading).

These results provide a clear answer to both the cross-linguistic and the structural question. First, the Observation of Isomorphism is not limited to the acquisition of English. Second, isomorphism does not follow from a one-to-one mapping between linear order and semantic scope but rather, from a one-to-one mapping between surface c-command relations and semantic scope. For further evidence that this preference is based on c-command relations and not linear order (i.e., either precedence or subsequence) or other factors, I refer to Lidz & Musolino (2003).

6. ISOMORPHISM AND THE COMPETENCE-PERFORMANCE DISTINCTION

In this section, I consider what I called the competence question, i.e. whether isomorphism reflects a grammatical difference between children and adults. I first present the grammatical account proposed by Musolino (1998), and adopted by Musolino et al. (2000). I then discuss more recent experimental evidence (Musolino, 2000; Musolino & Lidz, 2003), and I explain why these new results have led me to abandon the grammatical account I proposed in 1998.

6.1. Musolino's (1998) Grammatical Account

In their discussion of the competence-performance distinction, Musolino et al. (2000, 20), following Musolino (1998), argue that:

> The available evidence favors the grammatical hypothesis ... We argue, moreover, that isomorphism can be derived from the interaction of a learning principle, the subset principle, along with fundamental properties of UG ...

To see this, let us first consider sentences like *Every horse didn't jump over the fence*. Musolino et al., observe that while such sentences are ambiguous between an isomorphic (i.e., *none*) and a non-isomorphic (i.e., *not all*) interpretation in languages like English, they only permit an isomorphic (i.e., *none*) interpretation in languages like Chinese. Languages like Chinese therefore allow only a subset of the set of interpretations available in languages like English (i.e., *none* vs. *none* and *not all*, respectively). Following the logic of the subset principle, Berwick (1985), Musolino et al., argue that English-speaking children go through a 'Chinese-speaking' stage during which their grammar generates only the *none* interpretation of sentences like *Every horse didn't jump over the fence*.

Following the same logic, Musolino *and al.* argue that the subset principle can also be used to explain children's isomorphic interpretations of sentences like *The detective didn't find someone*. The authors' approach is based on a distinction, originally due to Hornstein (1984), between two kinds of quantified NPs (QNPs). According to Hornstein, some QNPs are assigned scope via a movement-based mechanism, i.e., type 1 QNPs (see Hornstein, 1995, for a specific proposal). In addition to the movement-based mechanism, other QNPs can also be assigned scope via a mechanism that does not involvement syntactic movement, i.e., type 2 QNPs (see Reinhart, 1997, for a specific proposal in terms of choice functions). Moreover, QNPs can only receive non-isomorphic interpretations with respect to negation when they are assigned scope via the non-movement mechanism. In other words, when the scope of a QNP is derived via (covert) syntactic movement, the resulting interpretation is always an isomorphic one. Thus, the options available to type 1 QNPs (i.e., taking scope via a movement-based mechanism) are a subset of those available to type 2 QNPs (taking scope via a movement-based and a non-movement-based mechanism). The logic of the subset principle therefore dictates that children initially hypothesize that QNPs are of type 1, and hence that they must be interpreted isomorphically with respect to negation.

6.2. Evidence against a Grammatical Account of Isomorphism

An alternative scenario, considered by Musolino et al., but then quickly rejected, would be that children and adults have similar grammars but that they display different preferences regarding the interpretation of sentences containing negation and quantified NPs, i.e., a performance account. It is interesting to observe in this respect that negative statements have been argued to be easier to process when certain felicity conditions are met[4] (Wason, 1965; Horn, 1989). Horn (1989, 172), citing Wason and others summarizes this idea as follows:

Very simply, the function of negative sentences is 'generally to emphasize that a fact is contrary to an expectation' (1965, 7). Negative statements by their nature 'assume and depend on a prior state of affairs, either existent or supposed. It is unlikely that the sentence "It is not x" would be uttered unless there were good reason to suppose that it might have been "x" or that someone thought that it might' (Cornish and Wason, 1970, 113). Thus, *5 is not even* is harder to process and takes longer to verify than *5 is odd*, but the difficulty is mitigated if we set up a 'context of denial': 4 is even {and / but} 5 is not even (cf. Greene 1970a, 18; Wason 1972, 28). Psychologically, if not ontologically, negation seems to require – or at least to strongly prefer – an affirmative context against which to operate.

This observation provides an interesting test for the grammatical account of isomorphism. To the extent that children's apparent inability to access non-isomorphic interpretations reflects a grammatical difference between children and adults, presenting children with sentences like *Every horse didn't jump over the fence* or *The detective didn't find someone* in a context which satisfies the felicity conditions described above should yield no significant improvement in performance. Conversely, if performance improves in such contexts, we would then have evidence against a competence explanation and in favor of a performance account.

These predictions were tested in an experiment by Musolino & Lidz (2003), based on Musolino (2000). The experiment had two conditions. The first condition was designed to replicate Musolino's (1998) finding regarding children's isomorphic interpretation of sentences like (17). In the second condition, children we presented with the same sentences as in (17) but, in order to satisfy the felicity conditions on the use of negative statements described above, these sentences were all preceded by affirmative statements which differed from their negative counterparts only in the object NP, as shown in (18):

(17) Every horse didn't jump over the fence.
(18) Every horse jumped over the log but every horse didn't jump over the fence.

In the story corresponding to (18), the three horses all jumped over the log and then, only two of them proceeded to also jump over the fence. Notice that if children interpret *Every horse didn't jump over the fence* in (18) to mean that none of the horses jumped over the fence, an isomorphic interpretation, they should reject the puppet statements and explain, as they did in the Musolino *et al.*, condition, that the puppet is wrong because two horses did jump over the fence. On the other hand, if children assign *Every horse didn't jump over the fence* in (18) a non-isomorphic interpretation, they should accept the puppet's statement since it is true that not all the horses jumped over the fence.

The subjects were 20 English-speaking 5-year-olds between the ages of 5;0 and 5;11 (mean 5;4) and 20 adult native speakers of English. Musolino & Lidz found that while adult subjects almost always accepted sentences like (17) and (18), i.e., 92.5% and 100% of the time respectively, children, who accepted sentences like (17) only 15% of the time, accepted sentences like (18) significantly more often, i.e., 60% of the time.[5] Moreover, when asked to justify their affirmative answers, children typically said that the puppet was right because one of the horses didn't jump over the fence while the two others did. Such justifications clearly show that children were indeed accessing a non-isomorphic interpretation.

Thus, in addition to replicating Musolino's original finding, these results demonstrate that children's ability to access the non-isomorphic interpretation of sentences like *Every horse didn't jump over the fence* dramatically improves when such sentences are preceded by affirmative statements. Showing that children's ability to access the not all, non-isomorphic interpretation of sentences like *Every N didn't VP* improves under certain contextual manipulations casts serious doubts on the grammatical account proposed by Musolino (1998).

6.3. The Limits of Isomorphism

So far, we have only considered the competence-performance distinction with respect to children's non-adult interpretation of sentences like *Every horse didn't jump over the* fence. Recall however that the Observation of Isomorphism is not limited to children's interpretation of universally quantified statements. What then are we to make of children's non-adult interpretations of sentences involving quantified NPs such as *some N* and *two N*?

In order to address this question, I tried to determine whether contextual manipulations such as the ones described above would have a similar effect on children's interpretations and could therefore shed some light on competence-performance issue. An additional manipulation consisted in replacing NPs like *two birds* by partitive NPs such as *two of the birds*. This manipulation is based on the intuition that the non-isomorphic interpretation obtains much more easily with partitives.

10 4-year-old children between the ages of 4;1 and 4;11 (mean 4;5) were tested on their interpretation of sentences like (19) which involve the same kind of contrast as sentences like (18). Sentences like (19) were used in the same context as the non-isomorphic condition of Lidz & Musolino (2002) described earlier:

(19) The Smurf caught all the cats but she didn't catch two birds.

In other words, the non-isomorphic interpretation of (19) was true in the context of the story, while the isomorphic interpretation was false. Another group of 12 children between the ages of 3;9 and 4;11 (mean 4;4) were tested on their interpretation of sentences like (20) in which the object NP is now a partitive:

(20) The Smurf didn't catch two of the birds.

Turning to the results, the manipulation in (19) had little effect on children's interpretation. Children in this condition accepted the puppet statement only 25% of the time (compared to 33% of the time in Lidz & Musolino's non-isomorphic condition). Moreover, children in this condition justified their negative answers in the same way that children in Lidz & Musolino's non-isomorphic condition did, namely by saying that the puppet was wrong because the Smurf had indeed caught two birds. By contrast, children in the partitive condition accepted sentences like (20) on a non-isomorphic interpretation significantly more often, i.e., 75% of the time in the partitive condition vs. 25% of the time in the case of sentences like (19). Moreover, in the partitive condition, when children were asked to explain why they thought that the puppet was right, they correctly pointed to the two birds that the Smurf didn't catch.

While this result clearly shows that children can, under certain circumstances, assign non-isomorphic interpretation, it bears only indirectly on the competence-performance issue regarding children's isomorphic interpretation of sentences containing numerally quantified NPs of the form *two N*. In other words, showing that children can assign non-isomorphic interpretations when the quantified NP is partitive doesn't tell us whether they know that such interpretations are also possible for NPs like *two N*.[6]

6.4. Turning Adults into Children

The results presented in section 6.2 provide evidence against a grammatical account of isomorphism. The strategy so far has been to show that under certain conditions, children can be made to look more like adults. Another way to achieve the same goal would be to show that adults can be 'turned into children' (e.g., Freeman, Sinha & Stedmon, 1982). This is what Musolino & Lidz (2003) did with respect to sentences containing negation and numerally quantified NPs. First, Musolino & Lidz showed that while adult speakers of English can easily access either scope interpretation of sentences like (21) in contexts in which one interpretation is true and the other is false (see section 5.1), they nevertheless display a preference for the isomorphic interpretation in a forced choice situation:

(21) Cookie Monster didn't eat two slices of pizza.

Moreover, Musolino & Lidz showed that the isomorphism effect typically displayed by children can also be seen in adults in the case of sentences like (22):

(22) Two frogs didn't jump over the rock.

Notice that this example can receive an isomorphic interpretation, i.e. *two > not*, on which the sentence can be paraphrased as *There are two frogs that didn't jump over the rock*. Alternatively, (22) can receive a non-isomorphic interpretation, i.e., *not > two*, on which it can be paraphrased as *It is not the case that two frogs jumped over the rock*.

Musolino & Lidz tested a group of 20 adult native speakers of English on their interpretation of sentences like (22) in a design similar to the one described in section 5.1 (i.e., one condition in which the isomorphic interpretation is true and the non-isomorphic condition is false and another condition is which this pattern is reversed). What Musolino & Lidz found is that adults displayed a significant preference for the isomorphic interpretation of sentences like (18), i.e., 100% acceptance rate in the isomorphic condition vs. only 27.5% in the non-isomorphic condition. Thus, the isomorphism effect typically seen in children can also be induced in adults, thereby providing additional evidence against a grammatical account of the phenomenon.

7. OVERCOMING ISOMORPHISM

In this section, I consider two related questions. The first one concerns the extent to which isomorphism represents a uniform phenomenon (see section 7.1). In section 7.2, I then turn to the developmental question, namely how children eventually manage to overcome their isomorphic tendencies.

7.1. Isomorphism: A Uniform Phenomenon?

Throughout this discussion, I have been implicitly assuming that the Observation of Isomorphism represents a uniform phenomenon. While this assumption may be warranted at the descriptive level, it is unclear whether children's non-adult behavior across the range of constructions investigated in this chapter reflects the operation of a single causal factor. To the extent that this is the case, one would expect to find that as soon as children's ability to access non-isomorphic interpretations becomes adult-like, its effects can be observed across the range of constructions discussed here. However, a closer consideration of the facts presented here suggests that this is not so. Recall that the 4-year-olds tested by Lidz & Musolino (2002) were able to access the non-isomorphic interpretation of sentences like *Cookie Monster didn't eat two slices of pizza* only 33% of the time while adults accessed such interpretations 93% of the time. Lidz & Musolino also tested a group of 12 5-year-olds and found that they could access the non-isomorphic interpretation of sentences like *Cookie Monster didn't eat two slices of pizza* 79% of the time. Statistical analysis revealed that the 5-year-olds' acceptance rate did not differ significantly from that of a control group of adults and therefore that by age 5, children were able to access non-isomorphic interpretations of sentences containing numerally quantified objects in an adult-like fashion. This however, stands in striking contrast to 5-year-olds' ability to access the non-isomorphic interpretation of sentences like *Every horse didn't jump over the fence*, i.e., 15% of the time in Musolino & Lidz' replication of Musolino's original result. Why then are 5-year-olds capable of accessing non-isomorphic interpretations in the case of sentences containing numerally quantified objects (i.e., *Cookie Monster didn't eat two slices of pizza*) but not in the case of sentences containing universally quantified subjects (i.e., *Every horse didn't jump over the fence*)?

One possibility may be linked to the fact that, from a theoretical perspective, isomorphism — or rather non-isomorphism — should not be regarded as a uniform phenomenon. While sentences like *Every horse didn't jump over the fence* and *Cookie Monster didn't eat two slices of pizza* can both be interpreted on a non-isomorphic interpretation, the grammatical mechanisms involved in the derivation of the non-isomorphic interpretation are generally regarded to be different in each case. That is, while interpreting the subject NP within the scope of negation in the case of *Every horse didn't jump over the fence* presumably involves reconstruction (i.e. interpreting the subject in its VP internal position and hence in the c-command domain of negation), interpreting the object as taking wide scope with respect to negation in *Cookie Monster didn't eat two slices of pizza* involves some form of quantifier raising (see Reinhart, 1997 for a specific proposal). It is in turn conceivable that children's sensitivity to these mechanisms develops on a different timetable; hence the observed asymmetry. Notice that this asymmetry could also be due to the different syntactic positions occupied by the quantified NPs (i.e., subject in the case of sentences like *Every horse didn't jump over the fence* vs. object in the case of *Cookie Monster didn't eat two slices of pizza*).

7.2. Overcoming Isomorphism: On the Way to Adulthood

Armed with a better understanding of isomorphism, we are now in a position to discuss what I called the developmental question. To be sure, explaining how children eventually manage to overcome their isomorphic tendencies necessitates a proper understanding of why they differ from adults in the first place. In this regard, the evidence discussed in the previous section suggests that the transition between the child's system and that of adults does not involve grammatical change per say. Rather, the difference between the two groups seems to lie in their respective sentence processing abilities. Moreover, prior considerations have led us to distinguish between sentences like *Every horse didn't jump over the fence* and *Cookie Monster didn't eat two slices of pizza*.

In the first case, it seems that children and adults display *opposite* preferences. That is, while children display a preference for the 'none', i.e. isomorphic interpretation, adults show a preference for the 'not all', non-isomorphic interpretation (see Musolino & Lidz, 2003 and Musolino & Lidz, in press for further evidence). The developmental question here amounts to explaining how children reverse their preferences in the course of development. One way to approach this question is to try to understand why adults have a preference for the non-isomorphic interpretation of sentences like *Every horse didn't jump over the fence*. One account, developed by Musolino & Lidz (2003), relies on the entailment relations holding between the alternative interpretations of such sentences. To be more specific, the *none* interpretation entails the *not all* interpretation, but not vice-versa (i.e., if it is true that none of the horses jumped over the fence, it necessarily follows that not all of them did, but not vice-versa). As is well-known in the pragmatics literature, entailment relations between alternative interpretations typically give rise to a kind of conversational inference known as scalar implicatures (Horn, 1972, 1989 among many others). Scalar implicatures arise in examples like (23) where the speaker's use of *some* typically indicates that s/he had reasons not to use a more informative term, i.e., *all*. The use of *some* in (23) therefore gives rise to the implicature in (24):

(23) Some of my friends liked the movie.
(24) Not all my friends liked the movie.

What defines informational strength here is the presence of entailment relations. So in the examples above, all of my friends liked the movie entails that some of my friends liked the movie, but not vice-versa. Notice now that by virtue of the entailment relations holding between the *none* and the *not all* reading of sentences like *Every horse didn't jump over the fence*, the same reasoning can be applied and one can thus explain adults' preference for the 'not all' reading of sentences like *Every horse didn't jump over the fence* in pragmatic terms (see Horn, 1989; Musolino & Lidz, 2003, for an account along these lines).

An interesting virtue of this approach is that it readily accounts for the fact that children and adults display opposite preferences in the case of sentences like *Every horse didn't jump over the fence*. Several recent experimental studies have now shown that preschoolers are by and large insensitive to scalar implicatures (Novek, 2001; Chierchia, *et al.*, 2001; Musolino & Lidz, 2003; Papafragou & Musolino, 2003). To the extent that the preference seen in adults for the *not all* reading of sentences like *Every horse didn't jump over the fence* is indeed due to scalar implicature, it should then come as no surprise that preschoolers, who have been independently shown to be insensitive to scalar implicature, display a preference for the opposite reading, i.e., the 'none' reading (for further discussion, see Musolino & Lidz, 2003). Seen in this light, children's difficulty with sentences like *Every horse didn't jump over the fence* loses its idiosyncratic character and can now been seen to follow from a much more general — and by now well documented — fact about 5-years-olds, namely their lack of sensitivity to the pragmatic consequences of entailment relations. Thus, in the case of sentences like *Every horse didn't jump over the fence*, the developmental question boils down to an account of children's developing pragmatic abilities (see Papafragou & Musolino, 2003 for further discussion).

In the second case, i.e., sentences like *Cookie Monster didn't eat two slices of pizza,* the isomorphic effect observed in children represents an *exaggerated* preference also observable in adults (see section 6.4). There are at least two ways in which this difference could be explained. On the assumption that there is a preference for one of the two readings of sentences like *Cookie Monster didn't eat two slices of pizza* — and, consequently, that the least preferred reading is more difficult to access, judging the truth of such statements presumably involves the following two components:

(i) The relative difficulty of obtaining each interpretation;
(ii) The ability to override this difficulty in order to obtain a reading which is true.

(i) can be viewed as the 'processing difficulty' associated with each interpretation and (ii) can be construed as a 'principle of charity', i.e., giving the puppet credit for speaking truthfully whenever this is possible. Given this state of affairs, there are now two ways in which the difference between children and adults can be accounted for. One possibility is that the difference hinges on (i). In other words, what is difficult for adults to process is even more difficult for children to process — hence the 'exaggerated' preference. Another possibility is that children and adults differ with respect to 'the principle of charity', i.e., (ii). On this scenario, (i) is the same for children and adults but for some reason, children do not apply the principle of charity in an adult-like manner. The data reviewed here, however, do not allow us to tease these two possibilities apart.

Indiana University

8. NOTES

[1] For a more detailed description of the TVJT, see Crain & Thornton (1998). In all the experiments described in this chapter, children witnessed stories that were acted out in front of them using small toys and props. Adult controls were shown the same stories as the ones witnessed by children but instead of having the stories acted out in front of them, they were shown video recordings of these stories. Finally, all the differences between children and adults reported as significant are significant at the .05 level.

[2] In fact, the puppet's statements in this condition used the future tense instead of the past tense, i.e. *Some girls won't ride on the merry-go-round* instead of *Some girls didn't ride on the merry-go-round*. This difference, however, does not affect the argument made here and is therefore irrelevant for the purposes of the present discussion.

[3] In fact, Lidz went to India and Musolino stayed in Philadelphia.

[4] I would like to thank Andrea Gualmini for pointing this out to me.

[5] Similar results were obtained when *but* was replaced by *and*, as in *Every horse jumped over the log and every horse didn't jump over the fence* (see Musolino & Lidz, 2003 for more details).

[6] For an account of the effect of partitivity on children's ability to access non-isomorphic interpretations, see Musolino & Gualmini (2003). Also see Krämer (2000) for further discussion of the isomorphism effect in the case of indefinites and for a criticism of Musolino's 1998 grammatical account. Finally, for additional evidence against Musolino's (1998) grammatical account in the case of sentences like *The detective didn't find someone*, see Gualmini (2003).

9. REFERENCES

Barwise, Jon, and Robin Cooper. "Generalized Quantifiers and Natural Language." *Linguistics and Philosophy* 75 (1981): 87–106.
van Benthem, Johan. *Essays in Logical Semantics*. Dordrecht: Reidel, 1986.
Berwick, Robert. *The Acquisition of Syntactic Knowledge*. Cambridge, MA: MIT Press, 1985.
Bloom, Paul. *How Children Learn the Meanings of Words*. Cambridge, MA: MIT Press, 2000.
Brooks, Patricia, and Martin Braine. "What do Children Know about the Universal Quantifiers *all* and *each*?" *Cognition* 60 (1996): 235–268.
Bucci, Wilma. "The Interpretation of Universal Affirmative Propositions: A Developmental Study." *Cognition* 6 (1978): 55–77.
Carey, Susan. "Cognitive Foundations of Arithmetic: Evolution and Ontogenesis." *Mind & Language* 16 (2001): 37–55.
Chierchia Gennaro, Stephen Crain, Maria Teresa Guasti, Andrea Gualmini, and Luisa Meroni. "The Acquisition of Disjunction: Evidence for a Grammatical View of Scalar Implicatures." In Anna H.-J. Do, Laura Dominguez, and Aimee Johnson (eds.) *Proceedings of the 25th*

Annual Boston University Conference on Language Development, 157–168. Somerville, MA: Cascadilla Press, 2001.
Chomsky, Noam. *Aspects of the Theory of Syntax*. Cambridge, MA: MIT Press, 1965.
Chomsky, Noam. *Knowledge of Language: Its Nature, Origin, and Use*. New York: Praeger, 1986.
Crain, Stephen. "Sense and Sense Ability in Child Language." In Catherine Howell, Sarah Fish, and Thea Keith-Lucas (eds.) *Proceedings of the 24th Annual Boston University Conference on Language Development*, 22–44. Somerville, MA: Cascadilla Press, 2000.
Crain, Stephen, and Rosalind Thornton. *Investigations in Universal Grammar: A Guide to Research on the Acquisition of Syntax and Semantics*. Cambridge, MA: The MIT Press, 1998
Crain, Stephen, Rosalind Thornton, Carol Boster, Laura Conway, Diane Lillo-Martin, and Elaine Woodams. "Quantification without Qualification." *Language Acquisition* 5 (1996): 83–153.
Drozd, Kenneth F. "Children's Weak Interpretation of Universally Quantified Sentences." In Melissa Bowerman and Stephen Levinson (eds.) *Conceptual Development and Language Acquisition*, 340–376. Cambridge: Cambridge University Press, 2001.
Drozd, Kenneth, and William Philip. "Event Quantification in Preschoolers' Comprehension of Negation." In Eve V. Clark (ed.) *Proceedings of the 24th Annual Stanford Child Language Research Forum*, Stanford: CSLI Publications, 1993.
Freeman, Norman H., Chris G. Sinha, and Jackie A. Stedmon. "All the Cars – Which Cars? From Word Meaning to Discourse Analysis." In Michael Beveridge (ed.) *Children Thinking Through Language*, 52–74. London: Edward Arnold, 1982.
Gualmini, Andrea. "*Some* Knowledge Children don't Lack." *Linguistics* (in press).
Horn, Laurence. *On the Semantic Properties of the Logical Operators in English*. Ph.D. Diss.UCLA, 1972.
Horn, Laurence. *A Natural History of Negation*. Chicago: The University of Chicago Press, 1989.
Hornstein, Norbert. *Logic as Grammar*. Cambridge, MA: The MIT Press, 1984.
Inhelder, Bärbel, and Jean Piaget. *The Growth of Logical Thinking from Childhood to Adolescence*. New York: Basic Books, 1958.
Inhelder, Bärbel, and Jean Piaget. *The Early Growth of Logic in the Child*. London: Routledge, 1964.
Jackendoff, Ray. *Semantic Interpretation in Generative Grammar*. Cambridge, MA: The MIT Press, 1972.
Keenan, Edward, and Jonathan Stavi. "A Semantic Characterization of Natural Language Determiners." *Linguistics and Philosophy* 9 (1986): 253–326.
Krämer, Irene. *Interpreting Indefinites: An Experimental Study of Children's Language Comprehension*. Ph.D. Diss., Universiteit Utrecht, 2000.
Lasnik, Howard. *Analyses of Negation in English*. Ph.D. Diss., MIT, 1972.
Lidz, Jeffrey. "The Morphosemantics of Object Case in Kannada." In Sonya Bird, Andrew Carnie, Jason D. Haugen, and Peter Norquest (eds.) *Proceedings of the West Coast Conference of Formal Linguistics 18*, 325–336. Cambridge, MA: Cascadilla Press, 1999.
Lidz, Jeffrey, and Julien Musolino. "Children's Command of Quantification." *Cognition* 84 (2002): 113–154.
Lidz, Jeffrey, and Julien Musolino. "Continuity in Linguistic Development: The Scope of Syntax and the Syntax of Scope." Ms., Northwestern University and Indiana University, 2003.
May, Robert. "The Grammar of Quantification." Ph.D. Diss., MIT, 1977.
Musolino, Julien. *Universal Grammar and the Acquisition of Semantic Knowledge: An Experimental Investigation into the Acquisition of Quantifier-Negation Interaction in English*. Ph.D. Diss., University of Maryland at College Park, 1998.

Musolino, Julien. "Universal Quantification and the Competence-Performance Distinction." paper presented at the annual Boston University Conference on Language Development, Boston, 2000.

Musolino, Julien, Stephen Crain, and Rosalind Thornton. "Navigating Negative Quantificational Space." *Linguistics* 38 (2000): 1–32.

Musolino, Julien, and Andrea Gualmini. "The Role of Partitivity in Child Language." Ms., Indiana University and MIT, 2003.

Musolino, Julien, and Jeffrey Lidz. "Why Children aren't Universally Successful with Quantification." Ms., Indiana University and Northwestern University, 2003.

Musolino, Julien, and Jeffrey Lidz. "The Scope of Isomorphism: Turning Adults into Children." *Language Acquisition* (in press).

Noveck, Ira. "When Children are more Logical than Adults: Experimental Investigations of Scalar Implicature." *Cognition* 78 (2001): 165–188.

O'Leary, Carrie, and Stephen Crain. "Negative Polarity Items (A Positive Result) Positive Polarity Items (A Negative Result)." Paper presented at the annual Boston University Conference on Language Development, Boston, 1994.

Papafragou, Anna, and Julien Musolino. "Scalar Implicatures: Experiments at the Semantics-Pragmatics Interface." *Cognition* 86 (2003): 253–282.

Philip, William. *Event Quantification in the Acquisition of Universal Quantification*. Ph.D. Diss., UMass, Amherst, 1995.

Reinhart, Tanya. "Quantifier Scope: How Labor is Divided between QR and Choice Functions." *Linguistics and Philosophy* 20 (1997): 335–397.

Roeper, Thomas, and Edward Matthei. "On the Acquisition of *all* and *some*." In *Papers and Reports on Child Language Development 9*, 63–74. Stanford: Stanford University Press, 1975.

Roeper Thomas, and Jill de Villiers. "The Emergence of Bound Variable Structures." In Erik Reuland and Werner Abraham (eds.) *Knowledge and Language*, 105–140. Dordrecht: Kluwer, 1993.

Thornton, Rosalind. "Children's Negative Questions: A Production/Comprehension Asymmetry." In Jennifer Fuller, Ho Han, and David Parkinson (eds.) *Proceedings of ESCOL '94*, 306–317. Ithaca: CLC Publications, 1995.

Wason, Peter. "The Contexts of Plausible Denial." *Journal of Verbal Learning and Verbal Behavior* 4 (1965): 7–11.

VEERLE VAN GEENHOVEN

TIME FOR CHILDREN

An Integrated Stage Model of Aspect and Tense

Abstract. Even though it is a well-established fact that aspect is "an early determining factor" (Bloom & Harner, 1989) in the development of time in child language, stage models of the acquisition of tense (Smith, 1980; Weist, 1986) do not integrate the development of aspect. I present an alternative stage model that integrates the development of tense in that of aspect. In particular, I argue that the early lexical aspectual distinction 'telic versus atelic' stimulates the development of grammatical aspect (imperfective, perfective, perfect, and prospective). Furthermore, a child's command of the relational meanings of grammatical aspect (Klein, 1994) is a necessary basis for his command of the relations expressed by present, past, and future tense.

1. INTRODUCTION

The acquisition of temporal expressions and their interpretation provides an interesting challenge both for developmental and semantic theories of time in language. A major point of interest in this area is the for acquisitionists well-known but by semanticists hardly known 'aspect before tense' hypothesis (Bloom *et al.*, 1980b). This hypothesis captures the idea that children acquire the aspectual distinction of telicity versus atelicity before they command tense. It was primarily based upon morpho-syntactic findings in French (Bronckart & Sinclair, 1973), Italian (Antinucci & Miller, 1976), and English (Bloom *et al.*, 1980b) child language and then observed in quite a few other languages (e.g., Greek, Hebrew, Turkish).

Another major topic in the study of time in child language is that at some point children develop the ability to express the deictic relations denoted by tense. To capture this development, one must understand the ways in which children acquire the temporal parameters (i.e., speech time, event time, and reference time) as well as the relations between these parameters (i.e., simultaneity, precedence, and posteriority). This has been investigated from a Reichenbachian perspective in Smith (1980) and Weist (1986), each of whom presented a stage model of a child's acquisition of time order and tense.

According to Smith (1980), the two subsystems of temporal reference, aspect and tense, integrate slowly. Yet, neither Smith's nor Weist's model accounts for how this integration proceeds. They regard aspect as a temporal system whose acquisition does not influence the acquisition of temporal parameters and of the relations between these parameters.

In this chapter, I defend the view that aspect clearly influences the development of tense. I show that the acquisition of lexical and grammatical aspect can very well be integrated into one stage model that captures the aspectual influences on the development of tense. In my view, the data that led to the original 'aspect before tense' hypothesis say at first something about how children express the inherent lexical aspect of verbs through particular temporal markers. Lexical aspect thus stimulates their use of temporal forms and what these forms can mean to them. Moreover, adopting Klein's (1994) relational interpretation of the grammatical aspects (i.e., imperfective, perfective, perfect, and prospective), I show how we can reinterpret the stepwise development of tense — as argued for by Weist — as the stepwise development of grammatical aspect. From this reinterpretation it follows automatically that present, past, and future tense each have an aspectual basis. A relational analysis of aspect and the widely accepted fact that time in child language is oriented towards the speech time are my prerequisites to show that aspect is the primary deictic relation in child language and not tense. Tense takes over this role when the notion of reference time has been acquired and decentred from the speech time. This decentring requires the competence to resolve temporal anaphora.

A relational analysis of grammatical aspect thus supports the 'aspect before tense' hypothesis. For example, I do not regard a child's earliest -*ed* as a past tense form but as a marker of the grammatical aspect 'perfective' that is directly associated with the lexical aspect 'telic'. In a second stage, -*ed* develops into a marker of the grammatical aspect 'perfect', that is, it becomes a marker of aspectual pastness. Children thus primarily express aspectual pastness and not, as often assumed, past tense. Similarly, children first command lexical future expressions from which they then develop an aspectual future (i.e., the grammatical aspect 'prospective') and only later a future tense (see Harner, 1982). I will show that the proposed developments from tense out of aspect have diachronic correspondents in German (see Klein, 1994) as well as a synchronic remnant in adult African-American English (see Terry, 2005).

The chapter is organized as follows. In the next section, I present the 'aspect before tense' hypothesis. The stage models of temporality set forth in Smith (1980) and Weist (1986) are presented in section 3, where I also discuss some unresolved problems related to these models. In section 4, I present my views on the interpretation of lexical aspect, grammatical aspect and tense, as well as some diachronic influences of aspect on the emergence of tense. These views provide the background of my integrated model of aspect and tense outlined in section 5. Section 6 concludes the chapter.

2. ASPECT BEFORE TENSE ?

Since Vendler (1967) it has become standard to classify verbs according to four event types, namely, states, activities, accomplishments and achievements. State and activity verbs have in common that they describe a temporally unbounded situation and, hence, they are atelic in nature. Accomplishment and achievement verbs are telic because they describe a process that leads up to a terminal point. Bronckart & Sinclair (1973) investigated the temporal system of French learners (age 2;11-8;7) and observed that younger children mostly describe

> actions that obtain a clear result ... in the *passé composé* ... and actions that do not lead to any result ... in the *présent* (1973, 126).

Similarly, Antinucci & Miller (1976) observed that Italian children in the age group 1;6-2;6 use the *passato prossimo* when talking about past events that are described with telic verbs. In contrast, state and activity verbs, which are not telic, are first never used in the past tense but in the present tense, then in the *imperfetto*. The following of their examples illustrate this observation:

(1) Papa *comprato* tanti giocattoli. (2;2)
    'Papa bought many toys.'

(2) Papa Natale *ha buttato giu* la cioccolata. (2;0)
    'P.N. threw down the chocolate.'

(3) *Corre* il cane. (1;9)
    'The dog is running.'
    È arrivato il cane.
    'The dog arrived.'

(4) Mother: E gli altri bambini?
    'And the other kids?'

   Child: *Giocavano*. (2;8)
    'They were playing.'
    Babbo Natale li *ha messi* nel sacco e dopo *piangevano*.
    'Santa Claus put them into the sack and then they were crying.'

In (1) and (2), we have the accomplishment verbs *comprare* 'buy' and *buttare giu* 'throw down' in the *passato prossimo*;[1] in (3), the child contrasts the present tense of the activity verb *correre* 'run' with the *passato prossimo* of the achievement verb *arrivare* 'arrive'; in (4), the activity verbs *giocare* 'play' and *piangere* 'cry' are in the *imperfetto* while *mettere in* 'put into' is in the *passato prossimo*.

In line with Antinucci & Miller's findings for Italian and the earlier findings for French by Bronckart & Sinclair, Bloom *et al.* (1980b) observed that English speaking children of the age group 1;10-2;4 associate *-ed*, which in adult English expresses the simple past ('past perfective'), with telic verbs, and atelic verbs with *-ing*, which in adult English expresses imperfective aspect. On Bloom *et al.*'s view, this early morphological contrast between *-ed* and *-ing* represents a child's early distinction between telic and atelic aspect and not a distinction between past and present tense. This grew into the 'aspect before tense' hypothesis: Lexical aspectual distinctions are mastered before the full tense system is.

Smith (1980) pointed out that the early association of telicity with a past tense form and of atelicity with an imperfective form cannot be understood as predicting that young children have no awareness of pastness. Weist *et al.* (1984) went one step further. They argued that if one adopts the 'aspect before tense' hypothesis one must basically conclude that children have a defective tense system as long as they have not completely acquired aspect. Investigating Polish children, Weist *et al.*, concluded that these children acquire aspect and tense morphology simultaneously. For him this was reason enough to reject the 'aspect before tense' hypothesis. Moreover, to capture the early notion of pastness, Weist (1986) developed a stage model of a child's tense system that was based upon the earlier stage model of the acquisition of time order presented in Smith (1980).

3. STAGE MODELS OF THE DEVELOPMENT OF TIME

In this section, I present Smith's and Weist's models of the acquisition of temporal parameters and relations. I discuss their major claims as well as some problems and relevant questions that these models leave unaddressed.

3.1. Smith's Stage Model of Time Order

Smith (1980) regards aspect and time order as the two crucial systems of temporal reference in adult language. Following Comrie (1976), imperfective aspect describes an event without considering its termination while perfective aspect describes an event as a whole. Whereas aspect involves the temporal contour of events, time order is "how events are ordered relative to a reference point (1980, 264)." In line with Reichenbach (1947), Smith argues that a command of the full temporal system of a language requires the ability to distinguish three temporal parameters, namely, the speech time (ST), the reference time (RT), and the event time (ET).[2]

Smith's assumptions that led to her stage model of early "time talk", are the following. First, the basic notions in a child's aspect system are 'perfective' and 'imperfective'. Second, Smith suggests that a child's early system of time includes only two temporal parameters and that this system is oriented towards the ST. While she recognizes the early association of telicity with a past tense form and of atelicity with an imperfective form, to her this must not mean that young children have no awareness of pastness. Her conclusion is that children have the notion of pastness by the age of 4;0 and express this by using past tense forms. Although a child's temporal system is simpler than that of an adult, Smith assumes that it is basically organized in an adult-like way. While a child keeps track of two temporal parameters only, he can still relate one parameter to the other by simultaneity or sequence. For a child, pastness means that a time precedes the ST.

Following Piaget, Smith adopts the view that at a first stage young children have an ego-centric world perspective and that they must learn to 'decentre' from this. According to Smith (1980, 266), "young children may thus be unable to talk about time other than present time" and their ability to decentre from the ST may be acquired in stages. In a first stage, children only use present tense while they are able to indicate aspectual distinctions. A clear indication of a child's disability to decentre is their use of a historical present to talk about a situation or an event in the past. Smith (1980, 275) suggests that

> the younger children in the French experiment took a view point like that of a historical present. This should not be surprising: it is common to find the historical present in children's early narratives ... It is not implausible that at one stage of their development children would talk about the past as if it were the present.

At a second stage, namely around age 4;0, a child can focus on an additional point of time that is distinct from the ST. He has now mastered the notion of pastness. Approaching the adult stage, a child adds a third temporal parameter to his system, namely, the RT. When this does not have a fixed meaning anymore, the child's temporal system has reached its destination.

3.2. Weist's Four-Stage Model of Tense

Weist (1986) presents a four-stage model of a child's acquisition of tense. Following Reichenbach, he regards tense as a relation between the ET of an utterance and the ST. Present tense is used in utterances that describe the situation in which the ET and the ST are simultaneous. Past tense utterances describe situations in which the ET precedes the ST, and future tense utterances situations in which the ET follows the ST. Tense is a deictic relation since it involves a relation to the ST, a deictic temporal parameter.

Weist (1986, 356) proposes that "children progress through a sequence of four temporal systems." The initial system is called the 'speech time system', which is a system in which both the ET and the RT are frozen at the ST. In this early period (age 1;0-1;6), child language is tenseless.[3] The 'event time system' is entered at the age of 1;8-2;0. In this second stage,

> there is a natural relationship between the internal perspective and speech time events, and between the external perspective and anterior events (1986, 365).

Children make a distinction between ongoing events at the ST and complete events that precede the ST. At this second stage, the RT coincides with the ST but given that the tense relations are said to hold between the ET and the ST this still leaves room for children to create all three of them. On Weist's view, the capacity of displacement (i.e., decentring) is required to express the notions of 'past' and 'future' as deictic relations, that is, as tenses.

The full range of tenses is acquired at a surprisingly early age. At the age of 3;0-3;2, a child enters a third stage, the 'restricted reference time system'. This stage is characterized by the onset of temporal adverbs and the use of temporal adverbial clauses. According to Weist, this onset indicates that a child must by now distinguish the RT from the ST, be it still restricted in that the RT is only a semi-independent, ET-oriented time point. This shows that children are still relating two points of time rather than three. The ability to relate three temporal parameters to one another is acquired when by the age of 4;0 a child arrives at the final stage, the 'free reference time system'. This arrival is signalled by the uses of the temporal connectives *before* and *after* and by the late development of the pluperfect.[4]

Like Smith, Weist regards aspect as contributing the global contour of an event. As such, it is not part of a child's growing ability to relate temporal parameters to each other in different ways. As we saw in the previous section, his position towards the 'aspect before tense' hypothesis is that this hypothesis wrongly predicts that children have a defective tense system.

3.3. Some Leftover Questions

I will address the following issues in Smith's and Weist's models: first, the early past tense forms, which they interpret as early past tense; second, the role of early aspect, which they leave unexplained; third, their interpretation of tense; and, finally, the onset of temporal adverbs and connectives, which they regard as triggers for the need of the RT.

3.3.1. Early Past Tense Forms

The fact that in many languages children associate lexical meaning with particular temporal morphemes cannot be ignored. For Weist (1986, 365), this association comes down to

> a natural relationship between the internal perspective (= imperfective aspect) and speech time events and between the external perspective (= perfective aspect) and anterior events.

Specifically, the relationship between perfective aspect and anterior events led him to integrate past tense into his model at a rather early stage, the second stage (age 1;6-2;6). According to Smith children command pastness well by the age of 4;0. Both authors regard early pastness as an early command of the precedence relation between a time and the ST. But does the fact that English learning children realize perfective aspect as -*ed* really indicate that they are able to express past tense? In other words, are a child's earliest uses of -*ed* really past tense forms? Smith (1980, 274) mentions the possibility that with -*ed* and similar 'tense' forms children "were describing the final stage of the actions they watched the experimenter perform." If Smith is right on this, this entails — as I will show in section 5 — that the earliest occurrences of -*ed* are to be interpreted as a 'present perfective' which is contrasted with earliest -*ing* as a 'present imperfective'.

3.3.2. The Role of Aspect in the Development of Tense

Bloom & Harner (1989) argue against Weist's conclusion that the 'aspect before tense' hypothesis predicts that a child's tense system does not develop and that it is defective. They point out that adopting the hypothesis

> does not require that children's use of aspect marking becomes fully developed before they learn tense distinctions, or even separate and sequential development of the two. Both systems develop together but aspect is an early determining factor (1989, 211).

Smith and Weist use the data on which the 'aspect before tense' hypothesis rests, to conclude that children have an early notion of pastness and anteriority. Yet, their models do not explain the associations themselves that a child creates between particular lexical aspects and particular temporal forms. According to Smith (1980, 266),

> it is also necessary for the two parts of the temporal reference system (time order and aspect) to integrate with each other, and this happens slowly.

Still, neither Smith nor Weist provides an account of how this integration proceeds. I think that this is mainly due to their nonrelational — in those days standard — perspective on grammatical aspect, which can at best be illustrated by the following quote from Comrie (1976, 5):

> Aspect is not concerned with relating the time of the situation to any other time-point, but rather with the internal temporal constituency of the one situation.

Since both the opponents and the proponents of the 'aspect before tense' hypothesis advocate the theoretical perspective that tense and aspect are two completely distinct systems, there is no point of contact for a theoretical account of a child's associations between aspect and tense.[5] Below, I present a complementary approach to aspect, namely Klein's (1994) relational analysis of grammatical aspect. This approach provides one of the crucial points of contact to understand the early aspect/tense associations.

3.3.3. Early Pastness

Smith's and Weist's views on temporal parameters and relations forces them to interpret pastness as a deictic relation between the ET and the ST, which is tense on Reichenbach's (1947) view. I argue below that we must first take a closer look at the temporal structure of verbs to get a better understanding of the contribution of lexical aspect in the development of time in language. In addition, we must adopt a relational perspective on grammatical aspect so that we can relate the development of aspect to the development of tense. Following Klein (1994), I will treat aspect as a relation between the ET and the RT and tense as a relation between the RT and the ST. All of this provides a novel set of tools to build a stage model in which we can recycle the existing empirical observations. For example, a relational perspective on grammatical aspect makes the notion of aspect very similar to the relational notion of tense. This offers room for a new understanding of early pastness as aspectual pastness and of early future as aspectual future. We can then postpone the full development of tense until a stage that is later than the very early one proposed by Weist.

3.3.4. The Onset of Temporal Adverbials and Connectives

Nelson (1991, 293-294) pointed out that

> the earliest temporal adverbials such as *today* and *yesterday* and adverbial clauses beginning with *when* are among the first to be used. ... The acquisition of the temporal prepositions *before* and *after* and the use of these terms to introduce subordinate clauses is typically delayed for a year or more after the use of temporal adverbs.

According to Weist (1986, 368),

the emergence of the prepositions 'before' and 'after' represents one important signal that children have developed the added flexibility which permits them to establish ST, ET, and RT at three related points in time.

Weist — and so does Smith — regards the onset of temporal adverbials and connectives as a clear indication of the fact that a child has identified the RT as a third temporal parameter. According to Weist, it is generally the case that temporal adverbs are used to establish the RT. He cites the early use of adverbs by Wawrzon, a Polish child age 2;6-2;8. Among these are the Polish correspondents of *today*, *yesterday*, *on Monday*. Weist takes these early adverbs as empirical evidence for his claim that at this age children enter the restricted RT system, which is the third stage in his model. However, it can be easily shown that the above temporal adverbs can also specify the ET (see Johnston, 1994; Klein, 1994). Following Klein, I assume that the RT is an element of the topic component, that is, an element of the presupposed material of an utterance [6] and that the ET is an element of its focus, that is, of the asserted material. Depending on whether a temporal adverb belongs to the topic of a utterance or to its focus, this adverb is a description of the RT or of the ET. Suppose we have the following sentence:

(5) Bill went to the dentist yesterday.

Testing which temporal parameter is or can be described by the adverb *yesterday*, (5) can be the answer to either of the following questions:

(6) What did Bill do yesterday?
(7) When did Bill go to the dentist?

In (6), *yesterday* is part of the question material and thus of the presupposed material of its answer. (5) can be the answer to (6), in which case *yesterday* describes the RT. In (7), we are asking for the time at which Bill went to the dentist. Again, (5) can be a correct answer, in which case *yesterday* describes the ET. Note that whether *yesterday* is interpreted as the specifier of the RT or of the ET is visible from the focus structure of (5). If the pitch accent is on *yesterday*, as illustrated in (5'), the adverb is more likely understood as an ET specifier; if it is not, as in (5"), *yesterday* is an RT specifier:

(5') Bill went to the dentist YEsterday.
(5") Bill went to the DENtist yesterday.

Given the ability of adverbs like *yesterday* to describe both the RT and the ET, there is no reason to follow Weist's conclusion that the onset of temporal adverbs indicates that the child's acquired an ability to identify the RT.

Rather, the onset of temporal adverbs indicates that a child is able or tries to describe a time. The empirical data available in the literature are insufficiently clear as to whether a child first tries to describe the ET and then the RT. From Smith's and Weist's models it seems to follow that a child is first able to describe the ET because it is this parameter which is displaced first. It is predicted that among the earliest temporal adverbials we should find typical ET specifiers rather than specifiers of the RT. I will return to this issue in section 5.2 below.

According to Weist, the onset of temporal adverbial clauses with the connectives *when* and at a later stage with *before* and *after* is a further indication of the fact that a child expresses his ability to distinguish the RT, first as an ET-oriented parameter and later as an independent one. I think that also here we can show that the onset of connectives is not necessarily related to entering an RT-stage. Consider the following examples:

(8) Bill went to the dentist when his aunt arrived.
(9) Bill went to the dentist before his aunt arrived.
(10) Bill went to the dentist after his aunt arrived.

On a standard view (see Stump, 1985; Rooth, 1985; de Swart, 1991), *when*, *before* and *after* express simultaneity, anteriority, and posteriority between the ET of the subordinate clause and the ET of matrix clause. Thus, in (8) the ET of Bill's going to the dentist coincides with the ET of his aunt's arrival while in (9) it precedes it and in (10) it follows it. To solve particular problems that arise in the interaction of *when*-, *before*-, and *after*-clauses with adverbs of quantification, focus, and aspect, I argued in Van Geenhoven (1999) that *when*, *before*, and *after* do not directly relate two ETs.[7] Rather, *when*-, *before*-, and *after*-clauses are temporal adverbs which can describe either the ET of a matrix or its RT. For example, the subordinate clauses in (8), (9), and (10) describe the RT of the matrix clauses (which is the RT of the whole utterance), if they answer the following questions, respectively:

(11) What did Bill do when his aunt arrived?
(12) What did Bill do before his aunt arrived?
(13) What did Bill do after his aunt arrived?

The subordinate clauses in (8), (9), and (10) describe the ET of the respective matrix clauses, if they are an appropriate answer to the question in (7), namely, if they describe the time at which Bill went to the dentist. From this short discussion of temporal connectives we can again conclude that their onset in child language does not necessarily indicate that children are able to distinguish the RT, first as a semi-independent and later as an independent temporal parameter. The earlier appearance of *when* and the later appearance of *before* and *after* seem to indicate only that the temporal relation 'simultaneity' is acquired before 'precedence' and 'posteriority' are.[8]

If not temporal adverbs and connectives trigger the acquisition of the ability to distinguish the RT as an additional temporal parameter, what then is the true trigger of this process? I will propose below that the independence of the RT is a consequence of having acquired the competence to resolve temporal anaphora. In other words, the independence of the RT mirrors the child's ability to interpret utterances in a larger temporal context.

4. THE INTERPRETATION OF ASPECT AND TENSE

In this section, I discuss the theoretical prerequisites on which I build a stage model that incorporates the development of both aspect and tense. These include my assumptions on the interpretation and representation of lexical aspect, grammatical aspect, and tense. The section closes with a discussion of some attested diachronic influences of aspect on tense.

4.1. Lexical Aspect

In the literature, different ways have been proposed to capture the coding of (a)telicity. Dowty (1979) proposed that atelic verbs and VPs can be categorized as 'subinterval', and telic verbs and VPs as 'nonsubinterval' (see also Bennett & Partee, 1977). A subinterval verb (or VP) has the property that if the sentence of which it is the matrix verb (or of which it is the VP) is true at some time t, then the sentence is true at every subinterval of t. Verbs and VPs that do not have this property are nonsubinterval. For example, the state VP *live in Paris* is subinterval since a sentence like *John lived in Paris* is true at a time t if at every subinterval of t John lived in Paris. The accomplishment VP *walk to Paris* is nonsubinterval since for *John walked to Paris* to be true at t it must not be the case that this sentence is true at every subinterval of t.

Building on Verkuyl (1972), Krifka (1989, 1992) distinguished atelic from telic verbs and predicates in terms of whether they are cumulative or quantized. A predicate P is quantized if and only if no entity which is P can be a proper subpart of another entity which is P. A predicate that is not quantized is cumulative. Within this perspective, accomplishment and achievement predicates come out as quantized while state and activity predicates come out as cumulative. For example, in *John walked to Paris* the accomplishment *walk to Paris* is quantized since no event of walking to Paris can be a subpart of an event of walking to Paris. In *John lived in Paris*, the state predicate *live in Paris* is cumulative since an event of living in Paris can be a subpart of an event of living in Paris.

While Dowty's approach focuses on the homogeneity of the temporal structure of situations described by atelic verbs and VPs, Krifka's approach focuses on the cumulativity or unboundedness of these expressions. For our present purposes, there is no reason to chose for one or the other, since both homogeneity and unboundedness are intrinsic properties of atelic expressions. Klein (1994) proposed to capture these properties in the lexical representation of state and activity verbs by saying that they are '1-state' verbs. For example, he represents the lexical homogeneity of the activity verb *dance* as a uninterrupted and unbounded line of plus signs:

(14) +++++++++++++++++++
     dance

Klein contrasts verbs with a homogeneous temporal structure with verbs who describe a change of state. An example is the accomplishment verb *clean*. *Clean* is what he calls a '2-state' verb and its representation involves two states, a source state and a target state:

(15)   SOURCE STATE   TARGET STATE
       (not clean)   (clean)
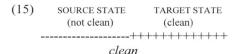
                 clean

One can regard the source state in this representation as the pretime of a change, namely, the state that exists before something has been cleaned. Similarly, one can regard the target state as the posttime of a change, namely, the state that exists after which something has been cleaned.[9] The notions 'pretime' and 'posttime' will turn out relevant in the interpretation and, hence, in the acquisition of particular aspects and tenses.[10]

4.2. The Relational Meaning of Grammatical Aspect

We saw that Smith and Weist adopt the viewpoint perspective on temporal aspect and regard aspect as a nonrelational temporal system (see section 3.3.2). Klein criticizes this way of defining grammatical aspect because the viewpoint definitions are metaphorical. Building on Reichenbach's three-parameter approach, Klein provides a more explicit characterization of aspect as the relation between the ET and the RT of an utterance. Consider the following examples:

(16) This morning, John cleaned the car.
(17) This morning, John was cleaning the car.

I assume that the topicalized adverbial *this morning* describes the RT of both utterances. Ignoring the past tense, we can say that the time of the cleaning event described by the perfective form *cleaned* in (16) is included in the time described by *this morning*. In other words, perfective aspect describes the situation in which the ET is included in the RT (ET $\subseteq$ RT). In (17), we have the opposite situation. The time of the cleaning described by the imperfective form *was cleaning* fully includes the time described by *this morning*. Imperfective aspect thus describes the situation in which the ET fully or properly includes the RT (ET $\supset$ RT). By relating the ET to the RT in this way, Klein thus provides a formal grasp of what it means to say that we have an internal or an external perspective on the temporal structure of an event.[11]

Imperfective and perfective aspect are both defined in terms of the relation 'simultaneity'. Logically, there are two more relations that can be realized between the ET and the RT, namely, precedence and posteriority. Consider therefore (18) and (19):

(18) This morning, John had cleaned the car.
(19) This morning, John was about to clean the car.

In (18), the time described by *this morning* is in the posttime of the time at which the cleaning took place. The perfect aspect expressed by *had cleaned* describes the situation in which the ET precedes the RT (ET < RT). In (19), the time described by *this morning* is in the pretime of the time at which the cleaning occurred. The prospective aspect expressed by the periphrastic form *was about to clean* describes the situation in which the ET follows the RT (ET > RT). Note that 'posttime' and 'pretime' are crucial notions in acquiring a full notion of aspect. This closes the discussion of the theoretical assumptions on grammatical aspect that I will adopt.

4.3. *The Relational Meaning of Tense*

By defining aspect in a relational way, its meaning gets much closer to tense, which is standardly interpreted as a temporal relation. The interpretation of tense as the deictic relation between the ET and the ST is a simplification of Reichenbach's (1947) three parameter approach to tense. On Reichenbach's view, the relation between the ET and the ST is indirect, in the sense that it is the result of the relation between the ET and the RT and the relation between the RT and the ST. Tense is thus a double relation.[12]

Klein (1994) disentangles this double relational view on tense by taking the relation between the ET and the RT to be the denotation of aspect, and the relation between the RT and the ST to be the denotation of tense. It is this interpretation of tense that I will adopt in this chapter.[13] Present tense is the case in which the RT includes the ST; past tense the case in which the RT precedes the ST; and future tense the case in which the RT follows the ST. Interestingly, on this interpretation of tense the RT is needed as an independent temporal parameter.

We can now give a complete picture of the aspect and tense systems that I adopt in this chapter. For explanatory purposes, I adopt Klein's representational tools. The temporal structure of (16) is represented by positioning its RT on the time axis in square '[...]' brackets and, relative to it, its ET in curly '{..}' brackets. Its ST is put immediately on time axis as 'ST'. The change of state that is part of the temporal structure of *clean* is combined with the aspect/tense configuration triggered by *cleaned* as follows:

(16')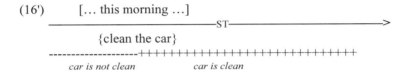

(17') represents the past imperfective (past progressive) *was cleaning* that we have in (17):

(17')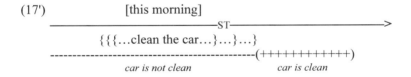

What is interesting is that while in the representation of perfective aspect in (16') the posttime of the cleaning event can be determined, this is not so in the representation of imperfective aspect: (17) does not say anything about whether the cleaning of the car has ever been finished. It is therefore not clear whether the ST is included in the ET or not. The imperfective operates on the source state expressed by the 2-stage verb *clean* and leaves the target state unaddressed.[14] Unaddressed target states are put in round '(...)' brackets.

4.4. Diachronic Aspectual Influences on Tense

Klein's theory of time in language allows for an insightful modelling of how the lexical and grammatical aspect systems have influenced the tense system diachronically. Klein (1994, 115) points out that

> in the development of so-called 'future tenses' in most modern European languages, we observe a transition from 'lexical future' to prospective aspect and finally to future tense.

The inner logic of this development he describes as follows. Instances of 'lexical future' are those cases in which the lexical content of a predicate describes an obligation or a willingness to do something, or a movement towards doing something. In English, this orientation towards the pretime of an upcoming ET was originally expressed by *shall* (obligation), *will* (volition), and *be going to* (movement). For example, *John shall come* literally meant that John has the obligation to come. The etymological correspondent of *shall* in German, namely *soll* (e.g., *Johann soll kommen*) still triggers this meaning. Similarly, *John is going to sleep* literally described a movement towards the location where John is planning to sleep. Again, its German correspondent *Johann geht schlafen* still has this literal meaning. The gradual loss of the original meaning of lexical future markers led to a loss of their pretime orientation in the sense that at some point the markers no longer described the pretime of an upcoming event but rather marked the relation of this pretime to the ET of the upcoming event. As such they became markers of prospective aspect, indicating that the RT precedes the ET. A representative in present day English is *be going to*. Present day English *shall* and *will* have gone one step further in that they now mark that the RT follows the ST. They have thus become markers of future tense.

Historical meaning shifts from aspect to tense can also be witnessed in meaning changes of perfect aspect forms. According to Klein (1994, 125),

> we often observe a transition of perfect aspect to past tense, that is, forms which at one time served to express perfect aspect now serve to express past tense. This development may begin with one verb type, for example 2-state verbs, and then slowly infect other verbs.

A case in point is the German *Perfekt* (e.g., *Johann ist gekommen* 'John came'), which has now adopted a past tense meaning. The *Präteritum* (e.g., *Johann kam*), which is the original past tense form, has only a reduced distribution as past tense expression.

What I will argue for below is that in the temporal forms of children we find meaning shifts that mirror the diachronic shift of perfect aspect to past tense meaning and of prospective aspect to future tense meaning.

5. A STAGE MODEL OF ASPECT AND TENSE

In this section, I show that the observations on which Smith's and Weist's models are based, are perfectly compatible with the idea that the acquisition of aspect influences and therefore precedes the acquisition of tense. This I do by presenting an alternative stage model of time in child language that is bases on the assumptions discussed in the previous section. The model provides novel answers to the questions of what early lexical aspect contributes to the development of time talk, of what early pastness and early future mean, and to the questions of when and why children identify the RT of an utterance as an independent parameter.

If we adopt Klein's minimal way of representing the temporal structure of verbs, an early command of lexical aspect comes down to an early capacity of distinguishing situations that have a homogeneous structure, from those that do not, as well as to an early capacity of distinguishing situations that involve a change of state from those that do not. I will show that these capacities also lead to a command of 'pretime' and 'posttime'.

If, in addition, we adopt a relational analysis for grammatical aspect as well as for tense, getting a command of grammatical aspect and of tense requires that a child must learn (at least) two things. First, in addition to the fixed 'here and now' in which a child finds himself and utters his speech, namely the ST, the child must learn to differentiate two more temporal parameters. That is, he must be able to distinguish the fact that *a situation talked about* can be located in the past, present, or future, from the fact that *the time talked about* can be located in the past, present, or future. In other words, he must learn to identify the ET on the time axis and he must learn to identify the RT on the time axis. Second, a child must learn the different ways of relating the ET to the RT and of relating the RT to the ST. In other words, he must learn to identify the four grammatical aspects as well as the three tenses.

5.1. Stage One: The Determining Role of Lexical Aspect

What comes in at the first stage in the development of temporal expressions is the fact that a child has an early notion of the lexical aspectual distinction 'telic versus atelic' or 'process versus result' (see Slobin, 1985; Swift, this volume). Moreover, given a child's orientation towards his 'here and now', there is reason to assume that at this first stage the three temporal parameters coincide. Specifically, if we assume with Smith and Weist that a child can keep track of two parameters only, we can say that at this first stage the three temporal parameters are instantiated as an ST/RT cluster, on the one hand, and an ET, on the other. If all temporal parameters coincide, the only temporal relation a child can create at this first stage is simultaneity, which entails that the ET does not move away from the ST/RT.

It is with these settings of his temporal parameters and the relation of simultaneity that a child's development of temporality begins. I represent a child's earliest atelic (1-state) verbs as in (20), and his telic (2-state) verbs as in (21):

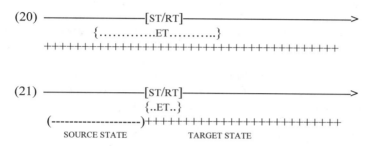

(20) represents the imperfective aspect expressions of a child, in which a verb has a homogeneous temporal structure. We see that the ET picks out a part of this structure and, moreover, that this ET properly includes the ST/RT cluster. The earliest progressive markers of an English learning child and the earliest present tenses of a young learner of French or Italian are thus interpreted as expressing the proper inclusion relation between the ET and the ST/RT. (20) also illustrates that at this first stage child language is tenseless. We saw that in Smith's view all tenses are present at this first stage while in Weist's view, the first stage is tenseless. I follow Weist in this respect: Having a notion of tense requires the ability to differentiate the RT from the ST even if the relation between them is one of simultaneity. Interestingly, since the RT is not distinguishable from the ST, a child's earliest temporal markers of aspect express a deictic relation. I call this 'present aspect'.

(21) captures the perfective aspect expressions of a child, in which a verb describes a change of state. Here, the ET picks out the target state of the verb. This target state orientation captures the fact that children do not recognize the source state of a 2-state verb, which I have captured by putting the source state in brackets. This fact was addressed by Smith (see section 3.3.1) and it is supported by the following fact from early Italian. Up to a certain age, as Antinucci & Miller observe, the participle that is regarded as a *passato prossimo* (see section 2) agrees with the object. (22) is a relevant example:

(22) *Presa* Checco campana. (2;1)
    'Took C. belt.'

In (22), Checco is the speaker. The correct adult utterance to express that Checco took the belt would have been *Ho preso la campana*, that is, without agreement between the object and the participle. The agreement in (22) shows that a child associates the resulting state expressed by the verb as a property of the object that is involved, namely that the belt was taken (see Borer & Wexler, 1992; Wittek, 2002).

(21) also illustrates that the earliest *-ed* forms in English — and so are the earliest occurrences of the *passato prossimo* in Italian and of the *passé composé* in French — are expressions of 'present aspect'. 'Present' is here an aspectual notion and not a notion of tense. While Smith and Weist remain silent on the question of what temporal parameters and relations mean to aspect, (20) and (21) clearly illustrate their relevance to the interpretation and, hence, to the acquisition of aspect — provided that we adopt a *relational* view on aspect. Even though at this first stage time talk is tenseless, the grammatical aspects that can be acquired are the ones expressing simultaneity, namely, imperfective and perfective aspect.

5.2. Stage Two: From Perfective to Perfect, from Imperfective to Prospective

According to Smith and Weist, children first differentiate the ET from the ST/RT cluster. Let us assume that this is the case. Then, in addition to simultaneity between the ET and the ST/RT cluster, children can now let the ET precede or follow this cluster in their speech. In Smith's and Weist's view, this means that at the end of this stage a child has learned to command the notion of tense. But not if we adopt Klein's theory, in which tense expresses a relation between the RT and the ST. Before I show what decentring the ET from the ST/RT cluster means in Klein's theory, I want to clarify first how a child learns to differentiate the ET from the ST/RT.

In my view, differentiating the ET from the ST/RT results from the fact that a child recognizes the source state of a telic verb. While in (21) the source state was still ignored, at a later point in his development a child is able to put the ET in the source state of a 2-state verb. We can represent this as follows:

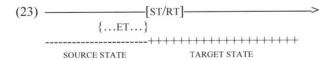

By recognizing the source state of a telic verb, a child learns the important notion of 'pretime' in that the ET lies in the pretime of a target state that holds at the ST/RT. A side effect of this situation is that the ET now precedes the ST/RT. In other words, a child is now able to express perfect aspect or aspectual pastness. An actual example of this acquired ability is when Italian learners correctly command that in *passato prossimo* constructions full object NPs do not agree with participles. Similarly, the *-ed*'s of an English learning child have now received the status of a perfect aspect form. I assume that children generalize their notion of perfect aspect to all types of verbs. This then yields a general command of perfect aspect, represented in (24):

(24) ─────────────[ST/RT]────────────────>
              {...ET...}

A child thus acquires his understanding of perfect aspect out of perfective aspect by integrating the notion of 'pretime' in his speech. An interesting question is whether this notion also has an impact on the development of a child's imperfective forms. I think that it does and I illustrate this in light of the early *imperfetto* in Italian (see section 2) and of the development of an early 'immediate future' in English, realized as *gonna* (*going to*) *infinitive*.

Young learners of Italian use the *passato prossimo* form to describe situations that involve a change of state and at some point they are able to identify the source state of this change (see (23)). At this point, these learners also use *imperfetto* forms ('past imperfective') to describe atelic situations. I suggest that these early *imperfetto* forms realize the following configuration:

(25) ─────────────[ST/RT]────────────────>
           {...ET...}...}...}...}...}
       ++++++++++++++++++++++++++++++++

Since they master the notion of pretime, children are now able to put the ET of their *imperfetto* utterances in the pretime of the ST/RT. Still, at this stage the *imperfetto* is not a marker of past tense. By putting the ET in the pretime of the ST/RT nothing is said about whether this ET precedes the ST/RT or not.

Children also develop their understanding of prospective aspect from an understanding of 'pretime' and imperfective aspect, in particular, out of the imperfective form *going to*, which expresses a lexical future (see section 4.4). As Harner (1982) points out, a child's earliest future expressions are all of the form *gonna* (*going to*) *infinitive*. I assume that if a child is using *going to* he is actually intending to go somewhere. In early realizations of sentences like *I am going to sleep*, *go to* is then an accomplishment verb and its target state is one in which the speaker has found a location to sleep. That is, the target state contains an involvement in another event, which has it own ET. I call this ET2. The imperfective aspect form *going* (*to*) expresses an orientation towards the source state of the accomplishment it expresses, which is simultaneously the pretime of ET2. This is captured as follows:

(26) ──────────[ST/RT]──────────────>
         {…..ET1…..}{…ET2…}

In (26), the ET described by *going to*, namely ET1, is in the pretime of an upcoming event time, namely, ET2. Losing its pretime orientation, *going to* becomes a prospective aspect marker in that it now marks that the ST/RT cluster precedes the upcoming ET2, as shown in (27):

(27) ──────────[ST/RT]──────────────>
                              {…ET2…}

I suggest that originally early occurrences of *will* are also lexical future expressions which first gain prospective aspect status. As we will see below, only at a later stage *will* receives its adult status of future tense marker.

Interestingly, by using Klein's relational definition of grammatical aspect to interpret Smith's and Weist's stepwise mastering of the temporal parameters and the relations between them, we arrive at the 'old' idea that aspect is mastered before tense. That is, by taking a novel route we arrive at the conclusion that a child commands perfect aspect before he commands past tense, and that a child commands prospective aspect — a so-called 'immediate future' — before he commands future tense. Children cannot command tense at this second stage because the ST and the RT are still a cluster. Note that this alternative way of arriving at the 'aspect before tense' hypothesis is compatible with Smith's observation that children have an early notion of pastness. In my view, this is aspectual pastness rather than pastness in terms of tense.

In the two stages presented so far, the important acquisitions are the notions of 'pretime' and 'posttime' on which the development of the relations 'precedence' and 'posteriority' rests. The primary ability to distinguish the ET from the ST/RT cluster — first in terms of including or being included, later in terms of precedence and posteriority — shows that a child's earliest temporal adverbs must be specifiers and operators of the ET (see section 3.3.4). Hence, they must be aspectual in nature. For German, this seems to be confirmed by early uses of *noch* 'still' (see Nederstigt, this volume), which is a continuative aspect marker, and by early occurrences of *wieder* 'again' (see Wittek, 2002), which is a marker of iterative aspect. Both aspect markers can be interpreted as operators on the ET (see Bennett & Partee, 1973; Dowty, 1979; Van Geenhoven, 2005). Similarly, the primary ability to relate temporal parameters by means of simultaneity and later by means of precedence and posteriority seems to be mirrored in the fact that *when*-clauses are used before *before*- and *after*-clauses are (see section 3.4.4).

5.3. Stage Three: From Deictic Aspect to Deictic Tense

By adopting a relational perspective on aspect, clustering the ST with the RT mirrors the fact that a child's grammatical aspect system is deictic in nature. According to Smith and Weist, it is only at a later stage that the RT is distinguished form the ST. Following Reichenbach, the need for a child to distinguish the RT as a third temporal parameter is related to his specific need to master the pluperfect (see fn. 4). If we adopt Klein's view on tense, the need for acquiring an independent RT follows from a general need to express past, present, and future tense. The question that immediately arises is why a child would develop a deictic system of tense if aspect can fulfil this role? My answer will be the following: Children do not develop tense because they need a deictic system. What they need is a system to anchor their utterances in larger temporal contexts. This brings us to the role of the RT and tense in the temporal system of adult speech.

Tense is more than a deictic system. If we adopt the view that tense is the relation between the RT and the ST of an utterance, it follows that tense is a *relational* system because of the relations it expresses. It also follows that it is a *deictic* system because of the involvement of the deictic element ST. But it also follows that tense is an *anaphoric* system because of the involvement of the RT, which is an anaphoric element. Building on Partee (1973), in which the interpretation of tense is linked to the interpretation of pronouns, Partee (1984, 243) points out that

> the reference time is at the heart of temporal anaphora ... and the similarity between tense morphemes and pronouns can be seen as a derivative phenomenon.

Partee's point is also in line with the view that the RT belongs to the presupposed material of an utterance (see section 3.3.4). The semantic correlation between presuppositions and anaphora in the nominal domain has been drawn in Heim (1982) and elaborated in van der Sandt (1992). In Van Geenhoven (1999), I have elaborated this correlation in the temporal domain by treating RTs as presuppositions that need to be resolved in van der Sandt's sense. This means that a RT requires an antecedent just like a pronoun requires an antecedent. When this antecedent is found, an utterance is anchored in a wider temporal context. This means that the ability to resolve the RT is basically the ability to interpret sentences at the level of discourse.

Returning to the goal of this chapter, which is to model the development of time, it follows that a child is able to differentiate the RT from the ST at the point at which he is able to embed utterances in a temporal context. A full understanding of the RT requires a command of discourse-level interpretive mechanisms, in particular, a command of relating anaphoric expressions to their appropriate antecedents (see Kamp & Reyle, 1993). Given that we know that the acquisition of anaphora resolution in the nominal domain is late (see Karmiloff-Smith, 1979; Wykes, 1981; Tyler, 1983; Yuill & Oakhill, 1991), I suggest that a child masters the role of the RT late as well. This late acquisition is the reason of why the RT is decentred from the ST only at a third stage. As long as child speech is tenseless, we basically say that child speech is not embedded in a discourse.

We now have a background against which we can explain the development of the tense system at a third stage. In (24) above, the interpretation of English *-ed* at the second stage is represented as a deictic perfect aspect. I suggest that by moving the RT out of the ST/RT into the pretime of the ST — because that is where the RT finds its antecedent — we get the following representation of a past tense meaning of *-ed*:

(28)   [...RT...]
——————————————ST——————————————>
        {...ET...}

The location of the ET has not been changed and the consequence of this is that *-ed* (and so do the Italian *passato prossimo* and the French *passé composé*) now receives its adult past perfective interpretation. Note that as soon as the RT is decentred from the ST, aspect has lost its deictic status.

Will was first interpreted as a tenseless prospective aspect marker (see (26)). Shifting the RT into the posttime of the ST — because here the RT finds its antecedent — results into the following representation of *will*-utterances:

(29)   [...RT...]
——————————————ST——————————————————————>
                                  {...ET...}

On its first future tense interpretation in (29) *will* is also a perfective aspect marker because the location of the ET remains the same.

Present tense is not acquired until a child is able to take apart the ST/RT cluster and to resolve the RT. Present tense, on the current perspective, is the case in which the RT finds its antecedent in the area of the ST and thus includes the ST. The late acquisition of present tense explains what Weist left unexplained, namely, why in English the present perfect is acquired late.

Interstingly, the child's development towards (28) and (29) mirrors the attested diachronic development of past and future tense out of perfect and prospective aspect. If past tense grows out of perfect aspect, it is predicted that the meaning of forms which express combinations of past tense and perfect aspect are acquired at an even later stage. This explains the late development of the pluperfect ('past perfect'). It is along the same line that I predict the late development of a 'future perfect' (e.g., *will have come*).

6. CONCLUSION

The first conclusion that I draw is that a command of temporal parameters and the relations between them is not necessarily synonymous with a command of tense. The development of these parameters and relations originates in an early understanding of lexical aspect and then serves as a basis of the development of a grammatical aspect system that is deictic.

Second, if we interpret the stepwise acquisition of temporal parameters and temporal relations in the way Smith and Weist have proposed by adopting a relational perspective on aspect, Smith's and Weist's stepwise acquisition supports the idea that aspect is acquired before tense. This conclusion is the opposite of what Weist argued for, namely, that the early development of creating relations between temporal parameters rejects the 'aspect before tense' hypothesis. Interestingly, the 'aspect before tense' hypothesis is supported by Smith's and Weist's claim that the ET is decentred from the ST before the RT is. Their claim is correct because displacing the RT requires the command of complex interpretive skills (anaphora resolution). Displacing the ET already begins earlier, namely, when children recognize the source state of a telic verb.

Third, mastering the aspect system is not the only prerequisite towards a full command of the tense system. A full command of tense assumes that the RT is regarded as an independent temporal parameter. This requires an ability to find the RT's antecedent so that an utterance can be embedded into the discourse of which it is a part.

Finally, a leading idea behind my integrated stage model is the diachronic development of tense out of aspect. There is a related prediction that I would like to address here. The prediction is that we expect that in the transitions between the different stages of a child's growing temporal system, a child's temporal forms are ambiguous in a way that we do not find in corresponding adult's forms. For example, we expect that in the third stage a child's *-ed* is ambiguous between a perfect aspect and a past tense interpretation. Given the fact that early time talk has never been investigated from this perspective, it would be premature to say that on the basis of the available child data we have evidence for or against this prediction. Yet, I would like to point out a related fact in adult language. Terry (2005) discusses Déchaine's (1993) observation that in African-American English V-*ed* sentences are ambiguous between a past perfective and a present perfect interpretation. This present perfect interpretation is close to the meaning of a Standard American English present perfect form. An example is (30):

(30) John ate the rutabagas.
    a.   'John ate the rutabagas.'
    b.   'John has eaten the rutabagas.'

From the perspective taken in this chapter, one could interpret this ambiguity as a consequence of the fact that although diachronically the simple past form *ate* has gained its past tense meaning out of a perfect aspect meaning, it did not lose this original aspectual meaning. The ambiguity of simple past forms in adult African-American English is then a synchronic correspondent of an ambiguity that we expect to find in a child's transition from the deictic aspect to the deictic tense stage.

Radboud Universiteit Nijmegen

7. ACKNOWLEDGEMENTS

A previous version of this chapter was presented at the 1998 workshop on *Acquisition and Variation in Syntax and Semantics* held at the SISSA, Trieste, Italy. I thank Wolfgang Klein and Carlota Smith for many helpful comments. This research was supported by the Max Planck Society, Munich, and by the Royal Netherlands Academy of Arts and Sciences.

8. NOTES

[1] Note that (1) lacks an auxiliary and thus a true tense marker. I return to this in section 5.2.

[2] Tense, in Smith's (1980) view, is the relation between the ST and the RT (1980, 265). In this respect she deviates from Reichenbach (1947), who treats tense as a relation between the ET and the ST which is mediated by the RT. Note that Smith (1991) adopts the dual approach that we also find in Kamp & Reyle (1993).

[3] This view clearly deviates from the one taken in Smith (1980), for whom the only tense at this primary stage is present tense.

[4] In Reichenbach's view, the RT is an additional ET needed to describe, among other things, the pluperfect as a past in the past.

[5] This becomes clear in the discussions in Rispoli & Bloom (1985), Smith & Weist (1987), and Bloom & Harner (1989).

[6] While Klein uses the term 'topic time', I use the term 'reference time'. The RT of an utterance is the time talked about while its ET is the time of the event or situation talked about.

[7] These interactions have been discussed at length in Stump (1985), Rooth (1985), de Swart (1991), and Johnston (1994).

[8] It would be interesting to rethink the acquisition of *before* and *after* from this perspective. See Clark (1971), French & Brown (1977), Bloom *et al.* (1980a), and Carni & French (1984).

[9] On Klein's view, achievement verbs (e.g., *find*) are also 2-state verbs. But see fn. 14.

[10] See also Johnston (1994) who introduces the related notions 'foremath' and 'aftermath'.

[11] Note that grammatical aspect markers have more than only a relational meaning. For example, imperfective aspect markers can express iteration, continuity, and habituality.

[12] An elaboration of tense as a double deictic relation can be found in Kamp & Reyle (1993).

[13] One of Klein's arguments against the view that tense is a relation between the ET and the ST is that this view cannot adequately capture that a state that holds before the ST could still hold at the ST. For example, if we utter *John was ill* it would be inadequate to interpret this sentence by saying that the ET at which John is ill was before the ST because John could still be ill at the ST.

[14] The fact that the imperfective picks out the source state of a 2-state verb leads to a problem in interpreting achievement verbs as 2-state verbs. Such an interpretation incorrectly predicts that a sentence like *John was discovering the solution when Mary called him* is well-formed because the meaning of the achievement verb *discover* contains a source state ('not discovered') that the imperfective can pick out. To me it seems that there is no inherent source state in the semantics of achievement verbs which explains that the above sentence is ill-formed. Instead, we can focus on their pretime. This would explain why prospective aspect is perfectly well compatible with achievement verbs (e.g., *John was about to discover the solution when Mary called him*).

9. REFERENCES

Antinucci, Francesco, and Ruth Miller. "How Children Talk about What Happened." *Journal of Child Language* 3 (1976): 167–189.

Bennett, Michael, and Barbara H. Partee. *Towards the Logic of Tense and Aspect in English*. Bloomington: Indiana University Linguistics Club, 1978.

Bloom, Lois, and Lorraine Harner. "On the Developmental Contour of Child Language: A Reply to Smith & Weist." *Journal of Child Language* 16 (1989): 207–216.

Bloom, Lois, Margaret Lahey, Lois Hood, Karin Lifter, and Kathleen Fiess. "Complex Sentences: Acquisition of Syntactic Connectives and the Semantic Relations They Encode." *Journal of Child Language* 7 (1980b): 235–261.

Bloom, Lois, Karin Lifter, and Jeremie Hafitz. "Semantics of Verbs and the Development of Verb Inflection in Child Language." *Language* 56 (1980b): 386–412.

Borer, Hagit, and Kenneth Wexler. "Bi-unique Relations and the Maturation of Grammatical Principles." *Natural Language and Linguistic Theory* 10 (1992): 147–189.

Bronckart, Jean-Paul, and Hermina Sinclair. "Time, Tense and Aspect." *Cognition* 2 (1973): 107–130.

Carni, Ellen, and Lucia A. French. "The Acquisition of *Before* and *After* Reconsidered: What Develops?" *Journal of Experimental Child Psychology* 37 (1984): 394–403.

Clark, Eve. "On the Acquisition of *before* and *after*." *Journal of Verbal Learning and Verbal Behavior* 10 (1971): 266–275.

Comrie, Bernard. *Aspect*. Cambridge: Cambridge University Press, 1976.

Déchaine, Rose-Marie. *Predicates Across Categories*. Ph.D. Diss., UMass, Amherst, 1993.

Dowty, David. *Word Meaning in Montague Grammar*. Dordrecht: Kluwer, 1979.

French, Lucia A., and Ann L. Brown. "Comprehension of *before and after* in Logical and Arbitrary Sequences." *Journal of Child Language* 4 (1977): 247–256.

Harner, Lorraine. "Talking about the Past and the Future." In William J. Friedman (ed.) *The Developmental Psychology of Time*, 141–169. New York: Academic Press, 1982.

Heim, Irene. *The Semantics of Definite and Indefinite Noun Phrases*. Ph.D. Diss., UMass, Amherst, 1982.

Johnston, Michael. *The Syntax and Semantics of Adverbial Adjuncts*. Ph.D. Diss., UC, Santa Cruz, 1994.

Kamp, Hans, and Uwe Reyle. *From Discourse to Logic*. Dordrecht: Kluwer, 1993.

Karmiloff-Smith, Annette. *A Functional Approach to Child Language: A Study of Determiners and Reference*. Cambridge: Cambridge University Press, 1979.

Klein, Wolfgang. *Time in Language*. London: Routledge, 1994.

Krifka, Manfred. "Nominal Reference, Temporal Constitution, and Quantification in Event Semantics." In Renate Bartsch, Johan van Benthem, and Peter van Emde-Boas (eds.) *Semantics and Contextual Expressions*, 75–115. Dordrecht: Foris, 1989.

Krifka, Manfred. "Thematic Roles as Links between Nominal Reference and Temporal Constitution." In Ivan A. Sag and Anna Szabolsci (eds.) *Lexical Matters*, 29–53. Stanford: CSLI Publications, 1992.

Nelson, Katherine. "The Matter of Time: Interdependencies between Language and Thought in Development." In Susan Gelman and James Byrnes (eds.) *Perspectives on Language and Thought*, 278–318. Cambridge: Cambridge University Press, 1991.

Partee, Barbara H. "Some Structural Analogies between Tenses and Pronouns in English." *The Journal of Philosophy* 70 (1973): 601–609.

Partee, Barbara H. "Nominal and Temporal Anaphora." *Linguistics and Philosophy* 70 (1984): 243–286.

Reichenbach, Hans. *Symbolic Logic*. New York: The Free Press, 1947.

Rispoli, Matthew, and Lois Bloom. "Incomplete and Continuing: Theoretical Issues in the Acquisition of Tense and Aspect." *Journal of Child Language* 12 (1985): 471–474.

Rooth, Mats. *Association with Focus*. Ph.D. Diss., UMass, Amherst, 1985.

van der Sandt, Rob. "Presupposition Projection and Anaphora Resolution." *Journal of Semantics* 9 (1992): 333–377.

Slobin, Dan I. "Crosslinguistic Evidence for the Language-Making Capacity." In Dan I. Slobin (ed.) *The Crosslinguistic Study of Language Acquisition, Volume II*, 111–220. Hillsdale, NJ: Lawrence Erlbaum, 1985.

Smith, Carlota. "The Acquisition of Time Talk: Relations between Child and Adult Grammars." *Journal of Child Language* 7 (1980): 263–278.

Smith, Carlota. *The Parameter of Aspect*. Dordrecht: Kluwer, 1991.

Smith, Carlota, and Richard Weist. "On the Temporal Contour of Child Language: A Reply to Bloom & Rispoli." *Journal of Child Language* 14 (1987): 387–392.

Stump, Gregory. *The Semantic Variability of Absolute Constructions*. Dordrecht: Reidel, 1985.

de Swart, Henriëtte. *Adverbs of Quantification: A Generalized Quantifier Approach*. Ph.D. Diss., RijksUniversiteit Groningen, 1991.

Terry, J. Michael. "The Simple Past and Present Perfect in African-American English." In Henk Verkuyl, Henriëtte de Swart, and Angeliek van Hout (eds.) *Perspectives on Aspect*, 217–232. Dordrecht: Springer, 2005.

Tyler, Lorraine K. "The Development of Discourse Mapping Processes: The Online Interpretation of Anaphoric Expressions." *Cognition* 13 (1983): 309–341.

Van Geenhoven, Veerle. "A Before-&-After Picture of *when-*, *before-*, and *after*-Clauses." In Tanya Matthews and Devon Strolovitch (eds.) *Proceedings of SALT 9*, 298–315. Ithaca: CLC Publications, 1999.

Van Geenhoven, Veerle. "Atelicity, Pluractionality, and Adverbial Quantification." In Henk Verkuyl, Henriëtte de Swart, and Angeliek van Hout (eds.) *Perspectives on Aspect*, 107–124. Dordrecht: Springer, 2005.

Vendler, Zeno. *Linguistics in Philosophy*. Ithaca: Cornell University Press, 1967.

Verkuyl, Henk. *On the Compositional Nature of the Aspects*. Dordrecht: Reidel, 1972.

Weist, Richard. "Tense and Aspect." In Paul Fletcher and Michael Garman (eds.) *Language Acquisition, 2nd Edition*, 356–374. Cambridge: Cambridge University Press, 1986.

Weist, Richard, Hanna Wysocka, Katarzyna Witkowska-Stadnik, Ewa Buczowska, and Emilia Konieczna. "The Defective Tense Hypothesis: On the Emergence of Tense and Aspect in Child Polish." *Journal of Child Language* 11 (1984): 347–374.

Wittek, Angelika. *Learning the Meaning of Change-of-State Verbs: A Case Study of German Child Language*. Berlin: Mouton-de Gruyter, 2002.

Wykes, Til. "Inference and Children's Comprehension of Pronouns." *Journal of Experimental Child Psychology* 32 (1981): 264–278.

Yuill, Nicola, and Jane Oakhill. *Children's Problems in Text Comprehension: An Experimental Investigation*. Cambridge: Cambridge University Press, 1991.

MARY SWIFT

STATE CHANGE AND TEMPORAL REFERENCE IN INUKTITUT CHILD LANGUAGE

Abstract. Early patterns of tense-aspect marking in child language crosslinguistically show that children tend to use past or perfective marking with verbs that express state change and present or imperfective marking with verbs that do not. Children acquiring Inuktitut, however, manifest this pattern not with the distribution of temporal markers, but solely on the basis of verb meaning and context of use, in accordance with the target language characteristic that unmarked verbs have default temporal interpretations based on their semantics. The Inuktitut data show how target language structure can influence the developmental sequence of tense-aspect marking, while the semantic processes underlying early temporal development crosslinguistically appear to be remarkably similar.

1. INTRODUCTION

The temporal distinction between perfective/past and imperfective/present time reference figures prominently in the early distributional patterns of tense-aspect morphology in child language crosslinguistically. Data from a number of typologically diverse languages, such as English (Bloom, Lifter & Hafitz, 1980), Hebrew (Berman, 1985), Italian (Antinucci & Miller, 1976), Mandarin (Li, 1990), Turkish (Aksu-Koç, 1988), and Warlpiri (Bavin, 1992) show that children demonstrate a strong early preference for the use of perfective/past marking with verbs that denote a change of state with clear results and imperfective/present marking with verbs that do not, suggesting a pattern of contrast in early tense-aspect marking based on state change, i.e., a 'state-change bias'.

Slobin (1985) addresses this crosslinguistic pattern in his basic child grammar hypothesis, proposing that contrasting temporal categories of PROCESS (nonpunctual, ongoing) and RESULT (punctual, completive) are part of a child's semantic predispositions. Whether PROCESS and RESULT are linguistically realized as aspect or tense marking depends on language-specific temporal encoding, so for example English has a contrast between the early use of progressive *-ing* and past *-ed*, as in *dropped*, *spilled* and *sleeping*, *running*. Slobin predicts that the categories of PROCESS and RESULT guide early grammatical encoding in child language such that the first perfective/past markers occur with resultative predicates.

This chapter addresses the distinction between perfective/past and imperfective/present time reference in the early speech of young children acquiring Inuktitut, a polysynthetic language spoken by the Inuit of arctic Quebec. In Inuktitut, the expression of this temporal distinction can be either unmarked or marked with overt morphology. An unmarked verb has a default temporal interpretation that depends on the meaning it encodes. Unmarked verbs that denote a discrete change of state have perfective/past time reference, i.e., reference to the completed state change, while unmarked verbs that do not denote a change of state have imperfective/present time reference, i.e., reference to an ongoing activity or current state. To extend this distinction between perfective/past and imperfective/present time reference beyond the lexically distributed contrast of the unmarked construction, the addition of overt morphology, such as aspectual markers that explicitly alter a verb's default interpretation of (un)boundedness, is required.

Spontaneous speech data from eight young children acquiring Inuktitut between ages 1;0 and 3;6 show that from an early age, Inuit children use temporally unmarked verbs in contexts of temporal reference that are consistent with the differences in the lexical semantics of the verb. That is, they use unmarked change of state verbs in reference to completed change of state events, and unmarked verbs that do not denote a change of state in reference to ongoing activities and current states. Thus young children acquiring Inuktitut use the same construction in contexts with different temporal reference.

Inuit children's early lexically distributed contrast with unmarked verbs indicates an early developmental preference for the bounded perspective for verbs that denote a discrete change of state, and the unbounded perspective for verbs that do not. This lexically distributed temporal contrast is demonstrated early on, but overt aspectual marking that manipulates the inherent (un)boundedness of verbal predicates appears only later, as does overt past marking.

The early distributional pattern of temporal reference in Inuktitut child language is semantically consistent with the state-change bias manifested in early patterns of tense-aspect marking reported crosslinguistically and with the expression of Slobin's contrast between PROCESS and RESULT. However, the temporal structure of Inuktitut gives rise to differences in Inuktitut child language with respect to the developmental pattern of overt tense-aspect marking observed in other languages. In Inuktitut, the state-change bias is expressed solely on the basis of verb meaning, without local cues of overt tense-aspect morphology onto which the notions of PROCESS and RESULT could be mapped. At the same time, Inuktitut has tense-aspect markers to express such notions, and they are required to express temporal viewpoints beyond those falling under the state-change bias. However, such markers appear in child speech only subsequent to the manifestation of the state-change bias with unmarked verbs. Finally, the first overt morphology used to express perfective/past in Inuktitut child language does not occur with resultative predicates, contra Slobin's (1985) prediction.

Relevant aspects of the Inuktitut temporal system are elaborated in section 2, within the temporal framework of Klein (1994). Methodological issues are summarized in section 3. The child speech data are presented in section 4, starting with the early state-change bias with unmarked verbs in section 4.1, then overt aspectual marking of completed activities and state change in progress in section 4.2, and finally the first overt past marking in section 4.3. The developmental patterns found in the Inuktitut data and their implications are summarized in section 5, and directions for future research are discussed.

2. STATE CHANGE AND TEMPORAL REFERENCE IN INUKTITUT

The Inuktitut temporal system is based on a future/nonfuture opposition (subsumed under a more general irrealis-realis opposition), where all future time reference must be overtly marked, and temporally unmarked verbs (i.e., main clause verbs that have no overt morphological marking for tense, aspect or modality) have nonfuture (either perfective/past or imperfective/present) time reference depending on the semantics of the verb, as noted above. The future/nonfuture opposition in Inuktitut contrasts with the past-nonpast system characteristic of languages in which a present tense form can be used with future time reference, such as German and Finnish (and, to a limited degree, in English, as in *The plane leaves tomorrow*).

The future/nonfuture temporal split in Inuktitut places perfective/past and imperfective/present time reference in the same nonfuture category, which is the unmarked member of the opposition. Thus the state-change bias described above is manifested without overt temporal marking in certain verb constructions in Inuktitut. The range of temporal reference implicit in temporally unmarked verbs is illustrated with the examples below:[1,2]

(1) a. *Anijuq.* *Completed change of state*
        ani-juq
        go.out-PAR.3sS
        'She went out.'

    b. *Pinasuttuq.* *Ongoing (in progress) activity*
        pinasuk-juq
        work-PAR.3sS
        'She is working.'

c. *Kaattuq.*   *Current state*
kaak-juq
be.hungry-PAR.3sS
'She is hungry.'

d. *Maniittuq.*   *Current location*
ma-ani-it-juq
here-LOC-be-PAR.3sS
'It is here.'

The examples in (1) illustrate how the temporal interpretation of unmarked verbs varies with verb meaning, although the verb construction (verb stem + inflectional ending) and the inflectional form remains the same. The example in (1a), *Anijuq* 'She went out', has perfective/past time reference with respect to the going out event. It is infelicitous to use the unmarked form if the subject has not yet left at the time of utterance. In contrast, the example in (1b), *Pinasuttuq* 'She is working', has imperfective/present time reference with respect to the working event. In this case, it is infelicitous to use this form if the event is not in progress at the time of utterance. The relevant factor for the determination of whether an unmarked verb has the perfective/past interpretation of (1a) or imperfective/present interpretation of (1b) is whether the verb stem denotes a discrete change of state. The examples with stative and locative verb stems in (1c) and (1d) have simple present interpretations; the verb stem in (1c) denotes a physical state, and the stem in (1d) denotes a location. Unmarked verbs can have more complex derived verb stems, as long as these contain no overt suffixes for temporal remoteness, aspect, or modality.[3]

The temporal contrast between perfective/past and imperfective/present is illustrated with the dialogue fragment in (2). The child asks where his mother and father are, and his aunt replies to each question with a temporally unmarked verb. The unmarked verb in (2b) is based on the verb stem *atai-* 'go out', which encodes a change of state, so it has completed event reference. The unmarked verb in (2d) is based on the verb stem *ammu-* 'sleep', which does not encode a change of state, so it has ongoing event reference:[4,5]

(2) a. *Aippagali?*   (Tumasi, 2;1)
aippaq-ga=li
companion-ABS.1Ssg=where
'Where (is) my companion (mother)?'

b.   *Ataipuq.* (Aunt)
     atai-vuq
     go.out-IND.3sS
     'She went out.'

c.   *Ataatagali*? (Tumasi, 2;1)
     ataata-ga=li
     father-ABS.1Ssg=where
     'Where (is) my father?'

d.   *Ammupuq.* (Aunt)
     ammu-vuq
     sleep-IND.3sS
     'He is sleeping.'

To capture the lexical distinction between ongoing and completed event reference in terms of whether or not a verb encodes a change of state, I adopt Klein's (1994) temporal framework,[6] which distinguishes lexical verb meaning in terms of the number of states encoded in the lexical content of a verb. The lexical content of a 1-state verb consists of a single state with no inherent boundaries, so no state change is encoded and the internal structure is homogenous. The lexical content of a 1-state verb, such as *pinasuk-* 'work', can be represented as in Figure 1:

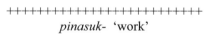
pinasuk- 'work'

Figure 1. *Lexical content of a 1-state verb stem*

In contrast, the lexical content of a 2-state verb encodes a change of state and so its internal structure is not homogenous, but comprised of a source state (before the state change) and a target state (after the state change). The lexical content of a 2-state predicate can be represented as in Figure 2:

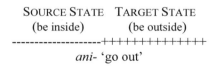
ani- 'go out'

Figure 2. *Lexical content of a 2-state verb stem*

Klein characterizes tense and aspect as relations between temporal intervals with the temporal parameters of Utterance Time (TU; the time the utterance occurs), Topic Time (TT; the time for which an assertion is made) and Situation Time (TSit; the time during which an event occurs). Tense is represented as a relation between TT and TU, and aspect (imperfective, perfective, prospective, perfect) is represented as a relation between TT and TSit.

The aspectual relation that holds between TT and TSit specifies how the lexical content of a predicate maps onto an event expression in discourse. For example, a perfective expression such as *Anijuq* 'She went out' expresses a state of affairs in which the going out event is finished at the time interval of the assertion, that is, TT includes TSit. An imperfective expression such as *Pinasuttuq* 'She is working' expresses a state of affairs in which the working event is going on at the time interval of the assertion, that is, TT is included in TSit. The temporal relations for perfective and imperfective aspect are summarized in Table 1:

Table 1. Perfective and imperfective relations

Inuktitut	Aspect	Aspectual Relation
Anijuq 'She went out'	Perfective	TT includes TSit
Pinasuttuq 'She is working'	Imperfective	TT included in TSit

The default temporal interpretations of the Inuktitut unmarked verb construction can be accounted for in the model described below, in which all and only the states represented in the lexical content of the verb map to the temporal interpretation of the unmarked construction. In this way, the difference in temporal interpretation of the unmarked construction with verb stems that do and do not encode state change follows from the difference in the meaning encoded in the verb (see Bohnemeyer & Swift, 2004 for an extended analysis).

Since a 1-state verb encodes a single unbounded state, its unmarked form in Inuktitut is used to assert a homogeneous event with no boundaries, so it has an imperfective temporal interpretation. An unmarked 1-state construction may be felicitously uttered as long as TT is included in TSit. The figure below illustrates the aspectual relationship defined by TT and TSit with the 1-state verb stem *pinasuk-* 'work' in the unmarked construction. TSit, in this case the time during which the working event occurs, is depicted graphically between {...} brackets, and TT, the time for which the assertion is made, is between [ ] brackets:

STATE CHANGE AND TEMPORAL REFERENCE IN CHILD INUKTITUT 199

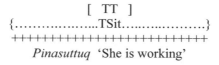

Pinasuttuq 'She is working'

Figure 3. *Default imperfective interpretation for unmarked 1-state verbs*

A 2-state verb in the unmarked construction is used to refer to a completed change of state event. The 2-state lexical content is not a homogenous internal structure since it embraces both the source state and the target state. For an unmarked 2-state verb to be felicitously uttered, the transition from source state to target state must be completed. Thus the default temporal interpretation is perfective, and the unmarked form may be felicitously uttered as long as TT includes TSit, the time of the going out event. The figure below illustrates the aspectual relationship defined by TT and TSit with the 2-state verb stem *ani-* 'go out' in the unmarked construction:

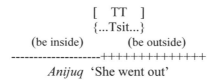

Anijuq 'She went out'

Figure 4. *Default perfective interpretation for unmarked 2-state verbs*

Since the default perfective and imperfective temporal interpretations in the Inuktitut unmarked verb construction depend on verb meaning, unmarked 2-state verbs can only be used in reference to completed state changes, and unmarked 1-state verbs can only be used in reference to ongoing activities and current states. To code completed and ongoing aspectual viewpoints across all verb types, such as a change of state in progress or the termination of an activity, overt aspectual suffixes must be added to the verb stem. The two aspectual markers addressed here are ingressive *-liq-* 'now, begin' and terminative *-jariiq-* 'finish', which are used to highlight initial and terminal boundaries, respectively.

The terminative marker *-jariiq-* 'finish' is used to refer to the completion of an ongoing activity, as in (3): [7]

(3) *Pinasugiirtuq.*
    pinasuk-jariiq-juq
    work-TERM-PAR.3sS
    'She has finished working.'

The addition of terminative -*jariiq*- alters the scope of TT to include the terminal boundary of TSit, but not the initial boundary. The meaning contribution of terminative -*jariiq*- with 1-state predicates can be depicted graphically as in Figure 5:

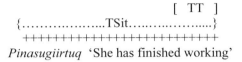

Pinasugiirtuq 'She has finished working'

Figure 5. *Terminative -jariiq- with 1-state verbs*

To refer to a change of state that has begun but not yet been completed, that is, state change in progress, the ingressive marker -*liq*- is added to the state change verb, as in (4):

(4) *Anilirtuq.*
 ani-liq-juq
 go.out-ING-PAR.3sS
 'She is (in the process of) going out.'

The addition of ingressive -*liq*- to 2-state verbs locates TT within the source state. When TT is located entirely within the source state, TT is included in TSit and the aspectual relation of the expression becomes imperfective. The meaning contribution of ingressive -*liq*- with 2-state verbs can be depicted graphically as in Figure 6:

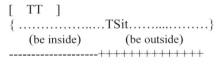

Anilirtuq 'She is (in the process of) going out/beginning to go out'

Figure 6. *Ingressive -liq- with 2-state verbs*

With 1-state verbs, ingressive -*liq*- contributes a temporal contrast with the previous moment, not unlike the English temporal adverb *now*, as in (5):

(5) *Pinasulirtuq.*
 pinasuk-liq-juq
 work-ING-PAR.3sS
 'Now she is working.'

The addition of ingressive -*liq*- to 1-state verbs highlights the initial portion of the event. Highlighting the initial portion of the homogenous representation does not change the default imperfective interpretation of the 1-state verb, but the addition of -*liq*- adds an implicature of contrast: Now she is working (but she wasn't before). The meaning contribution of -*liq*- with 1-state verbs can be depicted graphically as in Figure 7:

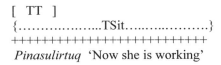

Pinasulirtuq 'Now she is working'

Figure 7. Ingressive -*liq*- with 1-state verbs

Tense in Inuktitut is marked with one of a number of temporal remoteness markers expressing several degrees of temporal remoteness in the past and future.[8] In Klein's framework, past tense is represented as a precedence relation between the time for which an assertion is made and the time of utterance, that is, TT precedes TU. (6) is an example of overtly marked past time reference in Inuktitut:

(6) *Pinasulaurtuq.*
     pinasuk-lauq-juq
     work-YESTERDAY.PAST-PAR.3sS
     'She worked yesterday.'

This section has illustrated different ways to express the encoding of the temporal contrast between perfective/past and imperfective/present in Inuktitut. First is the lexically distributed contrast of the unmarked verb construction, in which 2-state verbs have perfective interpretation and 1-state verbs have imperfective interpretation. Beyond this, overt temporal markers are required, such as the overt aspectual marking of boundedness with ingressive -*liq*- for the imperfective viewpoint with 2-state verbs and terminative -*jariiq*- for the perfective viewpoint with 1-state verbs, and the overt marking of past time reference. How the expression of the temporal contrast between perfective/past and imperfective/present develops at both the lexical level and at the level of overt temporal marking in the speech of young children learning Inuktitut is the focus of the remainder of the paper.

3. DATA COLLECTION AND METHODOLOGY

The data for this study are taken from two longitudinal spontaneous speech corpora collected by Crago (1988) and Allen (1996). The data represent the Tarramiut (Hudson Strait) dialect of Inuktitut, spoken by approximately 1500 Inuit in arctic Quebec. A focus on community programs promoting indigenous education and language use in this region have contributed to keeping Inuktitut the main language spoken in an increasingly bi- and trilingual (Inuktitut, English and French) environment. Inuktitut is still the first language of many children as well as the language of instruction for early primary education, although beyond the first years, formal instruction is conducted predominantly in English or French. In spite of the relatively strong profile of Inuktitut in arctic Quebec, especially in comparison to other indigenous language communities in Canada, Inuktitut is still considered at risk for long-term survival (Burnaby, 1996; Dorais, 1997).

The children in Crago's study (Jini, Lucasi, Sara and Tumasi) were videotaped for five hours every four months for one year. The children in Allen's study (Elijah, Lizzie, Louisa and Paul) were videotaped for four hours every month for nine months. Taken together, the corpora represent eight Inuit children with ages ranging from 1;0 up to 3;6, all acquiring Inuktitut as a first language. The child speech data, as well as speech from caregivers, siblings and peers who interacted with the children during taping, were transcribed by native speakers and coded as detailed in Crago (1988) and Allen (1996).

Because of differences in developmental complexity within similar age ranges, the child speech data presented here are grouped by verbal MLU [9] to illustrate patterns across successive stages of verbal development. The children and their ages by verbal MLU grouping are shown in Table 2:

Table 2. Data grouping by age and verbal MLU

MLU	Elijah	Lizzie	Paul	Louisa	Tumasi	Jini	Lucasi	Sara
1.00-1.49	--	--	--	--	1;9	1;0	1;8	1;4, 1;8
1.50-1.99	--	--	--	--	--	1;4	2;0, 2;4	--
2.00-2.49	--	--	--	--	--	1;8	2;8	1;11, 2;4
2.50-2.99	--	--	--	--	2;1	2;1	--	--
3.00-3.49	--	--	--	2;10	--	--	--	--
3.50-3.99	--	--	2;6	3;2	--	--	--	--
4.00-4.47	2;0	2;6, 2;10	2;11	3;6	--	--	--	--
4.50-5.49	2;5, 2;9	3;3	3;3	--	--	--	--	--

The child speech data were analyzed for developmental trends in temporal reference relevant to the expression of the temporal contrast between perfective/past and imperfective/present in both unmarked and overtly marked verbal utterances.

4. THE EXPRESSION OF PERFECTIVE/PAST AND IMPERFECTIVE/PRESENT IN INUKTITUT CHILD LANGUAGE

This section presents Inuktitut child speech data illustrating the development of the temporal contrast between perfective/past and imperfective/present first with the unmarked verb construction in 4.1, then with overt aspectual marking that manipulates event boundaries in 4.2, and finally with overt marking for past time reference in 4.3.

4.1. Temporally Unmarked Verbal Constructions

The morphologically simplest verbal construction in Inuktitut consists of a simple verb stem followed by the obligatory verbal inflection, as in the unmarked verbs illustrated in (1) above. Temporally unmarked verbs are among the first adult-like verbs used by Inuit children,[10] along with imperative verb forms, which can also have the simple structure of stem plus ending, but in this case the ending is in the imperative mood and thus not considered temporally unmarked (see fn. 3).

Analysis of the spontaneous speech data shows that Inuit children's use of temporally unmarked verbs is generally consistent with the target language. That is, children use unmarked 2-state verbs in reference to completed events involving a discrete change of state, discrete change of location, or object transfer, and they use unmarked 1-state verbs in reference to ongoing activities, current physical and emotional states, and stative location descriptions. Crucially, the children do not use unmarked 2-state verbs in reference to change of state events that are not completed, or unmarked 1-state verbs in reference to completed activities. Overt markers for these temporal perspectives appear only later (see sections 4.2 and 4.3). Use of unmarked verbs in child speech is illustrated below.

4.1.1. Unmarked 2-State Verbs

Examples (7) through (11) illustrate instances of unmarked 2-state verbs in reference to completed change of state events. The utterances in (7) and (8) illustrate some of the earliest instances of unmarked verbs in the Inuktitut child speech data. The unmarked construction with the 2-state verb stem *katak-* 'fall (inanimate)' in (7) was produced by Jini at age 1;4 when she tipped a carton of toys out onto the floor:

(7) *Katapu.* (Jini, 1;4)
     katak-vuq
     fall-IND.3sS
     'It fell.'

In (8), Jini uses an unmarked form of the 2-state verb stem *piiq-* 'remove, undo'. In the context surrounding this utterance, Jini's mother has dressed Jini's doll in trousers and told Jini not to take them off of the doll. Jini shakes the doll and when its trousers come off she produces the following utterance:

(8) *Piikpa.* (Jini, 1;4)
     piiq-va
     remove-INT.3sS
     'Did it come off?'

In the context surrounding the utterances in (9), Elijah is tossing balls of play-doh back and forth with a friend. One of the balls drops behind the table and Elijah produces the utterance in (9a) with the 2-state verb stem *katak-* 'fall (inanimate)'. His friend ducks under the table to get it, and Elijah produces the utterance in (9b) with the unmarked form of 2-state verb stem *tigu-* 'take':

(9) a.　　Katappuq.　　　　　　　　　　　(Elijah, 2;9)
　　　　　katak-vuq
　　　　　fall-IND.3sS
　　　　　'It fell.'

　　b.　　Tigujait?　　　　　　　　　　　(Elijah, 2;9)
　　　　　tigu-jait
　　　　　take-PAR.2sS.3sO
　　　　　'You got (lit. took) it?'

Tumasi produces the utterance in (10) when he submerges a dish in water in the sink, using the unmarked form of the 2-state locative verbalizer *-aq-* 'go by way of':

(10) *Imaappara.*　　　　　　　　　　　(Tumasi, 2;8)
　　　imaq-aq-vara
　　　water-go.by.way.of-IND.1sS.3sO
　　　'I dunked/sank it.'

Elijah produces the utterance in (11) with the unmarked form of *miluq-* 'hit with projectile' when he throws his cap at the researcher and hits his mark:

(11) *Milupara!*　　　　　　　　　　　(Elijah, 2;9)
　　　miluq-vara
　　　hit.with.projectile-IND.1sS.3sO
　　　'I hit her!'

4.1.2. Unmarked 1-State Verbs

Examples (12) through (16) illustrate children's use of unmarked 1-state verbs in reference to activities in progress.

Both of Jini's utterances below are in reference to a toy figure she is playing with. Jini produces the unmarked 1-state verb in (12) with the verb stem *tiituq-* 'drink tea' [11] when she is pretending that her toy figure is drinking tea, and she produces the unmarked 1-state verb with the baby word stem *ammu-* 'sleep' in (13) when she puts the toy to bed:

(12) *Tiiturpuq.*　　　　　　　　　　　(Jini, 1;8)
　　　tii-tuq-vuq
　　　tea-consume-IND.3sS
　　　'She's drinking tea.'

(13) *Ammutu maani.* (Jini, 1;8)
   ammu-juq   ma-ani
   sleep-PAR.3sS here-LOC
   'She's sleeping here.'

In the context of the utterance in (14), Elijah hears loud snoring noises coming from the sleeping platform and he uses the unmarked form of the 1-state verb stem *sinik-* 'sleep' to ask who is sleeping there:

(14) *Ataataga sinittu kinalu?* (Elijah, 2;0)
   ataata-ga   sinik-juq   kina=lu
   father-ABS.1Ssg sleep-PAR.3sS who=and
   'My father is sleeping, and who (else)?'

Paul makes the following comment to his father during one of his taping sessions, with the unmarked (passivized) form of 1-state verb *atjiliuq-* 'film':

(15) *Ataata atjiliuqtaujugut.* (Paul, 2;6)
   ataata   atjiliuq-jau-jugut
   father   film-PASS-PAR.1pS
   'Father, we're being filmed'

In the situation surrounding the utterance in (16), Lizzie's mother has asked Lizzie to sing, and Lizzie uses the unmarked construction with 1-state verb stem *pinnguaq-* 'play' to say that she doesn't want to sing because she is busy playing:

(16) *Ii gumanngitara. Pinnguarama.* [12] (Lizzie, 2;6)
   ii   guma-nngit-jara   pi-nnguaq-gama
   no   want-NEG-PAR.1sS.3sO   do-play-CTG.3sS
   'No, I don't want to (do) it. I'm playing'

Children also use the unmarked construction with nondynamic 1-state verb stems such as *kaak-* 'be hungry', *taqa-* 'be tired', and *ikkii-* 'be cold' in reference to physical states, e.g., as in (17), and with the locative copula *-it-* 'be' in reference to stative locations, as in (18):

(17) *Ikkiigama.* (Jini, 2;0)
   ikkii-gama
   be.cold-CTG.1sS
   'I'm cold.'

(18) *Anaana, tirqialiga naniittu.* (Elijah, 2;9)
　　 anaana　 tirqialik-ga　　 nani-it-tuq
　　 mother　 cap-ABS.1Ssg　 where-be-PAR.3sS
　　 'Mother, where's my cap?'

4.1.3. Contrastive Unmarked and Marked Verbs

The sequences of utterances in (19) and (20) below illustrate contrastive use of the same verb stem in both unmarked and overtly marked constructions in appropriately different contexts of temporal reference.
　　 In (19), Paul uses the 2-state verb stem *arqa-* 'get down', first marked with the marker of desiderative modality *-guma-* 'want to' in (19a), and then in the unmarked construction in (19c). In the context of these utterances, Paul has climbed on top of a cupboard. He tells his older brother Matthew that he wants to get down with the utterance in (19a), marking the verb with *-guma-* 'want to'. Matthew tells Paul to get down by himself, with the utterance in (19b). Paul then climbs down from the cupboard on his own. When he reaches the floor, he produces the unmarked construction with the 2-state verb stem *arqa-* 'get down' in (19c):

(19) a.　　 *Arqarumagama.*　　　　　　　　　　　 (Paul, 2;6)
　　　　　　 arqa-guma-gama
　　　　　　 get.down-want-CTG.1sS
　　　　　　 'I want to get down.'

　　　 b.　　 *Immini arqalirit.*
　　　　　　 imminik arqa-liq-git
　　　　　　 self　　 get.down-POL-IMP.2sS
　　　　　　 'Get down by yourself.'　　　　　　　 (Matthew)

　　　 c.　　 *Arqarama.*　　　　　　　　　　　　　 (Paul, 2;6)
　　　　　　 arqa-gama
　　　　　　 get.down-CTG.1sS
　　　　　　 'I got down.'

The alternation in (20) illustrates the 2-state verb stem *ukkuaq-* 'close' marked first with the prospective aspect marker *-si-* in (20b), and then in unmarked construction in (20c). In the context of this example, the door to the deep freezer is standing open. Paul's brother Matthew asks his mother to close it, in (20a). Paul tells Matthew that he is about to close it in (20b), marking the verb stem *ukkuaq-* 'close' with prospective *-si-*, as he moves to the door but has not yet closed it. When he closes the freezer door he produces the unmarked 2-state verb in (20c), in reference to the completed event:

(20) a. *Anaaana unaaluk ukkualauruk.* (Matthew)
anaana u-na=aluk
mother this.one-ABS.SG=EMPH
ukkuaq-lauq-guk
close-POL-IMP.2sS.3sO
'Mother, please close this one (the freezer door).'

b. *Ukkuasigakku.* (Paul, 2;11)
ukkuaq-si-gakku
close-PRSP-CTG.1sS.3sO
'I'm about to close it.'

c. *Ukkuarakku.* (Paul, 2;11)
ukkuaq-gakku
close-CTG.1sS.3sO
'I closed it.'

4.1.4. Summary of Unmarked Verbs in Inuktitut Child Speech

The data presented above illustrate Inuit children's use of temporally unmarked verbal constructions in appropriate referential contexts from as early as age 1;4. These examples show that children use unmarked 2-state verbs in reference to completed change of state and change of location events in (7) through (11), and unmarked 1-state verbs in reference to ongoing activities in (12) through (16), current states in (17), and stative location descriptions in (18). The alternations of unmarked and marked constructions in contrastive contexts of temporal reference in (19) and (20) provide additional evidence of children's understanding of the temporal forms and their meanings.

4.2. Overt Aspectual Marking of Perfective/Imperfective in Child Speech

This section examines the development of overt aspectual marking to manipulate the perfective/imperfective contrast in Inuktitut child speech, specifically the use of terminative *-jariiq-* to mark 1-state verbs as perfective and ingressive *-liq-* to mark 2-state verbs as imperfective.

4.2.1. Terminative -jariiq-

Terminative -*jariiq*- 'finish' is typically used to mark the completion of activities, as described in section 2. The occurrences of terminative -*jariiq*- in child speech are summarized in Table 3, which shows that -*jariiq*- is infrequent or nonexistent in the speech of most of the children except for Elijah, and most of the instances in his speech occur when he has a fairly developed level of verbal production.

Table 3. Terminative -jariiq- by subject and verbal MLU

MLU	Elijah	Lizzie	Paul	Louisa	Tumasi	Jini	Lucasi	Sara
1.00-1.49	--	--	--	--	0	0	0	0
1.50-1.99	--	--	--	--	--	0	0	--
2.00-2.49	--	--	--	--	--	0	1	0
2.50-2.99	--	--	--	--	0	0	--	--
3.00-3.49	--	--	--	0	--	--	--	--
3.50-3.99	--	--	1	1	--	--	--	--
4.00-4.47	1	1	0	2	--	--	--	--
4.50-5.49	9	0	0	--	--	--	--	--
Total	10	1	1	3	0	0	1	0

Terminative -*jariiq*- may appear either in an independent verb construction formed with the light verb root *pi*- 'do', as in (21), or as a suffix to a non-light verb stem, as in (22), in which case the initial syllable of the suffix is often deleted. Examples of -*jariiq*- from the child speech data are given below.

In the context of the utterances in (21), Lizzie wants to go outside to play. Her mother tells her to first ask the researcher if she has finished (her implicit reference is to the filming activity), with the utterance in (21a). Lizzie overrides her mother's request and produces the utterance in (21b), saying that she is finished (being filmed):

(21) a.   *Atii saanli pijariirqit lalauruk?*   (Lizzie's mother)
    atii   saanli   pi-jariiq-vit
    go.on   shanley   do-TERM-INT.2sS
    la-lauq-guk
    say-POL-IMP.2sS.3sO
    'Go on, say "Shanley, have you finished?"'

b. *Gumanngigakku. Pijariirtunga.* (Lizzie, 2;10)
    guma-nngit-gakku   pi-jariiq-junga
    want-NEG-CTG.1sS.3sO   do-TERM-PAR.1sS
    'Because I don't want to. I've finished.'

In the context of the utterance in (22), Elijah observes people outside the window and comments that school has just let out for the day; literally, they have finished learning:

(22) *Ilinniariirqu ilinniavimmitualuit.* (Elijah, 2;9)
     ilinniaq-jariiq-vut   ilinniavik-mi-it-juq-aluk-it
     learn-TERM-IND.3pS   school-LOC-be-NZ-EMPH-ABS.PL
     'Those who are at school have finished learning.'

In the context of Louisa's utterance in (23), Louisa wants to play with the video camera. She uses terminative *-jariiq-* in reference to the end of the researcher's filming activity. Louisa elides the verb stems in the forms below; the elided stem for the second verbal expression, which begins with terminative *-jariiq-*, is the 1-state verb stem *atjiliuq-* 'film':

(23) *Gumagama. Giirtuaguvit.* (Louisa, 3;6)
     guma-gama   jariiq-tuaq-guvit
     want-CTG.1sS   TERM-as.soon.as-CND.2sS
     'Because I want to (play with the camera). When you've finished (filming).'

The spontaneous speech data show that children are slow to begin to use terminative *-jariiq-* with 1-state verbs to mark the end of activities. Terminative *-jariiq-* appears with frequency in the speech of only the most verbally advanced of the children.

4.2.2. Ingressive *-liq-*

Ingressive *-liq-* 'now, begin' highlights the initial boundary of an event, as described in section 2. When combined with 1-state verbs, ingressive *-liq-* functions as a marker of temporal contrast, i.e., '(and) now'. With 2-state verbs, ingressive *-liq-* functions as an imperfective marker, since to begin but not complete a state change amounts to the change of state being in progress.

The occurrences of ingressive *-liq-* in child speech are summarized in Table 4: [13]

Table 4. Ingressive -liq- by subject and verbal MLU

MLU	Elijah	Lizzie	Paul	Louisa	Tumasi	Jini	Lucasi	Sara
1.00-1.49	--	--	--	--	0	0	0	0
1.50-1.99	--	--	--	--	--	0	0	--
2.00-2.49	--	--	--	--	--	0	0	0
2.50-2.99	--	--	--	--	1	0	--	--
3.00-3.49	--	--	--	0	--	--	--	--
3.50-3.99	--	--	1	4	--	--	--	--
4.00-4.47	0	4	0	1	--	--	--	--
4.50-5.49	23	7	4	--	--	--	--	--
Total	23	11	5	5	1	0	0	0

Ingressive -*liq*- is more frequent in child speech than terminative -*jariiq*-. However, most instances of -*liq*- in child speech are restricted to 1-state verb stems. Moreover, all children's first instances of this marker invariably occur with 1-state verbs. Only two of the older children, Lizzie and Louisa, use ingressive -*liq*- with 2-state verb stems to mark a change of state in progress (in (27) and (28)).

Examples (24) through (27) illustrate instances of ingressive -*liq*- with 1-state verbs in child speech as a marker of temporal contrast, i.e., '(and) now'. Lizzie produces the utterance in (24) at the moment the researcher arrives for the taping session:

(24) *Qallunaa tamaniilirqu.* (Lizzie, 2;10)
qallunaaq-ø ta-ma-ni-it-liq-vuq
white.person-ABS.SG ANA-here-LOC-be-ING-IND.3sS
'And now the white person is here.'

In the context of the utterance in (25), there is a puppy on the porch outside and Louisa wants to bring it inside, against her mother's wishes. Louisa's use of ingressive -*liq*- emphasizes the fact that the puppy has begun to whimper, although it was silent before:

(25) *Qimmiapi qialirtu.* (Louisa, 3;2)
qimmik-apik-ø qia-liq-juq
dog-DIM-ABS.SG cry-ING-PAR.3sS
'And now the little doggie is crying.'

In the context of the utterances in (26), Paul and his brother Matthew are trying to tear open a large cardboard box so they can play inside of it.

Matthew produces the utterance in (26a) before they tear it, and Paul produces the utterance in (26b) after they tear it open:

(26) a. *Alittusivavuk.* (Matthew)
         alittuq-si-vavuk
         tear-PRSP-IND.2dS.3sO
         'We two are about to tear it.'

   b.   *Alittursimalijaminik.* (Paul, 3;3)
         alittuq-sima-liq-jaq-minik
         tear-PERF-ING-PASS.NZ-MOD.4Ssp
         '(It is) one that has now been torn.'

In Inuktitut the suffixation added to a verb stem may contribute to whether the entire expression is 1-state or 2-state. In (26b) above, the 2-state stem *alittuq-* 'tear' is followed by the perfect suffix *-sima-* to form the 1-state stem *alittursima-* 'be torn'.

As noted above, there are very few examples of ingressive aspect *-liq-* in child speech used to mark a change of state in progress. Only Louisa and Lizzie use ingressive *-liq-* with 2-state verbs, illustrated in (27) and (28).

Louisa uses *-liq-* to get an in-progress interpretation with the 2-state verb stem *ani-* 'go out' in (27) below, produced as she wheels her tricycle through the door. At the time of utterance, Louisa has not yet left the house:

(27) *Una anilirtuq uvangalu.* (Louisa, 3;2)
     u-na   ani-liq-juq   uvanga=lu
     this.one-ABS.SG   go.out-ING-PAR.3sS   1.SG.ABS/ERG=and
     'This one (my tricycle) is going out with me.'

In the context of the utterances in (28), Lizzie has seen her friend playing outside and she wants to join her. Lizzie comes out of the bedroom carrying all the clothes that she wants to wear to go outside. Her mother laughs at this scene and asks her where she (thinks she) is going, in (28a). Lizzie responds in (28b) with the 2-state verb stem *ani-* 'go out' together with ingressive *-liq-* to mark the in-progress reading:

(28) a. *Namualuk?* (Lizzie's mother)
         namut-aluk
         whereto=EMPH
         'Where (are you going) to?'

b. *Anilirama.* (Lizzie, 2;10)
    ani-liq-gama
    go.out-ING-CTG.3sS
    'I'm (in the process of) going out!'

The circumstances surrounding Lizzie's utterance in (28b) suggest that she uses *-liq-* as a progressive marker for the going out event in progress that she has initiated by preparing to dress to go out, although she has not yet gone out the door.

The data presented in this section show that although ingressive *-liq-* is relatively frequent in child speech, it is used primarily as a marker of temporal contrast '(and) now' with 1-state verbs. Only two children, both with a verbal MLU of more than 3.5, use *-liq-* to mark an ongoing process with 2-state verbs. Children's use of *-liq-* with 1-state verbs demonstrates their facility with the form of the marker, while their delay in using *-liq-* with 2-state verbs suggests that it takes some time for the children to be able to recognize and highlight the source state of 2-state verbs.

4.3 First past marking

The data in section 4.1 show that Inuit children use unmarked 2-state verbs in the same contexts in which overt perfective/past markers are first reported for other languages, that is, in reference to completed state change events with clear results. Given this, it is not surprising that Inuit children's first overt marking of perfective/past appears with 1-state verbs, in contrast to the first uses of overt perfective/past marking reported for other languages and predicted by Slobin (1985). In Inuktitut, unmarked 1-state verbs are by default imperfective/present, so any reference to completed activities or to activities and states in the past requires overt marking. Since children's overt aspectual marking of boundedness for 1-state verbs (completed activities) was discussed in 4.2, this section will focus on early instances of past time marking in Inuktitut child speech, that is, instances of markers that specify a precedence relation between TT and TU.

The first uses of overt markers of perfective/past time reference in Inuktitut are late compared to overt future markers and temporally unmarked verbs. They are sporadic in child speech until children reach a verbal MLU level of 4.0, in contrast to the more frequent use of overt future markers starting at a verbal MLU level of 2.5 (Swift, 2004).

The earliest past marker to appear in the data is recent past *-kainnaq-* 'a moment ago'. An example is shown in (29) below. Louisa uses *-kainnaq-* and the negation suffix *-nngit-* with the 1-state stem *qia-* 'cry', in what appears to be an attempt to deny that she was just crying:

(29) *Qiakainnangi*. (Louisa, 2;10)
    qia-kainnaq-nngit
    cry-RCT.PAST-NEG
    '(I) wasn't crying (a moment ago).'

The first instance of overt past marking in Paul's speech is not in a resultative context. In the context of the utterance in (30), Paul's parents have been urging Paul to finish eating, pointing out that his older brother has already finished. Paul uses same day past -*qqau*- in his response below in an apparent reference to how his brother has been showing off for the video camera that day:

(30) *Takujauqqaumat*? (Paul, 2;6)
    taku-jau-qqau-mmat
    see-PASS-TODAY.PAST-CTG.3sS
    'Because he was seen (filmed) (earlier today)?'

The first instance of an overt past marker in Lizzie's speech is shown in (31). In the context surrounding this utterance, Lizzie points at a picture frame where a picture in the photo album had been, and produces the utterance below:

(31) *Maaniikainnamat*. (Lizzie, 2;6)
    ma-ani-it-kainnaq-mmat
    here-LOC-be-RCT.PAST-CTG.3sS
    'It was here (a moment ago).'

Inuktitut has at least five markers for degrees of temporal remoteness in the past, and some of them have aspectual interpretations as well (see Swift, 2001; 2004), which increases the complexity of a comprehensive account of early past marking. However, the available data suggest that early uses of overt past markers in Inuktitut child speech do not fit the pattern widely reported in the crosslinguistic literature, that is, that first past markers occur in reference to state change events with clear results.

5. DISCUSSION

This paper has addressed the development of the expression of perfective/past and imperfective/present temporal reference in children acquiring Inuktitut, a language in which the expression of that distinction is twofold: at the lexical level with temporally unmarked verbs, and at the morphological level with overt temporal markers.

At the lexical level, the data in section 4.1 show that from an early age, Inuit children use unmarked 2-state verbs for completed change of state reference, and unmarked 1-state verbs for ongoing activity and current state reference. The default perfective 2-state and imperfective 1-state interpretations of the unmarked verb construction is consistent with the early distributional pattern of tense-aspect marking reported crosslinguistically, but in Inuktitut children get this fundamental contrast in a sense 'for free' with the unmarked verb construction, that is, without the addition of overt tense-aspect morphology. As a result, children learning Inuktitut are faced with the task of figuring out what the relevant verb categories and their associated temporal interpretations are, without overt temporal morphology on which to map these distinctions. Their use of the unmarked forms to make a nascent distinction between completed change of state events and ongoing activities indicates an apparent sensitivity to state change as the result of lexical learning.

The case for lexical learning could of course also be made for children acquiring languages in which this temporal distinction is morphologically marked, for example as in English with progressive *-ing*, *-ed* and irregular past forms. However, for a language with obligatory tense-aspect marking on all perfective and imperfective forms, the relative contributions of lexical content and tense-aspect morphology to early verb categorization are more difficult to disentangle.

The relatively late development of the overt aspectual markers terminative *-jariiq-* and ingressive *-liq-* discussed in section 4.2 suggests that the default aspectual viewpoints of the unmarked construction, specifically the bounded perspective for 2-state predicates and the unbounded perspective for 1-state predicates, are more readily available to Inuit children and might be seen as more 'natural' than framing the event reference of 2-state expressions from an unbounded perspective and that of 1-state expressions from a bounded perspective.

The Inuktitut child language data show that the early preference for perfective reference to state change events and imperfective reference to non-change-of-state events observed crosslinguistically holds even if the verbs have no overt marking to indicate temporal interpretation. The Inuktitut data are consistent with the underlying semantics of Slobin's PROCESS and RESULT categories, but not with his concomitant prediction that first perfective/past time reference marking coincides with resultative predicates. The development of temporal reference in Inuktitut child language shows that the order in which overt tense-aspect marking emerges differs in accordance with the structure of the target language, though the semantic processes underlying temporal reference appear to be remarkably similar.

Although Inuit children appear to master the use of temporally unmarked verbs at an early age, the available spontaneous production data do not provide a complete picture of how children interpret the unmarked forms. Could the lack of morphological distinction between differences in temporal reference with 1- and 2-state unmarked verbs influence Inuit children's interpretation such that at some level, they interpret 1- and 2-state predicates similarly? For example, it is possible that Inuit children interpret the temporal reference of unmarked verbs as: 'the relevant state obtains at the time of utterance.' Unmarked 1-state verbs have only one state, which obtains at the time of utterance. For unmarked 2-state verbs, the relevant state is the one after the state change occurs, i.e., the target state. Thus Inuit children's correct use of unmarked 2-state constructions could be a comment on a present result state and not indicative of a notion of past. Comprehension data, such as data from experiments testing Inuit children's understanding of the notion of state change and its linguistic expression, would contribute to a more complete picture of how Inuit children interpret the temporal reference of unmarked 1- and 2-state verbs.

An intriguing question for future research would be to investigate whether Inuit children interpret unmarked change of state verbs as referring to the result (target) state only. If so, this could make for an interesting comparison with how children acquiring languages that overtly mark state change events with perfective/past morphology, such as English, conceptualize the reference of past-marked 2-state verbs. If these children conceptualize state change expressions as referring to the event itself, this would be a striking example of differences in event conceptualization guided by differences in the encoding of temporal concepts across languages.

University of Rochester

6. ACKNOWLEDGEMENTS

I am indebted to Shanley Allen and Martha Crago for making their Inuktitut spontaneous speech data available for analysis, and to the Inuit children and their families who participated in the data collection. I wish to thank the participants of the workshop on Semantics meets Acquisition, Jürgen Bohnemeyer, the editor and reviewers for comments. This research was supported by the Max Planck Society, Munich.

7. NOTES

[1] The following notation is used in the morphological glosses of examples. Nominal case: ABS = absolutive; ERG = ergative; LOC = locative; MOD = modalis. Verb mood: CND =

conditional; CTG = contingent; IMP = imperative; IND = indicative; INT = interrogative; PAR = participial (functionally equivalent to standard indicative in *Tarramiut*). Nominal inflection (e.g., ABS.SG): SG = singular; PL = plural.Verbal inflection (e.g., PAR.3sS): 1 = first person; 2 = second person; 3 = third person (disjoint); 4 = fourth person (third person coreferent); s = singular; d = dual; p = plural; S = subject; O = object. Possessed nominal inflection (e.g., ABS.1Ssg): 1 = first person possessor; S = singular possessor; sg = singular possessum. Prefix: ANA = anaphoric. Suffixes: ATP = antipassive; CAUS = causative; DIM = diminutive; EMPH = emphatic; ING = ingressive; NEG = negation; NZ = nominalizer; PASS = passive; PERF = perfect; POL = politeness (preceding imperative inflection); PRSP = prospective; TERM = terminative; RCT.PAST = recent past; TODAY.PAST = same day past, YESTERDAY.PAST = previous day past.

[2] Gender and animacy are not encoded in the verbal inflection, so decontextualized examples in 3rd person can be translated as he, she or it.

[3] Verbs in the imperative mood (which is, strictly speaking, optative, since the paradigm inflects for 1st, 2nd and 3rd person subjects) can also have the structure shown in (1), but the illocutionary force of the imperative ending contributes modal information (e.g., command, obligation, desire), so they are distinct from the temporally unmarked construction as discussed here. The same holds for certain subordinating mood inflections as used in complex clauses.

[4] Children's ages are represented in years;months. Pseudonyms are used for all speakers.

[5] The verb roots *atai-* 'go out' and *ammu-* 'sleep' are from a specialized lexicon of baby words (see Crago & Allen, 2001).

[6] For additional discussion of Klein (1994) see Van Geenhoven, this volume.

[7] The first syllable of *-jariiq-* is often deleted so it appears as *-riiq-* or *-giiq-*.

[8] The temporal remoteness system is elaborated in Swift (2001; 2004).

[9] An MLU (mean length of utterance) value is the mean of productive morphemes per utterance in a given speech sample. See Allen (1996) and Fortescue (1985) for discussion of the MLU measure in polysynthetic languages.

[10] See Crago & Allen (2001) for discussion of uninflected verbs in early Inuktitut.

[11] The verb stem *tiituq-* consists of the nominal root *tii-* 'tea' and the verbalizing suffix *-tuq-* 'consume'. As a denominal verb construction, it incorporates an unquantified theme argument, in this case *tii-*, hence, the expression in its unmarked form has a 1-state interpretation.

[12] Verb roots are sometimes elided in Inuktitut conversational speech, as is the case with *gumanngitara* 'I don't want to (do) it', where the word-initial *-guma-* 'want to' is a desiderative suffix (see Swift & Allen, 2002 for elaboration).

[13] Table 4 excludes occurrences of *-liq-* in verbs in the optative/imperative mood, where *-liq-* functions as a softener or politeness marker.

8. REFERENCES

Aksu-Koç, Ayhan. *The Acquisition of Aspect and Modality: The Case of Past Reference in Turkish*. Cambridge: Cambridge University Press, 1988.

Allen, Shanley E.M. *Aspects of Argument Structure Acquisition in Inuktitut*. Amsterdam: Benjamins, 1996.

Antinucci, Francesco, and Ruth Miller. "How Children Talk about What Happened." *Journal of Child Language* 3 (1976): 167–189.

Bavin, Edith L. "The Acquisition of Warlpiri." In Dan I. Slobin (ed.) *The Crosslinguistic Study of Language Acquisition, Volume III*, 309–371. Hillsdale, NJ: Lawrence Erlbaum, 1992.

Berman, Ruth. "The Acquisition of Hebrew." In Dan I. Slobin (ed.) *The Crosslinguistic Study of Language Acquisition, Volume I*, 255–371. Hillsdale, NJ: Lawrence Erlbaum, 1985.

Bloom, Lois, Karin Lifter, and Jeremie Hafitz. "Semantics of Verbs and the Development of Verb Inflection in Child Language." *Language* 56 (1980): 386–412.

Bohnemeyer, Jürgen, and Mary Swift. "Event Realization and Aspectual Interpretation." *Linguistics and Philosophy* 27 (2004): 263–296.

Burnaby, Barbara. "Aboriginal Language Maintenance, Development, and Enhancement: A Review of the Literature." In Gina Cantoni (ed.) *Stabilizing Indigenous Languages*, 22–40. Flagstaff: Northern Arizona University, 1996.

Crago, Martha B. *Cultural Context in Communicative Interaction of Young Inuit Children*. Ph.D. Diss., McGill University, 1988.

Crago, Martha B., and Shanley E.M. Allen. "Early Finiteness in Inuktitut: The Role of Language Structure and Input." *Language Acquisition* 9 (2001): 56–111.

Dorais, Louis-Jacques. *Quaqtaq: Modernity and Identity in an Inuit Community*. Toronto: University of Toronto Press, 1997.

Fortescue, Michael. "Learning to Speak Greenlandic: A Case Study of a Two-year-old's Morphology in a Polysynthetic Language." *First Language* 5 (1985): 101–114.

Klein, Wolfgang. *Time in Language*. London: Routledge, 1994.

Li, Ping. *Aspect and Aktionsart in Child Mandarin*. Ph.D. Diss., Rijksuniversiteit Leiden, 1990.

Slobin, Dan I. "Crosslinguistic Evidence for the Language-making Capacity." In Dan I. Slobin (ed.) *The Crosslinguistic Study of Language Acquisition, Volume II*, 111–220. Hillsdale, NJ: Lawrence Erlbaum, 1985.

Swift, Mary D. "The Morphological Encoding of Degrees of Temporal Remoteness in Inuktitut." In Mary Andronis, Christopher Ball, Heidi Elston, and Sylvain Neuvel (eds.) *CLS 37, The Panels: Languages of the Arctic. Papers from the 37th Meeting of the Chicago Linguistic Society, Volume II*, 289–304. Chicago: Chicago Linguistic Society, 2001.

Swift, Mary D. *Time in Child Inuktitut: A Developmental Study of an Eskimo-Aleut Language*. Berlin: Mouton de Gruyter, 2004.

Swift, Mary D., and Shanley E.M. Allen. "Verb Base Ellipsis in Inuktitut Conversational Discourse." *International Journal of American Linguistics* 68 (2002): 133–156.

MARIANNE STARREN

TEMPORAL ADVERBIALS AND EARLY TENSE AND ASPECT MARKERS IN THE ACQUISITION OF DUTCH

Abstract. This chapter examines how Turkish and Moroccan learners acquire the semantic and structural properties of the Dutch temporal reference system. The findings of this study demonstrate how these second language learners put early tense markers in utterance-initial position, in the topic component. In contrast, early aspect markers are embedded in front of the verb, in the focus component. Evidence is found that this development of verbal morphology is shaped by a parallel structural embedding of lexical adverbials in an earlier stage of acquisition. With respect to the 'aspect before tense' debate, I demonstrate that the first occurrences of morphosyntactic temporal marking emerge as grammatical aspect marking in the focus component of the learner utterances.

1. INTRODUCTION

In this chapter, the 'aspect before tense' hypothesis (Bloom *et al.*, 1980) is studied from a second language perspective. This hypothesis captures the idea that language learners acquire lexical and grammatical aspectual distinctions before they command tense. It has mainly been debated in the field of first language acquisition. Questions about how children learn to differentiate the Reichenbachian temporal parameters (event time ET, reference time RT, and time of speech ST) are addressed in two chapters about first language (L1) acquisition (see Swift, this volume; Van Geenhoven, this volume). This chapter discusses how adult second language learners, who already master the three temporal parameters from their L1, proceed in acquiring their second language's (L2) lexical and morphosyntactic means to express the relations between these parameters.

The general aim of this chapter is to describe and compare the acquisition of temporal reference by Turkish and Moroccan learners of Dutch from a longitudinal perspective, over a two-and-half-year period of language acquisition. The data is taken from the European Science Foundation's longitudinal and crosslinguistic database (Feldweg, 1993) and was collected from the onset of the acquisition process in the host countries. I describe in detail how these second language learners move from the initial *lexical* marking of temporal reference by temporal adverbials to a *morphosyntactic* tense and aspect marking at later stages. In doing so, I provide clear evidence for specific placement restrictions for temporal adverbials establishing temporal reference in the Dutch and French learner data. The temporal adverbial in the topic component has scope over the whole learner utterance, while the adverb in focus affects just the focus (see also Klein, this volume; Gretsch, this volume). The temporal adverbial in the focus component is put in front of the expression of the event or state expressed by the verb and its complements. I show how this topic-focus distribution of temporal adverbials recurs later in the process, with the same systematic shift between initial and non-initial position for early tense and aspect markings.

An essential question is whether learners first use iconic placing of scopal lexemes, adjacent to the material under scope, before they develop any of the morphosyntactic specifics of the target language in question. I hypothesize that the basic information structure, with its clear topic-focus partitioning and temporal adverbials specifying adjacent material under scope, functions as a skeleton for the learners' morphosyntactic development. The position of temporal adverbials functions as an anchor at which, in a later stage of acquisition, free morphemes expressing tense and aspect are adjoined. As a result, I propose a three-stage developmental model that shows how the structural and semantic properties of temporal adverbials shape the properties of early morphosyntactic tense and aspect markers in a later stage of development.

As far as semantic properties of these early tense and aspect markers are concerned, I propose that the learners' earliest experiments with verbal morphology express grammatical aspect distinctions (and not tense). Following Klein (1994), who builds on Reichenbach's three-parameter approach, I define tense and aspect as abstract temporal relations, which relate in different ways the three relevant time spans for expressing temporal relations. The temporal relation between the speech time (ST) and the reference time (RT) conveys tense. The temporal relationship between the event time (ET) and the reference time (RT) conveys aspect. I show that the learners of the present study, although all learning a tense-based target language, first develop a morphological encoding for marking the temporal relationship between ET and RT. On the basis of an analysis of some well-defined discourse contexts, I demonstrate that it is only in the later stages of acquisition that learners develop a morphological encoding for the expression of tense.

The chapter is organized as follows. In the next section I give an introduction to temporality in a second language. In section 3, I present the data and the informants. Section 4 describes the procedure of analysis of the learner data, which is a combination of a concordance/frequency (form-function) analysis and a discourse-oriented (function-form) analysis. In section 5, I list some features of the linguistic means for the expression of temporality in Dutch, Turkish and Moroccan Arabic. In section 6, I first present the three-stage model of acquisition of temporal reference. This is followed by the results of the empirical analyses of the structural and semantic properties of the (for the learners) most productive Dutch adverbial *altijd* 'always'. I then demonstrate my analyses of some early morphosyntactic tense and aspect markers that I found in the Dutch learner data. Section 7 is the concluding section.

2. TEMPORALITY IN A SECOND LANGUAGE

At the earliest stages of second language acquisition, temporal reference is established by means of a combination of discourse-pragmatic and lexical means. As several researchers (Dietrich *et al.*, 1995; Schumann, 1987; von Stutterheim, 1986) have previously found, learners in natural contexts first use implicit discourse-pragmatic means for temporal reference, then explicit temporal adverbials and at the later stages some learners develop a type of morphosyntactic tense and aspect marking (such as in *ik heb slapen* 'I have sleep', in example (1) below). Very few second language learners arrive at a final stage in which they are able to combine (proto)verbal tense and aspect markings into finite forms. Note that in the rest of this chapter I will refer to these early morphosyntactic tense and markings as protoverbal elements because they do not take all the features that full morphosyntactic auxiliaries and copulas show (person agreement, for example).

In this chapter, I propose for the development of temporal reference in Dutch by the Moroccan and Turkish learners of this study three stages going from lexical to finite verbal forms.

Stage 1: The Basic Lexical Stage. At this early stage learners use only lexical means to express temporality, there are no verbal markings. In these early learner utterances there is a structural embedding of temporal adverbials in two distinct positions, one for specification of the reference time (utterance initial position), the other one for the specification of the event time (adjacent to the VP or, in the very early stages, the 'word' denoting the event). As the learners start to use more verbal forms, they go over to the next stage.

Stage 2: The Free Morpheme Stage. Two distinct protoverbal markers are structurally embedded in two different positions. First, the free morphemes (*is/heeft* 'is/has') occur to mark the event time in a BEFORE-AFTER-AT-relation to the reference time, adjacent to the VP, to indicate the imperfective (with *is*) versus perfect(ive) (with *heeft*) aspectual character of the VP. These free morphemes indicating grammatical aspect occur in the focus component of the learner utterance. Then *is/was* occurs to mark the present versus past reference time in initial position, in order to mark tense.

Stage 3: The Packaging Stage. At this stage, which is only attained by a few learners, the earlier free morphemes are packaged in finite (auxiliary) verb forms.

In example (1) below, which comes from Ergün, a Turkish learner of Dutch, we see how beginning L2 speakers manage to anchor events in time by means of lexical items such as deictic adverbials (*vandaag* 'today', *vanmorgen* 'this morning'), direct speech, anaphoric (*dan* 'after'), and special discourse organization principles like mentioning events in their chronological order:

(1) *vandaag* hoofdpijn
     'today headache'
     ik ga niet naar fabriek
     'I go not to factory'
     ik *vanmorgen*
     'I this morning'
     half negen ik bellen
     'half past eight I phone'
     ja ik komt niet vandaag
     'yes I come not today'
     ik ben ziek
     'I am sick'
     vandaagavond zes uur
     'today evening six o'clock'
     ik *heb slapen*
     'I have sleep'
     dan klein beetje lopen
     'then a little bit walk'
     dan ik gaan naar cafee of zo
     'then I go to pub or something'

However, Ergün uses also one protoverbal element, namely the auxiliary-like *heb* in *ik heb slapen* 'I *have* sleep'. The exact meaning of this free morpheme has to be detected on the basis of very detailed analyses of the use of this morpheme in this and in much more other contexts. The difficulty in the analyses of these learner data, which often rely heavily on contextually given or previously established information and on presupposed shared knowledge, is to make the right inferences concerning the temporal information (see also Starren & van Hout, 1996). The example in (1) shows that the very nature of these natural data makes the coding of the distribution patterns of tense and aspect morphology very difficult. There are no clear morphosyntactic patterns. In fact, it is often the case that in these basic learner varieties, there is no verb at all or only bare root verbal forms (see also Starren, 1996; 2001). Therefore, for the analyses of these learner data, I present a combination of a form-oriented analysis and a concept–oriented discourse-analysis. In contrast to form-oriented analyses that are concentrated exclusively at morphological markings of temporality on the verb, a combination of these two types of analysis offers the possibility to find both explicit linguistic forms and implicit means used for establishing temporal reference in discourse. In the following section, I describe the collection and selection of the data. In section 4, I explain the procedure of analysis in detail.

3. THE DATA

The database in question is part of a larger database on untutored second language acquisition by adult immigrants, which is collected within the framework of an international project under the auspices of the European Science Foundation (ESF). In this project, data were collected simultaneously in Great Britain, Germany, The Netherlands, France and Sweden. For each target language (English, Swedish, German, Dutch, French), at least eight informants were followed and recorded in a variety of language activities for approximately three cycles of nine months, with one session per month on average. For this study, eight informants were selected from the total ESF database to provide a database representing a spectrum of different types of development: Mohamed, Fatima, HassanK, HassanL were all Moroccan speakers and Ergün, Mahmut, Abdullah and Osman were all Turkish speakers. This selection was made on the basis of earlier research (see Perdue, 1993a) in which Mohamed and Ergün were known to be relatively fast learners and Mahmut and Fatima relatively slow.

When the informants were first recorded, they were virtual beginners. Three similar data-collection cycles (Cycles 1, 2 and 3) of nine monthly encounters or sessions (Sessions 1-9) took place in which speech activities were repeated. During these sessions, a certain number of activities took place, such as narratives, film retellings, role-plays, and conversations (see Perdue, 1993a). In the presentation of the utterances, the session numbers precede the initials of the concerning informants: Ergün is ED, Mahmut is MA, Mohamed is MO, Fatima is FA, Osman is OS, Abdullah is AU, Hassan K is HK, Hassan M is HM. For example, code 1.3 ED indicates 'first cycle, third session from Ergün.'

For the discourse analyses, I had to select data from the total database. I opted for two types of data. The first is personal narratives (monologues), which seem to offer the richest temporal structure as it requires a deictic (with respect to the time of utterance) and anaphoric contextualization of events (in a sequence of utterances). The second type is film retellings, which permits checking the intended temporal reference of the informants (which in the early learner varieties often is implicit). The retelling of the silent film 'Modern Times' (see Perdue, 1993a) was used as the most structured type of narrative discourse data in the ESF project. The subtitle of the stimulus fragment of Charlie Chaplin's movie 'Modern Times' is 'Determined to return to prison.' It starts with a scene where Charlie Chaplin comes out of jail and finds work in a shipyard. Meanwhile a girl, alone and hungry, is watching a bakery van unloading bread at a bakery. As she steals a loaf of bread, another woman sees her stealing the bread and tells the baker, who in turn calls the police. In her flight the girl bumps into Charlie, and when the police arrive, he has the bread in his hands and takes the blame of the theft in order to return to jail. Below, I give an example of how a Moroccan learner of Dutch (Mohamed) retells this episode at the onset of the acquisition process (example 2a) and how he retells the same film episode at the end of the three years of data-collection (example (2b)):

(2) a. politie *komt* 1.9MO
'police comes'
pakt die meisje
'takes that girl'
die charlot *zegt*
'that charlot says'
ik *doet*
'I do'

b. toen hij loop in centrum 3.9MO
'then he walk in city'
toen *was* meisje heeft brood *stelen*
'then was girl bread steal'
toen vrouw *heeft* haar *gezien*
'then woman has her seen'
toen die meisje *gaat* snel *lopen*
'then the girl goes fast run'
toen allebei vallen
'then both fall'
maar toen *was* politie
'but then was police'
hij tegen die politie
'he to the police'
ik *heb* die brood uh/ja *gestelen* of zo
'I have that bread stolen or so'

In (2a), a basic form is used for retelling the sequence of events in chronological order, namely, the *root+t* form (*komt, pakt, zegt, doet*). In (2b), we see more complex verbal forms consisting of protoverbal markers in front of the main verb (*heeft stelen, gaat lopen, heb gestelen*). The forms in the retelling of this scene show how difficult it is to rely on forms alone; in one sequence Mohamed uses two times *heeft stelen* 'has stolen' and once *heb gestelen* 'has stolen' without a contrast in meaning. When uttering (2b), Mohamed is clearly in the middle of acquiring the past participle form of the verb and his stuttering reinforces the observation that he is creating complex forms. This juggling of forms is a clear indication that the learner is looking for a contrast to the basic form. However, it is difficult to judge whether the complex form is the result of a chunk or a real contrastive morphosyntactic construction.

4. THE PROCEDURE OF THE ANALYSIS

In order to give an inventory and classification of the structural and semantic properties of all the lexical and morphological devices used by each learner at each stage of acquisition, I first carried out a concordance analysis. I conducted computer-guided search analyses looking for forms of lexical and morphosyntactic devices in all the data available for the informants. I then analyzed and coded their semantic and structural properties in utterance and discourse context. In addition, I carried out in-depth concept-oriented discourse analyses over a subset of the total data set. For these analyses I took as a starting point a particular set of well-defined temporal concepts (such as 'simultaneity', 'past', 'present', 'future', '(im)perfectivity' etc.) and by reading through the transcripts line by line I analyzed how these temporal concepts are expressed by the learners. This is the only reliable way to detect nonstandard and nonexplicit devices of temporality.

4.1. The Concordance Analysis

The concordance technique for automatically searching for explicit standard linguistic devices expressing temporal reference (by means of automatic ocurrence programs) resulted in listings of relevant occurrences of specific temporal forms in a particular verbal context. I want to emphasize here that this concordance form-oriented strategy has three important disadvantages. First of all, this strategy does not show us which target language temporal adverbials are *not* used by the learner (either at a certain stage or not at all). Therefore, it was necessary to base my inquiry of the use of temporal adverbials in learner utterances on existing listings of Dutch adverbials as they are given in standard works on the use of the target language. For Dutch this is the *ANS* (Geerts *et al.*, 1984). I also used information from earlier research on Dutch temporal adverbials by Janssen (1994) and Oversteegen (1988) and my own intuitions about what words (or combination of words) could be cases of temporal reference in these learner varieties of Dutch.

Second, because *standard* linguistic devices for expressing temporal relations in Dutch and French were spotted in the occurrence lists, forms differing from these standard devices remain unincorporated or incorporated in the wrong way (see also Schenning, 1998). Take, for example, (3):

(3)   ik   gisteren   dokter gaan   vanmiddag   3.9MO
      I   yesterday doctor go   this afternoon
      'I went to the doctor yesterday afternoon.'

Instead of the standard form *gistermiddag*, Mahmut uses *gisteren vanmiddag*, which in Standard Dutch means 'yesterday this afternoon'. This composed deictic adverbial risks being coded as two individual deictic adverbials.

Third, temporal referential functions expressed in the L2 varieties without any overt temporal marking are not 'spotted' in the concordance list (see also von Stutterheim, 1986, 172). As is illustrated in example (4), Ankara functions here as temporal reference to the past because of shared situational knowledge.

(4)   Ankara   ik   trouw   1.3ED
      Ankara   I   marry
      'In Ankara I got married.'

The listener knows that Ankara is the place where Mahmut used to live. Therefore, spotting potentially interesting temporal adverbials and protoverbal markers in the output from word listings of the data was complemented by analyses of implicit methods of reference to temporality in discourse analyses.

The concordances are based on all nine sessions in all three cycles for the Turkish and Moroccan learners of Dutch. All 27 sessions (three cycles of 9 months) of all the informants are scanned for potential temporal forms. On the coding line I coded only the position of the temporal adverbial and/or the protoverbal marker. The semantic properties of these linguistic devices can only be judged in (still) more context. I indicated for each adverbial and/or protoverbal marker whether it is placed in the position before the topic-entity/subject (*ik* 'I') like *gisteren* 'yesterday' in example (5). This case I coded as 'POS1' (position 1). If the adverbial and/or protoverbal marker was put in another position I gave the code 'POS 2' (position 2), like *gisteren* 'yesterday' in the examples (6) and (7). In cases where there was no topic-entity mentioned, I did not code the position.

(5) gisteren ik gaat naar markt   2.3FC
     yesterday I go to market
     'Yesterday I went to the market.'

(6) ik gisteren slapen hele dag   2.2ED
     I yesterday sleep whole day
     'Yesterday I slept the whole day.'

(7) ik slapen tot drie uur gisteren   3.1OD
     I sleep till three o'clock yesterday
     'I slept till three o'clock yesterday.'

In earlier research on the utterance structure of adult learners, it was found that in the early stages of acquisition the event specification constitutes the focus of the utterance (Klein & Perdue, 1992, 312-314). The event is normally expressed by a verbal constituent (except for the earliest stages of acquisition where the whole utterance consists of nominals) and is usually placed after the topic information (as in example (5) above). At this basic level of language acquisition the topic information (adverbials of time and/or a topic entity, see Dimroth, 2000) is typically placed in initial position. This consistent ordering of topic-focus information mirrors in fact a basic information structure with topic elements setting the (temporal and spatial) stage on the left-hand side of the utterance and on the right-hand side the predicate. In the following I refer to the left-hand part of the learner utterances as the topic component and to the right-hand part as the focus component (see also Klein, this volume; Gretsch, this volume).

The output files of these automatic searches function as reference files for how one particular temporal adverbial or protoverbal marker behaves over time (over all sessions) for each individual learner as is shown in Table 1. The development of frequencies over time gives in the first instance only a rough idea which (standard) temporal adverbials and protoverbal markers were explicitly used and how many times at which cycle by each learner:

Table 1. Dutch temporal adverbials used by the main informants at each cycle

	Fatima			Mohamed			Ergun			Mahmut		
Cycle	I	II	III	I	II	III	I	II	III	I	II	III
al 'yet'	1 2	1 -	2 1	4 2	2 7	- 3	1 -	- 3	- 3	- 2	- -	- -
altijd 'always'	15 11	25 26	4 100	15 10	13 25	3 10	14 16	2 27	1 28	21 54	13 65	22 45
na 'after'	- -	3 1	- -	10 4	2 -	6 4	- -	- 1	- 1	1 -	1 -	- -
net 'just'	- -	- -	- -	- -	1 5	4 12	- -	- -	- -	- -	- 1	3 -
nog 'still'	8 16	22 23	7 79	7 24	26 12	3 51	8 5	10 32	9 80	11 13	13 15	2 50
nooit 'never'	- -	- -	- -	2 3	2 7	1 12	- -	- -	- -	- -	2 3	26 23
nou, nu 'now'	63 19	10 95	116 45	- -	- -	- -	5 12	2 12	7 11	5 2	3 12	26 10
vaak 'often'	- -	- -	- -	- -	- -	- -	1 -	- -	- -	- -	- -	- -
weer 'again'	- -	- -	- -	- 5	2 5	1 3	1 2	1 1	1 -	1 1	- 1	17 12

The concordance technique did not give sufficient information about how these temporal adverbials were used to express temporality. Therefore I needed an in-depth discourse analysis.

4.2. The Discourse Analysis

The discourse analysis was done by reading through all the personal narrative transcripts line by line, while coding for the expression of external and internal temporal properties by lexical adverbials, connectives, protoverbal markers and prepositional phrases (*in two weeks*) and/or pragmatic discourse means based on situational or contextual knowledge. Thus I followed, in the first instance, a form-oriented approach by tracing forms and giving them meanings in context.

4.2.1. The Coding of Temporal Adverbials

For the temporal adverbials (including nonstandard learner varieties of temporal adverbials) I coded the semantic characteristics of the adverbial in the utterance and the structural embedding of the adverbial in the utterance (POS 1/topic component or POS 2/focus component; see the concordance analysis above). For the semantic properties this means that I coded first the *type* of adverbial. In the present study, the following types of adverbials are distinguished:

TAP: Positional adverbials	(e.g., *yesterday, in two weeks*)
TAQ: freQuency adverbials	(e.g., *three times*)
TAD: adverbials of Duration	(e.g., *for four months*)
TAC: adverbials of Contrast	(e.g., *still, already, again*)

For the first type of adverbial, the positional adverbials TAP which specifies the *external* temporal relationship between two time spans, the coding system had to be the most complex. The position of the reference time RT is related to another time span on the time axis (the relatum) which is given in context in an anaphoric (*later*), deictic (*tomorrow*), or calendric way (*on the 8th of March*). The nature of the relatum was coded as follows:

AN: anaphoric relatum	(e.g., *two weeks later*)
DE: deictic relatum	(e.g., *in two weeks*)
CA: calendric relatum	(e.g., *after July 1967*)

To identify all the semantic properties of the temporal adverbials of the TAP-type, I also coded for each temporal adverbial if the anaphoric, deictic, or calendric relatum was in AFTER, BEFORE, or SIMULTANEOUS (AT) relation to the time talked about RT. For connectives which have by default an anaphoric relatum, I also coded the AFTER, BEFORE, or SIMULTANEOUS (AT) relation and their position in the utterance. For the other adverbials, I only coded the type of adverbial.

4.2.2. The Coding of Protoverbal Markers

The longitudinal design of this study and its onset early in the acquisition process allowed me to spot the earliest deviations from the base forms. If a learner uses in one interview only base infinitives and in the following interview an auxiliary-like verbal form in combination with these base forms (or fuses a morpheme with it), then there is reason to believe that the learner is trying to formalize whatever the concept is by morphosyntax-like linguistic means (see example (2), *steel* versus *heeft gestelen*).

Recall that I refer to these first experimentations on and around the verb as protoverbal markings. Protoverbal elements that occur 'independently' from another (lexical) verb in the topic component of an utterance and look like copulas are coded as 'proto-COP.' In that case, their positional code is 'POS 1', in parallel with the coding of temporal adverbials in the topic component. Note that in the case of early morphosyntactic tense and aspect markers, the protoverbal element can also remain in second position directly after the temporal adverbial in initial position and before the topic-entity/subject, as *is* 'is' after *dan* 'then' in example (8). Then they got also a POS2 code.

(8) dan   is   Charlie   bij hem   gestaan   1.5ED
    then is   Charlie   by him   stood
    'Then he stood close to him.'

When they occur in the focus component of an utterance as auxiliary-like morphemes in combination with another (main) verb, I consider them as 'proto-AUX' and they got the positional code 'POS2', as *gaat* in (9):

(9) toen   die meisje *gaat*   snel   lopen   3.9MK
    then   that girl goes   fast   run
    'Then she ran away quickly.'

There are also occurrences of two protoverbal elements in one utterance at two different positions (as in (10)): the first early morphosyntactic element, proto-COP, is placed in the topic component (*was*) and the second element, the proto-AUX, is placed in front of the verb in the focus component (*heeft*):

(10) toen   *was*   meisje   *heeft*   brood   stelen   3.9MK
     then   was   girl   has   bread   steal
     'Then the girl stole a loaf of bread.'

In order to understand the results of these two types of analyses, it will be helpful to first give a rather brief survey of some selected features of temporal adverbials and morphosyntactic tense and aspect markers in the source languages (namely, Turkish and Moroccan Arabic) and the target language (namely, Dutch) of the learners of the present study.

5. TEMPORALITY IN THE SOURCE AND TARGET LANGUAGES

Space precludes a detailed description of how the temporal aspectual systems work in the source and target languages of our informants; I confine myself to mentioning some global differences. The most important difference between the source and the target languages is that in Moroccan and Turkish many more aspectual notions are morphosyntactically encoded than in the target language Dutch and that tense marking is less basic than aspect marking. It is even said that Moroccan Arabic has no tense marking on the verb at all (Harrell, 1962; Caubet, 1982).

5.1. Temporality in Dutch

Dutch is a West Germanic language. Person and number are marked by the desinences of the finite verb (which is the lexical verb or a copula, an AUX or a modal verb). I use Geerts *et al.* (1984), Janssen (1994), and Boogaart (1999) as basic references for the description of Dutch.

The verb system is basically a tense system, i.e., the two conjugated verbal paradigms of the simple forms are built upon the present/past tense distinction (or present tense versus preterite tense, following Janssen, 1994):

(11) a. ik *werk*
'I am working/work.'
b. ik *werkte*
'I worked.'

The meaning of the two simple forms in (11) is present tense (RT = ST) in (11a) and past tense (RT < ST) in (11b). The relation between RT and ET for both cases is by default simultaneity. Therefore, there is no clear systematic morphosyntactically encoded contrast between RT IS INCLUDED IN ET (imperfective/progressive) and RT INCLUDES ET (perfective), like, for example, in English. However, there are two very productive periphrastic constructions in Dutch that I will call 'locatives'. These locative constructions can be used in all tenses. They are illustrated in (12):

(12) a. aan het INF
'on the INF'
b. zitten/liggen/staan/lopen/hangen te INF
'to sit/lie/stand/walk/hang to INF'

The finite verb appears in verb-second position in main clauses and in final position in subclauses. This means that in main clauses the auxiliary and the main verb are split up in two different positions, the auxiliary being in verb-second position and the main verb in utterance-final position.

As far as past tense reference is concerned, Dutch, like German, is said to suffer from "Präteritumsschwund", (see for example, Eisenberg, 1986). The preterite simple past form is in the process of being replaced by the present perfect complex verbal form. The Dutch perfect is constructed by the AUX of *hebben* 'to have' or *zijn* 'to be' plus a past participle, e.g., *hij heeft gewerkt* 'he has worked' and *hij is gekomen* 'he (is)/has come'. The choice of AUX depends on the particular verb and has to be learned individually. There is a strong debate going on in the literature (Boogaart, 1999; Janssen, 1954; Verkuyl, 1989) with respect to the meaning of the Dutch perfect.

As far as the position of the adverbials is concerned, in Dutch the adverbial can be placed in utterance-initial position (with inversion, ADV-FINITEVERB-SUBJECT-PREDICATE), as in (13):

(13) Vandaag eet   hij een appel.
      today   eats   he   an apple

In (14), we see that the adverbial can also be placed in the middle of the utterance (SUBJECT-FINITEVERB-ADV-PREDICATE):

(14) Hij moet   morgen   appels eten.
      he must   tomorrow   apples eat

Or, at the end (SUBJECT-FINITEVERB-PREDICATE-ADV) of the utterance, as is illustrated in (15):

(15) Hij eet   een appel vandaag.
      he eats   an apple   today

Temporal adverbials have scope properties just as quantifiers and negation particles do. The temporal components with which temporal adverbials interact vary according to their position in an utterance. The adverbials in the Dutch examples (16) and (17) exemplify the complex interaction of temporal adverbials:

(16) a. Op dinsdag nam Jan een pauze van 11 tot 12.
          'On Tuesday, John took a break from 11 to 12.'
      b. Jan nam pauze op dinsdag van 11 tot 12.
          'John took a break on Tuesday from 11 to 12.'

These utterances can be considered as answers to the following questions:

(17) a. Wat deed Jan op dinsdag?
          'What did John do on Tuesday?'
      b. Wanneer nam Jan een pauze?
          'When did John take a break?'

In (16a) the time for which an assertion is made (the reference time RT) is narrowed down to those days which are Tuesdays, and the assertion is John's break being from ten to twelve. In (16b), the RT is not narrowed down at all (except that it must include the time of speech ST) and the claim is the break being on Tuesday from ten to twelve. The RT-specification *on Tuesday* in (17a) contrasts with some other time about which a similar claim could be made, say *on Monday*. No such contrast is involved in (17b), where RT is not explicitly marked. This is an example of how the position of an adverbial has a direct influence on the semantic properties of the adverbial. Temporal adverbials can specify time spans: the RT or the ET. The time of speech is already given. The question is, which one of these two time spans is specified. The example above clearly shows that in these Dutch utterances, the temporal adverbial in initial position specifies the RT and the temporal adverbial in utterance-final position specifies ET.

5.2. Temporality in Turkish

Turkish is a so-called agglutinative language from the Altaic language family. The finite verb form is comprised of an invariant lexical stem and a string of affixed morphemes which agree phonetically with the root form. There are grammatical morphemes for voice (causative, reciprocal, reflexive, passive), modality, negation, tense, aspect, and person.

Turkish has explicit linguistic means for marking the temporal relation between RT and ST (tense) and ET to RT (aspect) and for indicating the relation between RT's in discourse. As in Dutch, tense is marked for each proposition of the discourse. The languages differ in the conflation of the aspectual categories; the Turkish system encodes aspectual distinctions that are different from the ones in Dutch. In combination with the present tense, there is a distinction between two aspects. One form, namely *-yor*, is used to express actions in progress (progressive RT included in ET), the other form, which is the aorist *-ir*, denotes continuing activity (one ET which is anchored at more then one RT).

Further devices for establishing temporal reference between RT and ST are positional adverbs (TAP) denoting points in time, *dün* 'yesterday', *simdi* 'now', *hemen* 'at once', and *sonra* 'later'. Frequentative and durative intervals are indicated by adverbials like *her zaman* 'always', and, for temporal contrasts, Turkish uses, for example, *gene* 'again'. In general, the adverbial system is similar to the Dutch system.

Neutral word order is SOV, with frequent deletion of subject pronouns, since person and number of subject are marked on the verb. For adverbials of time and place, the unmarked word order in Turkish is as follows: S (TAdv) OV (Erguvanli, 1984). In the absence of a subject NP, the time/place adverb occupies a sentence-initial topic position, setting the scene within which the predication is to hold. These adverbs may occur in topic (the sentence-initial position), focus (the immediately preverbal position), or background position (in Turkish, the postpredicate position) (Erguvanli, 1984).

5.3. Temporality in Moroccan Arabic

Moroccan Arabic is an Arabic dialect, which all native Moroccan speakers learn as their mother tongue before they begin formal education. It has often been said (Binnick, 1991; Caubet, 1986) that Moroccan Arabic has no explicit grammatical tense marking. Instead of referring to present and past times, the morphosyntactic markings on the verb indicate the completeness (perfect) or incompleteness (imperfect) of the event they refer to. In addition, there is a very productive active past participle which indicates the progressive aspectual viewpoint. This means that the temporal relation between RT and ST is not morphosyntactically encoded but that the temporal relation between RT and ET as completed or incompleted/ongoing is obligatorily marked at each utterance. It can be synthetized very roughly from the various descriptions of the Moroccan Arabic verbal system, that there are two verbal conjugations: one which is prefixed and indicates incompleteness and one which is suffixed and indicates completeness.

Inflected verb forms often combine into complex clusters, notably in connection with the auxiliary *ka:n* and what I call modifying verbs such as *bda* 'to begin', *bqa* 'to remain', *gadi* 'to be going to', etc. These complex verbal clusters are often combined with temporal adverbials (*di:ma* 'always', *daba* 'now', *l-ba:raH* 'yesterday'). It is this combination of various linguistic means which allows the speaker to express very subtle shades of temporal and aspectual meanings.

If you want to mark that an event is unbounded with respect to a particular RT such as ET in RT (which can be in the past, present, or future and this is specified by a temporal adverbial), you use one of the two imperfect prefixed forms depending on the actual prefixed *ka*-form (18) versus the 'pure' prefixed form non-actual distinction (19). The default reading is that the RT is present, otherwise, if the tense is not clear from context or a temporal adverbial, the AUX *ka:n* is added:

(18) *ka-y-ketbu*   RT is included in ET, actual reality reading
    'They are writing.'

(19) *ka:n y-ketb-u*   RT before ST and RT is included in ET
    'They were writing.'

The suffixed conjugation is roughly equivalent to the Dutch perfect. It sometimes indicates the aspectual post-state viewpoint of an event at RT, the anteriority of ET < RT, but in most cases it indicates a past tense, the anteriority of RT < ST:

(20)   *ketb-u*   (in the past, present or future RT)
       'They have written.'

With respect to the position of adverbials in Moroccan Arabic, it is very common to find an adverbial in sentence-initial position, particularly where it is temporal (e.g., *In the morning of August, 2nd, 1992*). The positioning of an adverbial element at the end is an indication that it may be taken up as the theme of the succeeding text (Holes, 1995, 208).

6. FROM SCOPE ADVERBIALS TO SYNTACTIC STRUCTURE

In this section I discuss the three-stage development for the acquisition of the target (Dutch) morphosyntactic tense and aspect system. I propose this stage-model, which contains the lexical stage, the free morpheme stage and the packaging stage, on the basis of my empirical analyses of occurrences of temporal adverbials and early protoverbal markers of tense and aspect in the learner data. I first give an overview of the stages at which the learners of the present study were stabilized. Then for each stage, I discuss the structural and semantic properties of the linguistic means used at each stage in more detail. On the basis of the concordance analyses the temporal adverbial *altijd* 'always' turns out to be the most productive adverbial. I describe, therefore, the structural and the semantic properties of this adverb in Dutch and in learner Dutch in a more elaborate way. For the free morpheme stage I concentrate on the most frequently used protoverbal markers, that is verbal forms of *to have* and *to be*, namely: *is, was* and *heeft* ('is', 'was' and 'has'). I show that in the last stage, the packaging stage, the learners try to cluster the free morphemes together with a main verb into a finite form (see also Klein, this volume). I show that the iconic embedding (based on scopal properties) of temporal adverbials and early free protoverbal markers is a framing factor for tense and aspect markings later in the development of temporal reference.

6.1. *The Three-Stage Model*

I propose the following three stages for the development of temporal reference in Dutch by the Moroccan and Turkish learners of this study.

   Stage 1: The Basic Lexical Stage. Fatima (Moroccan Arabic) fossilizes at this stage as she stays at only using lexical means e.g. temporal adverbials to express temporality. She increases her repertoire of temporal adverbials (see table 1, in section 4.1), which — as we will see below — allows her to express a limited number of aspectual distinctions by lexical contrast.

Stage 2: The Free Morpheme Stage. Mahmut, Osman and Abdullah stabilize at this stage, they spell out the notions of tense and aspect in free morphemes, showing no packaging (inflectional devices) of morphemes on auxiliaries or root forms. These learners use relatively fewer temporal adverbials than at stage 1. Two distinct protoverbal markers are structurally embedded in two different positions. First, the free morphemes (*is/heeft,* 'is'/ 'have') occur to mark the event time in a BEFORE-AFTER-AT-relation to the reference time, adjacent to the VP, to indicate the imperfective (with *is*) versus perfect(ive) (with *heeft*) aspectual character of the VP. These free morphemes indicating grammatical aspect occur in the focus component of the learner utterance. Then *is/was* occurs to mark the present versus past reference time in initial position, in order to mark tense.

Stage 3: The Packaging Stage. The packaging of different protoverbal markers (modality, tense and aspect) in finite (auxiliary) verb forms. HassanK, Ergün, HassanL and Mohamed try to package but fail.

6.2. The Lexical Stage

A first very general quantitative analysis of the data shows one adverbial to occur with an extremely high frequency, namely *altijd* 'always' (see Table 1 above). More interesting is the fact that further analysis revealed that Mahmut, Fatima and Zahra — learners who do not develop morphological means — manifest the highest frequencies on this adverbial.

I show below how different embeddings of *altijd* in the utterance organization lead to different interactions of this adverbial with other elements in the utterance, namely negation particles, definite and indefinite articles, tense and aspect and the lexical content of the predicate and its arguments. Different interactions give different readings and it seems that all learners in all stages are sensitive to the same general positional constraints. This I conclude on the basis of the structural properties of these adverbials which show two distributional patterns for the same temporal adverbials. That is, temporal adverbials which specify the RT are placed within the topic component of the utterance whereas temporal adverbials which specify the ET are placed within the focus component.

6.2.1. The Embedding of Temporal Adverbials in Learner Varieties

I show below that depending on how syntactic scope is organized in a particular language, the interaction of temporal adverbials with other elements in the utterance is established in different ways. Then I demonstrate, how these complex circumstances may pose severe learning difficulties for adult language learners. Nevertheless, the data demonstrate that learners in the different combinations of source and target languages studied here develop a clear and simple distributional system with their set of temporal adverbials to specify either reference times or event times.

A typical example of a learner using basic positional temporal adverbials to specify the RT can be found in:

(21) *gisteren*   ik   bergen   gaan   naar   2.3MO
      yesterday   I   mountains   go   to
      'Yesterday, I went to the mountains.'

In basic learner varieties, the relation within an utterance between ET and RT is by default transparent. ET and RT are assumed to be simultaneous (see Dietrich *et al.*, 1995). Learners at this stage do not have the morphosyntactic aspect markers, which could make the distinction between, for example, RT AFTER ET (perfect) and RT BEFORE ET. At this basic level of acquisition RT is always AT RT. If RT and ET in basic learner varieties are always simultaneous, any temporal adverbial could be said to specify both. How, then, can I obtain evidence for the claim that utterance initial temporal adverbials are indeed lexical specifications of RT instead of ET?

An important argument is the distribution of temporal adverbials in cases where an utterance contains *two* temporal adverbials, such as *maandag* 'Monday' and *negen uur* 'nine o'clock' in example (22) below. This is the case where adult learners place lexical specifications of RTs in initial position and specifications of ET in noninitial position close to the predicate, the event specification itself:

(22) *zaterdagzondag*   ik   niet   werkt   in Oosterhout   1.2HK
      Saturday-Sunday   I   not   work   in Oosterhout
      'I do not work in the weekends in Oosterhout.'
      maandag   is   opstaan   *negen uur*
      Monday   is   get up   nine o'clock
      'On Monday I have to get up at nine o'clock.'

Still more decisive evidence is provided in the next section by the distributional behavior of the most frequent adverbial for all learners at all stages: *always* (Dutch *altijd*). The frequencies of the concordance analyses (in Table 1) show immediately that Dutch *altijd* 'always' is a very productive adverbial.

6.2.2. The Embedding of 'altijd' in Dutch and in Learner Dutch

Before I demonstrate how the second language learners of the present study distribute the Dutch temporal adverbial *altijd* 'always' in their learner utterances, I discuss the distribution of *altijd* in Dutch.

Structural and Semantic Properties of 'altijd' in Dutch. I illustrate in (23i) and (23ii) below, the distributional analysis of Dutch *altijd* 'always' for a sentence like (23). Note that C is the variable for information that can be retrieved from context:

(23) Jan deed altijd de koelkast open.
 i. for all RT [C(RT)] there is a ET [jan deed de koelkast open at ET & AT (ET, RT)]
    'John always opened the fridge.'
 ii. there is a RT, ET [AT (ET, RT) & for all ET' [ET' in ET] [jan deed de koelkasr open at ET']]
    'John opened the fridge the whole time.'

In (23i) the quantificational adverb *altijd* binds the RT. In (23ii), there is one RT and a frequency adverb *altijd*. This *altijd* gets an iterative reading with telic predicates (accomplishments and achievements: e.g., *altijd verstoppen* 'always hiding'), and it gets a continuative reading with atelic predicates (states and activities: e.g., *altijd slapen* 'always sleeping').

The Embedding of 'altijd' in Learner Dutch. As can be seen from example (23) above, he temporal notions which can be obtained by different interactions of *always* do not have anything to do with a temporal *ordering* between RT and ET. They either express the 'frequency or the 'length' of RTs or ETs.

It is important to note here that only in learner varieties is it possible to specify (all) RTs by putting *always* in utterance-initial position. It must be stated here that the fronting of *always* is not a regular property of any of the target or source languages involved. In all of these languages, the occurrence of always in utterance-initial position is highly marked (strongly focused) or ungrammatical. The fronting of this adverb can only be described as the outcome of a general adult learner strategy.

Extensive analyses of the semantic and structural properties of *altijd* in the output files of the concordance analyses in combination with the discourse analysis gives a three-way classification of relevant meanings of *altijd* in terms of: quantification, continuity and frequency. I only present the target utterance containing the adverbial *altijd* without the surrounding context necessary for the right interpretation.

The first interpretation I discuss is the quantification of RT (see also Van Geenhoven, 1999; 2005). This reading is established by the utterance-initial position of the temporal adverbial *altijd* which has at this position the total utterance including the RT in its scope:

(24) altijd   ik   wakker   om acht uur   1.2MA
      always   I   awake   at eight o'clock
      'I am always (each morning) awake at eight o'clock.'

In (24) the event time of *to be awake at eight o'clock* and is hooked up to a series of reference times (quantified by the adverb *always* 'all time spans'). So, for all time spans which are part of the reference time RT (not morphologically marked on the verb) it is true/holds that in (22) Mahmut is/was/will be awake at eight o'clock.

In order to operate on the event itself, that is to say, to denote the intensity or frequency of the ET, the adverbial is placed in a non-initial position. This is illustrated by examples (25) and (26) below. These utterance structures typically denote a complex ET (consisting of separate phases of the event, quantified by *altijd*) linked to one RT (*gisteren-jaar, vandaag*), which yields an iterative reading. This is exactly the opposite of (24), where it is shown how one event time is linked to a series of RTs (quantified by *altijd*):

(25) *gisteren-jaar*   ik *altijd*   ongeluk   gedaan   2.2ED
      yesterday-year   I   always   accident done
      'Last year I had accidents, again and again.'

(26) *vandaag* ik *altijd*   weg   met auto   2.6FA
      today   I   always   gone   with car
      'Today I had to go away by car, again and again.'

The last notion I want to discuss here is the notion of continuity. Because *altijd* can be interpreted as indicating both the duration (all the time) of an event and the frequency of occurrence of an event, it is often difficult to choose between a durational and a frequency reading. As can be seen in the examples below, the reading depends on the lexical content of the predicate and its arguments (which may or may not be telic). In contrast to examples (25) and (26), the lexical content of utterances (27), (28), and (29) are all atelic (*drive, be ill, sleep, be tired, be wet*) leading to a continuity interpretation of *always*.

(27) auto vakantie beetje moeilijk   3.2ED
car holiday little bit difficult
drie dagen ik altijd auto rijen
three days I always car drive
'To go on holiday by car is difficult because for three days you do nothing but drive.'

(28) tot volgend jaar ik altijd ziek   2.1MK
til next year I always ill
'Til next year I'll be ill all the time.'

(29) vannacht ik geen slapen   2.1MO
tonight I none sleep
maar zij altijd slapen
but she always sleep
'Last night I did not sleep but she slept all the time.'

Since it is sometimes difficult to interpret what language learners mean, it can only be the integration of linguistic meaning proper and other sources of information (for example, previous utterances, situational perception, or general world knowledge) that makes it possible to construct (for the speaker) and to reconstruct (for the listener and the researcher) semantic representations. So, for the interpretation of the examples above (that is, to determine in which way the scope of *altijd* goes), I used a lot of contextual information which for reasons of space, is not all given here (the ESF-database is accessible for everyone).

It is worth pointing out that no occurrences were found in the basic stage of acquisition where *always* in utterance-initial position was used to specify event times in order to achieve a continuous or iterative reading. An utterance such as (25') never occurred in these learner varieties.

(25') altijd drie dagen ik auto rijden
always three days I car drive
*'It is always for three days that I drive the car.'

To sum up, learners at the basic variety level use temporal adverbials in both the topic and the focus component of the utterance, producing some lexical-aspectual contrasts. The adverb in topic has scope, to the right, over the whole utterance, while the adverb in focus affects just the focus.

6.3. The Free Morpheme Stage

In the positions where RTs and ETs are lexically specified in the earliest stages, morphosyntactic markers emerge in later acquisitional stages. In the case of the use of two auxiliary markers, those in utterance-initial position are related, as before, to the reference time which can be past, present, or future. Markers in front of the event specification (in the focus constituent) indicate the BEFORE, AFTER, or AT (simultaneity) relation of the event time to the reference time.

In Dutch (see 5.1), forms of the auxiliaries *to have* and *to be* are used as perfect and imperfective markers. In the target language, these auxiliaries take the tense morpheme to establish the reference to past and present (the situation for the future is more complex). The L2 learners of Dutch who reach the stage of more extensive grammaticalization (Mohamed, HassanK, HassanL, and Ergün), typically decompose these packaged verbal forms into separate protoverbal markers to express tense and aspect in a distinct way. As we can see in examples (30) and (31), these protoverbal markers appear in the same two distinct positions in the learner utterances as where the temporal adverbials emerged in the earlier basic lexical stage. This means that L2 learners put a proto-COP *is* (protoverbal form of the copula *zijn* 'to be', see 2) in initial position to mark a present reference time in relation to the utterance time:

(30)   nou   *is*   hij *is*   bezem trekken   3.9MO
       now   is   he   is   broom pull
       'Now he is in the process of pulling the broom.'

(31)   dan   *is* hij   *heeft* werk   aanvragen   2.9MK
       then is   he   has   work   ask
       'Then he is in the state after having asked for work.'

In both (30) and (31) there is a second protoverbal marker, in both cases adjacent to the VP. This marker (namely, proto-AUX, the protoverbal form of the auxiliary *is* or *have*) specifies the event time in relation to the reference time. In (30), the protoverb *is* marks an explicit simultaneous relation of the event time and the reference time, which yields an imperfective aspect. In (31), we see that in this position *is* can alternate with *heeft* (form of the auxiliary *hebben* 'have'). This form expresses a perfect(ive) aspectual relation between the ET and the RT. This means that the ET expressed by *work ask* is (partly) BEFORE the RT expressed by *then is*.

This analysis is corroborated by the fact that somewhat later in the process of acquisition, a past reference time specified by the free past tense morpheme *was* is used in utterance-initial position and in a paradigmatic relationship with the tense marker *is*:

(32) die   was   bij   Charlie   is   gestaan   3.4MK
     that   was   with   Charlie   is   stood
     'He was standing in the neighborhood of Charlie.'

(33) die meisje   was   nooit   heeft   verkering   2.4HK
     that girl   was   never   has   relation
     'That girl never had a relationship.'

The appearance of the past reference time marker *was* does not at all affect the occurrence of the aspectual markers *is* and *heeft*. These aspectual markers maintain their position near the verb itself. Note that in utterances where two protoverbal markers occur, the free morpheme *heeft* never occurs in initial position as a possible reference time marker.

The conclusion is that L2 learners use the iconic placing of temporal adverbials (i.e., direct adjacency to the material under scope) as a framework for anchoring free morphemes expressing tense and aspect. They do so before the morphosyntactic specifics of the target language are acquired.

6.4. The Packaging Stage

In the last stage of a stepwise acquisition process of morphosyntactic tense and aspect marking, the L2 learners have to learn how to package these free morphemes in complex finite verbal forms expressing both tense and aspect. The utterances in (34) below by HassanK, where he tries to merge tense and aspect morphemes with main verbs, are a good example of this last stage:

(34) a. ik   *was*   in Nederland   *kom*   3.4HK
         I   was   in Holland   come
     b. dan   die was   een jongen   bij ons op vakantie kwamen
         then   that was   a boy   to us   on vacation came
     c. was   in Marokko   gewoond   bij ons
         was   in Marokko   lived   with us
         'I came to Holland, then a boy came to us on vacation who had lived with us in Morocco.'

In (34a), we see how HassanK fails to integrate the free past tense morpheme *was* and the main verb *kom* 'come' which expresses the event itself. In Dutch, these two forms should be packaged into one complex verb form and this inflected verb should be placed in second position. In (34b) he combines the main verb *komen* with a past tense morpheme succesfully, which leads to the inflected verbal form *kwamen* (indicating a third person plural, but it also can be an unanalyzed past tense form). However, there is still a free past tense morpheme *was* in second position, which is the right (syntactic) position for the inflected form *kwamen*. In (34c), the past participle *gewoond* (perfect marking) is in the correct position but the utterance lacks the auxiliary *hebben* 'have' to complete the morphosyntactic perfect marking. In utterance-initial position a free past tense marker occurs which indicates a past reference time.

7. CONCLUSION

Two important conclusions can be drawn on the basis of these analyses. One is related to the structural properties of the temporal devices and the other one to the semantic properties. The overall picture that emerged from this study is that all learners of the present study went first through a stage in which adverbs, in combination with discourse-pragmatic means, established the most essential temporal relations. Those learners who left the basic lexical stage, developed free morphemes (proto-AUX and proto-COP) in order to express grammatical viewpoint aspect and tense. Proto-AUX were embedded adjacent to the verb in order to express the aspectual character of the verb and proto-COP were embedded in utterance-initial position to anchor the total utterance at the time axis (tense). Evidence was found that this development of verb morphology was shaped by the prior structural embedding of temporal adverbials. Time setting adverbials were placed in utterance-initial position to have scope over the total utterance. Adverbials that specified the aspectual character of the verb were placed adjacent to the verb. The position of temporal adverbials seems to function as an anchor at which, in a later stage of acquisition, free morphemes expressing tense and aspect could be joined.

As far as semantic properties are concerned, the diagnostics of some well-defined discourse-contexts showed that the earliest experiments with verbal morphology expressed aspectual viewpoint. The learners of the present study, although all learning a tense-based target language, developed a morphological encoding for aspect (proto-AUX) first and only later for tense (proto-COP).

8. REFERENCES

Binnick, Robert I. *Time and the Verb.* New York: Oxford University Press, 1991.
Bloom, Lois, Karin Lifter, and Jeremie Hafitz. "Semantics of Verbs and the Development of Verb Inflection in Child Language." *Language* 56 (1980): 386–412.

Boogaart, Ronny. *Aspect and Temporal Ordering: A Contrastive Analysis of Dutch and English.* Ph.D. Diss., Free University of Amsterdam, 1999.
Caubet, Dominique. "Systèmes Aspecto-Temporels en Arabe Maghrébin." *MAS-GELAS* 3 (1986): 97–132.
Dietrich, Rainer, Wolfgang Klein, and Colette Noyau. *The Acquisition of Temporality in a Second Language.* Amsterdam: Benjamins, 1995.
Dimroth, Christine, and Marzena Watorek. 'The Scope of Additive Particles in Basic Learner Languages." *Studies in Second Language Acquisition* 22 (2000): 307–336.
Eisenberg, Peter. *Grundriss der Deutschen Grammatik.* Stuttgart: Metzler, 1986.
Ergunvali, Eser. *The Function of Word Order in Turkish Grammar.* Berkeley: California Press. 1984.
Geerts, Guido, Walter Haeseryijn, Jacobus de Rooij, and Maarten C. van den Toorn. *Algemene Nederlandse Spraakkunst.* Groningen: Wolters-Noordhoff, 1984.
Harrell, Richard S. *A Short Reference Grammar of Moroccan Arabic.* Washington: Georgetown University, 1962.
Holes, Clive. *Modern Arabic: Structures, Functions and Varieties.* New York: Longman, 1995.
Janssen, Theo A. J. M. "Tense in Dutch: Eight Tenses or Two Tenses?" In Rolf Thieroff and Joachim Ballweg (eds.) *Tense Systems in European Languages*, 93–118. Tübingen: Niemeyer, 1994.
Klein, Wolfgang. *Time in Language.* London: Routledge, 1994.
Klein, Wolfgang, and Clive Perdue (eds.). *Utterance Structure: Developing Grammars Again.* Amsterdam: Benjamins, 1992.
MacWhinney, Brian. *The Childes Project.* New Jersey: Erlbaum, 1995.
Oversteegen, Leonoor. "Temporal Adverbials in a Two Track Theory of Time." In Veronika Ehrig and Heinz Vater (eds.) *Temporal Semantik.* 129–162, Tübingen: Niemeyer, 1994.
Perdue, Clive. *Adult Language Acquisition: Crosslinguistic Perspectives. Volume 1, Field Methods.* New York: Cambridge University Press, 1993a.
Perdue, Clive. *Adult Language Acquisition: Crosslinguistic Perspectives. Volume 2, The Results.* New York: Cambridge University Press, 1993b.
Reichenbach, Hans. *Symbolic Logic.* New York: The Free Press, 1947.
Schenning, Saskia. *Spatial Relations in Second Language Acquisition.* Tilburg: TUP, 1998.
Schumann, John. "The Expression of Temporality in Basilang Speech." *Studies in Second Language Acquisition* 9 (1987): 21–41.
Smith, Carlota. "The Acquisition of Time Talk: Relations between Child and Adult Grammars." *Journal of Child Language* 7 (1980): 263–278.
Starren, Marianne. "Temporal Adverbials as a Blocking Factor in the Grammaticalization Process of L2-Learners." In *CLS Proceedings 1996*, 1–16. Tilburg: TUP, 1996.
Starren, Marianne, and Roeland van Hout. "Temporality in Learner Discourse: What Temporal Adverbials Can and Cannot Express." *Zeitschrift für Literaturwissenschaft und Linguistik* 104 (1996): 34–50.
von Stutterheim, Christiane. *Temporalität in der Zweitsprache.* Berlin: de Gruyter, 1996.
Van Geenhoven, Veerle. "A Before-&-After Picture of *when-, before-,* and *after*-Clauses." In Tanya Matthews and Devon Strolovitch (eds.) *Proceedings of SALT IX*, 298–315. Ithaca: CLC Publications, 1999.
Van Geenhoven, Veerle. "Atelicity, Pluractionality, and Adverbial Quantification." In Henk Verkuyl, Henriëtte de Swart, and Angeliek van Hout (eds.) *Perspectives on Aspect*, 107–124. Dordrecht: Springer, 2005.
Vendler, Zeno. *Linguistics in Philosophy.* Ithaca: Cornell University Press, 1967.
Verkuyl, Henk. "Aspectual Classes and Aspectual Composition." *Linguistics and Philosophy* 12 (1989): 39–94.
Weist, Richard. "Tense and Aspect." In Paul Fletcher and Michael Garman (eds.) *Language Acquisition, 2nd Edition*, 356–374. Cambridge: Cambridge University Press, 1986.

WOLFGANG KLEIN

ON FINITENESS

Abstract. The distinction between finite and nonfinite verb forms is well-established but not particularly well-defined. It cannot just be a matter of verb morphology, because it is also made when there is hardly any morphological difference; by far most English verb forms can be finite as well as nonfinite. More importantly, many structural phenomena are clearly associated with the presence or absence of finiteness, a fact which is clearly reflected in the early stages of first and second language acquisition. In syntax, these include basic word order rules, gapping, the licensing of a grammatical subject and the licensing of expletives. In semantics, the specific interpretation of indefinite noun phrases is crucially linked to the presence of a finite element. These phenomena are surveyed, and it is argued that finiteness (a) links the descriptive content of the sentence (the 'sentence basis') to its topic component (in particular, to its topic time), and (b) it confines the illocutionary force to that topic component. In a declarative main clause, for example, the assertion is confined to a particular time, the topic time. It is shown that most of the syntactic and semantic effects connected to finiteness naturally follow from this assumption.

1. INTRODUCTION

As so many other concepts from our grammatical tradition, the notion of finiteness is used by everybody and understood by nobody. We were taught that the inflected forms *amo, amor, amavisses* are finite forms of the verb, whereas the inflected forms *amans, amaturus, amavisse* are nonfinite forms. No definition was given; instead, we were supposed to generalise from these and similar examples. Finiteness appears to be an inflectional category of the verb, along with tense, person, mood and others. This idea is problematic for at least two reasons. First, an inflectional category is not just a set of morphological changes; it is a cluster of formal and functional properties. But there is no apparent functional counterpart to the finite/nonfinite distinction, as there is a functional counterpart to the distinction between active and passive or between present tense and past tense. Second, the finite/nonfinite distinction between verb forms is also made for many languages in which its morphological marking is the exception rather than the rule. In English, all finite forms with very few exceptions such as *swam* or *are* can also be nonfinite forms and in which all nonfinite forms, except the *ing*-participle and some irregular forms such as *swum*, can also be finite forms. Nevertheless, we infallibly consider *left* in *He left* as finite, and in *He has left* as nonfinite. Why? Some irregular verb forms such as *must* are regularly categorized as finite, although they bear no inflection at all. Hence, finiteness should be more than just some changes in the form of the verb. But what? This is the question that I will address in this paper. It will be shown that finiteness has a number of syntactical and semantic consequences that cannot be derived from the fact that finite forms are marked for tense, person, mood and other verbal categories. Finiteness should be seen as a grammatical category in its own right.

This fact is clearly manifested in language acquisition. It has often been noted that children as well as adult learners regularly develop forms of linguistic organization which are characterized by the absence of finite verbs; this will be discussed in section 2. There are also many 'fully-fledged' languages without verb inflection, such as Chinese or Vietnamese. What is 'finiteness' in these languages? The same question may be asked for languages with a very rich inflection, such as all polysynthetic languages. The former are usually assumed to have no finiteness at all. This may be a premature conclusion, since the absence of inflection does not exclude the existence of other means to express the same function. As for polysynthetic languages, opinions on what is finite and what is nonfinite seem largely determined by the 'missionary's way' of grammatical analysis: a particular construction is labelled after a more or less close translation equivalent in Latin or English. This strategy has guided a great deal of our description of languages other than those for which traditional grammatical categories were originally proposed, that is, for Greek and Latin. It has lead us to call a 'perfect' form *veni* as well as *(I) have come* and *(ich) bin gekommen*, although neither their formal composition nor their functions are the same. Familiar categories such as perfect, passive, subject, direct object are but very preliminary attempts to lump together some functional and formal regularities, useful just by the very fact that they are so fuzzy and hence can be applied without any in-depth analysis. They should not be seen as theoretical notions, and any attempt to give them a 'precise definition' appears to be as hopeless and misguided as the attempt to give a precise definition to the Aristotelian classification of animals. They help us to bring together the phenomena to be investigated, no more, no less. This also holds for the notion of finiteness.

The paper has three parts. In section 2, I will review some relevant facts from first and second language acquisition. Sections 3 to 5 are devoted to a number of syntactical and semantical properties which go with finiteness; examples are primarily taken from German, since the distinction between finite and nonfinite is relatively clear and undisputed for most forms. In sections 6-9, I will try to bring these observations together; the result is an emergent picture of the role of finiteness in sentence structure. It does provide a formal theory of finiteness. It prepares such a theory. More problems will be raised than can be answered; but there is not much work on the notion of finiteness upon which one could build.

2. FINITENESS EFFECTS IN LANGUAGE ACQUISITION

In first as well as in second language acquisition, there is a characteristic stage in which speakers organise their utterances without finiteness marking. In what follows, I will briefly sketch the core facts; more detailed accounts are found in Dimroth & Lasser (2002).

2.1. First Language Acquisition: Root Infinitives

The first productive utterances of children are dominated by nonfinite verb forms. Here are a few examples from German: [1]

(1) a. Mein Kakao hinstelln (2;02)
 'my cocoa put-down'
 b. Max auch Pudding kochen (2;08)
 'Max also pudding cook'
 c. Ich erst ma das Buch angucken (2;11)
 'I first just the book watch'
 d. Eva Eis essen (2;02)
 'Eva ice cream eat'
 e. Andere Eis essen (2;03)
 'Other ice eat'
 f. Eis gesse (2;03)
 'Icecream eaten'

This fact, well-known since the days of Preyer and Stern, has recently become a matter of vivid discussion under the name of 'root infinitives' (i.e., infinites in root clauses). Over the last ten years, it has been addressed in numerous papers. In the present context, we will not re-examine this work (see Gretsch, this volume for a discussion and a new analysis, which is related in spirit to the present view on finiteness).

The lack of agreement in on-going research is partly due to the very unsatisfactory empirical basis. For German children at around age two, estimates on the share of root infinitive utterances vary between 15% and 100%.[1] This sharp fluctuation may reflect real variation between children; but for the most part, it is due to methodological problems. First, it is very difficult to decide what in a child's utterance is a root form or a productive sentence. Second, there is no clear criterion on when a verb form should be considered to be finite or nonfinite. Researchers tend to go the easy way here:

A form is 'finite' in child language, if its (closest) phonetic equivalent in adult language is finite, and it is nonfinite, if its (closest) phonetic equivalent in adult language is nonfinite. But formal resemblance to adult forms does not guarantee functional equivalence. Third, child production is often phonetically distorted and therefore in many ways ambiguous. Hence, it is anything but easy to draw clear conclusions about the role and development of finiteness in child language. Two points appear beyond doubt, however. First, children are highly sensitive to the distinction between finite and nonfinite forms. Second, they are also sensitive to syntactical consequences of this distinction; this is clearly reflected in the positional differences in which these forms appear.

2.2. Second Language Acquisition: From Nominal to Finite Utterance Organization

In second language acquisition, the existence of a nonfinite stage is less apparent. This is largely due to the fact that work in this field is still dominated by classroom research, in which the structure of the acquisition process largely reflects the way in which the material is presented to the learner. Thus, even the very first constructions taught are finite, and thus, it is no surprise if learners begin with finite sentences.

Second language acquisition outside the classroom reveals a very different picture. The largest investigation in this domain took place from 1981-1988 in France, Germany, Great Britain, The Netherlands and Sweden (for a comprehensive account, see Perdue 1993a,b). It was longitudinal and crosslinguistic. Its results are based on the productions of 40 adult learners of Dutch, English, French, German and Swedish, with varying native languages. All were recently arrived immigrants with legal status, and in daily contact with the language of their new social environment. All learners were observed and recorded over a period of about 30 months; various techniques of data collection were applied. The results give us at least some idea of what happens in 'natural' second language acquisition.

In general, this process is continuous and gradual, without really sharp boundaries between the various stages. But when looked at from some distance, it appears that there are three major steps in the way in which learners put their words together. We can call these steps 'nominal utterance organization', 'infinite utterance organization', and 'finite utterance organization', respectively. On the level of nominal utterance organization, productive utterances (i.e., except rote forms) are extremely simple and mainly consist of seemingly unconnected nouns, adverbs and particles. There are some verb forms used in a noun-like way, that is without the structuring power of the lexical content of verbs — such as argument structure, case role assignment, etc.

This is different in the second major stage in which all learners, irrespective of source or target language, develop a particular language form, the 'Basic Variety'. In the variety, verbs are regularly used, but they show up in only one form, mostly the infinitive or the bare stem. The structure of utterances is determined by a number of elementary organizational principles. In a nutshell, there are three such principles:

(a) The (infinite) verb is placed after the first noun phrase,
(b) The agent comes first, if there is more than one noun phrase,
(c) The focus comes last.

These three principles can be at variance, and then, the learner is faced with a problem; in fact, such conflicts seem to be a germ of further development. In general, however, the Basic Variety is a remarkably efficient communicative system which exploits the lexical content of verbs and adopts a simple constraint of information structure. What is completely absent, however, are 'finite' verb forms. These are developed by only two thirds of the fourty learners investigated in the project, and this development is very complex and varies from language pair to language pair.[2] It is not just a matter of inflectional morphology: the acquisition of finiteness also leads to a major restructuring of learner language (see Klein & Perdue, 1997).

The crucial point in the present context is this: second language learners, just as first language learners, clear distinguish between 'infinite utterance organization' and 'finite utterance organization'. Thus, the evidence from language acquisition, first and second, supports the notion that finiteness is not just tense or mood, let alone merely a matter of inflection - it is a major organising factor in the structure of utterance. This should be reflected in syntactic and semantic properties of all languages. We shall now examine this in a language with a quite transparent marking of finiteness, i.e., German.

3. FINITE AND NONFINITE FORMS IN GERMAN

The starting point of all verb forms, simple or complex, is the bare verb (abbreviated Vs) as a lexical unit, such as *lach-* 'laugh', *geh-* 'walk', *hol-* 'fetch'.[3] When integrated into some construction, Vs has to undergo some morphological operation which turns it into an inflected form. Such an inflected form can be finite, as the second person singular *lachst*, or nonfinite, as the infinitive *lachen* or the participle *gelacht*. Is Vs itself finite or nonfinite? The grammatical tradition has no opinion on this issue. In what follows, I shall say that it is 'nonfinite'. Then, of course, a distinction has to be made between Vs and those forms which are explicitly marked as nonfinite; the latter I will call 'infinite'. Hence, we have two types of nonfinite forms: those which are marked as infinite, and bare stems that are not finite but can be made finite by an appropriate operation; I shall say that such a form is 'FIN-linkable'. Infinite forms are not FIN-linkable unless they undergo further syntactical operations. In this regard, they are on a par with adjectives or nouns.

Forms such as *lachst* or *gelacht* are morphologically compound but syntactically simple. They can be combined with other verb forms, resulting in syntactically compound forms; these can be finite, such as *gelacht zu haben scheinst* 'seem (2nd person singular) to have laughed', or infinite, such as *gelacht zu haben scheinen* 'seem (infinitive) to have laughed'. There are numerous constraints on this composition, not to be considered in the present context. But one fact deserves to be noted:

(2) One finite element constraint:
A syntactically complex verb form can contain several infinite forms but maximally one finite form.

This restriction, which seems to be universal, is well-known but difficult to explain. Why is it possible to say in English *He must be able to dance* but not *He must can dance*, although finiteness is not even explicitly marked? The reason cannot be semantic incompatibility, since *be able to* and *can* both express ability. It could be a mere idiosyncrasy. Then, however, it would be surprising that we find this constraint in so many languages.

There are three infinite forms in German:

(3) a. Infinitum I: This is the 'bare infinitive' which, a few exceptions aside, is formed by attaching the suffix *-en* to Vs: *lach-* is turned into *lachen*.

b. Infinitum II: This is the so-called present participle or 'Partizip I'. It is formed by attaching the suffix *-end* to Vs: *lach-* becomes *lachend*.

c. Infinitum III: This is the so-called past participle or 'Partizip II'. Its form varies considerably, depending on the particular verb stem. Most commonly, *ge-* is prefixed and *-t* is attached as a suffix: *lach-* becomes *gelacht*. But there are many other possibilities.

The situation is much more complicated for finite verb forms, since they are regularly inflected for tense, mood, person, and number (not for voice). The latter two result from agreement and have no independent meaning, hence have no apparent connection to the function of finiteness — if it has an independent function at all.[4] This leaves us with two tenses, usually called *Präsens* and *Präteritum*, and three moods, usually called *Indikativ*, *Konjunktiv* and *Imperativ*. Hence, we have the following system (I give the form of the third person singular of *geh-*'walk' for Indikativ and Konjunktiv:

(4)
	Indikativ	Konjunktiv	Imperativ
Präsens	*geht*	*gehe*	*geh*
Präteritum	*ging*	*ginge*	—

There are many morphological variants which depend on the particular Vs. It is unclear whether the imperative should be considered to be finite or infinite. In fact, it is not easy to see on which grounds such a decision could be made; the traditional notion of 'finite form' is too ill-defined. Here, I will focus on the two forms of the *Indikativ* and only marginally deal with the *Konjunktiv*, whose functions are hard to determine and subject to much variation.

For the following discussion, a brief look at the composition of a finite form such as *geht* will be useful. This form has two components - the bare verb stem Vs *geh-* and a morphological marking *-t* which turns Vs into a finite form. Here, the carrier of finiteness is a simple affix. In other cases, however, the changes on Vs are very different, as illustrated by *ging*. I assume therefore that finiteness is represented by a more abstract operator whose application on Vs results into the finite form. This operator will be called FIN0 in the case of present forms and FIN< in the case of past forms (if the difference does not matter, FIN is used). Hence, *geht* is the result of applying FIN0 to *geh-*, whereas *ging* is the result of applying FIN< to *geh-*. FIN as well as Vs contribute to the entire meaning of the finite form. The contribution of Vs — its lexical content — is relatively clear: it provides an argument structure and assigns properties to its arguments, in this case, to its single argument. The contribution of FIN0 and FIN< is what is at issue here; somehow, it is related to 'tense', but it may have other functions, as well. In syntactically simple forms, such as *geht* or *ging*, the finite component and the lexical component are merged in one word. In syntactically compound finite forms, these two meaning components may be partly or fully distributed over two or more words. The latter case is exemplified by constructions with finite auxiliaries or copulae, such as *hat gelacht* 'has laughed' or *ist gegangen* 'has gone'. The finite forms *hat* and *ist* do not provide descriptive properties; these originate from the other part, here from the verb stem embedded in the past participle.

4. SYNTACTIC EFFECTS OF FINITENESS

There are at least three salient finiteness effects in syntax, to be discussed in turn.

4.1. Word Order

The basic word order of German follows three core rules, all of which are closely connected to the finite verb:

(5) a. In declarative main clauses, the finite verb is in second position (i.e., after the first 'main constituent').
 b. In subordinate clauses, the finite verb is in final position.
 c. In *yes-no* questions and in imperatives, the finite verb is in initial position.

There are a few exceptions, two of which are of interest here. First, there are hypothetical and counterfactual subordinates of the type *Käme Hans, ginge ich weg* 'If John came, I would leave'. Here, the finite verb is in initial position, just as in *yes-no* questions and imperative clauses. With these it shares the property that whatever is expressed, here the arrival of Hans, is not said to be true: these sentences are not assertive. This also applies to the second exception. These are main clauses of the type *Käme er nur nicht hierher!* 'Hopefully he won't come here!'. They express wishes, something like *I wish he didn't come here, but I am afraid he will*. We shall come back to these exceptions in section 8.

The rules in (5) have been stated for centuries in more or less the same way in every school grammar, and the first of them has given rise to the familiar notion that German is a V2-language. Now, this formulation is somehow ambivalent. A morphologically simple finite form merges two components, the lexical content from Vs, and finiteness from FIN. Which of these components is responsible for the three rules in (5)? It is finiteness, as becomes clear when lexical content and finiteness are not fused in one word:

(6) a. Dann hat er einen Kuchen gebacken.
 then has he a cake baked.
 b. obwohl er dann einen Kuchen gebacken hat.
 although he then a cake baked has.
 c. Hat er dann einen Kuchen gebacken?
 has he then a cake baked?
 Sei nicht so ängstlich!
 be not so shy!

Hence, the familiar word order rules of German have nothing to do with the verb as a lexical category. This impression comes from the fact that sometimes, Vs and FIN are fused in one word, and then the positional constraints on finiteness win over those of the lexical verb.

A similar argument can be made for another important grammatical constraint linked to the verb since Ross (1967) first introduced it: 'gapping', i.e., the omission of the verb in one of two parallel clauses, as in *John drank a beer and Peter — a wine*. As I have argued elsewhere, this type of ellipsis has nothing to do with the verb as a lexical category but with finiteness (Klein, 1981). If the carrier of finiteness is identical, it can be omitted on the second occurrence, as in *Hans ist gestern abgereist und Peter (ist) heute angekommen*. If, however, the lexical verb is identical, then it cannot be omitted: *Hans war gestern abgereist und Peter ist heute *(abgereist)*. It is possible, though, if the finite element is omitted, as well: *Hans ist gestern abgereist und Peter (ist) heute (abgereist)*. Hence, if finiteness falls, everything else can fall in appropriate context.

These observations on word order and gapping give rise to two comments. First, they show that the common classification of German and other languages as SOV, SVO, OSV is highly misleading. What matters for word order is not the lexical category V but finiteness — whatever it is. This fact casts some doubt on all typological classifications based on SOV, SVO and OSV word order. Second, if indeed finiteness and not the lexical verb is at the very heart of basic word order, then there is the natural question: Why is this so?

There is no straightforward answer. FIN carries tense. Under its traditional interpretation, tense indicates the temporal relation between the situation described by the sentence and the moment of speech. There is no obvious reason why this information should be given in second position in declarative main clauses and in final position in subordinate clauses. The same reasoning applies to the other category traditionally associated with finiteness, mood. A hint comes from the observation that FIN is in second position just in those cases in which the sentence has a kind of assertive function. This is not the case in subordinate clauses, in *yes-no* questions and in imperatives; nor is it the case in some other FIN-initial constructions like those noted after (5) above. This hypothetical association between 'assertive function' and the position of FIN is violated by another type of sentence not mentioned so far, *wh*-questions such as *Wen hat Hans angerufen?* 'Whom did Hans call?', *Wann kommt Hans?* 'When does Hans come?'. But first, these sentences have an explicit illocutionary marker which may suspend the assertive status. Second, they normally presuppose the truth of an underlying less specific proposition, here the proposition that Hans called someone, or that Hans will come. All that is at issue is *whom* he has called, and *when* he will come. No such presupposition is made in a *yes-no* question such as *Hat Hans angerufen?* 'Did Hans call?', or *Kommt Hans?* 'Is Hans coming?'.

Modern English has a similar but weaker association between the position of FIN and assertive status: subordinate clauses have FIN in second position, too, and in main clauses, the subject (which normally occupies the first position in English) may be preceded by a 'topicalized' constituent. Note, however, that the 'nonassertive' character of subordinate clauses may be due to the complementizer, and that topicalized constituents somehow deviate from the default structure: They exhibit a particular topic structure, a point that might be relevant for the role of finiteness.

4.2. Subject Licensing

There is a second familiar syntactic fact that is related to finiteness: in the absence of FIN, the argument position slots provided by Vs cannot be completely filled by appropriate noun phrases. In traditional terms, the grammatical subject requires the presence of a finite verb, or in more recent terms, only AGR licenses a nominative. I shall state it as in (7): [5]

(7) Subject licensing:
No grammatical subject without finiteness.

There are a few exceptions such as the ones given in (8):

(8) a. Ich und das Geschirr spülen —
I and the dishes clean
das muß ich mir erst mal überlegen.
that must I me first think about.
b. Ich das Geschirr spülen —
I the dishes clean
das muß ich mir erst mal überlegen.
that must I me first think about.

Why this constraint on the filling of one argument slot? After all, it is the lexical content of Vs, and not FIN, which provides these slots. Again, the answer is not obvious. If finiteness is just tense or mood, why should the possibility to have a grammatical subject hinge on the presence of tense or mood, let alone upon the presence of agreement features such as person or number? If there is no finite element, agreement is superfluous anyway. Hence, there must be something else in FIN that is responsible for this constraint.

The exceptional cases in (8) may give us a hint. First, sentences of this type have no assertive character. In a way, they just rise a possibility — the existence of a hypothetical situation which the speaker considers somewhat surprising but surely not excluded. Second, they only include given information. The possibility of this situation must have been mentioned before. Third, their intonation gives the impression of two topics: as for me and as to the possibility to clean the dishes — that is something I must first think upon. This observation is confirmed by the fact that in (8a), both components are separated by *und* 'and'. These observations are in no way conclusive; they tell us that constraint (7) has something to do with, first, the assertive character of an utterance, and second, with the topic status of the constituents.

The notion of grammatical subject, though used by everybody, is not well-defined. Typically, it combines three features (see, e.g., Keenan, 1976; Reis, 1982): case marking (nominative), agentivity, and topic-hood. None of these is obligatory. In German, there are subjects in the dative or in the accusative, there are nonagentive subjects, and there seem to be cases in which the subject is not topic (bearing in mind the notorious fuzziness of this notion). It might well be that constraint (7) is related to the third of these features but not to the others.

4.3. Expletive Licensing

Expletives, too, regularly require the presence of finiteness. Now, the term 'expletive' may refer to somewhat different phenomena across and also within languages. In what follows, I will consider only German *es*, which corresponds in many ways to English expletive *there*, but is much more common in presentational constructions.[6] Thus, *Es ritten drei Reiter in die Stadt* 'Three horseman rode into town' is as well possible as *Drei Reiter ritten in die Stadt*; sometimes, it is clearly preferred, as with *Es ging das Gerücht, daß Hans krank war* 'Rumour had it that Hans was ill' vs. *Das Gerücht ging, daß Hans krank war*. German expletive *es* cannot go with infinite verb forms. Again, the question why this is the case, and just as in the syntactic effects of finiteness observed so far, it does not seem plausible that this has to do with tense or mood. There is no full agreement on what the precise function of expletives is. It seems clear, first, that they are often used to express the existence of something, and second, that they lead to a peculiar information structure. Since expletives are not possible without finite verbs, it seems more plausible that these two functions are served by the combination of expletives and finiteness, rather than by the expletive alone. This points in precisely the same direction as the other syntactic facts.

We may sum up the observations of this section in three points:

(9) a. Finiteness is not just verb inflection: it clearly serves syntactic functions.
    b. These functions can apparently not be explained in terms of tense or mood.
    c. They rather seem to be connected to assertion and topichood, or, more generally speaking, with information structure.

So far about syntactic effects; let us turn now to semantics.

5. SEMANTIC EFFECTS OF FINITENESS

It has often been noted that verbs do not behave uninformingly with respect to indefinite noun phrases in object position:

(10) a. John found a unicorn.
     b. John sought a unicorn.

In (10b), the object NP has a specific and a nonspecific reading. So, John may have tried to find a particular unicorn — an entity which can have a proper name —, or he may have tried to find anything provided it is a unicorn. In (10a), only the first reading is available. Since the two utterances only differ in the lexical meaning of the verbs *to find* vs. *to seek*, it is generally assumed that the difference in the object NP readings is due to the lexical difference between these verbs. Verbs like *to find* are usually called 'transparent' (with respect to the object), and verbs like *to seek* are usually called 'opaque' (with respect to the object). It is also generally assumed that transparent verbs are the rule, and opaque verbs are the exception. This is in line with the common existential interpretation of indefinite NPs, such as *a unicorn, a proof of Fermat's Last Theorem* or *a former girl friend*. Thus, (10a) is understood to mean 'There is an x such that x is a unicorn and x was found by John'. Such an analysis is possible, too, for the specific reading of (10b), but not for its nonspecific reading. Hence, this reading requires a different analysis. Several proposals have been made to this effect; they are aptly surveyed, criticized and enriched by a new one in Zimmermann (1993).

Common to all of these proposals is the fact that the difference is considered to be due to the verb, more precisely to the lexical content of the verb. Now, the verbs in (10) are finite, hence, they include the Vs, the carrier of lexical content, as well as FIN, which carries tense, mood and perhaps something else. In principle, both components could be responsible for which readings are available. Consider now the following examples:

(11) Finding a unicorn — what a bizarre idea!
(12) It is the dream of each hunter to find a unicorn.
(13) In order to find a unicorn, the hunters first went to the forest of Broceliande.

In all of these cases, the normal reading of the object NP *a unicorn* is nonspecific (although a specific reading is not necessarily excluded). If, for example, (11) is true, then it is probably not meant that finding some particular unicorn, say the unicorn Senta, is a bizarre idea.

Apparently, transparent verbs such as *to find* show the transparency effect only when they are finite, as in (10a), but not when they are infinite, as in (11)–(13). A specific reading is enforced only by the presence of some 'higher' finite verb which governs nonfinite *find a unicorn*. This is not so suggestive in (11)–(13). Consider now the following examples:

(14) The hunter managed to find a unicorn.
(15) The hunters succeeded in finding a unicorn.

Clearly, these sentences have a specific reading (in fact, it looks as if they have only a specific reading). This effect disappears if the governing verb is not finite, either, as in (16):

(16) Succeeding in finding a unicorn is something that requires a lot of luck.

There is a straightforward conclusion:

(17) Finiteness constraint on specificity:
Indefinite noun phrases have a specific reading only if they are (directly or indirectly) in the scope of a finite verb.[7]

By 'directly', I mean that the NP is the argument of a finite verb, by 'indirectly', I mean that the NP is the argument of a nonfinite verb which, in turn, is in the scope of some finite element. This neither means that finiteness alone necessarily leads to a specific interpretation, nor does it mean that the lexical content of the verb which governs the indefinite NP is irrelevant. It only means that finiteness is indispensable for a specific reading. Why?

Again, it is hard to imagine that this effect of finiteness is a mere consequence of mood or tense, let alone agreement features which go with the finite verb. Intuitively, one of the differences between (9a) and (9b) is the fact that in (10a), there is a time at which a situation 'obtains' in which a unicorn is present; this is the time at which the unicorn has been found. In this particular example, this time is in the past. It could also be in the present or in the future. Hence, mere tense is not crucial. In (10b), no claim is made that there is a time at which a situation obtains in which a unicorn is present. But it is not excluded, either. Such a situation could have obtained at some earlier time, for example. It seems plausible that specificity results from precisely this difference: the term *a unicorn* is specific with respect to a particular time talked about. If there are three times about which such an assertion is made, then there should be three specific unicorns — specific relative to the asserted situation. This is indeed the case:

(18) a. Three times, John found a unicorn.
     b. Whenever John went out, he found a unicorn.

It is not excluded, of course, that this is the same unicorn in all cases, or in some of them. All that is said is this: The expression *a unicorn* is specific to a particular situation, which is claimed to obtain at some time. In (18a), such a claim is not made about one but about three times; in (18b), it is about an unspecific number of times. This is different in (18c):

(18) c. John found a unicorn three times.

Here, only one claim is made about some — possibly very long — temporal interval in the past. This time contains three sub-intervals, at each of which a unicorn was found. This must be the same unicorn. Hence, what matters is indeed the temporal interval about which the claim is made: if there is only one, then there is only one specific unicorn — although there are three finding situations. In other words, it is not the situation times that are crucial to specificity, but the times talked about.

These observations generalize to all number-specific indefinite NPs:

(19) a. Three times, John found two unicorns.
     b. John found two unicorns three times.

There are precisely two unicorns for each time talked about, for which it is asserted that John found them, just as there is precisely one in the case of (18c). It does not extend, however, to noun phrases which are not number-specific, such as bare plurals or mass nouns, since there is no specific number or amount for a particular time, about which the assertion is made.

What has this to do with finiteness? Infinite forms such as *to find a unicorn* or *finding a unicorn* describe a situation of unicorn finding (omitting the finder, though). They do not relate it to some time (or several times) talked about, and no assertion is made that such a finding situation obtains at this time (or these times). Hence, the term *a unicorn* cannot have a specific reading.[8] This appears much in line with the considerations from the preceding section about the function of finiteness.

6. WHAT IS FINITENESS I: THE CONTRASTIVE INTONATION TEST

How can we determine the meaning contribution, which an expression makes to the meaning of the entire construction to which it belongs? There is no royal way. The first and most obvious strategy is to ask our intuitions. We know what it means *to walk* or *to cook*, and we know what *a curtain* is and what *a shower* is. But the appeal to our intuitions often fails. First, it does not show the fine-grained structure of meanings. It may tell us, what the difference between *to go* and *to walk* is; but it does not tell us why *Where did he go?* is directional (a natural answer is *to the park*), whereas *Where did he walk?* can be directional, but normally is positional (the first answer is *in the park*). Second, it does not work very well with more functional meaning contributions. An appeal to our intuitions does not reveal us very much about what finiteness is.

A second and often more reliable test is to highlight the contrast of the relevant expression to expressions. Thus, if we say *John found THREE unicorns*, then this is understood to mark the particular fact that there were three, and not two or seven, unicorns. And when Conrad Hilton once put the gist of his life-long learning in the sentence *The shower curtain must be IN the shower*, then he highlighted the particular 'in-ness' of the spatial constellation, in contrast to the possibility that the curtain might be outside the shower.

What does this test reveal when we place contrastive intonation on FIN? Since a finite lexical verb conflates FIN and Vs, it is useful to begin with a case in which the finite element bears no descriptive content:

(20) The curtain WAS in the shower.

By uttering (20), the speaker claims that the curtain was in the shower. But this is also the case if the element *was* is not stressed at all, let alone is the only stressed element. The highlighted contrast can go in (at least) two directions, as illustrated by (21b) and (21b), respectively:

(21) a.   The curtain is in the shower. — That's wrong, the curtain WAS in the shower (but it isn't any longer).
     b.   The curtain was not in the shower. — That's wrong, the curtain WAS in the shower.

In the first case, the contrast relates to the particular time about which a claim is made here: The contrast is between *is* and *was* (or between *was* and *will be*). Hence, it is the time component of FIN which is highlighted by the contrastive intonation. This is in agreement with the traditional notion of finite verbs.[9]

In the second case, the time component is not at issue. The contrast seems to be between *was* and *was not*. What is highlighted, is the mere claim that the curtain's being in the shower at some unspecified time in the past is the case (in contrast to the possibility that the curtain's being in the shower at that time in the past is not the case). We may conclude therefore:

(22) FIN carries (at least) two distinct meaning components:
 1. The tense component: it marks past, in contrast to present or future;
 2. It marks that an assertion with respect to whatever is said is made — in contrast to the possibility that no such assertion is made.

In example (20), the finite element is a copula, which lacks inherent descriptive content. How is this when the lexical content and FIN are fused into a finite verb form, as in (23):

(23) John SOUGHT a unicorn.

This can at least express a two-fold contrast, as illustrated by

(24) a. John SOUGHT a unicorn, but he doesn't seek a unicorn/it any longer.
 b. John SOUGHT a unicorn, but he didn't find one/it.

In the first case, it is again the inherent tense component which is highlighted, and in the second, it is the particular lexical content of *seek* in contrast to, e.g., *find* or *shoot*. Is it also possible to highlight the mere claim of his seeking the unicorn by (23), in contrast to the possibility that he did not seek it at that time in the past? The answer is clearly negative. In order to do this, the finite component must be 'extracted' from the finite verb and given independent expression:

(24) c. The idea that he didn't seek a unicorn is wrong: John DID seek a unicorn.

The *do*-form in (24c) also carries tense — but it is not the tense contrast that is highlighted in (24a). It appears, therefore, that it is the basic function of the finite element to carry the 'assertive nature' of the utterance in question.

This idea is very close to Höhle's notion of verum-focus (Höhle, 1992; Jacobs, 1984). There is a crucial difference, however. As stated in (22), the contrast is between 'assertion made' and 'no assertion made'. The contrast as implied by verum-focus is between 'verum' and 'falsum'. The latter contrast presupposed the former: as long as no assertion is made — and I assume that this is the case in nonfinite constructions —, it does not make sense to speak about 'verum et falsum'. In other words, there is a difference between whether something is assertion-marked at all or not, and if the former is the case, the polarity of the assertion. Consider the two sentences *Hans behauptet, das Buch gelesen zu haben* 'Hans claims to have read the book' and *Hans bestreitet, das Buch gelesen zu haben* 'Hans denies to have read the book'. The proposition at issue is *Hans das Buch gelesen haben*. This is a mere description of a situation. The two matrix clauses relate this description to reality — either with positive or with negative polarity. So, the two matrix sentences have something in common — they introduce 'assertion-marking'; and they differ in something — the polarity of this marking.

The presence of FIN does not suffice to mark an utterance as assertive in this two-fold sense. It is a necessary, but not a sufficient condition. For a sentence like (20) to function as an assertion (with positive polarity), it must have a falling intonation. If it has an intonation rise between *was* and *in* and no fall until the end, then no assertion is made. Still, in contrast to a bare nonfinite description such as 'the curtain be in the shower', it is somehow 'assertion-related': the issue, so to speak, is raised, and it is just left open in which direction the assertion goes. What precisely is this assertion-markedness brought about by FIN? And what is the role of FIN, if the sentence does not make an assertion at all? Before examining these questions, we shall first briefly consider the relation between tense and the assertive role of FIN in simple declarative clauses, that is, in those cases in which indeed an assertion is made.

7. WHAT IS FINITENESS II: TENSE AND ASSERTION

Finiteness in German (and in related languages) minimally involves two meaning components: It carries tense and it carries assertion-markedness. How are these related to each other? According to its canonical definition, tense serves to locate the situation, which is described by the utterance, in the past, present, or future. Thus, in *Mika was sick*, Mika's sickness is placed into the past; in *Mika is sick*, it is said to be at, or to encompass, the time of utterance; and in *Mika will be sick*, it is in the future. This understanding of tense is common but false (see Klein, 1994 for an elaborate argument on this point). Suppose *Mika was sick* is said in answer to the question *Why didn't Mika come to the meeting this morning?* Then, it need not at all be the case that his sickness does not include the time of utterance. He could still be sick. The point is more obvious in sentences such as *The dog was dead*. It surely does not mean that the dog's being dead does not include the time of utterance. What is meant by the simple past is the fact that at some particular time span in the past, Mika was sick, and the dog was dead. An assertion is made only about this time span in the past, and it is simply left open whether the state obtaining at this time also obtains later or earlier. It is not the truth of his being sick or dead at a certain time that is crucial but the fact whether something is asserted about some time. Such a time span for which an assertion is made I call 'topic time', and it is the function of tense to mark whether the topic time precedes, contains or follows the time of utterance. The time of the situation itself may precede, contain, or follow the topic time. I think it is this relation between the topic time and the time of the situation, which is traditionally called 'aspect'. Aspect is often morphologically marked, although it need not be marked (just as little as tense, which is marked in English or German, but not, for example, in Chinese). A simple analysis of the English progressive is therefore that it marks that the topic time is included in the time of the situation (this is the aspectual component), whereas the simple form marks, that the topic time includes the time of the situation; the topic time in turn can be in the past, present, or future (this is the tense component). This naturally accounts for the intuition, that in the progressive, an event is presented 'from the inside', as 'on-going', whereas in the simple form, it is presented 'from the outside', as 'completed'. I will not elaborate this analysis here. What matters in the present context is the clear connection between tense, assertion and finiteness.

In declarative clauses, finiteness marks that (a) an assertion is made, and (b) this assertion is restricted to the 'topic time'. Tense indicates how the topic time is related to the utterance time. What is asserted is provided by the remainder of the sentence, that is, by its infinite part. This part I will call an 'assertable expression' or 'sentence base'. Minimally, a sentence base consists of a FIN-linkable element — i.e., a verb stem — and an appropriate filling of the argument slots (including the subject) provided by its lexical content. In German, in fact in all Indo-European languages, a sentence base can normally not be used as an independent main clause. There are a few exceptions, as illustrated in (8) above. They are not marked as asserted. This does not necessarily exclude that they are interpreted as an assertion. But then, this is just a matter of general context and world knowledge on the part of the interlocutor; there is, however, no explicit assertion marker, as FIN in the Indo-European languages.

8. TWO PROBLEMS

There is an obvious argument against this idea: not all finite sentences express an assertion. Essentially, there are two such cases, which will now be discussed in turn.

8.1. Nondeclarative Main Clauses

Nondeclarative main clauses may serve many functions, in particular:

(a) Imperatives: They do not express the speaker's opinion that something is true but that the addressee should perform an action which makes something true.
(b) *Yes-no* questions: They raise the question of whether something is true.
(c) Norm-creating statements, such as laws: They do not express that something is true but that something holds as a norm within a group of people.

Whereas imperatives and *yes-no* questions typically have a special (finite) form, normative statements are often identical in form to declaratives.

In all of these cases, there is a sentence base, as well: It gives a description of what should be made true (imperatives), is to be decided whether it is true (*yes-no* questions), or ought to hold (norm-creating statements). There is also a counterpart to the topic time. In the imperative, this topic time must be after the utterance time. There is no difference for questions. Norm-creating sentences also hold for the future; sometimes, they explicitly specify the beginning time. So, the crucial difference seems to rely on the notion of assertion.

This notion raises a number of terminological as well as substantial problems; see e.g., Stalnaker (1998). I take it to be a particular illocutionary role of utterances: something is asserted if the speaker marks that he or she takes it to be true in relation to a particular time and perhaps other factors. Imperatives, *yes-no* questions and norm-creating statements have a different illocutionary role, whose precise characterization is not an easy task. In a way, declaratives, imperatives and norm-creating statements have in common that something 'holds' or, as we also may say, 'is valid'. Whereas declaratives only indicate the speaker's conviction in this regard, both imperatives and norm-creating statements bring about this validity, if certain conditions are met. No attempt will be made here to specify this; I shall simply state that in all of these cases, the illocutionary role of the utterance is to mark 'validity'. *Yes-no* questions are different. They relate to truth, not to validity in a more general sense, and they are assertion-marked. I assume that they leave the polarity of the assertion open: this polarity becomes a topic in itself. We shall return to this point in section 9.

8.2. Subordinate Clauses

Subordinate clauses do not make an assertion either. Some of them do indeed reflect the speaker's opinion that the sentence base holds, others do not:

(25) a. I wonder why he called.
 b. I wonder if he called.
 c. That is the man who called.
 d. Do you think that he called?

In all four cases, the sentence base is *he call*. In (25a) and (25c), it is implied that this sentence base holds, whereas this is not the case in sentences (25b) and (25d). Whether a subordinate clause is assumed to hold depends on numerous factors — the complementizer, the matrix verb (some verbs are factive), illocutionary status of the main clause, and others. In any event, we cannot assume that subordinate clauses always involve an assertion or validity with respect to some topic time.

There are two possible solutions. First, there may be an operator higher than FIN which encodes validity. This operator can be realized on the surface in two ways, namely, by a complementizer, thus creating a subordinate clause, or by being projected on FIN, if no other target is available. Under this view, FIN itself initially carries only tense and mood, and so it continues in subordinate clauses. In declarative main clauses, it takes over validity. Let me call this the 'indirect carrier view'. The second analysis assumes that there is no such abstract operator, and that FIN always carries validity (as well as tense and mood). The meaning contribution of FIN can be overruled by the semantic contribution of higher operators, in particular complementizers. Depending on the particular complementizer and other factors (such as the matrix verb), FIN may preserve or loose its initial validity: *if* and *whether*, for example, suspend it, *why* and *relative pronouns* usually preserve it, and so on. We may call this the 'direct carrier view'.

Both solutions explain that subordinate clauses need not involve validity. The direct carrier view yields a uniform structure for subordinate clauses and main clauses. But it has the unpleasant property that just in the canonical case of an assertion, in declarative main clauses, the initial carrier of validity is not visible. There is no sufficient evidence to decide between these two solutions. In either case, FIN eventually *is* the carrier, and this is what matters here.

9. TOPIC COMPONENT, SENTENCE BASE AND FINITENESS

Let us return now to declarative clauses, in which finiteness serves (a) to mark that the sentence base is assertion-marked (with positive polarity), and (b) to mark how the topic time is related to the time of utterance. Consider now 26, uttered by someone right now:

(26) A priest attended.

Is this utterance true or false? Even if you know what the entire world is like, was like, or will be like, there is no reasonable answer to this question. It simply depends on which situation the speaker is talking about. If it happens to be the funeral of my grandfather, then the answer is *yes*. If it happens to be the death of Voltaire, the answer is *no*. Asserting some sentence base makes only sense if the situation talked about is identified. Various types of information can contribute to this situation identification. It may be provided

(a) by an explicit question, which includes the necessary information, for example *What did you notice at my grandfather's funeral* or *What do you know about Voltaire's death*;
(b) by contextual information, for example if the utterance is part of a longer text;
(c) by information which comes from the utterance itself.

Very often, all three types of information cooperate in order to identify the situation to which the assertion applies.

If this is correct, then a full finite sentence consists of three components. First, there must be a specification of the situation about which the utterance says something. This I will call the 'topic component'. Minimally, it includes a topic time (TT) this is the time to which the assertion (or whichever the illocutionary role is) is confined. It is plausible to assume that the topic component also contains a topic world and a topic place. Optionally, other elements can be added, for example a topic entity, typically realized by the grammatical subject. Second, there must be a 'sentence base', i.e., a nonfinite verb and minimally an appropriate filling of its argument slots. And third, there must be a marking which relates the sentence base to the topic component, i.e., finiteness. We may depict this as in (27):

(27)   UTTERANCE
        TOPIC COMPONENT   FIN   SENTENCE BASE
        topic topic topic (topic V_S and arguments
        time   place world   entity)

The way in which these components are packed into a full, finite sentence is highly language-specific. In German, there are constructions that immediately reflect these tripartite structure:

(28) a.   Es   hatte   jemand   für Dich angerufen.
            it   has   someone   for you called
      b.   Gestern   hatte   jemand   für Dich angerufen.
            yesterday   has   someone for you called
      c.   Dreimal   war   Schnee   gefallen.
            three-times   was   snow   fallen
      d.   Hier   war   Schnee   gefallen.
            here   was   snow   fallen

In (28a), the topic component is filled by a lexically empty element *es*: no information about TT or any other is given; the finiteness marker *hatte* indicates that TT precedes the speech time; the nonfinite component is *jemand für dich angerufen*; although this is not directly the sentence base in the sense explained above (it does not contain the bare stem but an infinite form marked as such, the past participle), we have a very close match. Utterance (28b) is much the same, except that the topic time is now lexically specified; note, however, that in German, an adverbial in this position can also specify the event time, i.e., the time of the call. Hence, there is no necessary relation between the initial position and topic function. In (28c), we have quantification over topic times: there are three topic situations about which something is said. In (28d), finally, a topic place rather than a topic time is indicated by the lexical element in first position.

This picture is rapidly blurred, if other syntactic operations come into play, for example, if more topic information is to be given, if the verb has more arguments, or if the finite component and the nonfinite component of the verb are fused in one form. I shall not try to follow this up but only make a few general comments (see Dimroth *et al.*, 2003, for a detailed analysis of how German and Dutch children acquire the specific patterns in their languages).

The connection of FIN with the topic time was examined in section 6. A case which makes this connection particularly clear is a court setting, in which the judge may ask the witness *What did you observe, when you entered the room?*. In this case, the witness is supposed to say something about exactly this time, and if he says *A man was on the floor. He was dead*, then this means that his assertion is confined to precisely this time. The time at which the man was on the floor, and the time at which he was and is dead is probably much longer. But this does not matter: the witness' testimony is only evaluated with respect to the topic time, as set by the question of the judge. The two other minimal elements of the topic component are much more speculative. If mood — the other category which is typically connected with FIN — indeed expresses hypotheticality, counterfactuality or, as in the case of imperatives, nonexistence but desirability of the situation, then we may say that the utterance is not about the real world or not *only* about the real world but about specific possible worlds; hence the world parameter. I am not aware of any language in which reference to space is grammaticalized in a way similar to time and — under the assumption just made — world; so, it may well be that this parallel assumed here is wrong. It would however make some sense that time and space serve a comparable function in the situation identification.

The sentence base minimally consists of a nonfinite verb stem and an appropriate filling of the argument slots. In the most straightforward case, sentence basis and topic component are clearly separated. It is also possible that parts of the descriptive information from the sentence base help to identify the situation talked about, in particular by marking one of its arguments as topic entity. Such an argument is often called subject. It should be clear, however, that there is a difference between subject as a lexically characterized element of the sentence base (e.g., the agent), and subject as a specific part of the topic component. These two properties may go hand in hand, and in fact, they often do. Under the assumption that the grammatical subject is indeed topic entity as well as semantic subject (i.e., as specified by the lexical content of the verb stem), then it becomes plausible why nonfinite sentences normally cannot have a subject (see section 4.2): no finiteness, no topic component, no topic entity.

Other expressions can be added to the sentence base, for example by adverbials. These, too, can contribute to the identification of the situation about which something is asserted. Temporal adverbials, for example, can but need not specify the topic time (note that FIN only gives a rather general restriction on how the topic time is situated on the time line). This is best illustrated with verb forms in which topic time and situation time are clearly separated, as in the pluperfect:

(29) a. At five, John had left the party.
b. John had left the party at five.

Both sentences involve a situation time (the time at which John left the party), and a topic time, at which the situation time is over. In (29a), the temporal adverbial *at five* specifies the topic time; the time of his leaving is not made explicit, but it must precede the topic time. In (29b), the temporal interval *at five* specifies the situation time; the topic time must be in the past (as marked by *had*), and it must be after the situation time; but its precise position on the time line is not indicated. Sometimes, both situation time and topic time can be specified by an adverbial, as in (30):

(30) a. On Monday, my office hour is from two to four.
     b. My office hour is on Monday from two to four.

In (30a), an assertion is made only about Mondays (not to a specific Monday, but any Monday), and it is asserted that at those topic times, the office hour is from two to four (in contrast to, for example, Tuesdays where it might be from seven to nine). In (30b), there is no explicit restriction to the time spans talked about; the assertion is more general, and it is said that the office hour in general is on Monday from two to four.

The question of whether a certain element from the entire sentence base contributes to the topic component or not, and how this is indicated — by word order, as in (29) and (30), by intonation, or by specific particles —, raises a variety of problems, three of which I would like to address briefly.

First, if elements from the sentence base are used to specify the topic component, then the simple equation between sentence base and assertable construction, and thus the clean cut illustrated in (27), breaks down. Within the sentence base, we must distinguish between an assertive and a nonassertive part. The latter includes those elements of the entire lexical content which contribute to the topic component. In the assertive part, these elements are replaced by variables, that is, elements which play a certain role in the structure (for example the role of an agentive argument) but are void of lexical content. Note that this is in a way the exact opposite of the classical focus analysis suggested by Akmajian, Jackendoff and others around 1970 and then taken up by numerous linguists.[11]

Second, the distinction between elements which contribute to the topic component and those which belong to the assertive part must not be confused with given vs. new information. There can be maintained topics as well as new topics. In a narrative, each sentence from the story line may report a new event and hence has a new topic time. In straightforward cases, this shift follows from the principle of chronological order (i.e., the order of mentioning corresponds to the order of events); but it may also be made explicit by temporal adverbials like *then, two years later*, etc. In picture descriptions or in route directions, there may be a similar chain of topic places introduced by adverbials such as *a bit to the left, at the next junction*, and so on. Each of these topic places is new with respect to the preceding utterance (see von Stutterheim, 1997). As a consequence, the assertive part as well as the nonassertive part can bear an intonational contrast, as in *To the right, there is a tree. To the left, there is a little creek.* This does not preclude a strong interaction between given and new information, on the one hand, and the two parts of the sentence base, on the other.

Third, many of the syntactic effects from section 4 turn out to be a reflex of this tripartite structure if we assume that the place where FIN is realized forms a watershed between the topic component and (the remainder of) the sentence base. This is not far-fetched given the fact that FIN expresses the relation between topic component and sentence base. Other principles may intervene. Thus, the topic component may be filled by an empty element. Nothing from the sentence base — not even the grammatical subject — belongs to the topic component; all it has is a topic time, which comes with finiteness marking itself. This leads to thetic constructions (Sasse, 1987): They have a subject with all lexical properties of the subject, but without topic status. Without finiteness, such an expletive element does not make sense, since there is no topic component at all, that could be filled by an expletive. This explains why expletives are licensed by finiteness.

10. CONCLUDING REMARKS

It was not the aim of this paper to present a theory of finiteness. I rather tried to bring together a number of observations that show that it is not just an epiphenomenon of verb inflection but plays a crucial role in the syntactical and semantic structure of utterances. These observations have also lead to an incipient picture of this structure which, when worked out in more detail, might help to understand a number of puzzling facts. These include the strong association between finiteness and the presence of subjects and expletives in Indo-European languages. Another one, noted under (2) in section 3, is the fact that syntactically compound verb forms can contain many infinite forms but maximally one finite form. It simply does not make sense to express more than one assertion relation (or, more generally speaking, validity relation) to the topic component of a sentence. Hence, this restriction finds a natural explanation. A third one concerns the loss of the 'transparent-opaque' distinction, if the relevant verb is not finite; if specificity is relative to a situation that is supposed to obtain at some topic time (or topic times), then nonfinite constructions cannot yield this specificity.

Examples came mainly from German. How is this in other languages? I believe that the distinction between a component that identifies the situation (or the situations) talked about and a component that provides a description of what might be valid at that time is found in all languages. I also believe that all languages have means to relate these components to each other. In Indo-European languages, this device is coupled with the lexical verb, and it often includes information about the time (and perhaps the world) talked about. Other languages use other means. In Chinese, for example, FIN is never coupled with verb inflection, since there is no verb inflection; instead, the function of finiteness is served by so-called aspectual particles which constrain the assertion to certain sub-intervals (see Klein *et al.*, 2000). Still other languages, such as Classical Arabic, combine elements which serve the function of FIN with the verb but differentiate between FIN-linkable elements with lexical content and without lexical content. In the latter case, the carrier of FIN can often be omitted, thus giving rise to copula-free predicative constructions. Within Indo-European languages, the interplay between the three components varies within certain limits. But I do not think that this variation, neither the more general variation in how languages realize this tripartite structure, affects the general picture sketched here.

Max Planck Institute for Psycholinguistics, Nijmegen

11. ACKNOWLEDGEMENTS

This paper brings together a number of observations presented on various occasions, notably Dimroth & Klein (1996), Klein (1994, 1998) and a talk held at the conference 'Semantics meets acquisition' at the Max-Planck-Institut für Psycholinguistik, March 2000. I wish to thank the members of the MPI group 'The acquisition of scope relations', in particular Christine Dimroth, for numerous discussions on these issues. Helpful comments also came from Nigel Duffield, Clive Perdue, the reviewers and the editor.

12. NOTES

[1] The first three of these examples are from the Simone-Corpus (quoted after Lasser, 1997, 15), the last three from my daughter Eva.

[2] Lasser (1997, 127-181) surveys this evidence and carefully reanalyses the most comprehensive German corpus to date, the Simone tapes. She also demonstrates that a great deal of the child's infinite constructions are also found in the adult language.

[3] See, for example, Becker & Dietrich (1996) for a fine-grained study of how the development of finiteness marking and negation evolves in advanced learner varieties.

[4] Vs can be morphological compounds, as in *aufess-* 'eat up', *weggeh-* 'go away'; this is not relevant in the present context.

[5] In the light of the Western grammatical tradition, this view may be premature. The classical definition of '(de)finite' inflectional forms according to Priscian (1494, 86) includes 'person' as a feature. Maas (2000) examines this historical background and argues that 'person' may be the most important feature of finiteness. For reasons that will become clear later, I do not share this view; but I agree that it is in line with the traditional notion.

[6] The traditional definition of the restriction suffers from the notorious fuzziness of the notion 'grammatical subject'. The definition in terms of case licensing suffers from the fact that the constraint is also operative when the relevant NP does not require nominative but accusative or dative, as in *Mich friert* 'I am freezing' or *Mir graut* 'I have a horror'. None of them has any explanatory value; they just state the facts.

⁷ The functions of the English expletive *there* are served by two expressions in German. If the existence or nonexistence of some entity is asserted, as in *There are no pianos in Peoria*, German has a fixed form *es gibt*: *Es gibt in Peoria keine Klaviere*. Here, word order can be changed, but *es* cannot be omitted: *In Peoria gibt es keine Klaviere*. Presentational usage of *there*, as in *There came a man into a bar* corresponds to *es* + finite verb. Here, *es* can be omitted when word order is changed: *Es kam ein Mann in eine Bar - ein Mann kam in eine Bar - in eine Bar kam ein Mann*. It is this latter *es* in which we are interested here.

⁸ It is not easy to see how this constraint could be implemented in a formal account. It would not suffice, however, to add an intentional operator to all nonfinite forms (a possibility suggested by a reviewer); additional measures would have to be taken in order to ensure that this operator does not affect other types of noun phrases, and that its effect is reverted as soon as the indefinite object noun phrase is in the scope of finiteness.

⁹ We observe the same effect if the verb is finite but the clause does not make an assertion for other reasons, for example the *if*-clause in *If I find a unicorn, I will be famous*. (Thanks to an anonymous reviewer, who pointed out this example).

¹⁰ It is not easy to tell whether there is also a 'mood contrast', as would be predicted by the traditional idea that finite verbs also express mood, except perhaps if a different mood expresses counterfactuality: *Er WAR nicht hier - er WÄRE hier* 'He was NOT here - he WOULD BE here'. But even so, such a correction sounds somewhat odd, although not as odd as *Er ist nicht hier - er sei hier* 'he is not here - he (ought to) be here'. I shall not follow up this point here.

¹¹ Throughout this paper, I tried to avoid the term 'focus', not because I believe that this is an irrelevant notion but because I find it increasingly problematic. Typically, the focus is a prosodically prominent element of a sentence. But topic elements can bear a contrastive intonation, too. They can also encode new information, and they involve 'alternatives'. I do not think, either, that a sentence can in general be partitioned into a 'presupposed part' (the topic) and a 'nonpresupposed part' (the focus). The notion of presupposition, derived from the full sentence by replacing the focus by a variable and existentially quantifying over this variable, makes sense in some cases, but is highly problematic in others. Take, for example, a sentence such as *Hans war NICHT hier* 'Hans was NOT here', where the focus is on *nicht*. This sentence cannot have the presupposition *Hans war hier* 'Hans was here'. Even if we assume that *nicht* is replaced by a kind of polarity variable, then the resulting structure would only say that this sentence has a polarity. This is no presupposition in the usual sense.

13. REFERENCES

Becker, Angelika, and Rainer Dietrich. "The Acquisition of Scope in L2 German." *Zeitschrift für Literaturwissenschaft und Linguistik* 104 (1996): 115–140.

Dimroth, Christine, Petra Gretsch, Peter Jordens, Clive Perdue, and Marianne Starren. "Finiteness in Germanic languages: A Stage Model for First and Second Language Development." In Christine Dimroth and Marianne Starren (eds.) *Information Structure and the Dynamics of Language Acquisition*, 65–93. Amsterdam: Benjamins, 2003.

Dimroth, Christine, and Wolfgang Klein. 1996. "Fokuspartikel in Lernervarietäten: Ein Analyserahmen und einige Beispiele." *Zeitschrift für Literaturwissenschaft und Linguistik* 104 (1996): 73–114.

Dimroth, Christine, and Ingeborg Lasser. "Finite Options. How L1 and L2 Learners Cope With the Acquisition of Finiteness." *Linguistics* 40 (2002).

Höhle, Tilman. "Über Verum-Fokus im Deutschen." In Joachim Jacobs (ed.) *Informationsstruktur und Grammatik*, 112–141. Opladen: Westdeutscher Verlag, 1992.

Jacobs, Joachim. "Funktionale Satzperspektive und Illokutionssemantik." *Linguistische Berichte* 91 (1984): 89–134.

Keenan, Edward. "Towards a Universal Definition of Subject." In Charles Li (ed.) *Subject and Topic*, 303–334. New York: Academic Press, 1976.

Klein, Wolfgang. "Some Rules of Regular Ellipsis in German." In Wolfgang Klein and Willem Levelt (eds.) *Crossing the Boundaries in Linguistics: A Festschrift for Manfred Bierwisch*, 51–78. Dordrecht: Reidel, 1981.

Klein, Wolfgang. *Time in Language.* London: Routledge, 1994.

Klein, Wolfgang, and Clive Perdue. "The Basic Variety, or: Couldn't Natural Language be much Simpler?" *Second Language Research* 13 (1997): 301–347.

Klein, Wolfgang, Li Ping, and Henriëtte Hendricks. "Aspect and Assertion in Mandarin Chinese." *Natural Language and Linguistic Theory* 18 (2000): 723–770.

Lasser, Inge. *Finiteness in Adult and Child German.* Ph.D. Diss., City University of New York, 1997.

Maas, Utz. "Finit und Infinit. Eine Typologische Bestandsaufnahme." Paper presented at the Jahrestagung der deutschen Gesellschaft für Sprachwissenschaft, Mannheim, 2000.

Perdue, Clive. *Adult Language Acquisition: Crosslinguistic Perspectives. Volume 1, Field Methods.* Cambridge: Cambridge University Press, 1993a.

Perdue, Clive. *Adult Language Acquisition: Crosslinguistic Perspectives. Volume 2, The Results.* Cambridge: Cambridge University Press, 1993b.

Priscianus. *Opera.* Venedig: Bonetus Locatellus, 1496.

Reis, Marga. "Zum Subjektbegriff im Deutschen." In Werner Abraham (ed.) *Satzglieder im Deutschen*, 171–211. Tübingen: Niemeyer, 1982.

Ross, John Robert. *Constraints on Variables in Syntax.* Ph.D. Diss., MIT, 1967.

Sasse, Hansjürgen. "The Thetic/Categorical Distinction Revisited." *Linguistics* 25 (1987): 511–580.

Stalnaker, Robert C. "Assertion." In Asa Kasher (ed.) *Speech Act Theory and Particular Speech Acts*, 232–249. London: Routledge, 1998.

von Stutterheim, Christiane. *Einige Prinzipien des Textaufbaus.* Tübingen: Niemeyer, 1997.

Zimmermann, Thomas. "On the Proper Treatment of Opacity in Certain Verbs." *Natural Language Semantics* 1 (1993): 149–179.

PETRA GRETSCH

FUNCTIONS OF FINITENESS IN CHILD LANGUAGE

Abstract. This chapter compares the interpretation of finite with the interpretation of infinitival utterances in early first language acquisition. I propose a universal bifurcation of world-referencing within the verbal and nominal domain which relates different form types to different interpretations. Grammatical default settings such as [+ finite] or [+ citation case] are linked to a world-referencing pointing to the actual world, whereas non-default settings such as [– finite] or [+ oblique case] are linked to a world-referencing involving distant worlds, i.e., future worlds, past worlds, and wish worlds. This bifurcation constitutes the starting point for a series of further differentiations in a cell fission model of child language development.

1. INTRODUCTION

Consider the following examples, of the German speaking children Max and Benny: [1,2]

(1) (Max turns to the tape recorder) (Max, 2;09,00)
des n n   ma   n n sanne   anHÖRN\ den ANmachen\
that n n once   n n sanne   to-listen-INF that on-make-INF
'I want to listen to that Susanne, switch it on.'

(2) (Max puts a toy-pig into the barn) (Max, 2;09,00)
ich   MACH   des   in stall\
I   make-FIN   that   into barn
'I will put that into the barn.'

(3) (Benny wants the interlocutor to take the racket) (Benny, 2;10,28)
du   SO   halten\   so\
you   this-way hold-INF   this-way
'You should hold the racket this way.'

(4) (Benny stops playing badminton) (Benny, 2;10,28)
ich   geh   jetzt   weg\
I   go-FIN   now   away
'I am leaving now.'

273
V. Van Geenhoven (ed.), Semantics in Acquisition, 273–302.
© 2006 Springer. Printed in the Netherlands.

This small set of data illustrates that children care about morphological forms for the expression of specific temporal or modal functions. Wishes or imperatives prefer infinitival structures, whereas real-world facts related to the 'here-and-now' tend to finite forms. This peculiar distributional property of early child language has been already described in the study of Hoekstra & Jordens (1994) but has never found an explanation. What could be a reason for this early differentiation in the process of acquisition?

This chapter gives an answer to this question and argues for an interpretive differentiation of [+/– finite] forms from the start of grammatical structures in child language onwards. This view is empirically supported by a qualitative and quantitative analysis of data from early German child language. Theoretical considerations and facts from the data analysis lead to a new developmental model that is based on the idea of 'cell fissions'. These fissions concern the domain of morpho-syntactic structures as well as the domain of interpretations. I will show that it is the major fission between [+/– finite] in early verb forms which is central to express temporal reference different from the default 'here and now' reference.

More precisely, the following questions will be pursued. First, to what extent do form types matter with respect to temporal interpretations? Second, how is a specific temporal interpretation related to a specific form? Third, do these correlations form obligatory links between grammatical features or do they express only tendencies of co-occurrence? And fourth, which role does finiteness play at this early stage in child language acquisition?

With respect to the notion of finiteness, I adopt Klein's view on finiteness as a multi-level phenomenon (see Klein, 1998, this volume). This account is based on Klein's conception of the temporal relations of tense and aspect (see Klein, 1994). It serves as a starting point for a multi-level analysis of data of the type as exemplified above in relating aspects of morphological form with aspects of semantic interpretation. The theoretical insights on finiteness are cast into a developmental model of cell fissions which allows for a more and more fine-grained expression of temporal reference over time. This model captures the empirical findings in a compact and flexible manner.

This chapter is structured in the following way. In section 2, I discuss relevant methodological issues that lay open the criteria for the classification of the data. Section 3 introduces the data analysis and gives additional statistical information about the significance of specific form-meaning relations. These findings are then contrasted with developmental hypotheses on early form-meaning relations made in the literature. In section 4, my own account, the cell fission model, is presented. In a last step, this developmental model will be generalized to include the nominal domain. This generalization is empirically backed up by first data on the acquisition of case in Czech.

2. METHODOLOGICAL ISSUES

When does a morphological form count as finite or as infinitival in a child's utterances? And, how do we determine the intention of a child's utterance if a classification of the semantic interpretation is at stake? Before we can take a closer look at the child data, these two questions have to be answered with sufficient precision to yield us a robust tool for the classification of child language. So, this section deals with the sharpening of methodological tools for the assessment of morphological form and the assessment of interpretation, subsequently.

Here is a terminological a priori in place. I label [– finite] marked verbs as *infinitive forms*; corresponding utterance structures which exhibit an infinitive verbal form but no finite marked verb are labelled as *infinitival structures*. To avoid confusions, I disregard from the ambiguous term 'root infinitives' as used widely in the literature since it is ambiguous between verbal form and utterance structure. I adhere to Klein's terminology (Klein, this volume) in distinguishing a tripartite classification that comprises of finite structures, infinitival structures, and verb-free structures.

2.1. The Assessment of Morphological Form

Considering (1) through (4), the application of this classification this seems to be an easy task. Obviously, it is not as unproblematic as the examples suggest since examples are usually chosen because of their relative clarity. I am convinced that the amazing incompatibility of empirically obtained proportions for finite vs. infinitival utterance structures in German child language are due to a gross variability in methodology, not to speak of general misunderstandings concerning the interpretation of these heterogeneous results.

Regarding the form characteristics of [+/– finite] morphology, the German target language offers three criteria for this distinction. First, the shape of the morphological form itself; second, the positioning of the verbal element in the utterance; and third, the positioning of verbal prefixes and verbal particles in relation to the rest of the verbal part. All these criteria are comparably easy to classify in target-adequate utterances, because at least the first two of them conspire in adult language. But the application of this formal grid to child language is less easy.

One reason for possible confoundings constitutes the fact that the *-en* ending of the infinitive morphology is shared by the 1st and 3rd plural morphology of tensed verb forms in target German. Considering that child utterances are short and topologically often unreliable, the positional factor can hardly be decisive here. Problems of homonymous inflectional elements are worse in southern dialects of German. Since the protagonists of our empirical sketch, Max and Benny, are raised in Swabia (a region in the South of Germany), they are faced with an additional homonymy between the dialectal -*e* ending of the regional infinitival form and the tensed 1st singular form.

To analyze their data, the following procedure has been used. I classify a verbal element as an infinitive if the pronunciation of the verb-ending shows a potential target-conform -*en* or -*e/-a* realization (the latter are the dialectal variants). Further, the positioning of the verb must not contradict German placement patterns if the general picture of an individual acquisitional path allows the assumption that the basic rules of German topology are acquired.[3] For the infinitival classification, this means that the positioning factor indicates an attempt to position the verbal element at hand close to the end of the utterance (verb-final placement). Verbal particles of infinitives have to occur affixed to their verbal host. For infinitives, it is also possible to occur as one-word utterances. Obviously, the phonological realization allows for a distinction in these cases. Moreover, the context of the utterance is taken into account insofar as it indicates repetitions, direct citations, memorized song texts, etc., which point to a particular classification.

With respect to the finite classification, the requirements are broadened compared to those of the target language in the following way. A verb is finite if the pronunciation of the verb-ending shows either a target-adequate form or possibly also an inadequate agreement (not excluding -*en* or -*e/-a* realization of the verb-ending). Thus, agreement errors are allowed for. Concerning the positioning factor, a finite marked verb might be placed in verb-first, verb-second, or in another position if an individual-based systematicity can be observed. In the case of Benny, his system allows also for a verb-third positioning of finite elements during our crucial period. Therefore, the acquisition of the strict verb-second placement of German assertive root clauses is not a precondition for verbal elements to count as finite. The placement of verbal particles plays no role if the agreement marking is adequate and the *non*-verb-end positioning of the verb unambiguous. Note here, that this categorization of form achieves a maximal independence from interpretive factors.

Apart from the [+/– finite] split, another utterance structure is of major importance, especially if we are concerned with utterances of young children: the verb-free utterance organization. If we are interested in the relation between forms to interpretations in child language, this truly non-finite type must not be neglected. Therefore, a tripartite differentiation of morphological utterance forms will be used for the analysis of the data. But before we can come to the analysis, I will shortly discuss the assessment of interpretation.

2.2. The Assessment of Interpretation

Turning to the interpretive partitioning, the following four categories have been distinguished to classify the utterances: requests/wishes, narratives, existentials/descriptions, and comments on ongoing events. This illocutionary classification implies a close relationship to the temporal reference embodied in the characteristics of the respective class. It is not only temporal reference that is of interest here, but also the issue of world referencing as becomes manifest in requests. Following Klein (this volume), the relationship between illocutionary force and world referencing is stated as follows:

> If mood ... indeed expresses hypotheticality, counterfactuality or, as in the case of imperatives, non-existence but desirability of the situation, then we may say that the utterance is not about the 'real world' or not *only* about the 'real world' but about specific possible worlds; hence, the world parameter.

In the following, I will discuss these four different illocutionary categories focusing on their repercussions on time/world reference. The category of requests and wishes encompasses all utterances of a child, which signal the intention of the child to obtain a specific state of affairs. This state of affairs is not given at the moment of speech (see examples (1) and (3) in the introduction). Hence, requests and wishes point in their temporal reference to a (potential) posterior time or — speaking in possible worlds — to a wish-world. The fulfillment of the request or wish by an agent, i.e., the interlocutor or the child itself, is accompanied by satisfaction on the child's side, i.e., further repetitions of this sort of utterance stop. I am aware that the actual wish or desire expressed by the child holds at the moment of speech as a psychological real concept. So, imperatives and desideratives are bi-phasic in displaying a 'wish-time' and a 'fulfillment-time' in the successful case. Nevertheless, I assume together with Klein that it is the existence or non-existence of a particular situation at the moment of speech that controls the time/world reference parameter.

The next category, the one of narratives, comprises of personal narrations on the child's side. The state of affairs is by definition set in the past, so they induce clear reference to an anterior time. Concrete temporal pointers as e.g., *yesterday, last month* etc. are typically omitted in early child language. So, parental help is often needed to clarify doubtful interpretations of these sequences, see the following example:

(5) (Benny is telling about a Punch and Judy show in which the witch
    'Wackelzahn' played a role) (Benny, 2;10,28)
    die der wackelZAHN   mit hex   war au noch   da\
    the the loose-tooth   with witch   was also PRT   there
    'Witch Wackelzahn was there, too.'

The category of existentials and descriptions subsumes labeling functions (*feuerwehrmann* 'fireman') and picture descriptions of picture books (*desisne uhr* 'this-is-a watch'); they crucially do not involve any action or agent. Their temporal reference embodies reference to the moment of speech and consequently, their world referencing relates to the actual world. The notion actual world means here 'actual' from the perspective of the child. This includes actual play worlds and worlds as laid out in picture books. In this respect, the concept of the actual world is broadened to include a child's current imaginational world that is treated as actual by the interlocutors.

The last category, commenting on ongoing events, requires the joint attention of child and interlocutor towards an action to which the utterance refers to directly, cf. the examples (2) and (4) from above. Thus, a pre-established common focus of attention for child and interlocutor sets the temporal frame for the utterance interpretation that is set close to the moment of speech as the term 'ongoing' suggests. This includes crucially a shared real world experience, which gets commented on.

These four categories of interpretation constitute the grid for a classification of time/world referencing in child language. Other a-temporal categories are excluded to keep the analysis as unambiguous and simple as possible. Among these excluded categories, questions form the most prominent class. Likewise, exclamatives are omitted since their characteristics of form and interpretation do not enlighten our issue at hand. I exclude also structures with imperative morphology since they constitute a *tertium datur* within the inflectional paradigm and they are thus neither strictly finite nor infinitival. Moreover, imperative marked structures form a closed class at the developmental stage analyzed here and can thus be neglected.

In addition, the following list of occurrences is excluded from the analysis: onomatopoeic utterances, discourse fillers like *hm, äh,* immediate repetitions of the input, unanalyzable sequences, *yes-no* answers and utterances with unclear interpretation.

Last but not least the category of context-coherent elliptical answers following turn-adjacent questions has to be excluded although it constitutes a frequent category in child language. In my opinion, this is the most crucial difference to other methodological approaches. The reason for excluding them is that we never know for sure whether a child has already acquired the mechanisms for grammatical adjacency ellipsis (acknowledging steps of silent acquisition). If so, this would render these infinitival structures to be possibly embedded under a matrix verb.

Again, the guiding idea is to reach complete independence of the interpretive classification from formal factors. The exclusion of potentially elliptical answers takes this credo sadly effectively into account since it reduces the amount of analyzable data drastically.

Now, we are equipped with sufficient background information about the classification procedure and we can turn to the inspection of the data.

3. TWO DEVELOPMENTAL PATHS

In this section, we will follow the two developmental paths of Max and Benny on their way towards the German target. First, I present some general information concerning the database. This includes also a first quantitative overview about the differentiation of morphological forms across data points. Second, examples illustrate the array of temporal and modal interpretations found with finite and infinitive forms. Here, the earlier given quantitative information allows the reader to weigh the examples according to their relative frequency. Third, the data analysis casts the biases and tendencies found in the data into percentages. Fourth, statistical information tells us which of the involved form-interpretation relations are significant across development and which are not. Finally, a short discussion of the data compares these findings with claims made in the literature on acquisition.

3.1. The Database

The data are taken from the Tübinger corpus of the DFG-project on the 'Acquisition of complex sentences' collected under the header of R. Tracy. The analysis is based on 2209 child utterances in total. After the exclusion of all the disturbing categories mentioned above, 846 utterances are left to be included in the analysis, 357 child utterances had to be excluded due to their adjacency elliptical nature. The absolute numbers with respect to different form categories at different data points can be read off from Figure 1 below. The age window covered for the two children ranges from 2;6 to 2;11 for Max, and from 2;2 to 3;0 for Benny. So, both learners exhibit a relatively slow development which is the reason that their 'root infinitive stage', i.e., the stage where finite and infinitive forms coexist across utterances, occurs comparatively late in the second half of the second year of life.

Three data points have been chosen for the analysis within the individual time window. These points represent more or less the onset, the peak and the offset of their root infinitive stage in the respective developmental paths. This can be read off from the proportions of their occurrence compared to verb-free and finite utterance structures. Compare the diagrams below which depict this development for Max and for Benny:

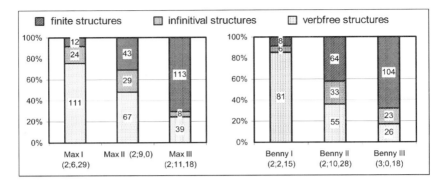

Figure 1. The proportion of utterance structures across development

A developmental progression in the realm of syntactic structuring can be inferred from the decrease of verb-free utterance structures and the increase of finite marked structures. Infinitival structures occur concomitantly to this structural shifting and their frequency peak lies interestingly at the center of this process.

3.2. Examples

In the following, several examples illustrate the array of form-interpretation relations as found in the data. I will restrict the examples to finite and infinitival utterance structures and omit the case of verb-free structures. Nevertheless, it has to be stressed that all four interpretative categories discussed above (requests, narratives, descriptions, and comments on ongoing events) do also occur in verbless counterpart structures.

The following set of examples has been selected to focus on the question which of these four interpretative categories from above can be conveyed by an infinitival utterance structure:

(6) (Max wants Mickey Mouse to wash his hands)   (Max, 2;11,18)
 schnell händ waschen\
 quickly hand-PL wash-INF
 'Mickey Mouse, wash your hands quickly!'

(7) (Benny wants the interlocutor to lie down again) (Benny, 3;00,18)
 etz dich wieder HINlegen\
 now you again down-lie-INF
 'Now, lie down again!'

(8) (Benny is throwing a toy fish back into the water) (Benny, 3;00,18)
    du   wieder   wasser   neigehe\   hopp/
    you   again   water   into-go-INF   hop
    'You are going back into the water. Hop!'

(9) (Benny tells about his visit to a fairy-tale garden) (Benny, 2;10,28)
    dann   dann   einmal   RUMspringen\   LAUS\
    then   then   once   around-jump-INF   Klaus
    'Then, I was once jumping around with Klaus.'

(10) (The interlocutor holds a Lego-brick in her hands) (Max, 2;09,00)
    n   des   auch-n   dach   sein\
    n   that   also-a   roof   be-INF
    'This is/should be also a roof.'

(11) (Benny is sitting)   (Benny, 2;10,28)
    etz   endlich   SITzen
    now   finally   sit-INF
    'Now, I am finally sitting.'

(12) (Max is closing the cover of the toy-toilet)   (Max, 2;09,00)
    des   ZUmachen\
    this   close-make-INF
    'I am closing this.'

(13) (Benny tries to throw the ball across the hedge) (Benny, 2;10,28)
    etz   da   HOCH   schieße\
    now   there   high   throw-INF
    'Now, I throw it on top of the hedge.'

The examples in (6), (7), and (8) are requests or wishes from the child's side; (9) is a narrative; descriptions or states of affairs are expressed under (10) and (11); and comments on ongoing events are illustrated by (12) and (13). Since this type of early child data consists mainly of concrete play-situations, narratives are generally very rare. Thus, I have not found any infinitival narratives in Max' data. Note also, that infinitival structures do not exclude the occurrence of an overt subject, as is, e.g., the case in (8).

Now, let us turn to the finite utterance structures and their variety of interpretative categories:

(14) (Max wants to have the tractor) (Max, 2;09,00)
  ich will-eh   TRAKtroa\
  I   want-FIN-the tractor
  'I want the tractor'

(15) (Benny wants to fish for the mermaid in a play) (Benny, 3;00,18)
  will   die meerjungfrau das du hast
  want-FIN the mermaid   that you have-FIN
  net   die meerjungfrau\
  not the mermaid
  'I want to have the mermaid so that you do not have it.'

(16) (Max tells about an earlier play-accident) (Max, 2;11,18)
  ich hab   auch WEHgetan\
  I   have-FIN also   hurt
  'I hurt myself, too.'

(17) (Benny tells about his ride on a merry-go-round) (Benny, 3;00,18)
  da   hab ich –   dann die rote GANZ schnell fährt\
  there have-FIN I – then the red very fast ride-FIN
  'There, I rode in/on the red one very fast.'

(18) (Max states about the casualty after a play-accident) (Max, 2;09,00)
  des   lebt   noch\
  that live-FIN still
  'That one is still alive.'

(19) (Benny states that the interlocutor has a mum) (Benny, 3;00,18)
  du   etz   hat   eine MAmi\
  you now have-FIN   a mummy
  'You have a mummy.'

(20) (Max puts Mickey Mouse on the play-trailer) (Max, 2;11,19)
  so   MICKImaus fährt   mit\
  well Mickey Mouse come-FIN   along
  'Well, Mickey Mouse come along.'

(21) (Benny is acting as a lion, eating another cookie) (Benny, 3;00,18)
  namnam\   ich   freß   NOCH was
  yummy-yummy I   devour another one
  'Yummy yummy, I will devour another one.'

The examples in (14) through (21) constitute the finite mirror image to the ones in (6) through (13) above. Due to the differentiated methodological grid, target-inadequate topological ordering does not exclude a classification as finite. So, surface structure V3-ordering is allowed for, as e.g., in (15) and (19). The V2-placement pattern and the emergence of finite morphology are not necessarily coupled in the acquisition process, as the data show.

Concerning the interpretative classification, (14) and (15) express requests, (16) and (17) are narratives, (18) and (19) form descriptions, and (20) and (21) are comments on ongoing events in play situations. Now, the reader might wonder how one argues for form-interpretation correlations in the face of this structural variety of child data. This is the point where biases and tendencies have to be taken into account. The distribution of infinitival and finite utterance structures across all interpretative categories is not equal. It differs within and across time.

This distribution indicates also that the form-interpretation correlations in child language are more flexible than feature-bound grammar systems allow for. A grammatical rule as for example 'infinitive morphology triggers modal interpretation' fails to capture the complete set of actual occurrences of form-interpretation correlations. Nevertheless, rules like this have been suggested in the literature to explain the modal bias of the infinitive form. This point is elaborated in the discussion section below. But before we can come to that we have to examine the relevant biases and tendencies in more detail.

3.3. Data Analysis

To this aim, the two figures below represent the encountered form-interpretation relations of the analyzed utterances of Max and Benny, respectively. Each bar represents the distribution of interpretations within a data point, i.e., within the analyzable utterances of one session. Each figure is divided into four diagrams which represent the form-interpretation correlations for the utterance total, all verb-free utterance structures, all infinitival structures and last but not least, all finite structures.

In the first diagram of Figure 2 below, labeled 'the utterance total', the overall distribution is depicted for each data point. This interpretive segmentation of the utterance total gives the background against which the interpretational biases of individual forms can be judged. This background information is crucial due to the drastic differences in the individual frequency of the interpretational categories involved as shown by the extremely low numbers of the category 'narrative'. For the visualization of the correlations, I separated in Figure 2 and Figure 3 the overview about the formal distribution from the interpretational distribution. Therefore, the changes between the proportions across the three data points have to be interpreted against the steady shift of form types from verb-free to finite marked utterances as shown in Figure 1. Figure 2 captures the interpretational distribution across time for Max:

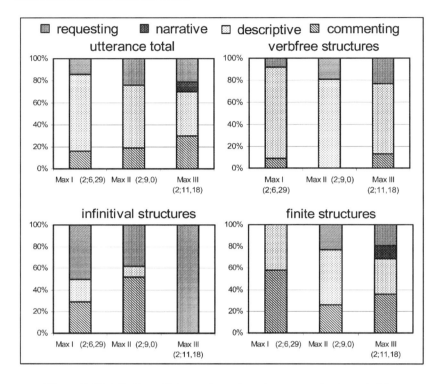

Figure 2. Distribution of interpretive categories across structures in Max

A comparison of the first diagram, labeled 'utterance total', with the second one, labeled 'verb-free structures', shows the interpretive distribution of verbless utterances within and across data points. For the verbless category this is not very spectacular since its interpretive distribution differs hardly from that of the utterance total. Apart from the missing commenting category at data point two and the missing narratives at data point three, the bars are equal. Hence, verb-free structures are not related to a specific interpretation.

Comparing this with the third diagram, the contrast in distribution is remarkable. Concerning the descriptive category, it hardly plays a role within the form type of infinitival utterances. Narratives do not occur as was found before within the verb-free category.

The last diagram represents the distribution of interpretations within finite utterances. Again, a different picture emerges. Finite utterance structures prefer first of all comments and descriptive expressions. Later, the request interpretation enters the finite-marked stage. With respect to data point three, a comparison with the distribution of the utterance total is particularly interesting since there is hardly any difference. So, finite utterances take over the full range *and* the distributional properties of the utterance total.

Summarizing, a systematic differentiation of form-interpretation correlations emerges, though not in all form types. With differentiation, I mean a particular distribution of biases and more or less strong tendencies. With respect to finite structures, they first avoid request interpretations before they allow for an unbiased representation. Infinitival structures, on the other hand, attract request interpretation and to a lesser extent also comment interpretation. Verb-free structures stay unbiased towards any interpretation through the whole developmental window.

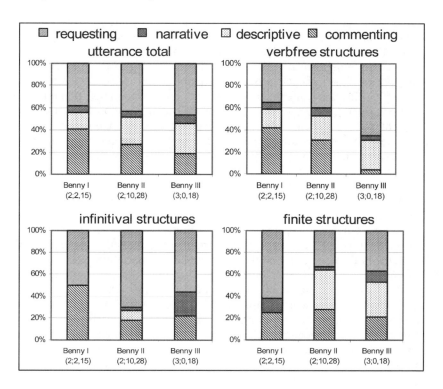

Figure 3. Distribution of interpretive categories across structures in Benny

In Figure 3, the interpretational distribution of the utterance total is again presented in the first diagram, and then the distribution of verb-free structures, infinitival structures, and finite structures. The overall picture of Benny's development strengthens the observation that at the beginning of the relevant age window the category of verbless utterances in the second diagram represents best the distribution of interpretation of the utterance total. This category of verbless utterances changes only with respect to a decrease in comment interpretation across the three different data points. As was found for Max, the distribution of interpretational categories within the form type of infinitival utterances differs from the verb-free category in practically excluding descriptive interpretations and in attracting request interpretation. In Benny's case, narratives are among the favored interpretations of infinitival forms, too.

Regarding the distribution of interpretations within finite utterances (the last diagram), the first data point excludes again descriptive expressions but shows request interpretations, narratives and comments. The further development within that form type attracts descriptive interpretations as one would expect after the emergence of (nearly always finite) copula constructions. In contrast to Max' progression, the request/wish interpretation within finite forms is relatively strong and narratives exist from the first data point onwards. A comparison of data point three across structure types reveals that the finite utterance type mirrors the distributional properties of the utterance total. Hence, finite utterances become eventually the default type not only by their sheer magnitude but also by their correlational properties. This is in line with the findings for Max. But generally speaking, the differentiation across form types in Benny's data is not as striking as was the case with Max.

If we compare the two developmental pictures, no major differences appear. Benny's case weakens slightly the tendency of finite structures to avoid request interpretations before allowing for an unbiased representation. The second tendency, i.e., the fact that infinitival structures attract request interpretation and, to a lesser extent, comment interpretation, is confirmed, but Benny's data suggest also that the category of narratives can belong to this favored list of interpretations. Regarding the third tendency, i.e., that verb-free structures stay unbiased towards any interpretation through the whole developmental window, this can be refined to disfavor more and more the category 'commenting on ongoing events' as action verbs get included into the active lexicon of the child. In general, the inter-individual commonalities are much stronger than their differences. Now, the question is how strong these commonalities are with respect to the claim made here, namely that finite forms correlate with a 'here-and-now' bound interpretation whereas infinitive forms correlate with a non 'here-and-now' interpretation. This is the point where a statistical analysis is called for.

3.4. Statistics

In order to test the main results from above statistically, the pooled data of Max and Benny were subjected to a χ^2-analysis. To repeat, the general case made here in this chapter is that finite utterance organization attracts 'here-and-now' reference to a significant degree. This is assumed to be complemented by a significant degree of pairings between infinitival structures and non 'here-and-now' reference.[4] As stated before in the methodological section, the interpretive categories embody by definition temporal reference and world reference. 'Here-and-now' based interpretations are related to descriptions/ existentials and to comments on ongoing events. On the other hand, narratives and requests express a 'not-here-and-now' reference. This way the interpretive categories were split in two halves of time/world referencing. This split reaches significance for the infinitival domain ($\chi^2 = 5.9$ for $p< .05$, df = 1, critical value = 3.84) and even a stronger significance for the finite form type ($\chi^2 = 23.2$ for $p< .05$).

A second split is obtained if we divide the 'not-here-and-now'-based reference into forward and backward pointing of temporal reference. Requests point into a possible or desired future, while narratives point into the past. By means of this second split we can test the often observed modal bias of the infinitive form. How strong is the correlation between infinitival utterance organization and request/wish interpretation?

Surprisingly, the χ^2-analysis revealed that the split between [+/− modal] is highly significant within the finite form category ($\chi^2 = 67.16$ for $p< .05$, df = 1, critical value = 3.84), whereas the alleged overwhelming bias of infinitival utterances towards modal interpretation is not significant in the pooled data here ($\chi^2 = 0.78$ for $p< .05$). This depicts clearly a 'Anti-Modal Reference Effect' of finite utterances instead of a 'Modal Reference Effect' for infinitival structures. Even if we split our data across the two children, Max and Benny, a significant value of modal interpretations within the infinitive segment is neither reached for Max nor Benny.

3.5. Discussion of the Data

The empirical picture as sketched above modifies general assumptions on early finite and infinitival child language considerably. The assumption discussed most in the literature states that the interpretation of infinitival structures, the so-called root infinitives, shows a bias towards a modal interpretation. A modal bias of the infinitival utterance organization has been found in data from Jordens (1990, 2002), Boser *et al.* (1992), Whitman (1994), Ingram & Thompson (1996), and Hoekstra & Hyams (1998), and is assumed to constitute a robust empirical fact. But this robust fact has hardly ever been tested statistically. Instead of this modal bias, I found an 'Anti-Modal Reference Effect' of finite utterances to be statistically significant.

This casts some doubt on all developmental models that focus on the alleged modal bias of infinitival structures. Boser *et al.* (1992) proposed a dropped modal in TNS position. This perspective is complemented by the assumption of Whitman (1994) that an empty dummy modal gets inserted in infinitival structures. Hoekstra & Hyams (1999) argue for a direct form-function link between the infinitive morphology itself and modality, which captures the observed 'Modal Reference Effect' of infinitival structures. In Jordens (2002), the second relatum of this link is not labeled modality but specified with the semantic feature [+ intention]. These 'modal-focused models' are faced with three major problems according to our empirical analysis: First, the infinitival utterance organization is not exclusively related to modal interpretations (see also e.g., Becker & Hyams, 2000, where one child shows 43% non-modal interpretations in her infinitival structures and Schaner-Wolles, 2000, where a child shows up to 48.1% non-modal root infinitives).[5] How can any other interpretations be reconciled within the developmental models sketched above? Second, verbless structures can also convey modal interpretations. Which type of mechanism should allow them to be modal if a direct encoding of a modality feature is obviously excluded in these structures? And third, if the allegedly modal bias of infinitival structures is not significant statistically, neither within nor across individual developments, why then fix features for non-significant relations? Note, too, that there is also a major theoretical problem attached to this sort of models: What happens if a morphological form is target-inadequately set to an interpretive value like [+ modal]: How can a child retreat from such a misleading parameter-setting in the further course of development?

A broader interpretational range has been taken into account in the work of Behrens (1993) and Lasser (1997), where it is claimed that infinitive forms convey non-completed interpretations. In these accounts, comments of ongoing events and other 'here-and-now' related illocutions are included in the array of interpretations for infinitival structures, but utterances with pastness effect as, e.g., personal narrations are excluded. A special case of this broader interpretation of infinitival child utterances is found in Schaner-Wolles (2000) who states that modal root infinitives refer to the future and non-modal root infinitives refer to the present. If the infinitive-marked verb occurs in V2-position it is seen as a morphological substitute form for present tense. This view is not corroborated by our data since infinitival structures do occur as narratives, too. The general exclusion of non-completed interpretations or past interpretations is not borne out by the data. Thus, this broader interpretational range is still not broad enough to model the data adequately.

Other accounts argue precisely that the notion of finiteness is absent in early child language. Thus, the difference between infinitival and finite structures can have no repercussions on interpretational matters. For example, in Jordens (1990) it is claimed that only infinitive verbs are used productively, whereas finite verbs display only a small fraction of different verb types. Therefore finite verbs are unanalyzed and learned holistically. This points to a lack of grammatical finiteness and abstract grammatical relations like head movement in an early stage of child language. Hence, this category has to be acquired subsequently to the 'root infinitive stage'. Following this line of reasoning significant differences such as the 'Anti-Modal-Reference Effect' should rest on the differentiation between analytically and holistically learned verb forms. It might well be that these two developmental strategies, the holistic learning and the analytic learning, play different roles in acquiring one-state or two-state verbs but it is then totally unclear how this differentiation should lead to significant interpretational correlations. Within the data discussed above, the set of finite verbs is productive at least from the second data point onwards.

In a more recent study by Jordens (2002, 687), it is argued for Dutch that "in early child Dutch finiteness is not yet part of the children's productive grammatical system." This view is not corroborated by my analysis as described above. Three factors might lead to this incompatibility between the two analyses. First, Dutch child language involves a bigger set of illocutionary force indicating operators which are holistically learned as e.g. *unne* for 'want' or *mag-ikke* for 'may I'. In this respect, Dutch child language acquisition is closer to the case of English than to the case of German. Second, learning strategies between children can differ to a greater extent than usually acknowledged since this sort of inter-individual variation is always a drawback for the formulation of developmental theories. More longitudinal studies are needed in both languages to evaluate these cross-linguistic and/or inter-individual differences. Third, the early ability to differentiate between [+/– finite] need not necessarily imply that the whole grammatical system involving the abstract category finiteness is in place.

In my view, the interpretation of data across the literature is heterogeneous due to, on the one hand, small sample sizes which are not subjected to a statistical analysis, and, on the other hand, different criteria of methodological classification. As mentioned in Klein (this volume), the estimates on the share of German root infinitive utterances vary between 15% and 100% around the age of two. The developmental accounts suggested so far can not model adequately the range of inter-individual differences, on the one hand, and the range of associations between specific morphological forms and their temporal meanings in early child language, on the other hand. This is, because these accounts can not deal with biases and tendencies in general or they ignore the first or the latter variation completely. Hence, the next section investigates more closely how an empirically adequate and flexible model could look like.

4. A GENERALIZED MODEL OF FORMS TO MEANINGS

This section introduces a model of the acquisition of form-meaning relations in early child language. This model is based on an account on finiteness as sketched in Klein (this volume). Therefore, I present first a short summary of the relevant implications of Klein's account on finiteness. Second, I introduce the *cell fission model* (CFM). The flexibility of this model allows to cast biases and tendencies as found in the data into the dynamics of cell growth whereby the cells model the relations between forms and meanings in a more and more fine-grained manner. In a third step, a more detailed description of the first and the second cell fission is presented for the case of German child language. Fourth, this model is complemented with an independent, second mechanism of temporal reference, a plain pragmatic process of temporal resolution. This pragmatic override mechanism occurs in utterances with joint focus of attention of both interlocutors. The combination of the CFM and this pragmatic mechanism allows for an adequate modelling of the empirics.

In step five, the CFM is generalized so that it includes the development of form-interpretation relations in other domains as well. To this aim, I discuss first data on the acquisition of case that illustrates a first developmental phase within the nominal domain. The similarities of findings within the nominal and the verbal domain indicate that the basic principle concerning the mapping of forms to meanings is the same. The essence of this mechanism is captured in the *Principle of Default-Boundedness*. The implementation of this principle within the CFM yields a developmental system with the advantage to be domain-independent, fool-proof, and cross-linguistically applicable.

4.1. Klein's Framework of Finiteness

As has become clear in the data section, it is the [+/– finite] distinction that controls somehow the interpretation of an utterance. In this section, I will inquire into the nature of this relation and I will be more particular about the 'somehow' part.

Klein's general framework (see Klein, 1994; 1998; this volume) introduces a relational account for the definition of grammatical tense and grammatical aspect. The three temporal parameters time of utterance (TU), situation time (TSit) and topic time (TT) conspire pair-wise in these two definitions: Grammatical tense is defined as the relation between TT and TU whereas grammatical aspect is defined as the relation between TT and TSit.

Turning to the role of the grammatical category finiteness, Klein assumes that it is the finiteness element that links the purely descriptive sentence base to a time span, about which an assertion (as the basic case of illocutionary act) is made. That time span is captured in the topic time parameter TT. As a result, [+ finite] marked utterances bear a grammatical assertion potential. The abstract finiteness element is interpreted as an operator that takes scope over the asserted part of a sentence. It is claimed that the grammatical potential of exerting assertive force (i.e., the grammatical finiteness category) and the category where tense-morphology surfaces are two different grammatical categories which only happen to fall morphologically together in the Germanic languages. An example like *Jim DID climb* illustrates this point in being ambiguous between highlighting the temporal factor (contrasting past tense with another tense) or the assertion factor comparable to a verum-focus construction. Consequently, the role of finiteness neither reduces to agreement inflection, nor to tense (or aspect) inflection only. If finiteness is grammatically specified (as either [+ finite] or [– finite]) it surfaces as a morphologically visible element on the matrix verb in Indo-European languages. Still, the category finiteness itself can not be reduced to the morphosyntactic level of grammar since it serves also as the grammatical anchor of TT and with it as the carrier of the assertion potential within the domain of interpretation.

Summarizing, the grammatical finiteness operator controls the assertive force of a sentence. This assertive force holds for a specified temporal interval, namely, the time about which an assertion is made. This interval is called 'topic time' (TT). Without the specification of TT no exertion of assertive force is possible. This way, the finiteness operator mediates between the topic component of an utterance, including TT, and the asserted part.

For the complete grammatical finiteness system to be operative, knowledge about the morphological paradigm, about syntactic dependencies and the verb-second rule, about the licensing of subjects, etc. has to be acquired. At the relevant stage of child language analyzed here, there exists no evidence to support the assumption that this whole set is already learned. Still, we find significant differences with respect to the interpretation of [+ finite] and [– finite] structures which indicate that the finiteness distinction matters.

Therefore, the following question arises: How do [+/– finite] marked structures relate to a specific temporal interpretation in early acquisition? Since utterance structures marked for [+ finite] associate with assertive force and, crucially, with a TT specification as a prerequisite in Klein's account, they relate to the assertable. For a child, the assertable amounts to the actual world and its 'here-and-now' reference. In a complementary way, the marking [– finite] *refuses* distinctly a built-in assertive force or a TT specification. Thus, it relates to the nonassertable, i.e., worlds other than the actual world. Children thereby functionalize early verbal morphology. Later in acquisition, this functionalizing aspect of morphology is replaced with a grammaticalizing aspect. Then, the [+/– finite] distinction per se reflects no interpretational distinction anymore but signals grammatical dependencies. Nevertheless, the early functionalizing aspect of morphology survives in the fringes of the target system as e.g. in infinitival requests like *Sofort hinlegen!* 'Lie down immediately!' (see Lasser, 1997). In effect, this functionalizing of morphology is therefore not target inadequate but target-adequate for a restricted domain within the grammar.

Concerning the third formal category of verbless structures, a grammatically induced expression of assertion is impossible and with it a grammatical specification of TT. Finiteness plays no role in these structures. This under-specification results in a strong context-dependence of verb-free structures. They are truly unbiased regarding the time/world parameter and rely on external factors for their temporal interpretation as long as temporal adverbials or other lexical elements that can be temporally interpreted do not occur in these structures.

4.2. The Cell Fission Model

The metaphor 'cell fission' allows us to convey useful biological connotations into linguistics and into language development, in particular. Cells exist in different sizes, if necessity arises they can split in half. This process takes place recursively until it is actively stopped. Moreover, this process leads to a differentiation in form and, correspondingly, also in the functionality of the whole system. These characteristics among others render a cell fission model (CFM) for an explanative account on child language development attractive.

In language acquisition, the system strives for a one-to-one correspondence between formal and interpretational aspects of cells. This old idea has been cast for example in Clark's 'Principle of Contrast' which states that the child expects that a difference in form implies difference in function (see Clark, 1987). Every now and then, the relation between forms to interpretations cannot be based on a one-to-one correspondence due to differences in the individual developmental pace of the related domains. This way, deviations from the targeted one-to-one correspondence trigger new developmental steps and constitute thereby one of the driving forces of acquisition. Cell fissions occur if enough material has been accumulated within the original cell for two separate cells to be self-contained. This involves a procedure of first collecting material and then splitting it up which leads to a minor or major restructuring of the system.

Within the domain of verbal morphology in Indo-European languages, the formal split between [+/– finite] marked structures constitutes the first step into productive verbal morphology. Subsequently, the imperative morphology is singled out. In a later step, the morphological opposition of present and past tense is realized with early participle forms of telic verbs as precursor forms. Eventually, a major restructuring of the system allows for grammatical tense and grammatical aspect to become productive.

Concerning the domain of temporal interpretation, a first bifurcation separates the 'here-and-now' from the 'not-here-and-now'. The 'not-here-and-now' has then to be split into a temporally backward pointing and forward pointing area. This results into a differentiation between anteriority and posteriority. Posteriority comprises of potential futures which intermingle with desired futures if crosscut with the [+/– modality] axis. In a series of steps, temporality gets separated from aspects of modality and modality itself becomes multi-faceted as regulated in the target system. Concomitantly to the cell fissions within the temporal domain, three temporal parameters (TU, TT, TSit) have to be segregated and defined. Their independence of each other enables the system of grammatical tense and grammatical aspect to be interpreted in a target-like manner.

The mapping of 'formal' cells to 'interpretational' cells is controlled by a guiding principle that relates grammatical default forms to default interpretations in a target-conform manner as long as no other grammatical rules intervene:

Principle of Default-Boundedness (PDB):
(i) Grammatical default forms relate to default interpretations
(ii) Grammatical non-default forms relate to non-default interpretations

Thus, the distribution can not be picked randomly. Differences across individual developmental paths are due to possible differences in the form-interpretation pairings that result from the formal or the interpretational domain taking the lead.

The temporal sequence of cell discoveries is ordered by a salience hierarchy. The more salient a formal or interpretational category, the earlier it is cell-wise segregated and thus defined. If we consider the case of English for a moment, differences in verbal morphology are less prominent. This might be the reason for the request interpretation to be signalled by the early holistic *wanna* ('want+to') construction. Due to a lack of inflectional saliency, children have to fall back on other means to fill in the formal cell equivalent (for a discussion of the CFM within a broader crosslinguistic perspective, see Gretsch, 2004).

4.3. The Cell Fission Model Applied to German Child Language

For our case of German child language, I discuss the first and the second fission more detailed. In the *first formal fission*, the two most salient morphological differentiations are separated resulting in a split between [+/−finite] marked verbs or structures. In the *first interpretative fission*, the two most salient time/world differentiations are separated resulting in a split between the actual world and the non-actual world (the 'here-and-now' and the 'not-here-and-now'). Two 'formal' cells plus two 'interpretational' cells allow for a simple one-to-one correspondence of forms to interpretations. Following the PDB, [+ finite] structures which exhibit the grammatical default marking map onto the 'here-and-now', i.e., the actual world, as the default of the time/world parameter. Thereby, the latter default setting takes the central egocentricity — not only of children — into account. This relational distribution is in general already target-adequate, although relevant grammatical restrictions are missing.

Following our finiteness account, the determination of an assertive force and a corresponding TT provide the missing theoretical link between [+finite] structures and the actual world. Finite structures attract therefore 'assertable' interpretations whereas infinitival structures imply the opposite. The latter structures refuse the setting of an assertive force and relate thus to the 'nonassertable' which points to the (set of) non-actual world(s). The first fission of the CFM uses only a binary set of temporal parameters. As I argued elsewhere (see Gretsch, 2004), this set comprises of TU and a conglomerate parameter of TT/TSit. If this conglomerate parameter TT/TSit is not fixed to the 'here-and-now' (default interpretation) it can point to a preceding or following temporal interval with respect to the 'here-and-now' (non-default interpretation). This non-default interpretation subsumes thus references with a pastness effect and those with a future/irrealis effect.

This is precisely what we find in the data from section 3 which show a significant correlation between [+ finite] and 'here-and-now' interpretation and a significant correlation between [− finite] and interpretations involving time-world continua distant from the 'here-and-now'. In contrast to this, a distinction based on a modality split only could not be corroborated by the statistical analysis. Note in addition, that the form type of verbless utterances differs from the [– finite] marking in not refusing any assertive component. So, to be verb-free implies complete non-specification with regard to TT setting and assertion. This is borne out by the data where the form type of verbless utterances and their interpretations mirrors more or less the distributional properties of the utterance total, showing no special bias.

Summing up, it is the morphological [+/– finite] distinction that enables the German learning child to convey a first differentiation in linguistically relevant world-referencing.

The *second fission* within the realm of form-interpretation correlations adds a temporal directionality to the concept of distant worlds leading to a morphological differentiation of past- and futureness. The child is then faced with the following problem: How to distribute three coarse temporal distinctions (anteriority, posteriority, present) onto the two morphological forms [+/– finite]? This situation triggers the search for an adequate formal marker. In German, this problem is solved by the emergence of past participle markings that induce a perfective aspect interpretation. This perfective aspect interpretation leads to an encoding of anteriority similar to the *-ed* interpretation in early child English (see Van Geenhoven, this volume). This development frees the infinitive form from covering interpretations with anterior temporal reference. This is the point in development where infinitival structures attract mainly modality-related interpretations. From then on, the child's linguistic system is able to encode the two temporal directions, backward and forward, plus the 'here-and-now' reference exclusively via verbal morphology. A one-to-one correspondence of forms to interpretations is established again allowing now for an unambiguous anterior, posterior and present reference. Still, no more than two basic temporal parameters (TU and the TT/TSit conglomerate) are needed to express this tripartite temporal differentiation. It is only in a later step that TT and TSit become disentangled and give way to a target-like tripartite temporal parameter system.

Depending on the pace of cell fissions within an individual developmental path, this stage of a possible strong modal bias of infinitival structures may last longer or shorter. This is also what is reflected in the data. Whereas Max shows a strong modality bias only around the age of 2;11, this is less evident for Benny. Interestingly, the statistics for the modal bias of infinitival structures is neither significant in the pooled data, nor in the individual data from Max and Benny. Remember that we found a 'Anti-Modal Reference Effect' of finite utterances instead of a 'Modal Reference Effect' for infinitival structures. The heterogeneity of percentages found across children (here and in the literature) has a twofold explanation within the CFM. First, data from the developmental interval labeled as the 'root infinitive stage' might comprise of different phases within the CFM or of only a short snapshot of one of the cell fission stages. Second, the subsequent cell fission stages may last longer or shorter within an individual.

The CFM-induced correlations are subjected to two opposing directions during the process of acquisition: On the one hand, the more forms are available, the stronger the corresponding interpretation that can be attached to an individual form. On the other hand, formal splits as [+/− finite] have eventually to weaken their interpretational correlate to allow for their exclusively grammatical role in the core grammar — neglecting the peripheral case of adult infinitival structures for a moment. Hence, the linguistic system of a child gains its individuality within the acquisitional space as put up by these opposing forces.

With regard to the range of the inter-individual differences as presented here, they do not demarcate by far the boundaries of the acquisitional space but indicate only two possible trajectories through it. Nevertheless, it is already evident from this sketched miniature space that the strength of the link between individual formal and interpretive cells varies considerably in intra-individual and inter-individual development depending on the stage of cell partitionings and their mappings.

So far, the CFM satisfies the statistical aspects of the empirical analysis. But there exists yet another puzzle in the data. According to the CFM, finite and infinitival structures form a mirror image of each other. The data as sketched above in section 2 are much more complex and refractory, not to say contradictory to this view. One of the central remaining questions is: How can the CFM account for the large percentage of infinitival structures, which relate nevertheless to the 'here-and-now'? This problem finds an explanation in a twofold mechanism of temporal reference described in the next section.

4.4. Two Mechanisms of Temporal Reference [6]

I claim that the mechanism for specifying time/world reference in utterances which entail a joint focus of attention between interlocutors is different from the mechanism in those utterances where this joint focus is not available. Joint focus implies joint topical parameters (topic time, topic place, topic entity) which make any overt specification of TT and with it of TSit obsolete. In effect, two different mechanisms of temporal reference are available (in development as well as at the target stage). On the one hand, a grammatical based mechanism is controlled by the form-interpretation mappings according to a particular cell fission state within the CFM. On the other hand, a pragmatic based mechanism resolves the issue of temporal reference if a joint focus of attention sets a TT contextually, as for example in (12) above. The contextual setting frees the speech in these situations from any referencing need. As a result, a differentiation has to be made between interpretations where a TT specification is actively refused (CFM) and interpretations where a TT specification is not needed because of the simultaneity of language and action referred to (pragmatic resolution).

The existence of a pragmatic mechanism of temporal reference is corroborated by verb-free structures. Verb-free structures, too, can express comments on ongoing actions. Since these structures do not exhibit any formal marker on which the temporal interpretation could hinge, only a pragmatic resolution process is feasible. This process always overrides the formal aspect of utterance structures. Hence, joint focus utterances are expected to behave randomly with respect to the choice of form — a pattern that we find not only in child language but in adult language, too.

Combining the CFM and the pragmatic mechanism of temporal reference yields a parsimonious and elegant system to model the heterogeneous data. The tendencies and biases of the data found here and elsewhere are cast into a more and more fine-grained grid of emerging form-interpretation correlations which feed the grammatical based mechanism of TT specification. In addition, a stable pragmatic override mechanism accompanies the developmental cell fission process. Moreover, the CFM itself has to rely on a subsequent pragmatic disambiguation procedure for an interpretation to be successful if the interpretive cells are (still) highly underspecified. The lesser the number of cells, the broader is their coverage and thus their multi-functionality concerning potential interpretations. This mirrors the empirically well-known fact that early child language is highly context dependent. Even if a system of temporal referencing may already provide crude directions for a temporal interpretation, a disambiguation, i.e., a more detailed specification of TT, is usually needed. This is where context information is called for.

If we grant that TT specification and world referencing are (indirectly) a property of the finiteness element, as argued above, then one of the crucial implications of this conception is that the basics of this finiteness category are already operative in early child language — at least as early as the so-called root infinitive stage. This does not imply that the acquisition process of the finiteness category has come to an end. Other relevant factors related to finiteness are still lacking as e.g., the verb-second rule or the licensing of subjects. This can be directly read off from the examples above. Hence, another advantage of the CFM is the disentangling of grammatical and interpretive aspects of the category finiteness for the acquisition process.

In a last step, the general applicability of the CFM is tested by a totally different set of data, namely, nominal case marking in Czech.

4.5. Generalizing the Model

Strong similarities between the verbal and the nominal domain indicate an interesting test area for a generalized CFM: nominal phrases can bear a temporal reference, too, if not even "nominal tense" (Lecarme, 1999). Some languages allow for case-marked nominals with a corresponding time/world reference similar to the one we observed for the [+/– finite] opposition. One of these languages is Czech.

In Czech, the nominative case used as a 'root nominative structure' associates with 'here-and-now' reference whereas the accusative case signals distancy from the 'here-and-now'. In parallel to the verbal domain, default case is linked to default temporal reference ('here-and-now'), whereas non-default case relates to non-default reference ('not-here-and-now') following the Principle of Default-Boundedness (PDB). For an illustration, compare the following examples from a Czech child, Martina, from the Smolík corpus collected in Prague:

(22) (Martina wants to look at another book) (Martina, 1;11)
ešte   knížku\   [...]   ne   ist\
more   book-ACC   no   read-INF
'I want to have another book. [...], I do not want to read the one I have.'

(23) (Martina does not want to read that book) (Martina, 1;11)
<tam> tam   máš   knížku\
here   you have   the-book-ACC
'Here, you have the book.'

(24) (Martina and her mother look at the requested book) (Martina, 1;11)
knížka\
book-NOM
'This is the/a book.'

If no verb frame controls the distribution of case across nominal phrases, nominals in requesting utterances, and nominals in structures with assertive interpretation differ in their case marking. This is illustrated by (24) for the requesting case, the accusative, and (26) for the assertive case, the nominative. Note that this distribution is completely target-adequate and not a particularity of child language. The choice of the corresponding case marking for world reference is obligatory. The example (25) shows the occurrence of a target-adequate marked accusative nominal within a verb frame. As soon as case marked nominals become integrated into larger verb dominated phrases in child language, they loose their interpretational correlate of temporal/world reference.

As with the verbal differentiation, children pick up this pattern and use it according to the CFM from early on, i.e., from the first productive case opposition onwards. The reliable usage of the nominative and the accusative case marking is indicated at this developmental stage by their target-adequate forms across different verb frames.

This parallelism of the effects of verbal inflection and case marking on interpretation calls for an explanation. Within the CFM, salient formal oppositions are mapped onto salient interpretive oppositions. The mapping itself is controlled by the PDB. CFM plus PDB allow us to model empirical data and their interpretive biases as different as the development of the German inflectional system and the development of the Czech case system.

5. CONCLUSION

The analysis of German child data on the acquisition of verbal inflectional patterns shows that an interpretive differentiation between finite and infinitival structures is made from the first steps into grammar onwards. Several hypotheses from the literature cast this differentiation into rigid grammatical rules or into formulations about particular biases between a verbal form and a related, typical interpretation. The so-called modal bias of root infinitive structures is an example. These hypotheses fail in the face of a complex and refractory empirical situation.

It was the first aim of this paper to analyse the data situation with the aid of a transparent methodological assessment procedure and to subject the data base to a statistical analysis in order to test assumptions about relevant correlations between verbal forms and their temporal interpretations. The statistics show a significant correlation between infinitival utterance structures and a temporal interpretation involving a 'not-here-and-now' interpretation, as well as an even stronger correlation between finite structures and a temporal 'here-and-now' interpretation. Interestingly, the modal bias hypothesis was neither significant for the pooled database nor for the individual data. Nevertheless, a correlation between finite structures and non-modal interpretations, i.e., past and present interpretations, reached significance. These facts establish rather a 'Anti-Modal Reference Effect' of finite utterances instead of a 'Modal Reference Effect' of infinitival structures.

The second aim of this paper was to introduce a new theoretical account of the acquisition of verbal inflectional patterns that can model the subtle empirical picture adequately. I claim that a cell fission model (CFM) as developed here captures the data best due to its flexible dynamics within and across developmental stages. The core fission of the CFM is based on theoretical considerations on the category of finiteness following the framework of Klein (this volume). In this multi-level conception of finiteness, the finiteness operator links the assertive part of a sentence to a topic time, i.e., the time for which an assertion holds. Thus, finite structures relate to what can be asserted. For children, assertable information amounts to information about the actual world and its 'here-and-now' reference. This explains why finite structures relate to the actual world whereas infinitival structures do not.

Within the CFM, the mapping from forms to interpretations is controlled by a principle which makes use of default hierarchies. This Principle of Default-Boundedness states that grammatical default forms relate to default interpretations, whereas non-default forms relate to non-default interpretations. This principle allows for an adequate modelling of the data when complemented with a second mechanism of temporal referencing for utterances with a joint focus of attention. Moreover, the generality of this principle allows for a broad coverage. Hence, first insights into the development of nominal case in Czech exhibit an interesting parallel between the nominal and the verbal domain in acquisition. As a result, the CFM represents a systematic developmental frame to capture the emergence of forms and their associated interpretations with crossdomain and crosslinguistic applicability.

Max-Planck-Institut für Psycholinguistik, Nijmegen

6. ACKNOWLEDGEMENTS

I want to thank the audiences of the conference 'Semantics meets acquisition' at the Max-Planck-Institut für Psycholinguistik, March 2000 as well as the members of the MPI group 'The acquisition of scope relations' for their valuable comments. I am particularly grateful to Maria Bittner for directing me to the nominal parallel. With respect to the body of empirical data on child language, I am indebted to Rosemarie Tracy and Filip Smolík for granting me access to the German and Czech data, respectively. This paper benefited very much from the criticisms of the editor and two anonymous reviewers. I also like to thank Barbara Schmiedtová who commented on an earlier version of this paper.

7. NOTES

[1] Context information is given in brackets; likewise the age of the child on the right side. The slashes at the end of a child utterance signal intonation contours, so '\' signals a falling contour;

capitalizing signals main stress. The abbreviations used are: INF for 'infinitival form', FIN for 'finite form', PRT for 'particle', PL for 'plural', NOM for 'nominative', ACC for 'accusative'.

[2] The data analyzed for this chapter are taken from transcripts of Max and Benny from the Tübingen corpus, collected by Rosemarie Tracy and her collaborators of a DFG-project at the University of Tübingen.

[3] As will become clear in the data section, the acquisition of verbal morphology and the acquisition of topological positioning proceeds not always hand in hand. Depending on the individual style of acquisition, the time lag between the two may exceed even a year. Generally, the positioning of infinitive marked verbs is easier to acquire than the positioning of the finite marked verb with its peculiar verb-second property.

[4] Since the verbless category does not exhibit any strong tendencies towards specific favored forms, it was excluded from the χ^2-analysis. Note though, that this does not imply that the earlier distinction between infinitival and truly non-finite, verb-free forms is obsolete.

[5] In contrast to the study cited before, her study focuses precisely on the relationship between verb placement and different interpretations of root infinitives.

[6] 'Two mechanisms of temporal reference' means 'two' that are directly related to our explanandum. Obviously, there are more mechanisms of temporal reference to be acquired. A very important mechanism involves temporal adverbials of various sorts and temporal NPs as e.g., *im Urlaub* ('on vacation'). The exclusive usage of these temporal devices (omitting verbal morphology completely) is less typical for child language but very common in second language acquisition at a specific stage, called the conceptual ordering stage (see Dimroth *et al.*, 2003; Gretsch, 2003).

8. REFERENCES

Becker, Misha, and Nina Hyams. "Modal Reference in Children's Root Infinitives." In Eve C. Clark (ed.) *Proceedings of the 30th Annual Child Language Research Forum*, 113–122. Stanford: CSLI, 2000.

Behrens, Heike. *Temporal Reference in German Child Language. Form and Function of Early Verb Use.* Ph.D. Diss., University of Amsterdam, 1993.

Boser, Katharina, Barbara Lust, Lynn Santelmann, and John Whitman. "The Syntax of CP and V2 in Early Child German: The Strong Continuity Hypothesis." In Kimberley Broderick (ed.) *Proceedings of NELS 22*, 51–66. Amherst: GSLA, 1992.

Clark, Eve C. "The Principle of Contrast: A Constraint on Language Acquisition." In Brian MacWhinney (ed.) *Mechanisms of Language Acquisition*, 1–33. Hillsdale, NJ: Lawrence Erlbaum Associates, 1987.

Dimroth, Christine, and Ingeborg Lasser. *Finite Options: How L1 and L2 Learners Cope With the Acquisition of Finiteness, Linguistics* 40 (2002).

Dimroth, Christine, and Marianne Starren. *Information Structure and the Dynamics of Language Acquisition.* Amsterdam: John Benjamins, 2003.

Dimroth, Christine, Petra Gretsch, Peter Jordens, Clive Perdue, and Marianne Starren. "Finiteness in Germanic Languages: A Stage Model for First and Second Language Development." In Christine Dimroth and Marianne Starren (eds.), 65–93.

Gretsch, Petra. "On the Similarities of L1 and L2 Acquisition: How German Children Anchor Utterances in Time." In Christine Dimroth and Marianne Starren (eds.), 95–117.

Gretsch, Petra. "What does Finiteness Mean to Children? A Cross-linguistic Perspective on Root Infinitives." *Linguistics* 42 (2004): 419–468.

Hoekstra, Teun, and Peter Jordens. "From Adjunct to Head." In Teun Hoekstra and Bonnie Schwartz (eds.) *Language Acquisition Studies in Generative Grammar: Papers in Honor of Kenneth Wexler from the GLOW Workshops*, 119–150. Amsterdam: John Benjamins, 1994.

Ingram, David, and William Thompson. "Early Syntactic Acquisition in German: Evidence for the Modal Hypothesis." *Language* 72 (1996): 97–120.

Jordens, Peter. "The Acquisition of Verb Placement in Dutch and German." *Linguistics* 28 (1990): 1407–1448.
Jordens, Peter. "Finiteness in Early Child Dutch." In Christine Dimroth and Ingeborg Lasser (eds.), 687–765.
Klein, Wolfgang. *Time in Language.* London, New York: Routledge, 1994.
Klein, Wolfgang. "Assertion and Finiteness." In Norbert Dittmar and Zvi Penner (eds.) *Issues in the Theory of Language Acquisition: Essays in Honor of Jürgen Weissenborn,* 225–245. Bern: Lang, 1998.
Lecarme, Jacqueline. "Nominal Tense and Tense Theory." In Francis Corblin, Carmen Dobrovie-Sorin, and Jean-Marie Marandin (eds.) *Empirical Issues in Formal Syntax and Semantics 2,* 333–354. The Hague: Holland Academic Graphics, 1999.
Lasser, Ingeborg. *Finiteness in Adult and Child German.* Ph.D. Diss., CUNY, New York, 1997.
Lasser, Ingeborg. "The Roots of Root Infinitives." In Christine Dimroth and Ingeborg Lasser (eds.), 767–796.
Schaner-Wolles, Chris. "Am Anfang ist das Verb, finit markiert ist es erst später: Zum erstsprachlichen Erwerb von Finitheit im Deutschen." Paper presented at the Annual DGfS Meeting, Marburg, 2000.
Whitman, John. "In Defense of the Strong Continuity Account of the Acquisition of Verb-Second." In Barbara Lust, Margarita Suñer, and John Whitman (eds.) *Syntactic Theory and First Language Acquisition: Cross-Linguistic Perspectives. Volume 1, Heads, Projections, and Learnability,* 273–287. Hillsdale, NJ: Lawrence Erlbaum, 1994.

ULRIKE NEDERSTIGT

ADDITIVE PARTICLES AND SCOPE MARKING IN CHILD GERMAN

Abstract. Focus particles are rather complex linguistic items; despite their complexity focus particles appear very early in child German. This chapter investigates the use of the additive focus particles *auch* 'also' and *noch* 'still, also' in the natural child production data of a monolingual German girl in order to determine how children mark the relation between the particle and its domain of application. The results show that the child use of the two particles is very adult-like and that the child clearly distinguishes between the two particles.

1. INTRODUCTION

In German, as in most languages, focus particles such as *auch* 'also', *noch* 'still, also', or *nur* 'only' are optional elements. Still, they show up very early in child language, a fact that may be due to their eminent communicative importance. Though structurally optional, focus particles strongly interact with other elements of the utterance in which they appear; this is clearly reflected by various positional and intonational constraints. Previous work on the acquisition of such particles (Crain, Philip, Drozd, Roeper & Matsuoka, 1992; Drozd & Van Loosbroek, 1998; Bergsma, 1999, this volume; Philip, 2000) is only concerned with the comprehension of these particles at a rather advanced age. However, among the early child utterances we find utterances like the following: [1]

(1) a. Grossvater   auch   (1;10,29)
       Granddad   also
       'Granddad, too.'

    b. noch   ein   Haus   (1;05,15)
       still   a   house
       'Another house.'

The studies on the comprehension of focus particles set in after children have been using them productively for more than a year. This is partly due to the experimental nature of these studies and the fact that it is difficult to get children under the age of three to participate in an experiment.

There are also a few studies (Penner, Tracy & Wymann, 1999; Penner, Tracy & Weissenborn, 2000; Hulk, 2002) on the production of focus particles in child language, however just as the studies on comprehension mentioned above they reduce the scope properties of focus particles to the particle's syntactic scope. They fail to consider the complex interaction of the syntactic, semantic, pragmatic and prosodic properties of these particles and the utterances in which they occur that are vital for the interpretation of particles like *auch* 'also' and *noch* 'still, also'. However, the child utterances in (1) are very similar to the adult *auch*- and *noch*-utterances below:

(2) a. ja,   die Seite   auch [2]
        yes   this page   also
        'Yes, this page, too.'

    b. und   dann noch   so rote Scheiben
        and   then still   such red disc
        'And then another red disc.'

The question is whether children make use of the same linguistic means to mark the scope of particles such as *auch* 'also'. Or put differently, are children aware of the complex interaction between the syntax, semantics, pragmatics and prosody in focus particle utterances and if not, how do they mark the scope relation between the particle and that part of the utterance that is affected by the particle.

A related question is whether children apply the analysis of one particle to other particles of whether they analyze different particles individually. Penner *et al.* (2000) who looked at the acquisition of *auch* 'also' observed that the first focus particle to appear in child German is *auch* 'also'; other particles appear somewhat later. Penner *et al.*, suggested that other (additive) particles might be acquired by means of analogy. This would mean that *auch* 'also' and *noch* 'still, also', at least in the beginning, are used in the same way.

This chapter presents the results of a study on the acquisition of *auch* 'also' and *noch* 'still, also' in the spontaneous production data of a monolingual German girl between the age of 1;10 and 3;06. The chapter is organized as follows: In the next section, the properties of *auch* 'also' and *noch* 'still, also' in adult German are described and the terminology that is used throughout this chapter is explained. Based on the properties of *auch* 'also' and *noch* 'still, also' described in section 2, the child's learning tasked is described in section 3. In section 4, the corpus data and the method used in this study are described. After the presentation of the results in section 5, the results are discussed.

2. THE PROPERTIES OF *AUCH* AND *NOCH* IN GERMAN

In this section, the properties of *auch* and *noch* are discussed in terms of their syntax, semantics and phonology. The two particles are treated separately: Section 2.1 is concerned with the particle *auch*, section 2.2 with *noch*.

2.1. Auch

Focus particles are relational items whose meaningful interpretation is possible only after the successful identification of the domain of application of the particle, i.e., that part of the utterances that is actually affected by the particle.[3] In an utterance like (3), which is interpreted as 'Tom ate an apple and Tom did not eat anything but an apple', [*Apfel*] is the domain of application of *nur* 'only': [4]

(3) Tom hat nur [einen APFEL] gegessen.
     'Tom ate only an apple.'

In utterances like (3), the domain of application is contrasted with alternatives to [*Apfel*], i.e., other things Tom might have eaten. Those alternatives together with the domain form the so-called set of alternatives. The particle sets up a relation between the domain and other members from the set of alternatives. The nature of this relation is dependent on the meaning of the particle itself. In (3), this relation is one of exclusion, whereas it is one of inclusion in (4):

(4) Tom hat auch [einen APFEL] gegessen.
     'Tom also ate an apple.'

Apart from general context, two factors are important for the identification of the domain of application of a focus particle: the position of the particle within the utterance and the prosodic structure of the utterance. The utterances in (4) and (5) differ not only with respect to the domain of the particle, but also with respect to the particle's position within the utterance:

(5) Auch [TOM] hat einen Apfel gegessen.
     'Tom, too, ate an apple.'

The position of *auch* 'also' seems to be responsible for the different domains of application since *auch* 'also' directly precedes its respective domain. In German, a particle like *auch* 'also' can be inserted in almost any position within an utterance as the one in (6). This is illustrated in (7):

(6) Tom   hat   gestern   einen Apfel   gegessen.
     Tom   has   yesterday   an apple   eaten
     'Yesterday, Tom ate an apple.'

(7) a. Auch [TOM] hat gestern einen Apfel gegessen.
        'Also Tom ate an apple yesterday.'
    b. Tom hat auch [GESTERN] einen Apfel gegessen.
        'Yesterday Tom ate an apple, too.'
    c. Tom hat gestern auch [einen APFEL] gegessen.
        'Yesterday Tom also ate an apple.'
    d. Tom hat gestern einen Apfel auch [GEGESSEN].
        'Tom also ate an apple yesterday.'
    e. *Tom hat auch gestern [einen APFEL] gegessen.
        'Yesterday Tom also ate an apple.'

In (7a) through (7d), the domain of application is identified via the location of the particle that precedes its domain and is adjacent to it. The example in (7e) shows that in German, it is not possible to have a distant domain if the particle precedes its domain of application. Furthermore, the particle has to be adjacent to its domain.

There is a general consensus in the literature concerning the close interaction between focus particles and the focus of an utterance (that is why they are called focus particles). It is typically assumed that the domain of application and the focus of an utterance concur. In (7a), *Tom* is not only the domain of *auch* 'also', but also the focus of the utterance, and the same is true for the other examples in (7). The notion of prosody is regularly associated with the notion of focus because in languages like German, Dutch or English the focus part of an utterance is marked by a pitch accent (see Uhmann, 1991; Féry, 1992). This is why the domain of application and, hence, the focus in the above examples in (7) are accented.

Focus is seen as a prerequisite for the interpretation of focus particles. Thus, von Stechow (1991, 807) states that "[e]very focussing particle must have at least one focus associated in its scope." The precise nature of the interaction between particle and focus is a matter of dispute. Rooth (1992; 1996) argues that the set of alternatives necessary for the interpretation of focus particles is introduced by the focus of the utterance. The focus is seen to introduce a free variable that has to find an antecedent or has to be otherwise given a pragmatically construed value for which the proposition — in case of additive particles — also holds.

However, Dimroth (1998) and Krifka (1999) argued that in an utterance like (8) the domain of application does not concur with the focus of the utterance:

(8) [TOM] hat AUCH einen Apfel gegessen.
'Tom ate an apple, too.'

In this example, the particle follows its domain of application and carries a pitch accent. Given the additional pitch accent on the domain of application, examples like this have traditionally been analyzed in parallel to utterances in which the domain follows the particle. The domain is considered to be a topicalized focus (see Altmann, 1976a, 1976b; Jacobs, 1983; König, 1991). Positional variation is explained in terms of movement. Reis & Rosengren (1998, 248) showed that this movement account is untenable. Dimroth (1998) and Krifka (1999) suggested that the pitch accent on the domain is that of a contrastive topic, i.e., it is one element from a list of elements under discussion:

(9) A: Was haben Tom und Lisa gegessen?
'What did Tom and Lisa eat?'
B: TOM hat einen APFEL gegessen.
'Tom ate an apple.'

In (9), both *Tom* and *Lisa* are under discussion, but speaker B only gives a partial answer to speaker A's question. This partiality is indicated by a pitch accent on *Tom*. The interpretation of *einen Apfel* 'an apple' has focus status and consequently receives a pitch accent. In utterances with stressed *auch* 'also', the domain of application is a contrastive topic; it is not the only element under discussion. This means that not only foci, but also contrastive topics can be responsible for the establishment of the set of alternatives necessary for the interpretation of focus particles, they can also function as domain of application of focus particles.

Dimroth (1998) and Krifka (1999) further argued that the particle in utterances like (9) functions as the focus of the utterance. This is based on the assumption that an utterance with stressed *auch* 'also' is an answer to a polarity question. A polarity question can trigger two possible answers, affirmation or negation. Consequently, the set of alternatives is of the following kind: {yes; no}. In case of a negative answer, the negation particle receives a pitch accent and has focus status as in the following example:

(10) [Tom] hat NICHT einen Apfel gegessen.
'Tom did not eat an apple.'

German, unlike Dutch[5], lacks an overt affirmative marker which could be accented. However, since the set of alternatives in (8) and (9) consists of the alternatives *yes* and *no* or, put differently, of the alternatives affirmation and negation, and the affirmation could be expressed by *auch* 'also', it seems plausible to analyze *auch* 'also' in parallel to *nicht* 'not' in (9) and assume that the particle is the focus of the utterance.

This means that there are two different usage patterns for *auch* 'also' that differ at least in the position the particle takes with respect to its domain of application and the pitch accent location. In the focus analysis, the particle precedes its domain; the domain corresponds to the focus of the utterance and carries a pitch accent. In the topic analysis, the particle follows its domain, its carries a pitch accent and has focus status. The difference in intonation between those two patterns allows us to clearly distinguish between the utterances in (4) and (8) that would be ambiguous without information about their prosody. In Nederstigt (2001), I showed that both patterns are common in adult spoken German, but that *auch* 'also' following its domain of application is used more frequently than *auch* 'also' preceding its domain of application, 72% of the *auch*-utterances I analyzed had a particle following its domain, whereas the particle preceded its domain in only 16% of the utterances. There were also *auch*-utterances in which the domain of application of *auch* 'also' was not part of the particle-utterance. However, looking at the examples in Nederstigt (2001) the position within the utterances of *auch* 'also' in post-position seems to be restricted to the position within the verbal bracket, i.e., the middle field as in the following example:

(11) Oh, das freut [mich] AUCH sehr, dass wir da zusammen hinfahren können.
'Oh, I'm looking forward to being able to go there together with you, too.'

2.2. *Noch*

In the literature on German focus particles distinctions are made between *additive* such as *auch* 'also' and *restrictive* focus particles such as *nur* 'only' on the one hand, and 'scalar' particles like *sogar* 'even' and 'non-scalar' particles like *ebenso* 'also', on the other. The general assumption is that the particles within one of the above categories function in more or less the same way. However, the analysis of the properties of the respective category of particles is typically restricted to the analysis of only one of the particles, in the case of additive particles this particle is *auch* 'also'. Given this assumption little attention has been paid to other additive particles, we find little on *noch* 'still, also' as focus particle.[6] In Nederstigt (2001), I found a number of differences between *auch* 'also' and the focus particle use of *noch* 'still, also'. Whereas I found the clear relation between the position of the particle, that of the domain of application and the position of the pitch accent described above for *auch*-utterances, the same relation was not found for *noch* 'still, also'. In *noch*-utterances the relation between the particle and its domain seems to be of a different nature. Irrespective of whether the particle precedes, follows, or is located within its domain of application and whether it is adjacent or non-adjacent, it is the domain that carries a pitch accent. I also found utterance like the one in (12) in which *noch* 'still, also' in preposition was accented (10% of the *noch*-utterances):

(12) Tom hat NOCH [einen Apfel] gegessen.
 'Tom ate another apple.'

In these utterances, the particle always preceded its domain and the set of alternatives in these utterances is restricted to tokens of the same type, i.e., the set of alternatives in an utterance like the one above only consists of tokens of the apple type.

Dimroth (2002) argued that stressed *noch* 'still, also' preceding its domain of application has to be analyzed in parallel to utterances with stressed *auch* 'also', claiming that *noch* 'still, also' here also adds topic constituents. Under the assumption that (12) is only feasible if there are two distinctive apple eating events that take place at different times, she argued that *noch* 'still, also' does not add one apple to an already existing one, but a topic time to an already existing topic time. What, according to Dimroth (2002), is under discussion in an utterance like (12) are two events of eating an apple; these events take place at different times which is reflected by the different topic times of the utterance. *Noch* 'still, also' then adds one topic time to another. The contrast between the two apples is not taken into account. This is seen in parallel to an utterance like the one in (8). According to Dimroth (2002) what is under discussion in this utterance are two events of apple eating; these events are characterized by the fact that there are two people eating an apple, Tom and someone else. There is also a contrast between the apples that where eaten, but this contrast is ignored, just as the contrast between the two apples in the *noch*-utterance.

Dimroth's line of reasoning is problematic because the addition expressed by *noch* does not necessarily involve two different topic times. Compare the following example:

(13) Jan hat eine VW, einen Mercedes, einen Audi und ich glaube
 NOCH [einen VW].
 'Jan owns a VW, a Mercedes, an Audi, and I think another VW.'

In this example, the speaker lists the different cars owned by Jan. There is only one topic time because Jan owns several cars at the same time. The use of stressed *noch* is feasible in this utterance because one VW was mentioned before the one referred to in the *noch* 'still, also' part of the utterance, but this is not related to the topic time.

Another problem is that if stressed *noch* 'still, also' were the focus of an utterance, we would expect that, in an appropriate context, the particle can stand on its own, for example in an answer to a question about the topic that functions as its domain of application. But *noch* 'still, also' on its own cannot answer a question about the topic time that functions as its domain of application, expressing the addition of this topic time. Even *noch* together with the topic time that functions as its domain, *noch* 'still, also' cannot answer a question about this topic time. *Noch gestern* 'Still yesterday' could be an answer to the question *When did Peter play football?* but it could not be interpreted as 'also yesterday'; it would have to be interpreted as 'only yesterday'. For stressed *auch* 'also', this is possible, as shown in the following dialogue:

(14) A: Frankreich hat gestern beim Fußball verloren.
           'France lost yesterday's soccer match.'
      B: Und Italien?
           'And Italy?'
      A: Auch.
           'Also.'

Here, *auch* 'also' is an answer to a question about its domain of application, *auch* 'also' expresses that Italy too, lost a soccer match.

We have already seen that the set of alternatives of the domain of stressed *noch* 'still, also' differs from the sets of alternatives of the domain of application of unstressed *noch* 'still, also'; in the former case, the domain consists of tokens of the same type. I propose that, rather than adding topic times, stressed *noch* 'still, also' marks the fact that its domain of application is a token of the same type as a previously mentioned entity. The domain of stressed *noch* 'still, also' as well as that of unstressed *noch* 'still, also' is the focus of the utterance because in both cases the domain is contrasted with other, previously mentioned entities. Since the entity added by stressed *noch* 'still, also' is a different token of the same type as mentioned before, a pitch accent cannot serve to distinguish between the two tokens because it does not mark them as different. Consequently, the contrast between the two is not marked on the focus or domain itself, but by a pitch accent on the particle. As soon as the contrast is marked otherwise, it is no longer possible to stress the particle. Consider the following example:

(15) Tom will noch [MEHR Äpfel].
'Tom wants even more apples.'

In this example, the contrast between *Äpfel* 'apples' and a set of apples mentioned previously in the context is marked by *mehr* 'more'. Here, the contrast is not placed on *noch* 'still, also', but on *mehr* 'more' which serves to distinguish between the two tokens of the same type.

This means that *noch* 'still, also' does not interact with the topic of an utterance. Its domain of application is restricted to focus constituents, but this focus can be of a particular sort, namely a token of the same type as a previously mentioned entity. This is marked by a pitch accent on the particle itself.

3. THE CHILD'S LEARNING TASK

In section 2, we saw that the properties of *auch* and *noch* are rather complex, which results in an equally complex learning task for the child. The child has to learn that there are basically two usage patterns for *auch*, one in which the particle precedes its domain of application and one in which the particle follows its domain of application. In order to master the first pattern the child will have to learn that the particle can appear at almost any position within the utterance depending on the position of its domain of application because the particle has to be adjacent to its domain. The child will not only have to learn that the domain of application of *auch* concurs with the focus of the utterance and that this focus is marked by means of a pitch accent, but also that a focus establishes a set of alternatives necessary for the interpretation of *auch*. The second pattern is equally complex. The child has to learn that the particle follows its domain of application, that the particle is accented and the focus of the utterances. Furthermore, she has to learn that the felicitous use of this pattern requires a set of alternatives to be under discussion and that these alternatives have to be established prior to the *auch*-utterance. She will also have to learn that the position of *auch* within the utterances is far more restricted than that of *auch* preceding its domain of application; *auch* in post-position seems to be restricted to the German middle-field position. The fact that the domain of application in these patterns can, but does not have to be accented makes this pattern even more complicated to learn.

The learning task for *noch* is somewhat different. The child has to learn that the particle can appear in various positions within an utterance, that it can follow or precede its domain of application, and that it can also be located within its domain. She has to learn that the domain of application concurs with the focus of the utterance and that, just as for *auch*, the focus is responsible for the establishment of the set of alternatives needed for the interpretation of *noch*. In addition, the child has to learn that a pitch accent on the particle is used to indicate that the set of alternatives consists of tokens of the same type. The learning task is complicated by the fact that *noch* is not only used as a focus particle, but also as temporal adverb and as comparative particle.

In the remainder of this chapter, we look at the acquisition of *auch* and of the focus particle use of *noch*, and their scope properties in terms of the position of the particles with respect to their domain of application, and the relation between this position and the location of the pitch accent.

4. DATA AND METHOD

The present study is based on the Caroline Corpus, a longitudinal study of a monolingual girl between 0;10 and 2;03.[7] It includes transcriptions and audio material of mother and child interactions, daily routines such as eating, getting dressed, changing nappies, etc. and play, games, looking at picture books, etc. On average, two to three recordings were made per week. For the present study the recordings were digitized, and the *auch*- and *noch*-utterances found in the transcripts were sound-linked to the digitized sound files in order to facilitate the intonation analysis of the child utterances. The corpus contains more than 23.000 child utterances, 868 of which are *auch*- and 1.055 *noch*-utterances.

The starting point for the analysis of *auch* and *noch* in child language was the identification of the domain of application of the two particles on the basis of the context of the utterance. Their additive meaning played a central role here. The idea is that the domain of the two particles is added to an already existing entity:

(16) Tom hat auch einen Apfel gegessen.
 'Tom has eaten an apple, too.'

In (16) there are at least three possible domains, namely [*Tom*], [*einen Apfel*] and [*einen Apfel gegessen*]. If we adopt the idea of an open formula we get three different open formulae depending on the domain of *auch* in (16):

(17) a.　　　*x* hat auch einen Apfel gegessen.
　　 b.　　　Tom hat auch *x* gegessen.
　　 c.　　　Tom hat auch *x*.

Ideally, we should be able to find one utterance among the utterances preceding (16) that corresponds to one of the open formulae in (17), where *x* is filled by an element other than the domain. Of course, this corresponding utterance is without the additive particle. Hence, we should be able to find one of the following types of utterances in the context preceding (16):[8]

(18) a.　　　*Lisa* hat einen Apfel gegessen.
　　　　　　 'Lisa ate an apple.'

　　 b.　　　Tom hat *eine Birne* gegessen.
　　　　　　 'Tom ate a pear.'

　　 c.　　　Tom hat *ein Glass Milch getrunken*.
　　　　　　 'Tom drank a glass of milk.'

Depending on the formula that is matched by an utterance from the context, the domain of application of *auch* in (16) can be determined.

Once the domain was identified, the data were coded for the position of the particle with respect to its domain, i.e., whether it precedes or follows its domain, and for the placement of pitch accent(s). The position of the pitch accent was determined based on auditory perception and by a speech analysis program that performed pitch analysis (F0-analysis). Figure 1 gives an example of the output of the speech analysis program for the utterance *will noch zwei Bücher* '(I) want two more books'. The *x*-axis of the graph represents the time-axis; the *y*-axis of the upper part represents the intensity in decibels and that of the lower part the pitch in hertz:

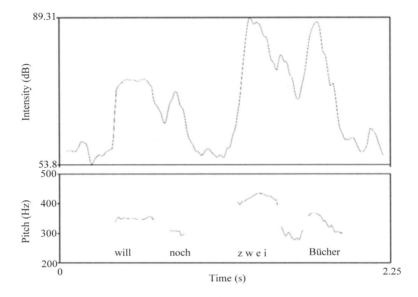

Figure 1. Speech analysis program output

There is a clear rise on *zwei* 'two' and the intensity increases at this point. The part of the wave form between *zwei* 'two' and *Bücher* 'books' is blurred by background noise, a problem that could not be avoided using natural production data, and this often led to the exclusion of individual utterances from the analysis.

5. RESULTS

This section reports the results of the analysis of child language. Section 5.1 looks at the position of *auch* and *noch* with respect to its domain, and section 5.2 looks at relation between this position and the location of the pitch accent within the utterances.

Caroline's first *auch*-utterances appear at the age of 1;06,02 and their frequency increases after 1;09. *Noch* first appears at the age of 1;09,06 and becomes more frequent after 1;10. Figure 2 illustrates the quantitative development of Caroline's *auch*- and *noch*-utterances. Initially *auch* is more frequent than *noch*, but the situation changes between 2;03 and 2;05 when *noch* becomes more frequent:[9]

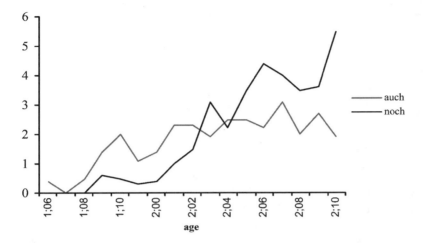

Figure 2. Quantitative development of 'auch' and 'noch' in the Caroline Corpus

A number of *auch*- and *noch*-utterances in the corpus had to be excluded from the analysis because they were partly unintelligible, they overlapped with other speakers or noise or the child was playing with her voice. A total of 489 *auch*-utterances and 566 *noch*-utterances, of which 331 were additive in meaning, remained for the analysis.

5.1. The Position of the Particle with respect to its Domain of Application

Table 1 shows the position *auch* and *noch* take with respect to their domain, i.e., their sequential order. It reveals a number of differences between the two particles that are discussed in more detail below:

Table 1. Position of the particle with respect to its domain of application

	preceding	following	in-between	domain outside
auch N= 489	10%	**62%**	-	**28%**
noch N= 331	**70%**	21%	6%	3%

Auch predominantly follows its domain of application (in 62% of all *auch*-utterances), whereas *auch* in pre-position is relatively infrequent, only 10%

of the *auch*-utterances are of this type. Conspicuous is the rather large percentage of utterances in which the domain of application is not part of the particle utterance. Typical examples are of the following kind:

(19) hast   ein #   aeh   will
     have   one   aeh   want
     auch   eine Maus   machen.   (2;09,10)
     also   a mouse   make
     'Have you one # aeh (I) want to make a mouse too.'

(20) auch   baun   (1;09,07)
     also   build
     '(I want to) build too.'

In examples like (19) and (20), the domain of application can be determined by the available context: In (19), Caroline and her mother are drawing and talking about what to draw next. Her mother tells Caroline that she is going to draw a mouse. Caroline also wants to draw a mouse. In (20), Caroline is asked whether she wants to build something with building blocks or look at a book. Caroline first tells her mother that she (i.e., the mother) has to build something and then says that she herself wants to build something, too.

Table 1 also reveals that for *noch*-utterances, the number of utterances in which the domain is not part of the particle-utterance is very low (3%). This type of utterance seems to be restricted to *wh*-questions that lack the *wh*-question word. Compare the following examples:

(21) Gouda   und   noch?   (2;07,19)
     Gouda   and   still
     'Gouda-cheese and (what) else?'

(22) sagt   der   a # noch?   (2;05,08)
     says   he   a still?
     '(What) else does he say?'

Other than *auch*, the majority of the *noch*-utterances with additive meaning (70%) have a particle that precedes its domain of application, but *noch* follows its domain in only 20% of the utterances. In 6% of the utterances the particle is located within the domain; this pattern is particular to *noch* because it does not occur for *auch*-utterances.

Though Caroline uses both particles in a pre- as well as in a post-position, if we look at the distribution of the two usage patterns, her use of *auch* seems to differ from that of *noch*.

5.2. Position of the Particle and the Location of the Pitch Accent

5.2.1. 'Auch'

In section 5.1, we have already seen that there are far more utterances in which *auch* follows its domain than utterances in which it precedes its domain. The following table presents the results of the analysis of the pitch accent location in these utterances:[10]

Table 2. Relation between the position of 'auch' and the location of the pitch accent

auch	preceding N=49	following N=304	domain outside N=136
particle	4%	72%	76%
particle&domain	20%	10%	-
particle&other	4%	14%	20%
domain	70%	1%	-
other	2%	3%	4%
total	100%	100%	100%

Most utterances in which *auch* precedes its domain (70%) carry a pitch accent within the domain of application, as in the following examples:

(23) auch   [AUTOS]   (2;02,15)
     also   cars
     'Cars too.'

(24) da   muss   auch [LOEWE]#   sein   und und
     there   must   also lion   be   and and
     Max   ist   ein # ein ein   Tiger   (2;09,17)
     Max   is   a a a   tiger
     'There must also be (a) lion and Max is a tiger.'

20% of the utterances in which *auch* precedes its domain have a pitch accent within the domain as well as on the particle as in these examples:

(25) ich   AUCH   [SOWAS]   (2;02,03)
     I   also   such a thing
     'I (want) something like this, too.'

(26) AUCH   [die SCHILDkröte]
     also   the turtle

Beine   im Wasser?   (2;04,01)
legs   in-the water
'The turtle also (has its) legs in the water?'

Thus, a total of 80% of the utterances in which *auch* precedes its domain, carry a pitch accent within the domain of application. In Caroline's *auch*-utterances in which the particle precedes its domain of application, we find the clear correlation between the position of the particle and the location of the pitch accent described in section 2.1. Both accent patterns, i.e., a pitch accent on the domain and an accent on the domain as well as on the particle can be found among her early *auch*-utterances around the age of 1;10 and from that age onwards throughout the data.

Though less obvious, the results in Table 2 also reveal a clear relation between the position of the particle and the pitch accent placement for utterance in which the particle follows its domain of application. Most of these utterances (72%) carry a pitch accent on the particle as in (27) and (28):

(27) Großvater   AUCH   (1;10,29)
     grandfather   also
     'Grandfather too.'

(28) [ich]   AUCH   bunten   Sternenhimmel   (2;02,10)
     I   also   coloured starry-sky
     'I (draw) a starry sky too.'

Many verbless utterances were found among the early *auch*-utterances, and they can be found throughout the data. Caroline's initial assumption seems to be that the particle has to be adjacent to its domain of application. Even when she starts using finite verbs, she places the particle directly adjacent to its domain as in (29) and (30), a pattern that is not possible in the adult target main clause utterances:[11]

(29) [Elefant]AUCH   [ich]   AUCH   tanz   (2;01,21)
     elephant also   I   also   dance
     'Elephant and me dance, too.'

(30) [Max]   AUCH   kann   schon
     Max   also   can   already
     neiden   meine Schere   (2;01,28)
     cut   my scissors
     'Max can already cut with my scissors, too.'

This pattern co-exists for some time with the correct adult target pattern in which the particle follows the finite verb and that appears around 2;03. By the age of 2;07, the above pattern is completely replaced with the target illustrated in (31) and (32):

(31) nein # [die] waren AUCH böse (3;04,00)
no they were also naughty
'No, they were naughty, too.'

(32) [ich] will AUCH (2;05,30)
I want also
'I want (this), too.'

The remaining utterances with *auch* in post-position carry either a pitch accent on the particle as well as on some unrelated element that is not part of the domain of application (see the examples in (33) and (34)), or they carry a pitch accent on the particle as well as within the domain of application (see the examples (35) and (36) below):

(33) ne [die] aehm mag AUCH NICHT (2;07,27)
well it aeh like also not
'Well, (he) doesn't like this either.'

(34) [ich] AUCH alle DELben (1;10,29)
I also all yellow
'I (want) all the yellow ones too'

(35) [des von LENA] AUCH annemalt (2;04,17)
that from Lena also coloured
'(I) also coloured the one from Lena.'

(36) nein [KRUEMEL] heisst das AUCH (2;07,22)
no Kruemel is called that also
'No, (he) is also called Kruemel.'

Both types of utterances are among the early *auch*-utterances, i.e., utterances that are used between 1;09 and 1;11 and keep being used.

In sum, we find that 97% of the utterances in which *auch* follows its domain of application carry a pitch accent on the particle.

Table 2 also reveals that there are utterances with *auch* in post-position in which some unrelated element carries a pitch accent; this type of utterance stays very infrequent and accounts to not more than 3% of the utterances. An example is (37):

(37) wenn [ich] auch neun BIN? (2;08,17)
if/when I also nine am?
'If I am nine too?'

In Table 2, we find a rather high number of *auch*-utterances in which the domain of application is not part of the *auch*-utterance itself. On the assumption that focus particles are relational items, one would expect that the domain of application has to be part of the utterance and cannot be left out. In principle, these utterances behave like those in which *auch* follows its domain of application. The particle carries the pitch accent. In 76% of the utterances it is only the particle that carries the pitch accent, as in the examples in (38) and (39):

(38) AUCH Öl (2;02,09)
also oil
'(I want) oil too.'

(39) waschen AUCH waschen AUCH (1;09,03)
wash also wash also
'(We need to) wash (this) too.'

The remaining 21% of the *auch*-utterances of this type carry a pitch accent on the particle as well as some other unrelated element, as in (39) and (40):

(40) AUCH NICH (2;10,22)
also not
'(That one) neither.'

(41) ehja # AUCH BAUN AUCH BAUN (1;09,07)
aeh also build also build
'(I want to) build too.'

Summing up, we can say that Caroline's *auch*-utterances show up in two basic patterns: one in which the particle precedes its accented domain, and one in which the accented particle follows its domain of application. Utterances in which the domain of application of *auch* is not part of the actual utterance are treated similarly to utterances in which *auch* follows its domain.

5.2.2. 'Noch'

The distribution of pitch accents in *noch*-utterances differs considerably from that in *auch*-utterances. Table 3 shows that the majority of *noch*-utterances has a pitch accent within the domain of application:

Table 3. *Relation between the position of 'noch' and the location of the pitch accent*

	preceding N=232	following N=68	in-between N=21	domain outside N=10
particle	33%	19%	5%	80%
particle&domain	1%	2%	-	-
domain	63%	72%	90%	-
domain&other	-	-	5%	20%
other	3%	7%	-	-
total	100%	100%	100%	100%

The results displayed in table 3 are now discussed in detail. If *noch* precedes its domain of application, most utterances (63%) carry a pitch accent within the domain. Note that the pitch accent within the domain can be on the NP, as in (42), as well as on the determiner, as in (43), depending on the relevant contrast. These utterances constitute the early *noch*-utterances, they appear first at 1;10,26:

(42) noch [ein BUCH] dieses (2;03,00)
     still a book this
     'Another book this one.'

(43) will noch [ZWEI Bücher] (2;03,22)
     want still two books
     '(I) want two more books.'

About a third of the utterances (33%) in which *noch* precedes its domain carry a pitch accent on the particle itself. In all those utterances, *noch* has an 'another' reading rather than an 'also' reading which means that the set of alternatives is restricted to tokens of he same type (see section 2.2). Though the properties of these utterances are quite complex, they are as early as 2;01,15:

(44) NOCH [eins] (2;01,22)
     still one
     'Another one.'

(45) NOCH   [ein Haus]   mal   ich   (2;03,02)
    still   a house   draw   I
    'I will draw another house.'

The remaining 3% of the utterances in which the particle precedes its domain of application carry a pitch accent on some unrelated element as in the example below. These utterances do not appear before 2;05,01:

(46) noch   [ein]   AUFdrehen   (2;05,26)
    still   one   unscrew
    'Open another one.'

The function of the pitch accent in utterances like the one in (46) is yet unclear to me and will have to be investigated further.

With 21% the overall frequency of utterances in which *noch* follows its domain of application is, compared to *auch*, rather low. Most of these utterances (72%) carry a pitch accent within the domain, as in (47) and (48). They appear first at 1;11,08, but do not become frequent before 2;02,04:

(47) nee   nur   [EIN Lied]   kann ich noch   (2;10,13)
    no   only   one song   can I still
    'No, I can also sing only one song.'

(48) [EIN Buch]   noch #   [EIN # Buch]   noch   (2;02,04)
    one book   still   one book   still
    'One more book, one more book.'

Though initially *noch* is always adjacent to its domain, there are two utterances in which the particle follows its domain but precedes the finite verb. These two utterances do not seem to form a precursor of the sequence 'domain – finite verb – particle' as in the case of *auch*, because this type of *noch*-utterance does not appear before 2;07,01.

Table 3 shows that 19% of the utterances in which *noch* follows its domain of application, carry a pitch accent on the particle as in (49) and (50):

(49) [was]   NOCH?   (2;03,12)
    what   still?
    'What else?'

(50) nee   und [wer] NOCH   krabbelt immer Hand?   (2;07,01)
     no   and who still   crawls always hand
     'No, and who else crawls always (on a) hand?'

Utterances like this are usually questions with final *noch*. Here, the pitch accent does not lead to an 'another' interpretation of *noch*. This type of utterance does not appear before 2;05,01.

Utterances in which the particle is located within its domain of application are very rare among Caroline's *noch*-utterances (a total of 21 utterances) and they do not appear before the age of 2;05,01. The late occurrence may be due to the fact that this pattern requires a relatively complex utterance structure which only appears once the mean length of utterance (MLU) increases. In 91% of the utterances in which the particle is located within the domain, the pitch accent is also located within the domain of application, as in (51) and (52):

(51) nee   [ein bisschen]   noch   [zu PAPI]   (2;09,07)
     no   a little   still   to Daddy
     'No, (I) want to be a little with Daddy.'

(52) nee [du doch]   noch   [des KISSEN holen der Ayche]   (2;08,15)
     no you MP   still   the cushion get the Ayche
     'No, you also have to get the cushion for Ayche.'

Table 3 also shows that utterances in which the domain of application is not part of the utterances are also rare (10 utterances); they do not appear before 2;05,20 and disappear after 2;08,14. The pitch accent is almost exclusively located on the particle that is usually in final position. Typically, these utterances are *wh*-questions without a question word, as in the following examples:

(53) Gouda   und   NOCH?   (2;07,19)
     Gouda   and   still
     'Gouda and (what) else?'

(54) sagt   der   a #   NOCH?   (2;05,08)
     says   he   a   still
     '(What) else does he say?'

In sum, the majority of Caroline's *noch*-utterances carry a pitch accent within the domain of application irrespective of the position of the particle with respect to its domain of application. In utterances in which the accented particle precedes its domain the set of alternatives is restricted to tokens of the same type just as in the adult target.

6. CONCLUSION AND DISCUSSION

The study presented in this chapter tried to determine the way in which the scope relation between the additive focus particles *auch* and *noch* and their respective domains of application are marked in early child German. The results show that scope marking in child language is much like that of the adult target, particularly when we look at the supra-segmental and positional information used to identify the particle's domain of application.

In the child's *auch*-utterances, the particle can precede or follow its domain of application. In the former case, the domain of application typically carries a pitch accent whereas in the latter, it is the particle that carries the pitch accent. With the exception of utterances in which the particle in post-position directly precedes the finite verb, the *auch*-utterances are much like those found in adult spoken German (Nederstigt, 2001). Even the distribution of *auch* in post- and pre-position is similar to the distribution in adult spoken German. In both cases, *auch* in post-position is more frequent than *auch* in pre-position. However, in child language, utterances in which the domain of application is not part of the particle utterance are more frequent than in adult language (28% of the *auch*-utterances in child language compared to 12% in adult language (Nederstigt, 2001, 423). In these utterances, the domain of application is established in the context, it either exists in the non-verbal context or is established in the verbal context preceding the *auch*-utterance. This fact could probably explain the higher frequency of these utterances in child language. The child is able to express complex relations, for example between objects, with relatively few words because she can utilize contextual information to do so. With a two-word utterance like the one in (36), AUCH *Öl* '(I want some) oil, too', and the relevant context (e.g., a dinner table situation where someone pours salad-oil over her salad, so the oil is visible in the non-verbal context) Caroline can express that she wants to have some oil over her salad, too.

In Caroline's *noch*-utterances, it is the domain of application that carries a pitch accent in most of the utterances, irrespective of whether the particle precedes, follows or is located within its domain. Again, in terms of the position of the particle and the location of the pitch accent, these utterances are much like those found in adult German. Caroline also used utterances in which the accented particle precedes its domain of application. In all of these utterances the set of alternatives is restricted to tokens of the same type. This means that the child clearly distinguishes between utterances with stressed and unstressed *noch*. In terms of the position of the particle with respect to its domain of application and the location of the pitch accent, Caroline's *auch*- and *noch*-utterances are much like those of adults.

The literature on focus particles suggests that the domain of application of these particles concurs with the focus of the utterances in which these particles occur. Dimroth (1998) and Krifka (1999) challenged this view and argued that the domain of particle like *auch* could also be a topic. Though the present study did not investigate whether the domain of application of the two particles had focus or topic status, it seems to support the assumptions made by Dimroth (1998) and Krifka (1999). Studies that deal with focus typically work with constructed examples with a predetermined topic-focus structure or use the intonation of semi-natural data such as read out texts to determine the focus of an utterance. The latter approach is problematic because contrastive topics can also by be marked by a means of a pitch accent, the former does not work for natural speech data. In lack of a suitable analytical framework the present study did not attempt to determine whether the domains of application of the two particles are the topics or foci of the respective utterances. However, the general assumption is that utterances consist of a topic and a focus part, but whereas the topic part of an utterance can be left out, the focus part cannot be left out. Among Caroline's *auch*-utterances were utterances in which the domain of application was not part of the particle utterance. If the domains of the particles concurred with the focus of these utterances, it could not be left out because as focus it had to be part of the utterance. Given that *auch*-utterances in which the domain of application is not part of the particle utterance not only appear in child language, but also in adult spoken German, these utterance are clear empirical evidence for the fact the topics can also function as domain of application of *auch*.

The results show that the child clearly distinguished between the different usages patterns for *auch* and *noch*, and she also clearly distinguished between the two particles, i.e., she employs different usage patterns for both particles. This clear differentiation suggests that *noch*, which appears somewhat later than *auch*, is not acquired by means of analogy as suggested by Penner *et al.* (1999) because the acquisition by means of analogy would result in the same usage patterns for both particles, but this is not what was found in this study. Further research will have to be carried out in order to determine how children learn to use these particles.

The results presented in this chapter seem to contradict the findings of a comprehension study by Bergsma (this volume). Bergsma looked at the comprehension of the Dutch focus particle *ook* 'also'. The properties of this Dutch particle are similar to the properties of German *auch*. The particle can precede as well as follow its domain, in the former case the particle's domain of application is accented; in the latter the particle carries a pitch accent.

Bergsma used a picture verification task to see how children interpret utterances of the following type (Bergsma, this volume; the small caps print is mine):

(55) a. Ook [de JONGEN]_F aait de hond.
'The boy too pets the dog.'
b. De jongen aait ook [de HOND]_F.
'The boy also pets the dog.'
c. [De jongen]_F aait OOK de hond.
'The boy too pets the dog.'

Children were presented with one of these utterances and had to select one of three pictures that matches the respective utterance. Even by the age of 7;11, the children did not seem to have an adult-like interpretation of utterances as in (55). Utterances of the type in (55c) seem to be particularly difficult for the children; they do not consistently interpret *de jongen* as the particles domain of application. In her 1999 study on the acquisition of *alleen,* Bergsma showed that contextual information improved children's interpretation of the particles and, consequently, Bergsma presented the children with contextual information before the experiment. She introduced a boy and a dog to the child and also presented her with alternatives to the boy and the dog, so that the alternatives needed for the interpretation of the particle were available to the child. However, the mere presentation of possible alternatives to *de jongen* 'the boy' does not seem sufficient here. Even for an adult the utterance in (55c) does not seem to be an adequate description of a picture in which a boy and a girl are petting a dog, unless it has been made clear in the context preceding the *ook*-utterances that there are alternatives to the boy who are actually petting a dog. Without this information the use of (55c) does seem to offer an adequate description of a picture in which a girl and a boy are petting a dog. So, the results presented by Bergsma could be an artifact to the experimental setup she used. However, further research will have to be done because (55a) is an adequate description of a picture in which a boy and a girl are petting a dog even without additional contextual information and most children get the correct interpretation for sentences like this. The differences could be related to the fact that in (55a) the focus concurs with the domain and with a topic in (55c), this could be an explanation for why the additional information is needed in (55c) but not in (55a).

Radboud Universiteit Nijmegen

7. ACKNOWLEDGEMENTS

The Max Planck Society supported the research reported in this chapter. I would like to thank Christine Dimroth, Petra Gretsch, Wolfgang Klein, Clive Perdue and Christiane von Stutterheim for their help. I would also like to thank two anonymous reviewers and the editor of this volume for valuable comments on an earlier version of this chapter. Of course, the remaining errors are my own.

8. NOTES

[1] The age of the child is given in year, months and days. For example, 1;10,29 stands for the age of 1 year, 10 months and 29 days.

[2] The adult examples are taken from the corpus of the 'Sonderforschungsbereich 360' at the University of Bielefeld, Germany.

[3] That part of the utterance whose interpretation is affected by the focus particle is often called the 'focus of the particle' (see Rooth, 1985; 1992). However, the terminology in this respect is far from clear (for a discussion see Dimroth, 1998). Given that in German the part whose interpretation is affected by the particle does not necessarily have to be the focus of the utterance, I prefer to call this part the 'domain of application'.

[4] Square bracket mark the domain of application, small caps print marks a pitch accent.

[5] Dutch has the explicit affirmative marker *wel* 'affirmative do' that forms a contrast to the negative marker *niet* 'not' as in the following example:

    A: Is Jan op school geweest? 'Did Jan go to school?'
    B: Jan is NIET op school, geweest. 'Jan did NOT go to school.'
    C: Jan is WEL op school geweest. 'Jan DID go to school.'

[6] *Noch* 'still, also' can also be used as a temporal particle, as in *Tom schläft noch* 'Tom is still sleeping' and receive a comparative meaning as in *Tom ist noch größer als Jan* 'Tom is even taller than Jan'. These uses of *noch* 'still, also' can be clearly distinguished from the focus particle use of *noch* 'still, also'. Since this study aims at a comparison between *auch* 'also' and *noch* 'still, also' only the focus particle use of *noch* is considered here.

[7] There are a number of corpora documenting the acquisition of German but none of the corpora appeared to suitable for this study because either the frequency of the recordings was to low, the recordings started at an age when children were already using the particles frequently; or the audio files of the corpora were not suited for an analysis of the intonation of the child utterances.

[8] The element that fills the open formula is underlined.

[9] Figure 2 includes all *auch*- and *noch*-utterances, however temporal and comparative *noch* are not productively used until the age of 2;07.

[10] In the following, only utterance types that occur more than five times in the corpus are discussed.

[11] In main clause utterances in German the finite verb appears in the second position in the sentence, in subordinated clauses the finite verb appears in utterance final position. I consider the examples in (28) a main clause utterance despite the fact that the verb lacks the correct finite morphology. In fact, some German dialects omit finiteness marking in examples like this. This is also true for the dialect Caroline's parents speak.

9. REFERENCES

Altmann, Hans. *Die Gradpartikeln im Deutschen: Untersuchungen zu ihrer Syntax, Semantik und Pragmatik*. Tübingen: Niemeyer, 1976a.
Altmann, Hans. "Gradpartikeln und Topikalisierung." In Kurt Braunmüler and Wilfried Kürschner (eds.) *Grammatik: Akten des 10. Linguistischen Kolloquiums Tübingen 1975*, 233–243. Tübingen: Niemeyer, 1976b.
Bergsma, Wenda. "Children's Interpretation of Dutch Sentences with the Focus Particle *alleen*." In Ingeborg Lasser (ed.) *The Process of Language Acquisition*, 263–280. Frankfurt/Berlin: Peter Lang Verlag, 1999.
Crain, Stephen, William Philip, Kenneth Drozd, Tom Roeper, and Kazumi Matsuoka. "Only in Child Language." Unpublished manuscript, University of Connecticut, Storrs, 1992.
Dimroth, Christine. *Fokuspartikeln und Informationsgliederung im Diskurs*. Ph.D. Diss., Freie Universität Berlin, 1998.
Dimroth, Christine. "Topic, Assertions and Additive Words: How L2 Learners Get from Information Structure to Target Language Syntax." *Linguistics* 40 (2002): 891–923.
Drozd, Kenneth, and Eric Van Loosbroek. "Dutch Children's Interpretation of Focus Particle Constructions." Poster presented at the 23rd Annual Boston University Conference on Language Development, Boston, 1998.
Féry, Caroline. *Focus, Topic and Intonation in German*. Tübingen: Universität Tübingen, 1992.
Hulk, Aafke. "Merging Scope-Particles: Word Order Variation and the Acquisition of 'aussi' and 'ook' in a Bilingual Context." In Christine Dimroth and Marianne Starren (eds.) *Information Structure and the Dynamics of Language Acquisition*, 211–234. Amsterdam: Benjamins, in press.
Jacobs, Joachim. *Fokus und Skalen: Zur Syntax und Semantik der Gradpartikeln im Deutschen*. Tübingen: Niemeyer, 1983.
König, Ekkehart. *The Meaning of Focus Particles: A Comparative Perspective*. London, New York: Routledge, 1991.
Krifka, Manfred. "Additive Particles under Stress." In Devon Strolovitch and Aaron Lawson (eds.) *Proceedings of SALT 8*, 111–128. Ithaca: CLC Publications, 1999.
Nederstigt, Ulrike. "Prosody: A Clue for the Interpretation of the Additive Focus Particles *auch* and *noch*." *Linguistische Berichte* 18 (2001): 415–440.
Penner, Zvi, Rosemarie Tracy, and Jürgen Weissenborn. "Where Scrambling Begins: Triggering Object Scrambling at the Early Stage in German and Bernese Swiss." In Susan Powers and Christine Hamann (eds.) *The Acquisition of Scrambling and Cliticization*, 127–164. Dordrecht: Kluwer Academic Publishers, 2000.
Penner, Zvi, Rosemarie Tracy, and Karin Wymann. "Die Rolle der Fokuspartikel *auch* im frühen kindlichen Lexikon." In Jörg Maibauer and Monika Rothweiler (eds.) *Das Lexikon im Spracherwerb*, 229–251. Dordrecht: Kluwer, 1999.
Philip, William. "Children Want Only A Right-Conservative Determiner." In Paul de Lacy and Anita Nowak (eds.) *UMOP 24*, 221–243. Amherst: GLSA, 2000
Reis, Marga, and Inga Rosengren. "A Modular Approach to the Grammar of Additive Particles: The Case of German *auch*." *Journal of Semantics* 14 (1997): 237–309.
Rooth, Mats. *Association with Focus*. Ph.D. Diss., University of Massachusetts, Amherst, 1985.
Rooth, Mats. "Association with Focus or Association with Presupposition?" In Peter Bosch and Rob van der Sandt (eds.) *Focus, Linguistic, Cognitive, and Computational Perspectives*, 332–344. Cambridge: Cambridge University Press, 1992.
von Stechow, Arnim. "Current Issues in the Theory of Focus." In Arnim von Stechow and Dieter Wunderlich (eds.) *Semantics: An International Handbook of Contemporary Research*, 804–824. Berlin: de Gruyter, 1991.
Uhmann, Susanne. *Fokusphonologie: Eine Analyse deutscher Intonation im Rahmen der nichtlinearen Phonologie*. Tübingen: Niemeyer, 1991.

WENDA BERGSMA

(UN)STRESSED *OOK* IN CHILD DUTCH

Abstract. This chapter presents the results of a comprehension experiment investigating Dutch children's understanding of sentences with the additive focus particle *ook* 'also, too'. Unlike children's comprehension of sentences that contain restrictive particles like *only*, the way children understand utterances with additive focus particles has not been previously investigated. Therefore, the results reported in this chapter can be regarded as an interesting contribution to acquisition research. The results presented here can be considered as a first step towards an understanding of how children interpret sentences that include additive focus particles.

1. INTRODUCTION

While investigating Dutch children's understanding of sentences that include the focus particle *ook* 'also, too', this chapter presents an answer to two questions. The first question concerns the kind of semantic contribution of the particle *ook* 'also, too' to the sentence it occurs in. Consider for instance the Dutch sentence in (1):

(1) Ook Peter eet een appel.
     'Peter too is eating an apple.'

The semantic contribution of *ook* to the sentence in (1) is that somebody other than Peter is eating an apple. Or, to put it in semantic terms, sentence (1) presupposes that somebody other than Peter is eating an apple. This presupposition should be fulfilled, otherwise sentence (1) cannot be uttered felicitously. For child Dutch, this raises the interesting questions of whether and, more importantly, how children take this presuppositional contribution of *ook* into account when interpreting sentences that contain the particle.

The second question concerns the syntactic position that the particle *ook* occupies in the sentence. In this chapter, two different syntactic postions of *ook* are investigated, i.e., *ook* in presubject and in postverbal position. If *ook* 'also, too' appears in presubject position, as in (1), the only constituent that can be modified by the particle is the subject NP. This means that a sentence like (1) can receive only one interpretation. However, if the particle *ook* 'also, too' appears in postverbal position it can modify several constituents in the sentence, depending on which constituent is taken to be the modified constituent of *ook*. This is illustrated in (2):

(2) Peter eet ook een appel.
 'Peter is also eating an apple.'

In (2), *ook* appears in postverbal position. From this position it can modify different constituents in the sentence. This means that a sentence like (2) can be assigned different interpretations. W.r.t. child Dutch, the semantic difference between *ook* in presubject postion and *ook* in postverbal position raises the question of whether children are sensitive to this difference. In other words, do Dutch children know that sentences with *ook* in presubject position are unambiguous, whereas sentences with *ook* in postverbal position can receive different interpretations, depending on what counts as the modified constituent of the particle *ook*? If children are sensitive to this semantic difference between *ook* in presubject position versus postverbal position, how is this difference exposed?

Whereas the chapter on focus particles by Nederstigt deals with questions concerning children's production of utterances with additive focus particles, this chapter presents an answer to the two questions mentioned above. Both questions concern Dutch children's comprehension of sentences that contain the additive focus particle *ook*.

The chapter is organized as follows. Section 2 starts with a short description of the use of the focus particle *ook* in adult Dutch and adresses the question of what children have to learn about the use of *ook* in adult Dutch. Section 3 reports a comprehension experiment investigating Dutch children's understanding of sentences with the particle *ook*. Section 4 presents the results of this experiment. Section 5 proposes a possible account for children's difficulties when interpreting *ook* in postverbal position. Section 6 concludes the chapter.

2. THE CHILD'S TARGET: *OOK* IN ADULT DUTCH

Focus particles in Dutch include words like *alleen* 'only', *ook* 'also, too', *maar* 'but' and *zelfs* 'even'. Categorically, these words can be used in different ways, as illustrated for *alleen* 'only' in (3):

(3) a. Alleen Peter werkt.
 'Only Peter is working.'

 b. Peter werkt alleen.
 'Peter is only working/Peter is working alone.'

Sentence (3a) is unambiguous. In this case, *alleen* can be used only as a focus particle, modifying the subject NP *Peter*, rendering the interpretation that the only person who is working, is Peter. In contrast, sentence (3b) can receive different interpretations. Here, *alleen* can either be used as a focus particle or as an adverb. If it is used as a focus particle, *alleen* can modify the verb *werkt* 'is working' to convey the interpretation that the only thing Peter does is working, or it can modify the subject NP *Peter* rendering the interpretation that Peter is the only person who is working. If *alleen* is used as an adverb, then sentence (3b) receives the interpretation that Peter works on his own. This chapter concentrates on the use of these words as focus particles.

In the literature on focus particles, it has often been observed that focus particles can occur in different syntactic positions within the sentence (e.g., König, 1991; Bayer, 1996; Reis & Rosengren, 1997). For Dutch, this positional variability is illustrated below:

(4) Jan heeft Marie aan Peter voorgesteld.
'John introduced Mary to Peter.'

In (4), focus particles like *ook* 'also, too' can be inserted in different syntactic positions, as exemplified in (5):

(5) a. Ook Jan heeft Marie aan Peter voorgesteld.
'John too introduced Mary to Peter.'

b. Jan heeft ook Marie aan Peter voorgesteld.
'John also introduced Mary to Peter.'

c. Jan heeft Marie ook aan Peter voorgesteld.
'John also introduced Mary to Peter.'

d. Jan heeft Marie aan Peter ook voorgesteld.
'John also introduced Mary to Peter.'

This positional variability is not restricted to the Dutch particle *ook* occur in the same syntactic positions, as shown in (6) and (7):

(6) a. Alleen Jan heeft Marie aan Peter voorgesteld.
'Only John introduced Mary to Peter.'

b. Jan heeft alleen Marie aan Peter voorgesteld.
'John only introduced Mary to Peter.'

c. Jan heeft Marie alleen aan Peter voorgesteld.
'John only introduced Mary to Peter.'

d. Jan heeft Marie alleen aan Peter voorgesteld.
'John only introduced Mary to Peter.'

(7) a. Zelfs Jan heeft Marie aan Peter voorgesteld.
'Even John introduced Mary to Peter.'

b. Jan heeft zelfs Marie aan Peter voorgesteld.
'John even introduced Mary to Peter.'

c. Jan heeft Marie zelfs aan Peter voorgesteld.
'John even introduced Mary to Peter.'

d. Jan heeft Marie aan Peter zelfs voorgesteld.
'John even introduced Mary to Peter.'

The examples in (5) through (7) do not only show that focus particles in Dutch can occur in different syntactic positions within the sentence, but they also illustrate that these particles normally precede the constituents they modify. The constituent that is modified by the particle is typically marked by focus. Depending on what is taken to be the modified constituent of the particle, the sentence can receive one or more interpretations. This also depends on the syntactic position of the particle in the sentence. For instance, if the focus particle *ook* precedes the subject NP, the only constituent that can be modified by the particle is the subject NP. This is indicated by focus on this NP. This is illustrated in (8):[1]

(8) Ook [Hans]$_F$ heeft een slechte film gezien.
'Hans too saw a bad movie.'

This means that a sentence like (8) can receive only the interpretation presented in (9):

(9) 'Hans and somebody other than Hans saw a bad movie.'

If the focus particle *ook* does not appear in presubject position, it can modify more than one constituent in the sentence, resulting in different possible interpretations. For instance, if *ook* appears before the VP, it can modify the subject NP, the VP or a (sub)constituent within the VP, depending on what counts as the modified constituent of the particle:

(10) Hans heeft ook een slechte film gezien.
'Hans also saw a bad movie.'

In (10), the focus particle *ook* occurs in postverbal position. From this position, the particle can modify at least four different (sub)constituents in the sentence. This means that this sentence can be assigned no less than four interpretations. These are presented in (11):

(11) a. [Hans]_F heeft ook een slechte film gezien.
'Hans too saw a bad movie.'
Interpretation: Hans and somebody other than Hans saw a bad movie.

b. Hans heeft ook [een slechte film gezien]_F.
'Hans also saw a bad movie.'
Interpretation: Hans saw a bad movie and Hans did something else.

c. Hans heeft ook [een slechte film]_F gezien.
'Hans also saw a bad movie.'
Interpretation: Hans saw a bad movie and Hans saw something else.

d. Hans heeft ook een slechte film [gezien]_F.
'Hans also saw a bad movie.'
Interpretation: Hans saw a bad movie and Hans did something else to a bad movie.

First, if the particle *ook* modifies the subject NP, as in (11a), then (10) receives the interpretation that Hans and somebody other than Hans saw a bad movie. Second, if *ook* modifies the VP, as in (11b), then (10) gets the reading that Hans saw a bad movie and Hans did something else. A third possibility is that *ook* modifies the object NP, as in (11c). In this case, (10) receives the interpretation that Hans saw a bad movie and Hans saw something else. Finally, the particle *ook* can modify the verb, as in (11d). If *ook* modifies this subconstituent of the VP, then (10) receives the interpretation that Hans saw a bad movie and Hans did something else to a bad movie.

Whereas focus particles like *alleen* 'only' and *zelfs* 'even' typically conform to the pattern outlined above, the focus particle *ook* 'also, too' shows a more complex behaviour. Either the constituent that is modified by *ook* is marked by focus or the particle itself receives stress. This stressing behaviour is not restricted to the Dutch particle *ook*. In the literature on focus particles, it has often been observed that particular additive particles can have unstressed as well as stressed variants, e.g., *also*, *too* in English and *auch* 'also, too' in German (König, 1991; Reis & Rosengren, 1997; Hoeksema & Zwarts, 1991). In standard theories on focus particles, this stressing behaviour of additive particles has hardly been accounted for. Exceptions are Dimroth (1998) and Krifka (1999).

If the constituent that is modified by *ook* is marked by focus, then the particle typically precedes its modified constituent. If *ook* receives stress, then the particle typically follows the constituent it modifies. Consider the following Dutch examples:

(12) a.   Ook Inge heeft een bos bloemen gekocht.
'Inge too bought a bunch of flowers.'

b.   Inge heeft ook een bos bloemen gekocht.
'Inge also bought a bunch of flowers.'

In (12a), the particle *ook* precedes the subject NP. In this case, the only constituent that can be modified by the particle is the subject NP, as indicated by focus on this NP:

(13) Ook [Inge]$_F$ heeft een bos bloemen gekocht.

The only interpretation that is available for this sentence, is the one in which Inge and somebody other than Inge bought a bunch of flowers. This interpretation corresponds with the one presented in (14):

(14) Inge and somebody other than Inge bought a bunch of flowers.

In (12b), the particle *ook* appears in postverbal position. From this position, the particle can modify several constituents in the sentence, resulting in at least three different interpretations. These different interpretations are summarized in (15):

(15) a.   Inge heeft ook [een bos bloemen gekocht]$_F$.
'Inge also bought a bunch of flowers.'

>
> Interpretation: Inge bought a bunch of flowers and Inge did something else.

b. Inge heeft ook [een bos bloemen]$_F$ gekocht.
'Inge also bought a bunch of flowers.'
Interpretation: Inge bought a bunch of flowers and Inge bought something else.

c. Inge heeft ook een bos bloemen [gekocht]$_F$.
'Inge also bought a bunch of flowers.'
Interpretation: Inge bought a bunch of flowers and Inge did something else to a bunch of flowers.

Note that if the particle *ook* in (12b) itself receives stress, then the constituent that is modified by the particle is followed by the particle, here the subject NP *Inge*. In this case, (12b) receives the same semantic interpretation as (12a), i.e., Inge and somebody other than Inge bought a bunch of flowers.

Summarizing, the examples in (12) illustrate a semantic difference between unstressed *ook*, on the one hand, and stressed *ook*, on the other. If the particle *ook* is not marked by stress, then it typically precedes its modified constituent. In this case, its modified constituent is marked by focus. In this situation, *ook* behaves in a similar way as focus particles like *alleen* 'only' and *zelfs* 'even'. If the particle itself receives stress, then the constituent that is modified by *ook* typically appears to the left of the particle.

In child Dutch, the semantic difference between unstressed and stressed *ook* raises some important questions. First, do children know that the Dutch focus particle *ook* can be stressed? Second, do children realize that unstressed *ook* semantically differs from stressed *ook*? Third, are children aware of the correlation between the syntactic position of *ook* and the possibility of stress on the particle? Fourth, if children know the differences between unstressed *ook* and stressed *ook*, when and how do they acquire them? In order to answer these questions, I conducted the comprehension experiment presented in the next section. Given that children's comprehension of additive focus particles has not been investigated before, the results of this experiment provide some first answers to the questions mentioned above.

3. THE *OOK* EXPERIMENT

In this section, I present the comprehension experiment which investigates Dutch children's understanding of sentences with the focus particle *ook*. The section is structured as follows. Section 3.1 presents the predictions on which the *ook* experiment is based. Section 3.2 describes the number of children who participated in the experiment. Section 3.3 gives a description of the method that was used. Section 3.4 reports the procedure that was followed during the whole experiment. Section 3.5 discusses a remark about how intonation was controlled.

3.1. Predictions

As mentioned in the introduction, this chapter tries to find an answer to two different questions. Here, I reformulate both questions as two predictions. These predictions form the basis of the experiment presented in this chapter.[2]

The first question concerns the presuppositional contribution of *ook* to sentences like in (1), here repeated in (16):

(16) Ook Peter eet een appel.
 'Peter too is eating an apple.'

The presuppositional contribution of *ook* to (16) is that somebody other than Peter is eating an apple. In other words, sentence (16) presupposes that somebody other than Peter is eating an apple. For child Dutch, this raises the question of whether children know that they have to take this presuppositional contribution of *ook* into account when asked to interpret sentences that contain *ook*. With respect to this question, I predict that children initially ignore this presuppositional contribution of *ook*. This prediction is stated in (17):

(17) Prediction 1:
 Initially, children ignore the presuppositional contribution of *ook* 'also, too' in their interpretation of sentences that contain *ook*.

The basis for the prediction presented in (17) concerns the presuppositional nature of the particle *ook*. Whereas a truth-conditional particle like *alleen* 'only' can alter the truth value of a sentence, this does not hold for a presuppositional particle like *ook*. This means that a sentence with *ook* cannot be true or false in a particular context. Given a certain context, a sentence with *ook* can only be felicitous or not. For children, this semantic contribution of *ook* might be difficult to grasp. If children find it difficult to interpret the presuppositional contribution of *ook*, children may find it easier to simply ignore this presuppositional contribution of *ook*.

The second question involves the syntactic position of the particle *ook*, in particular, the difference between *ook* in presubject position and *ook* in postverbal position. If *ook* appears in presubject position, as in (16), the only constituent that can be modified by the particle is the subject NP. However, if the particle *ook* occurs in postverbal position, as in (18), it can modify more than one constituent within the sentence, depending on whether the particle is marked by stress or not:

(18) Peter eet ook een appel.
'Peter is also eating an apple.'

Given this semantic difference between *ook* in presubject and in postverbal position, I predict that children find it more difficult to identify the modified constituent of *ook* in sentences with *ook* in postverbal position than in sentences with *ook* in presubject position. This is captured in (19):

(19) Prediction 2:
Initially, children find it more difficult to determine the modified constituent of *ook* 'also, too' in sentences with *ook* in postverbal position than in sentences with *ook* in presubject position.

Prediction 2 is based on the assumption that children have more difficulties in interpreting ambiguous sentences than in interpreting unambiguous sentences. If a sentence can receive only one interpretation, the only thing children have to do is to determine this interpretation. However, if a sentence can be assigned different interpretations, children need to figure out these different interpretations. This might be more difficult for children. This means that children may find it easier to interpret sentences with *ook* in presubject position than sentences with *ook* in postverbal position.

3.2. Subjects

In my comprehension experiment, 44 children from an elementary school in Steenwijk, The Netherlands, participated. Their ages ranged from four years and two months to seven years and eleven months. Table 1 presents the number of subjects divided across three different age groups:[3]

Table 1. Number of children per age group

Age group	Number of children
4;02 - 5;04	15
5;05 - 6;04	15
6;05 - 7;11	14
Total	44

3.3. Method

The method I used was a Picture Selection task. The task of the children was to select pictures corresponding to three types of test sentences, as in (20):[4]

(20) a. Ook [de jongen]_F aait de hond.
'The boy too is petting the dog.'

b. De jongen aait ook [de hond]_F.
'They boy is also petting the dog.'

c. [De jongen]_F aait OOK de hond.
'The boy too is petting the dog.'

In (20), square brackets mark the modified constituent of the particle *ook* 'also, too' and small caps print indicates stress on the particle. As mentioned above, the interpretation of sentences with the focus particle *ook* depends on the syntactic position of *ook* as well as the presence of stress on *ook*.

In (20a), the particle *ook* occurs in presubject position. In this case, the only constituent that can be modified by the particle is the subject NP. This is indicated by focus on this NP. This means that the only interpretation that is available for this sentence is the one in which the boy and somebody other than the boy is petting the dog. This interpretation is presented in (21) and I refer to it as 'Subject Interpretation':

(21) Subject Interpretation:
The boy and somebody other than the boy is petting the dog.

In (20b), the particle *ook* appears in postverbal position. In this sentence, focus on the object NP marks this NP as the modified constituent of the particle, rendering the interpretation for (20b) that the boy is petting the dog and he is petting something other than the dog. This interpretation is given in (22) and I call it 'Object Interpretation':

(22) Object Interpretation:
The boy is petting the dog and he is petting something other than the dog.

In (20c), the particle *ook* occurs again in postverbal position. However, whereas in (20b) the focus on the object NP marks this NP as the modified constituent of the particle, in (20c) the stress on the particle indicates that the modified constituent of *ook* appears to the left of the particle, i.e., the subject

NP. This means that (20c) receives the same semantic interpretation as (20a), i.e., the boy and somebody other than the boy petted the dog. This is the Subject Interpretation presented in (21).

3.4. The Procedure and an Example

During the experiment, the experimenter followed the same procedure for each item. First, the experimenter showed the child an introduction picture, for instance a picture with a boy, a girl, a dog and a cat. Then, the experimenter told the child a short story about the picture in Figure 1:

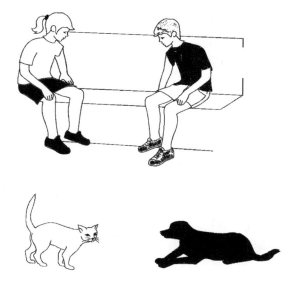

Figure 1

Kijk, hier zie je een jongen, een meisje, een hond en een kat. Als de jongen en het meisje het leuk vinden, dan kunnen ze de hond en de kat gaan aaien. Wie zou er gaan aaien: de jongen of het meisje of allebei? Wat zou er geaaid worden: de hond of de kat of allebei? Laten we het plaatje in de box doen, dan kunnen we Tommie gaan vragen of hij in de box kan kijken om te zien wat er gebeurt.

['Look, here you see a boy, a girl, a dog and a cat. If the boy and the girl feel like doing that, they can pet the dog and the cat. Who will be petting: the boy or the girl or both? What will be petted: the dog or the cat or both? Let's put the picture into the box, then we can ask Tommie to look inside the box to see what happens.']

After the experimenter told the child this story about the picture, the experimenter asked the child to put this picture inside the box of the handpuppet Tommie. Before the experimenter started the experiment, the experimenter explained to the child that this handpuppet Tommie is so smart that he can look inside this box and can tell the experimenter and the child what is happening inside this box. After the child put the introduction picture inside this box, the experimenter asked the handpuppet Tommie to tell what happens. In this case, Tommie looked inside the box and said:

> Ik zie wat er gebeurt. ['I can see what happens.']
>
> Ook de jongen aait de hond. ['The boy too is petting the dog.'] (test sentence)[5]

Then the experimenter presented three different pictures to the child and asked the child to select the picture that corresponds to the sentence uttered by the handpuppet Tommie, in this case the sentence *Ook de jongen aait de hond* 'The boy too is petting the dog'.

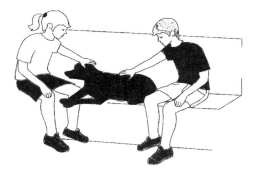

Figure 2

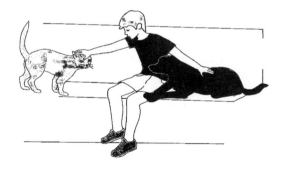

Figure 3

Figure 4

After the child selected the corresponding picture, the experimenter asked the child to put this picture inside the box of the handpuppet as well.

3.5. Control Intonation

In order to control for intonation, each sentence of the handpuppet Tommie was spoken by one native speaker of Dutch (female, twenty-one years old) and recorded in a palm-size computer. In the beak of the handpuppet, a little loudspeaker was installed that was connected to the computer. By clicking on the appropriate item on the screen of the computer, each sentence of the handpuppet could be played.

4. RESULTS

In this section, I present the results of my experiment. It consists of two parts. First, I present the results of the experiment with respect to Prediction 1 (see (17)). Then I report the findings regarding Prediction 2 (see (19)).

4.1. Prediction 1

The task of the children in the above experiment was to select pictures corresponding to three types of test sentences, for convenience repeated here as (23):

(23) a. Ook [de jongen]$_F$ aait de hond.
'The boy too is petting the dog.'

b. De jongen aait ook [de hond]$_F$.
'The boy is also petting the dog.'

c. [De jongen]$_F$ aait OOK de hond.
'The boy too is petting the dog.'

The children were asked to make a choice between three different pictures for each type of test sentence. For instance, when asked to select a picture for sentences like (23a), the experimenter showed the child three different pictures. The first picture in Figure 2 showed the boy and the girl both petting the dog. This picture correlates with an expected Subject Interpretation for sentences like (23a). The second picture in Figure 3 showed the boy petting the dog and the cat, corresponding with an unexpected Object Interpretation for this type of sentence. The third picture in Figure 4 was included in order to test Prediction 1, repeated here in (24):

(24) Prediction 1:
Initially, children ignore the presuppositional contribution of *ook* 'also, too' in their interpretation of sentences that contain *ook* 'also, too'.

The picture in Figure 4 showed the boy petting the dog. If children ignored the presuppositional contribution of *ook* 'also, too' as predicted by Prediction 1, then they would select this picture as the corresponding picture for sentences of the type (23a). Table 2 presents the number of children who always selected this third picture for each type of test sentence in (23):[6]

Table 2. Number of children who always selected the third picture

Age group	Number of children
4;02 - 5;04	8 (15) (53,3%)
5;05 - 6;04	6 (15) (40,0%)
6;05 - 7;11	1 (14) (7,1%)
Total	15 (44) (34,1%)

For the children in the youngest age group, Table 2 shows that eight of the fifteen children consistently selected the third picture (Figure 4) for the three different types of test sentences (53,3%). For the children in the older age groups, Table 2 reveals that fewer children always selected this picture as the corresponding picture. Whereas six of the fifteen children from the middle age group chose the third picture for each type of test sentence (40,0%), only one child in the oldest age group always selected this picture (7,1%). These results confirm Prediction 1: Children initially ignore the presuppositional contribution of *ook* 'also, too' in their understanding of sentences that contain the particle *ook*.[7]

4.2. Prediction 2

The findings presented in section 4.1 show that children initially ignore the presuppositional contribution of *ook*. At a certain point in their language development, children learn how the particle *ook* contributes to the sentence it occurs in. The question of how children master this is not answered by the results presented in section 4.1. This must be investigated in further research. One clue that children certainly can help in acquiring the presuppositional contribution of *ook* involves the kind of context in which a sentence with *ook* is used. Children must learn that a sentence with *ook* can only be used in a certain context. For instance, a sentence like *Ook Peter eet een appel* 'Peter too is eating an apple' can only be uttered in a context in which somebody other than Peter is eating an apple. If this presupposition is not satisfied, then *Ook Peter eet een appel* 'Peter too is eating an apple' cannot be used felicitously. The role of contextual factors can therefore be considered as an important clue for acquiring the semantic contribution of *ook*.

Another issue that children need to learn about the contribution of *ook* concerns the difference between *ook* in presubject position and *ook* in postverbal position. Or, more precisely, what kind of interpretations do children assign to sentences like in (23). Do they assign a Subject Interpretation to sentences like (23a) and (23c) and an Object Interpretation to sentences of the type (23b) like adults? Or, in terms of the picture selection task, do children select the picture corresponding with a subject reading for sentences like (23a) and (23c) and the picture corresponding with an object reading for sentences like (23b)? In order to answer these questions, I investigated the results of the children who did not consistently select the third picture. These children either selected the picture corresponding with a subject interpretation or the picture corresponding with an object interpretation when asked to select pictures for sentences like in (23). The number of these children was 29. Table 3 presents the number of these children divided across three different age groups:

Table 3. Number of children per age group

Age group	Number of children
4;02 - 5;04	7
5;05 - 6;04	9
6;05 - 7;11	13
Total	29

Table 4 below presents the results of the children captured in Table 3. The percentages denoted by 'Subject' correspond to the number of expected selections for sentences like (23a), i.e., the number of times at which children selected the picture corresponding with a subject interpretation. The percentages marked by 'Object' correlate with the number of expected selections for sentences of the type (23b), i.e., the number of times at which children selected the picture denoting an object interpretation. Finally, the percentages denoted by 'Particle' correspond to the number of expected selections for sentences like (23c), i.e., the number of times at which children selected the picture corresponding with a subject interpretation:

Table 4. Expected selections per sentence type [8]

Age group	Subject (23a)	Object (23b)	Particle (23c)
(4;02) – (5;04)	75,0%	35,7%	50,0%
(5;05) – (6;04)	84,4%	53,1%	59,4%
(6;05) – (7;11)	77,1%	60,4%	50,0%
Average	78,8%	49,8%	53,1%

Table 4 shows that for sentences like (23a), i.e., sentences with *ook* 'also, too' in presubject position, children selected the expected picture corresponding to a subject interpretation almost 80% of the time. In contrast, for sentences like (23b) and (23c), i.e., sentences with *ook* in postverbal position, children did not show a clear pattern regarding which picture to choose. When asked to select pictures for those sentences, children from the three different age groups randomly selected from three different pictures a picture that either corresponded to a subject interpretation or a picture that corresponded to an object interpretation. This contrast between children's understanding of sentences with *ook* in presubject position and their understanding of sentences with *ook* in postverbal position supports Prediction 2, repeated here as (25):

(25) Prediction 2:
Initially, children find it more difficult to determine the modified constituent of *ook* 'also, too' in sentences with *ook* in postverbal position than in sentences with *ook* in presubject position.

5. A POSSIBLE ACCOUNT

In order to explain children's difficulties in interpreting sentences with *ook* 'also, too' in postverbal position, I suggest an account in terms of three semantic differences between *ook* in presubject position and *ook* in postverbal position. First, if the particle *ook* appears in presubject position, then the sentence can receive only one interpretation. In contrast, if *ook* appears in postverbal position, several interpretations are possible, depending on what counts as the modified constituent of *ook*. This means that sentences with *ook* in presubject position are unambiguous, whereas sentences with *ook* in postverbal position can be regarded as ambiguous. Assuming that children find it more difficult to interpret ambiguous sentences than unambiguous sentences, this explains children's difficulties in interpreting sentences with *ook* in postverbal position.

A second and related difference that plays a role concerns the possibility of stress on the particle in postverbal position. Whereas *ook* cannot be stressed in presubject position, in postverbal position the particle *ook* can either occur stressed or unstressed, resulting in different kind of constituents that can be modified by *ook*. If the particle *ook* is not marked by stress, then the constituent that is modified by *ook* typically appears to the right of the particle. In those cases, the modified constituent is marked by focus. However, if the particle itself receives stress, then the modified constituent of *ook* typically occurs to the left of the particle. This kind of ambiguity forms an additional reason for children's difficulties in interpreting sentences with *ook* in postverbal position.

A third difference between presubject *ook* and postverbal *ook* involves the interpretation of the stress on the particle. The fact that children ignore the stress on the particle indicates that children do not know how to interpret the stress on the particle. In order to explain this, I suggest that children find it more difficult to interpret the stress on the particle itself than focus on the modified constituent of *ook*. Whereas focus on the modified constituent of *ook* contrasts this constituent with other possible alternatives from a given set of alternatives, the way stressed *ook* is contrasted with other alternatives is less clear. Therefore, children have more problems in identifying the stress on the particle itself.

6. CONCLUSION

The results of the picture selection task reported in this chapter show that Dutch children initially ignore the presuppositional contribution of the particle *ook* 'also, too' in their interpretation of sentences that contain the particle. Whereas eight of the fifteen children from the youngest age group always selected the third picture for sentences that include *ook*, only one child from the oldest age group consistently selected this third picture for those sentences.[9] These findings support Prediction 1. However, the question of how children learn the presuppositional contribution of *ook* is not answered by those findings. This question forms an issue for further research.

An additional conclusion that can be drawn from the results of the picture selection task presented in this chapter, concerns Dutch children's understanding of sentences with *ook* in presubject position and their comprehension of sentences with *ook* in postverbal position. It was predicted that Dutch children find it more difficult to identify the modified constituent of *ook* in sentences with *ook* in postverbal position than in sentences with *ook* in presubject position. The results reported here confirm this prediction. For sentences in which *ook* appears in presubject position, all of the children frequently selected the expected picture, i.e., the picture corresponding to a subject interpretation. In contrast, for sentences in which *ook* occurs in postverbal position, children did not show a clear pattern regarding which picture to choose. When asked to select pictures for sentences with *ook* in postverbal position, children from all age groups randomly selected a picture that either corresponded to a subject interpretation or a picture correlating with an object interpretation. This discrepancy between Dutch children's understanding of sentences with *ook* in presubject position and their comprehension of sentences with *ook* in postverbal position provide evidence for the second prediction presented in this paper.

In order to explain Dutch children's difficulties in interpreting sentences with *ook* in postverbal position, this chapter suggests an account in terms of three semantic differences between *ook* in presubject position and *ook* in postverbal position. Based upon these semantic differences, this account says that children find it more difficult to identify the modified constituent of *ook* in sentences with *ook* in postverbal position than in sentences with *ook* in presubject position.

Instituut voor Taal- en Studiebegeleiding, Laren

7. NOTES

[1] In the examples, [...]$_F$ stands for the modified constituent of the particle marked by focus.

[2] Recall that the experiment presented in this chapter is the first study investigating how children comprehend sentences with additive focus particles like *ook* 'also, too'. Therefore, the predictions presented in this section are not related to other predictions known from other acquisition studies.

[3] The results of the children presented in this study should be compared with the interpretation of sentences with the particle *ook* 'also, too' by Dutch adults. This needs to be included in further research.

[4] Of each type of test sentence in (20), four items were tested (total 12 test items). Each item contained a different verb and a different subject NP and object NP. In addition, two training, eight control and eight filler items were included. In total, the experiment consisted of 30 items.

[5] One of the reviewers pointed out that the test sentences are not felicitous in the context in which they are presented. According to this reviewer, this means that this experiment does not only investigate how children interpret *ook* 'also, too', but simultaneously how they react to non-felicity. This would be problematic. I agree with the observation that a sentence with *ook* can only be uttered in a certain context. As mentioned in the introduction, the presupposition triggered by *ook* should be satisfied, otherwise a sentence with *ook* cannot be uttered felicitously. However, one the aims of the experiment presented was to find out whether children are sensitive to the presuppositional contribution of *ook*. This explains the experimental set-up.

[6] The responses of the other children are discussed in the next section.

[7] The decrease in the number of children selecting the third picture was statistically not significant. Although this difference was not significant, it shows a certain tendency between the age group and the selection of the third picture (Figure 4).

[8] Due to the low number of subjects, the percentages of expected selections per sentence type statistically do not differ from each other. This means that the percentages reported in Table 4 can only indicate certain tendencies, for instance an increase in the correct object interpretation from 35,7% to 60,4%.

[9] Recall that this kind of picture was included in order to test Prediction 1.

8. REFERENCES

Bayer, Josef. *Directionality and Logical Form. On the Scope of Focusing Particles and Wh-in-Situ*. Dordrecht: Kluwer, 1996.

Bergsma, Wenda. "Children's Interpretation of Dutch Sentences with the Focus Particle *alleen*." In Ingeborg Lasser (ed.) *The Process of Language Acquisition*, 263–280. Frankfurt/Berlin: Peter Lang Verlag, 1999.

Crain, Stephen, Weijia Ni, and Laura Conway. "Learning, Parsing and Modularity." In Charles Clifton, Lyn Frazier, and Keith Rayner (eds.) *Perspectives on Sentence Processing*, 443–467. Hillsdale: Lawrence Erlbaum, 1994.

Crain, Stephen, William Philip, Kenneth F. Drozd, Thomas Roeper, and Kazumi Matsuoka. *Only in Child Language*. Unpublished manuscript. University of Connecticut and University of Massachusetts, Amherst, 1992.

Dimroth, Christine. *Fokuspartikeln und Informationsgliederung im Diskurs*. Ph.D. Diss., Freie Universität Berlin, 1998.
Drozd, Kenneth F., and Erik Van Loosbroek. "Dutch Children's Interpretation of Focus Particle Constructions." Poster presented at *The 23rd Annual Boston University Conference on Language Development*. Boston, 1998.
Hoeksema, Jack, and Frans Zwarts. "Some Remarks on Focus Adverbs." *Journal of Semantics* 8 (1991): 51–70.
König, Ekkehard. *The Meaning of Focus Particles: A Comparative Perspective*. London: Routledge, 1991.
Krifka, Manfred. "Additive Particles under Stress." In Devon Strolovitch and Aaron Lawson (eds.) *Proceedings of SALT 8*, 111–128. Ithaca: CLC Publications, 1998.
Philip, William. *Children Want Only a Right-Conservative Determiner*, Unpublished Ms., 1999.
Reis, Marga, and Inger Rosengren. "A Modular Approach to the Grammar of Additive Particles: The Case of German *auch*." *Journal of Semantics* 14 (1997): 237–309.

SUBJECT INDEX

A

accomplishment 169, 177, 178, 185, 238
achievement 169, 170, 177, 190, 191, 238
activity 32, 33, 169, 170, 177, 178, 194, 195, 199, 209, 210, 215, 233
adjective 19, 21, 22, 25, 29, 40, 46, 48, 53, 57, 111, 250
adjunct 14
adverb 40, 46, 86, 116, 143, 175, 200, 220, 223, 235, 238–240, 312, 331
  quantificational 238
  temporal 86, 175, 200, 312
adverbial 27, 66, 86, 172, 174, 176, 179, 220, 221, 226–230, 230, 232–239, 266–268
after 172, 174, 176, 177, 186, 221, 229, 236, 237, 241
agglutinating 5
all 2, 22, 92, 111, 115, 116, 120, 138, 142–144, 147, 148, 150–152, 156, 162, 163
alle 2, 121–126, 138
alleen 124, 326, 330–332, 334–336
alternatives 7, 8, 271, 305–307, 309–312, 321, 324, 326, 346
altijd 221, 235–240
ambiguity 3, 21, 22, 145, 146, 190, 345
anaphora 168, 177, 187–189
  temporal 168, 177, 187
anaphoric 38, 45, 52, 53, 187, 217, 222, 223, 229
antecedent 24, 32, 45, 56, 103, 187–189, 306
anteriority 173, 176, 235, 293, 295
article 22, 24, 25, 33, 34, 38, 48–50, 58, 59, 61
aspect 5, 6, 14, 15, 20, 21, 78, 141, 150, 167–174, 176–191, 193–196, 198, 207, 212, 215, 219–222, 230, 231, 233, 235–237, 241–243, 262, 274, 291–293, 295,
  grammatical 15, 167, 168, 174, 177–179, 181, 182, 186, 187, 189, 190, 219–221, 236, 291, 293
  imperfective 170, 173, 179, 180, 183, 185, 190, 198, 241
  lexical 168, 174, 177, 182, 189
  perfect 179, 181, 184–186, 188–190
  perfective 78, 170, 173, 179, 180, 183–185, 188, 295
  prospective 179, 181, 185, 186, 188, 191, 207
  temporal 6, 178
assertion 15, 98, 198, 201, 233, 245, 256, 258, 260–266, 268–271, 291, 292, 295, 300
atelic 6, 15, 167, 169, 170, 177, 178, 182, 183, 185, 238, 239
atelicity 167, 170, 171
auch 16, 247, 281, 282, 303–322, 324, 325, 327, 334

B

background 7, 8, 21, 90, 145, 168, 188, 234, 270, 279, 283, 314
bare 4, 5, 10, 11, 24, 31–34, 38, 45, 47, 50, 52, 56–58, 60, 61, 223, 249–251, 258, 261, 266
before 86, 172, 174–177, 186, 219, 221, 229, 236, 237, 241
boundedness 51, 194, 201, 213, 290, 293, 298, 300

C

cell fission model 273, 274, 290, 292, 294, 299
Childes 75, 142

349

350   SUBJECT INDEX

Chinese 31, 58, 62, 75, 156, 246, 262, 269
clause 14, 27, 51, 54–56, 65–67, 70–72, 74, 75, 78, 82, 176, 195, 245, 262, 264, 271, 318, 327
complement 14, 65, 67, 71, 72, 74, 78
   relative 67
   subordinate 27, 176, 264
clitic 27, 60
collective 120–127, 130–134, 136, 137
common ground 98
competence 117, 120, 135, 141–144, 149, 150, 155, 157–159, 168, 177
complement 14, 65–67, 71, 72, 74, 78, 87
complementizer 75, 76, 81, 87, 254, 264
compositionality 37, 39, 42–44, 59, 60, 94, 95, 102
compound 41, 42, 53, 250, 251, 269
comprehension 16, 91, 96, 115, 137, 138, 142–144, 147, 149, 216, 303, 304, 325, 329, 330, 335, 337, 346
conditions 55, 61, 84, 90, 92, 95, 96, 99, 100, 103, 111, 118, 119, 122, 124–127, 130–136, 138, 139, 143, 153, 156, 157, 159, 2
   felicity 95, 96, 99, 100, 103, 138, 143, 156, 157
   truth 61, 92, 111, 118, 135, 139
connective 172, 174–177, 228, 229
conservativity 94, 95, 102, 104, 105, 111
context 3, 4, 8, 11, 14, 19, 21, 22, 27, 30, 33, 52, 53, 56, 57, 60, 89, 91, 95–99, 101, 104–107, 110, 111, 115–138, 157–159, 177, 187, 193, 204, 206, 207, 209–212, 214, 225, 226, 228, 229, 234, 238, 239, 247, 249, 250, 253, 262, 270, 276, 278, 292, 297, 300, 305, 310–313, 316, 324, 326, 336, 343, 347
continuative 186, 238
crosslinguistic 1, 3–6, 10, 12, 13, 15, 94, 193, 214, 219, 248, 289, 294, 300

cumulative 177, 178
Czech 13, 274, 297–300

D

definite 25, 29, 31–34, 37, 45–49, 56, 59, 61, 130, 236
deictic 33, 46, 55, 167, 168, 172, 174, 179, 183, 187–190, 222, 223, 226, 229
denotation 11, 39, 102, 103, 135, 180
desiderative 207, 217
determiner 3, 4, 17, 37, 48, 50, 56, 58, 61, 62, 92, 94, 95, 102, 104, 116, 122, 135, 143, 321
   conservative 94, 104–106
discourse 12, 22, 45, 49, 57, 61, 91, 92, 94, 95, 98, 99, 101, 102, 106, 107, 109, 115, 116, 118–120, 127, 135–139, 187–189, 198, 220–226, 228, 233, 238, 243, 278
distributive 120–127, 130–132, 134–136, 138
Dutch 6, 7, 9–11, 13–16, 65–69, 71–77, 83–87, 121, 122, 127, 138, 219–226, 228, 230–233, 235, 237, 238, 241, 242, 248, 266, 289, 306, 325, 327, 329–332, 334–336, 341, 346, 347

E

ellipsis 24, 32, 33, 253, 278
English 2–8, 10, 11, 13, 14, 17, 20, 21, 23–27, 29, 31, 33, 34, 38, 40, 42, 44, 45, 50, 51, 61, 62, 65, 66–69, 71–78, 82–87, 90, 138, 141, 144, 148, 150–156, 158–160, 167, 168, 170, 173, 181, 183–185, 188–190, 193, 195, 200, 202, 215, 216, 223, 231, 245, 246, 248, 250, 254, 255, 262, 271, 289, 293, 295, 306, 334
   African-American 168, 189, 190
   American 31, 33
   British 31
   Old 25
entailment 109, 162, 163
   downward 109

SUBJECT INDEX 351

episodic 6
event 19, 61, 66, 67, 69, 70, 72, 76, 77,
 86, 92–95, 101, 102, 109, 111,
 167, 169–172, 177–181, 185, 186,
 190, 196–199, 201, 203, 208, 210,
 213, 215, 216, 219–221, 227,
 234–237, 239–242, 262, 264, 266
every 3, 89–96, 100–112, 115–123,
 128–130, 134–136, 138, 139, 141–
 147, 149–151, 156–158, 161–164
exhaustive pairing 90, 102, 115–120,
 123–126, 130, 133–136, 138, 139
experimental 12, 14, 48, 73, 86, 89, 90,
 91, 96, 99, 101, 103, 106, 107,
 109, 111, 115, 117, 118, 122, 123,
 127, 130, 135, 144–145, 147, 155,
 163, 303, 326, 347
expletive 34, 45, 46, 48, 49, 56, 61,
 255, 269, 271

F

felicity 94–97, 99, 100, 102, 103, 115,
 117, 138, 143, 156, 157
finiteness 13, 15, 16, 245–259, 261,
 262, 265–267, 269–271, 273, 274,
 289–292, 294, 297, 300, 327
Finnish 195
focus 2, 3, 7–9, 13, 15, 16, 22, 31, 101,
 144, 171, 175, 176, 191, 201, 202,
 213, 219–221, 227, 229, 230, 234,
 236, 240, 241, 249, 251, 261, 268,
 271, 278, 280, 288, 290, 291, 296,
 297, 300, 303–308, 310–312, 320,
 324–327, 329–335, 338, 345, 347
French 24, 25, 42, 87, 97, 167, 169–
 171, 183, 184, 188, 190, 202, 220,
 223, 226, 248
functional 16, 23, 24, 39, 40, 116, 245,
 246, 248, 259

G

gapping 245, 253
generic 11, 33, 45, 48, 138, 139
German 2, 3, 6, 13, 16, 17, 23, 27, 44,
 168, 181, 186, 195, 223, 231,
 246–250, 252, 253, 255, 261, 262,
 266, 269–271, 273–276, 279, 289,
 290, 294, 295, 299, 300, 303–308,
 311, 334, 325, 327, 334
Greek 27, 38, 48, 167, 246

H

habitual 6, 26
Hindi 26

I

iedere 10, 121–134, 137–139
illocutionary 217, 245, 253, 263–265,
 277, 289, 291
imperative 203, 217, 251, 252, 263,
 278, 293
implicature 162, 163, 201
indefinite 3, 10–12, 17, 22, 32, 33, 46,
 49, 53, 59, 61, 102, 236, 245,
 256–258, 271
individual 4, 9, 11, 22, 118, 120–123,
 143, 226, 227, 276, 279, 283, 288,
 293, 295, 296, 299, 301, 314
inference 47, 96, 107, 162
infinitival 16, 22, 25, 273–276, 278,
 280, 281, 283–289, 292, 294–296,
 299–301
infinitive 29, 87, 185, 247, 249, 250,
 275, 276, 279, 283, 287–289, 295,
 297, 299, 301
 optional 18, 303
 root 247, 279, 289, 295, 297, 299
inflectional 5, 24, 26, 29, 196, 236,
 245, 249, 270, 275, 278, 294, 299
ingressive 199–201, 208, 210–213,
 215, 217
innate 3, 4, 59
innateness 2, 3
intensional 65, 72
interface 1, 4, 5, 9, 13
 syntax-semantics 1, 4, 5, 13
interpretive 1, 2, 4–6, 12, 66, 146, 187,
 189, 274, 276, 278, 283–285,
 287–288, 296, 297, 299

intonation 2, 31, 255, 259–261, 268, 271, 300, 308, 312, 325, 327, 336, 341
  contrastive 259, 260, 371
Inuktitut 5, 13, 15, 193–195, 198, 199, 201–204, 208, 212–217
isomorphism 144, 148–150, 152, 154–162, 164
Italian 13, 32, 62, 97, 167, 169, 170, 183, 185, 188, 193
item 29, 49, 74, 82, 87, 339, 341, 347
  lexical 29, 87
  negative polarity 74, 87
iterative 186, 238–240

J

Japanese 13, 14, 24, 31, 65–77, 81–86

K

Kannada 144, 154, 155
Kekchi 25
kind 4, 10, 11, 13, 38, 40, 45–49, 51, 52, 56, 57, 61, 85, 90, 91, 97, 104, 116, 120, 142, 150, 154, 158, 162, 253, 271, 307, 316, 329, 343, 345, 347

L

Latin 23, 26, 38, 246
learnability 93, 99, 101, 106
learner 1–6, 13, 14, 16, 22, 24, 25, 34, 183, 219–229, 235–238, 240, 241, 248, 249, 270
lexical 8, 15, 19, 21–25, 28–32, 34, 35, 43, 60, 67, 82, 87, 111, 120, 145, 146, 149, 152, 154, 167, 168, 170, 173, 174, 177, 178, 181, 182, 185, 186, 189, 194, 197–199, 201, 214, 215, 219, 221, 222, 225, 228, 229, 231, 233, 235–237, 239, 241, 243, 249, 251–254, 256, 257, 259, 260, 262, 266–270, 292
linear 22, 75, 150, 152, 154, 155

M

many 104–106, 111, 119, 143
modal 22, 17, 217, 231, 274, 279, 283, 287–289, 295, 299
mood 203, 216, 217, 245, 246, 249, 251, 253–257, 264, 267, 271, 277
Moroccan 15, 219, 221, 223, 224, 226, 230, 231, 234, 235
morphology 5, 15, 25, 26, 29, 38, 43, 45, 50, 62, 66, 87, 170, 193–195, 215, 216, 219, 220, 222, 243, 245, 249, 275, 278, 283, 288, 291–295, 301, 327
  inflectional 5, 29, 249
morphosyntax 229

N

negation 2, 10, 12, 14, 17, 22, 25, 62, 74, 75, 87, 139, 144, 145, 146, 147, 149, 150, 151, 154, 155, 156, 157, 159, 161, 165, 213, 217
noch 16, 186, 272, 282, 03, 304, 305, 308, 309–312, 314–316, 321, 327, 328,
nonfinite 245–248, 250, 257, 261, 265, 266, 267, 271
nonspecific 13, 32, 37–38, 45–46, 50, 57–59, 61, 256–257
noun 19–22, 24–26, 29, 31–34, 37, 41–42, 44–45, 47, 49–50, 52, 56–58, 60, 90, 101–103, 111, 116, 135, 143, 187, 233, 245, 248–250, 254, 257–258, 271
  bare 45, 47, 56–58, 61
not 2, 10, 12, 25, 33, 82, 145–148, 150–152, 156–157, 160, 162–163, 180, 225, 260

O

ook 9, 16, 325–326, 329–338, 340, 342–343, 345–347
only 8, 16, 71, 267, 277, 329, 348

SUBJECT INDEX

P

parameter 3, 171–172, 175–177, 180, 182, 187, 189, 220, 267, 277, 288, 291–292, 294–295
   semantic 4, 7, 17, 62
particle 8–9, 16, 23, 29, 34, 300–301, 303–309, 311–312, 315–327, 329–338, 343–347
   exclusive 8, 92, 109–110, 301
   focus 7–9, 13, 16, 303–308, 312, 320, 324–325, 327, 329–335, 338, 347
   inclusive 8
   restrictive 8, 16, 308, 329
partitive 138, 158–159
performance 73, 84–85, 89, 92, 96, 101–102, 109, 112, 117–120, 126, 132–136, 144, 149, 155, 157–159
phonological 28, 30–31, 142, 276
picture selection task 338, 343, 346
pitch accent 16, 175, 306–309, 311–314, 317–325, 327
plausible dissent 96–100, 102–103, 112, 115, 117–118, 120–121, 123, 126–127, 129–130, 132–135, 138
plural 11, 25–27, 29, 31, 111, 130, 217, 243, 301
Polish 13–14, 65–71, 77–78, 81–87, 170, 175
polysynthetic 5, 15, 194, 217, 246
posteriority 167, 176–177, 179, 186, 293, 295
posttime 178–180, 182, 186, 188
preposition 23–24, 27, 111, 309
presupposition 8, 11, 39, 61, 109, 118–119, 126, 136, 254, 271, 329, 343, 347
presuppositional 101, 119–121, 123, 127–130, 136, 138, 329, 336, 342–343, 346–347
pretime 178–179, 181–182, 184–186, 188, 191
production 16, 143, 209, 216, 248, 303–304, 314, 330
progressive 6, 180, 183, 193, 215, 231, 233, 234, 262

property 4, 11–12, 47, 50–51, 94, 107, 109, 127–135, 141, 145, 177, 184, 238, 252, 264, 274, 297, 301
proposition 8, 98, 102, 112, 117, 136, 233, 261, 306
prosodic 3, 23, 304–305
protoverbal 221–222, 225–230, 235–236, 241–242

Q

quantification 7, 12, 14, 92–94, 101–104, 108–109, 111, 117–121, 123, 126–129, 132–133, 135–138, 143, 176, 238–239, 266
   domain of 118–120, 123, 126–129, 132–133, 135–137, 143
quantifier 2–4, 11, 21, 23, 89–90, 92–96, 100, 102–107, 109–111, 115–123, 126–127, 129–130, 133, 135–136, 138, 141, 144, 161
   universal 3, 7, 12, 14, 89–90, 92–96, 100, 102–103, 105–107, 109–111, 115, 117–118, 120–121, 127, 129, 133, 135–136, 138, 1 43–144
   weak 14, 105, 143
quantized 177

R

referential 13, 22, 56, 61, 99, 137, 208, 226
restriction 34, 55, 102, 118–119, 135, 250, 267–270
resultative 34, 193, 195, 214–215

S

salience 101–104, 107, 111–112, 293–294, 299
salient 33, 99, 102–103, 106, 136–137, 252, 293–294, 299
Salish 49

scope 2–4, 8–12, 14, 16, 21–22, 32, 53, 67, 105, 110, 118–119, 123, 134, 137, 139, 141, 145–146, 147, 149, 150–156, 159, 161, 200, 220, 232, 235–236, 239–240, 242–243, 257, 270–271, 291, 300, 304, 306, 312, 324
  nuclear 105, 110, 118–119, 123, 137
simultaneity 167, 171, 176–177, 179, 183–184, 186, 225, 231, 241, 297
Spanish 27, 32
specific 1, 3, 13, 28, 31, 37, 45–46, 48–50, 58–60, 149, 156, 161–162, 187, 220, 225, 245, 253, 256–259, 266–268, 274, 277, 284, 290, 292, 301
stage 6, 11, 15, 47, 49, 50, 52, 60, 66, 75, 98, 145, 149, 156, 167–168, 170–177, 180, 182–190, 219–222, 225, 227, 235–237, 240–243, 247–249, 274, 278–279, 285, 289, 291, 295–297, 299, 301
state 20, 28, 33, 57, 154, 157, 163, 169, 177–178, 180–185, 189–191, 193–201, 204–208, 210–217, 220, 235, 241, 254, 262–263, 270, 277, 289, 296
state change 193–194, 5, 7–8, 200, 210, 213, 215–216
stress 2, 9, 13, 31, 45, 301, 310, 334–335, 337–338, 345–346, 348
structural 5, 11–12, 15, 150, 152, 154–155, 219–221, 225, 229, 235–236, 238, 243, 245, 280, 283
structure 1–5, 7–8, 13–15, 23–24, 28–29, 37, 39, 43–44, 50, 59, 61–62, 72, 75, 102, 111, 143, 174, 178–180, 182–183, 193–194, 197, 199, 203, 217, 220, 223, 227, 235, 246, 248–249, 251, 254–256, 259, 266, 268–271, 275–276, 280, 283, 286, 298, 305, 323, 325
  focus 3, 175, 325
  focus-background 8
  theme-rheme 102
Swahili 25

symmetrical 90, 92–95, 102, 106, 110, 115

T

Tarramiut 202, 217
telic 15, 167–170, 177, 183–184, 189, 238–239, 293
telicity 167, 170–171, 177
temporality 13, 15, 168, 183, 220–221, 223, 225–226, 228, 230–231, 233–234, 236, 293
tense 5–7, 14–15, 19, 21–22, 24, 27–28, 44–45, 65–67, 70–73, 78, 87, 164, 167–174, 177, 179–191, 193–195, 198, 201, 215, 219–220, 222, 230–231, 233–236, 241, 243, 245–246, 249, 251, 253–258, 260–262, 264, 288, 291, 293, 298
  aspect before 14–15, 167–169, 170, 172–174, 186, 189, 219
  future 15, 70, 164, 167–168, 171, 180–181, 186–188
  past 14, 22, 27, 65–67, 73, 78, 87, 164, 168–171, 173, 179–181, 185–186, 188–190, 201, 231, 235, 241–243, 245, 291, 293
  present 6, 7, 66–67, 71, 78, 87, 169–171, 180, 188, 190, 195, 231, 233, 245, 288
  sequence of 13, 27, 66, 72, 193
terminative 199–201, 209–211, 215, 217
thematic role 22
Theory of Mind 65, 68, 72
time 5, 14–15, 27, 34, 43, 56–59, 66–68, 70–71, 76–77, 80, 86–87, 93, 95, 97, 99, 102–103, 115, 118, 131, 148, 152, 158–159, 161, 167–177, 179–182, 184, 186–187, 189–190, 193–196, 198–199, 201, 203, 212–213, 216, 219–222, 227, 229, 233, 236, 238–243, 244, 257–269, 274, 277–278, 283–284, 287, 291–292, 294, 296, 298, 300–301, 309–310, 313–314, 319, 344
  event 66–67, 70, 76–77, 86, 167, 171–172, 186, 219–221, 236, 239, 241, 266

reference 167–168, 171–172, 187, 190, 219–221, 229, 233, 236, 239, 241–243
situation 67, 70, 198, 267, 268, 291
speech 167, 168, 171–173, 220, 266
topic 15, 190, 198, 245, 262–269, 291, 296, 300, 309–310
utterance 66, 68, 70, 87, 198, 241, 262–263
truth-conditional 20–21, 336
truth value judgment task 96, 98, 102, 106, 110, 147
Turkish 5, 15, 25, 167, 193, 219, 221–223, 226, 230, 233–235

U

unboundedness 178
Universal Grammar 2, 37, 94, 111

V

variation 1, 4–7, 58, 60–61, 66, 127, 190, 247, 251, 270, 289–290, 307
crosslinguistic 1, 4–5
semantic 4, 6–7
variety 5–7, 12–13, 20–21, 34, 38, 53–54, 59, 61, 72, 143, 223, 240, 249, 268, 281, 283

verb 6, 11, 15, 24, 34, 40, 47, 65–66, 72, 76, 78, 82, 92–93, 110, 154, 169–170, 177–178, 180–181, 183–185, 189, 191, 193–201, 203–212, 215–217, 219–220, 222–223, 225, 229–236, 239, 242–243, 245–257, 259–260, 262, 264–267, 269–271, 274–276, 278, 280, 283–286, 288–289, 291–292, 295, 297, 298–299, 301, 319, 322, 324, 327, 331, 333, 347
attitude 65, 72
verum-focus 261, 291
Vietnamese 246

W

when 136, 174, 176–177, 191, 253, 266, 310
wh-movement 74–75, 81–82, 87
wh-question 74, 81
wieder 186, 280–281
word-order 40

Y

yes-no question 97–98, 122, 254

STUDIES IN THEORETICAL PSYCHOLINGUISTICS

1. L. Solan: *Pronominal Reference.* Child Language and the Theory of Grammar. 1983 ISBN 90-277-1495-9
2. B. Lust (ed.): *Studies in the Acquisition of Anaphora.* Volume I: Defining the Constraints. 1986 ISBN 90-277-2121-1; Pb 90-277-2122-X
3. N. M. Hyams: *Language Acquisition and the Theory of Parameters.* 1986 ISBN 90-277-2218-8; Pb 90-277-2219-6
4. T. Roeper and E. Williams (eds.): *Parameter Setting.* 1987 ISBN 90-277-2315-X; Pb 90-277-2316-8
5. S. Flynn: *A Parameter-Setting Model of L2 Acquisition.* Experimental Studies in Anaphora. 1987 ISBN 90-277-2374-5; Pb 90-277-2375-3
6. B. Lust (ed.): *Studies in the Acquisition of Anaphora.* Volume II: Applying the Constraints. 1987 ISBN 1-55608-022-0; Pb 1-55608-023-9
7. G. N. Carlson and M. K. Tanenhaus (eds.): *Linguistic Structure in Language Processing.* 1989 ISBN 1-55608-074-3; Pb 1-55608-075-1
8. S. Flynn and W. O'Neil (eds.): *Linguistic Theory in Second Language Acquisition.* 1988 ISBN 1-55608-084-0; Pb 1-55608-085-9
9. R. J. Matthews and W. Demopoulos (eds.): *Learnability and Linguistic Theory.* 1989 ISBN 0-7923-0247-8; Pb 0-7923-0558-2
10. L. Frazier and J. de Villiers (eds.): *Language Processing and Language Acquisition.* 1990 ISBN 0-7923-0659-7; Pb 0-7923-0660-0
11. J.A. Padilla: *On the Definition of Binding Domains in Spanish.* Evidence from Child Language. 1990 ISBN 0-7923-0744-5
12. M. de Vincenzi: *Syntactic Parsing Strategies in Italian.* The Minimal Chain Principle. 1991 ISBN 0-7923-1274-0; Pb 0-7923-1275-9
13. D.C. Lillo-Martin: *Universal Grammar and American Sign Language.* Setting the Null Argument Parameters. 1991 ISBN 0-7923-1419-0
14. A.E. Pierce: *Language Acquisition and Syntactic Theory.* A Comparative Analysis of French and English Child Grammars. 1992 ISBN 0-7923-1553-7
15. H. Goodluck and M. Rochemont (eds.): *Island Constraints.* Theory, Acquisition and Processing. 1992 ISBN 0-7923-1689-4
16. J.M. Meisel (ed.): *The Acquisition of Verb Placement.* Functional Categories and V2 Phenomena in Language Acquisition. 1992 ISBN 0-7923-1906-0
17. E.C. Klein: *Toward Second Language Acquisition.* A Study of Null-Prep. 1993 ISBN 0-7923-2463-3

STUDIES IN THEORETICAL PSYCHOLINGUISTICS

18. J.L. Packard: *A Linguistic Investigation of Aphasic Chinese Speech.* 1993
    ISBN 0-7923-2466-8
19. J. Archibald: *Language Learnability and L2 Phonology:* The Acquisition of Metrical Parameters. 1993 ISBN 0-7923-2486-2
20. M.W. Crocker: *Computational Psycholinguistics.* An Interdisciplinary Approach to the Study of Language. 1996 ISBN 0-7923-3802-2; Pb 0-7923-3806-5
21. J.D. Fodor and F. Ferreira (eds.): *Reanalysis in Sentence Processing.* 1998
    ISBN 0-7923-5099-5
22. L. Frazier: *On Sentence Interpretation.* 1999 ISBN 0-7923-5508-3
23. S. Avrutin: *Development of the Syntax-Discourse Interface.* 1999
    ISBN 0-7923-5936-4
24. B. Hemforth and L. Konieczny (eds.): *German Sentence Processing.* 2000
    ISBN 0-7923-6104-0
25. M. De Vincenzi and V. Lombardo (eds.): *Cross-linguistic Perspectives on Language Processing.* 2000 ISBN 0-7923-6146-6
26. S.M. Powers and C. Hamann (eds.): *The Acquisition of Scrambling and Cliticization.* 2000 ISBN 0-7923-6249-7
27. M. Schönenberger: *Embedded V-to-C in child grammar: The acquisition of verb placement in Swiss German.* 2001 ISBN 0-7923-7086-4
28. M. Walsh Dickey: *The Processing of Tense.* Psycholinguistic Studies on the Interpretation of Tense and Temporal Relations. 2001
    ISBN 1-4020-0184-3; Pb 1-4020-0185-1
29. C. Hamann: *From Syntax to Discourse.* Pronominal Clitics, Null Subjects and Infinitives in Child Language. 2002 ISBN 1-4020-0439-7; Pb 1-4020-0440-0
30. S. Nooteboom, F. Weerman and F. Wijnen (eds.): *Storage and Computation in the Language Faculty.* 2002 ISBN 1-4020-0526-1; Pb 1-4020-0527-X
31. A.T. Pérez-Leroux and J. Muñoz Liceras (eds.): *The Acquisition of Spanish Morphosyntax.* The L1 / L2 Connection. 2002
    ISBN 1-4020-0974-7; Pb 1-4020-0975-5
32. H. Verkuyl, H. De Swart and A. Van Hout (eds.): *Perspectives on Aspect.* 2005
    ISBN 1-4020-3230-7; Pb 1-4020-3231-5
33. N. Gagarina and I. Gülzow (eds.) *The Acquisition of Verbs and their Grammar.* 2006 ISBN 1-4020-4334-1; Pb 1-4020-4336-8

STUDIES IN THEORETICAL PSYCHOLINGUISTICS

34. M. Bader and J. Bayer: *Case and Linking in Language Comprehension*. Evidence from German. 2006   ISBN 1-4020-4343-0
35. V. Van Geenhoven (ed.): *Semantics in Acquisition*. 2006   ISBN 1-4020-4484-4